OFFICIAL REPORT

OF THE

THIRTEENTH INTERNATIONAL

CHRISTIAN ENDEAVOR CONVENTION

HELD IN

SAENGERFEST HALL AND TENT

CLEVELAND, OHIO, JULY 11 – 15, 1894.

First Fruits Press
Wilmore, Kentucky
c2015

First Fruits Press
The Academic Open Press of Asbury Theological Seminary
204 N. Lexington Ave., Wilmore, KY 40390
859-858-2236
first.fruits@asburyseminary.edu
asbury.to/firstfruits

OFFICIAL REPORT

OF THE

THIRTEENTH INTERNATIONAL

Christian Endeavor Convention

HELD IN

SAENGERFEST HALL AND TENT

CLEVELAND, OHIO, JULY 11-15, 1894

Copyrighted 1894 by U. S. C. E.

PUBLISHED BY
UNITED SOCIETY OF CHRISTIAN ENDEAVOR
646 WASHINGTON STREET, BOSTON, MASS.
1894

Officers and Trustees of the United Society of Christian Endeavor.

1 President F. E. Clark, D.D.
2 Gen. Sec. John Willis Baer.
3 Treasurer William Shaw.
4 Rev. J. Z. Tyler.
5 Rev. R. W. Brokaw.
6 Rev. W. J. Darby, D.D.
7 Rev. H. B. Grose.
8 Bishop Samuel Fallows, D.D.
9 Rev. J. F. Cowan.
10 Rev. M. Rhodes, D.D.
11 Rev. J. T. Beckley, D.D.
12 Rev. M. M. Binford.
13 Rev. James L. Hill, D.D.
14 Rev. C. A. Dickinson.
15 Rev. William Patterson.
16 Rev. J. M. Lowden.
17 Prof. James Lewis Howe, Ph. D.
18 Rev. Canon J. B. Richardson.
19 Rev. H. C. Farrar, D.D.
20 Rev. P. S. Henson, D.D.
21 Rev. W. W. Andrews, Ph. D.
22 Rev. N. Boynton.
23 William R. Harper, LL. D.
24 Hon. John Wanamaker.
25 Rev. Gilby C. Kelly, D.D.
26 Mr. W. J. Van Patten.
27 Rev. David J. Burrell, D.D.
28 Auditor Fred H. Kidder.
29 Rev. Teunis S. Hamlin, D.D.
30 Rev. Wayland Hoyt, D.D.
31 Rev. Rufus W. Miller.
32 Rev. John H. Barrows, D.D.
33 Mr. W. H. Pennell.
34 Rev. W. H. McMillan, D.D.
35 Rev. E. R. Dille, D.D.
36 Williston Church, Portland, Me.

Thirteenth International Convention

OF THE

YOUNG PEOPLE'S SOCIETIES

OF

CHRISTIAN ENDEAVOR.

CLEVELAND, O., JULY 11–15, 1894.

WHITE and gold everywhere! Flags, festoons, streamers, and banners decorated in profusion public and private buildings, business blocks, and residences. Storekeepers vied with each other in making displays of their goods which should most beautifully combine the two colors. Florists filled their windows with white and yellow daisies, Japan lilies, and golden-rod. Jewelers devoted their show windows to the most ingenious arrangements of silver and gold. Dry goods dealers displayed a wealth of white and yellow silks, ribbons, and fabrics of all kinds. Booksellers gave a conspicuous place to their "white and gold" editions. Some stores provided electric illuminations at night which emphasized the same combination; and even the fireworks at the "Siege of Vicksburg" recognized the prevailing custom. Prettiest of all, great numbers of young ladies adopted for their home and street costumes white dresses with golden-hued belt and trimmings.

White and gold are the colors of the Cleveland Christian Endeavor Local Union. The citizens of Cleveland took this method of expressing their welcome to the delegates who came to the Thirteenth International Christian Endeavor Convention.

It should be said, also, that everywhere interwoven with the white and gold were the national colors. The great electric light mast in the Public Square, with its numerous stays, was heavily hung with United States flags. So, also, were the cross-wires of the electric street railway down town. Looking up almost any principal street there could be seen great stretches of color on either side, the folds of "Old Glory" everywhere intermingled with white and gold.

And all this exuberance and brilliancy of outward display was simply the threshold to the real, genuine, and substantial welcome which the delegates received. When the Ohio delegates stormed the New York Convention in 1892 with their irresistible refrain, "Pass along the watchword, Cleveland, '94," it was felt that the enthusiasm there manifested gave promise of great things for the convention of 1894, and the promise was amply fulfilled. The committees of arrangement for all the great Christian Endeavor Conventions have done nobly, but the palm for superlative excellence must be unquestionably awarded to the Committee of '94. The committee was appointed and began its work two years before the convention was held. Plans were carefully laid and systematic work at once undertaken. First of all, the Christian Endeavorers of Cleveland were given an actual proprietorship in the convention. Every member of every one of the eighty Christian Endeavor societies in the city was asked to contribute a specified sum towards the expenses of the convention, the amount to be paid within one year. This gave the young people of Cleveland a personal interest in the Convention which they would not have had if the expense fund had been raised among the business men of the city, as has usually been the case. Moreover, the personal services of every one, so far as possible, were enlisted in the work of preparation. Gratuitous service was invariably asked and invariably rendered with cheerfulness. As the convention approached, explicit directions were sent out to every society relating to its part in the entertainment of the delegates; and these directions were carried out with admirable promptness and dispatch. As a single illustration, a party of 345 delegates from Pennsylvania were received at the church constituting their headquarters, passed through the rooms where assignments were made, and every one was duly assigned and given a card of introduction to his or her host — the whole delegation being thus taken care of in only fifteen minutes' time. Places of entertainment were secured for 40,000 delegates, and a much larger number could have been accommodated. The work of the various sub-committees was most admirable, every possible convenience being afforded for the comfort of the delegates and the successful carrying on of the great convention.

A week before the convention met, things looked exceedingly unfavorable for a large attendance. The great railroad strike, tying up so many of the Western lines, and with its attending circumstances of riot and bloodshed, threatened to reduce the attendance of delegates to a very small proportion of what had been anticipated; and, indeed, in some quarters there was actual talk of postponing the convention. It was decided, however, that the convention must be held whether delegates were able to reach Cleveland or not. As matters turned out, while the strike prevented a great many from attending the convention, even some whole delegations being kept away, the enrollment of delegates from *outside Cleveland* and vicinity, as reported by the Registration Committee Saturday, reached the number of 18,790, while members of local societies and churches registered and received badges to the number of over 21,000 more, — a total of 40,000 delegates and visitors in attendance upon the convention. Monday, Dr. Tyler announced that additional registration cards had come in, making the total number of delegates from outside of Cleveland over 20,000.

On arriving at Cleveland the delegates were met by members of the reception committee, wearing white yachting caps with gold trimmings, by whom they were escorted to their respective State headquarters, where they registered and received their programmes and convention badges. The Cleveland badge was one of the most beautiful which has yet been designed, consisting of two diamond-shaped pieces of white celluloid tied with a yellow ribbon and containing six sheets of fine paper, each bearing two photo-engravings of Cleveland views. The face of the badge bore the "C.E." monogram, surrounded by a laurel wreath, and on the back was a picture of the Garfield monument, with the lettering, "Thirteenth International Christian Endeavor Convention, Cleveland, July 11–15, 1894." The programme, with covers in white and gold, was very handsomely designed, and contained, besides the order of exercises for the several sessions, a number of Scripture selections for responsive reading, and about sixty hymns selected from the new hymn-book, "Christian Endeavor Hymns," by Ira D. Sankey.

The convention, as at Montreal last year, divided its principal sessions between two places, — the Saengerfest Building and a mammoth tent formerly belonging to Barnum's Circus. The Saengerfest Building, located at the junction of Wilson and Scoville Avenues, is an immense structure originally designed for great convocations of the German singing societies. The interior is arranged in the shape of a huge amphitheater, or half-circle, the speakers' platform being in the geometrical center, the choir seats rising immediately at the rear, and the seats for pastors extending on either side. The reporters' tables, accommodating one hundred representatives of the press, were on the floor of the hall, in front and on either side of the speakers' stand. The hall was very prettily decorated with the Cleveland colors, and with flags of all nations, masses of palms and other potted plants being placed along the front of the platform. The speakers' stand was draped with the American and English flags and the Y. P. S. C. E. pennant which first greeted Dr. Clark at Australia on his voyage around the world. Over the choir gallery was hung an immense banner bearing the society's motto, "For Christ and the Church." The hall was provided with seating accommodations for 10,000 people, and the acoustic properties were for the most part very good.

The tent was pitched at the corner of Wilson and Cedar Avenues, "only three blocks from the hall;" but they were three of the longest blocks that most of the delegates had ever experienced. It was unfortunate that the cross-town street railway could not be completed in time for the convention; but the work was unavoidably delayed on account of the coal miners' strike, the company not being able to secure the rails. However, the delegates made the best of this inconvenience; and certainly the walk between the two auditoriums was a very pleasant one. The tent was 320 × 190 feet in size, and 55 feet high, seating about 12,000 people. The speakers' stand was at one end of the tent, the choir seats and pastors' seats being placed on either side. Of necessity, the decorations in the tent were less elaborate than in the hall; but the auditorium proved to be a very comfortable one, especially in the evening sessions, and the speakers were heard even more easily than in the hall.

WEDNESDAY, JULY 11.

MEETING OF THE TRUSTEES.

First on the programme of the convention came the meeting of the Board of Trustees of the United Society, held at noon at the Hotel Stillman, the headquarters of the officers and trustees. Here came the first great disappointment of the convention. President Francis E. Clark, who for several weeks had been under the care of a physician, but who hoped up to the last moment that he might be able to attend the convention, was positively forbidden by his physician to undertake the journey. His absence was deeply deplored, and many were the prayers offered up during the convention for his speedy recovery.

At this meeting of the trustees there were present the following: General Secretary John Willis Baer; Treasurer William Shaw; Rev. C. A. Dickinson, Rev. R. W. Brokaw, Rev. J. F. Cowan, Rev. Teunis S. Hamlin, Rev. J. T. Beckley, Prof. J. L. Howe, Rev. J. Z. Tyler, Rev. Canon J. B. Richardson, Rev. J. M. Lowden, Rev. J. L. Hill, Rev. H. B. Grose, Mr. W. H. Pennell, Rev. William Patterson, Rev. H. C. Farrar, Rev. W. H. McMillen, Rev. W. J. Darby, Rev. M. Rhodes, Rev. G. C. Kelly, Rev. R. W. Miller, Rev. M. M. Binford. Later during the convention Bishop Samuel Fallows, Rev. Wayland Hoyt, and Pres. W. R. Harper arrived.

Rev. C. A. Dickinson was made president *pro tem.*, and the annual report of President Clark was read by the clerk as follows : —

To the Members of the Board of Trustees of the United Society of Christian Endeavor: —

Dear Friends, The past year has been a year of the right hand of the Most High. Never before have we come to this annual meeting with more reason for gratitude and thankfulness as a United Society. There has been a larger gain numerically than in any twelve months of our history. Better than that, I believe there has been a large and substantial gain in the principles for which we stand. The societies have come to see that Christian Endeavor stands for Christian citizenship and missionary effort, and for world-wide fellowship, as never before; and these forward movements are only the outgrowth of the pledge and the consecration meeting and the work for the Master which always have and always will characterize Christian Endeavor as fundamental and essential features. The growth of the society in other lands has been quite as encouraging as in our own country. In England the advance has been phenomenal, a hundred societies recently being added in a single week; and the convention recently held in London was as enthusiastic, as earnest, and as characteristically Christian Endeavor as any ever held in this country. In China the news has just come that at a recent Christian Endeavor gathering in Shanghai more people were present than a veteran missionary has ever seen in a Chinese Christian gathering. Chairs were brought in, and all available space was occupied about the pulpit, and even the steps of the pulpit were filled. The meeting was a "revelation to many of the English speaking friends, who had no idea that there were so many capable native Christians in Shanghai."

A recent mail brought news that in Japan there are now fifty-seven fully equipped Christian Endeavor societies, and that they are to hold their national convention in Tokio while we hold ours in Cleveland. From India we hear that the constitution has been translated into six languages already, and that it is being rendered into Canarese, so that now the Christian Endeavor principles can be read in Tamil, Telugu, Hindi, Marathi, Bengali, and Hindustani. The young people's society connected with the Church

Missionary Society of the Church of England in India, has seen the advantages of Christian Endeavor and has voluntarily given up its organization and name, and has taken the Christian Endeavor name and methods, because it stands for the larger fellowship. So that, on the whole, though there are still problems demanding our attention, there is still much to encourage and cheer us. The State conventions this year, with but few exceptions, have been larger, more enthusiastic, and attended by better results, I believe, than ever before. May the coming year show that the blessing of God is resting upon our efforts in even larger measure, and to this end may we be guided in all things to know and do his will.

Respectfully submitted,
F. E. CLARK, <i>President.</i>

After the reading of the report a group picture of the trustees was taken for the *Golden Rule.* The remainder of the afternoon was spent in listening to the representatives of the cities which were seeking the convention for 1896. The most promiment of these were Baltimore, Washington, and Asbury Park. The trustees then adjourned until the following morning without deciding the question.

WEDNESDAY EVENING.

PRELIMINARY MEETINGS.

A new feature of the convention this year was the appointment of no less than fifteen preliminary meetings, held in as many different churches of the city, with addresses by well-known Christian Endeavor workers. The meetings were in all cases well attended, in some instances the churches being so overcrowded that overflow meetings were held.

First Congregational Church.

An immense throng attended the exercises at this church, hundreds being unable to gain admittance. The church was beautifully decorated, the colors of the Detroit delegation (blue and white), which was entertained by this church, being added to the national colors and those of the Cleveland union. Rev. John W. Malcolm, the pastor of the church, presided. The programme announced that Bishop Fallows was to speak at this meeting, but a telegram received from him announced that he was delayed on account of the strike. Rev. William Patterson of Toronto was therefore first introduced. His subject was " Christian Endeavor Enthusiasm," — a subject which he happily illustrated in the delivery of an inspiring address.

Rev. J. Lester Wells, of Jersey City, N.J., was the next speaker, his subject being

Christian Endeavor among the Life Savers.

Address of Rev. J. Lester Wells.

The beginning of the work of the Christian Endeavor Society in Life-saving Stations, Lighthouses, and Light-ships, is one of recent date. Only about two years have passed since the cause was officially inaugurated, and now it assumes vast proportions.

The International Committee, which includes representatives from all coast States and Canada, was appointed in New York at the Convention of 1892. At Montreal, 1893, representatives for England, Scotland, Ireland, and Wales were added. As the way is open representatives will be secured for every nation on earth.

In addition to the present countries represented, we should extend our work South to Mexico, Central America, West India Islands, South America, New Zealand, Victoria, South Shetland, and all islands of the Western Hemisphere. Then, from Great Britain as a starting point, in the Eastern Hemisphere, to France, Spain, Italy, the coasts of the Mediterranean, Black and Caspian Seas, Africa, Madagascar, India, Arabia, China, Japan, eastern and southern coasts of Asia, Australia, and neighboring islands, northern shore of Siberia, Sweden, Norway, and wherever life-saving stations are established or lighthouses and light-ships are located.

We have been encouraged on every hand, and kindly considerations for this work have been accorded by the Prime Minister of England, Hon. William E. Gladstone, by Her Majesty the Queen of England through her Secretary, by the President and Vice-President of the United States, and many others.

From the first meetings held and work done, along the New Jersey sea-board, when Rev. S. Edward Young preached at Sandy Hook and other life-saving stations, the cause has extended to thousands of miles of coast in the United States, to Canada, and to the United Kingdom of Great Britain.

KEEPERS AND SURFMEN.

The value of the service of the surfmen in rescuing lives and saving property cannot be overestimated. The establishment and regulation of these Stations by the Government prove their importance. Hon. Sumner I. Kimball, of Washington, D.C., General Superintendent of the National Life-Saving Service, who has commended the Y.P.S.C.E. work in the stations and given us valuable suggestions, has furnished facts and statistics to help the Committee in their work. There are ten thousand miles of sea and lake coast in the United States, not counting Alaska.

In every dangerous place life-saving stations have been located and manned with sturdy crews.

The men are drilled in the work of rescuing passengers and the strictest discipline enforced. They are taught all the methods of resuscitating half-drowned persons, and, in short, instructed in every phase of the work. Hundreds of stations are isolated from settlements, some on islands many miles from the main land, or on some sand-bar, difficult of access. The distances range from one to seventy-five miles from any cities or towns. For this reason the keepers and surfmen are cut off from home, family, and friends the larger portion of the year.

In the awful hurricane of 1880, which brought ruin and devastation to the New Jersey Coast, strewing her banks with broken wrecks and pieces of ships, three crews, when the tempest was the highest, in the darkness of the night, with their bodies covered with ice, and with but little light from their lanterns, worked their apparatus successfully and rescued the passengers on four ships, without a single accident. For such heroism the State Legislature passed resolutions praising the skill and bravery of keepers and surfmen.

The heroism and skill of those men who command the thousands of lighthouses and light-ships are equally praiseworthy. The tens of thousands of lives rescued and the millions of dollars worth of property saved by those heroes have brought to them the admiration of the world.

METHODS.

It was found that their wages were small ; and among the first steps was the securing an increase in their stipend. Rev. S. Edward Young interceded with Congress, and secured better wages for their valuable service. We then issued a circular to Christian Endeavor Societies, especially to those adjacent to the stations, stating that as " the surfmen were debarred throughout a larger portion of the year, by the isolation of their lonely tasks, from home and religious influences, they, in general, would appreciate services of song and prayer, and that there was no organization that could take charge of the matter so effectively as the Christian Endeavor Societies. It was recommended that local unions along the ocean and lake fronts arrange monthly visits to the stations within their bounds, always remembering that the men are engaged in a work too important for subordination to the convenience of any individual or society." It was also recommended that it would be well to confer by letter or in person with the keeper of each station regarding the most convenient hour for himself and the crew, with the understanding that stormy weather annuls the appointment. The Christian Endeavorers were also invited to send comfort bags, books, magazines, papers, leaflets, woolen wristlets, — called pulse warmers by the crews, — mufflers, mits, socks, yarn caps, and the like. In the comfort bags, which are made of strong ticking 12 x 14 inches, with a string shirred in at the top, so as to open and close at will, may be put buttons, needles, thread of different sizes, pocket scissors, knife, bandages, small bunch of white cotton, court and sticking plaster, coarse and fine combs, brush, pair of woolen wristlets, tooth-brush, automatic pencil, box of letter paper and envelopes, safety pins, a package of story leaflets, a Testament, and a bright, cheery letter, written to the recipient. Anything may be put in the bag that will comfort the surfman, who daily hazards his life, far away from home, mother, and sister; or the lighthouse keeper, upon whom ships freighted with precious lives depend for safety.

In coming into communication with the societies I took immediate steps to come into correspondence with the stations and lighthouse keepers, and so forwarded a circular with blanks, for answers to a few questions, stating, in the prelude, that the Christian Endeavor Societies, representing a million and a half of young people, desired to give help and a good cheer to the brave men of the life-saving stations, and would be glad if they would fill out the blanks and return answers to such questions as would inform us as to what could be done for their spiritual, physical, and intellectual good.

It is gratifying to record that the most cordial letters with answers came from the keepers, and grateful thanks expressed to Christian Endeavorers for their kindly interest. Letters poured in by the hundreds from societies, inquiring concerning the work, and volunteering to help the life-savers. As soon as possible I put the societies into communication with the stations in such a way as to distribute the help as equally as possible. Through the recommendations at Washington, comfort bags for the lighthouses and light-ships are sent, through the inspectors of the different divisions in the United States. In the Dominion of Canada a similar arrangement has been made.

RESULTS.

It is impossible to record in detail the results of this noble work. In fact, the work is too new to look for large returns; and yet we have facts sufficient to show that the cause moves grandly on, and that it has the hearty interest of the United Society of Christian Endeavor. Of all the crews heard from, only three thought it not best to hold meetings in their stations, and their reasons were considered satisfactory. Fifty-three stations the first year had regular services, two Sabbath-schools and one church organized. One station reported two meetings in two years, and another only one in six years, and would be thankful for them every week. Some of the stations being in or near villages, the surfmen attend church there. Earnest efforts have been made along this line, and the workers, in one instance, went fourteen miles in a row-boat to hold services in a station.

In the reports from the keepers, the general feeling expressed is delight at the thought of having the Endeavorers come to them in song and prayer, and cordially extend their thanks for all such visits. A large number of stations are almost inaccessible, owing to their being located so far away from any settlement; but they appreciate the spirit of the young people in desiring to cheer and bless them.

With reference to the intellectual work, hundreds of books have been sent; and I might say thousands of papers, magazines, and leaflets have found their way in boxes and packages to the life-savers. In some instances copies of the *Golden Rule* have been mailed regularly to them. Much good literature has been secured for the surfmen through the Chicago Christian Endeavor Literature Exchange.

Owing to the trying times of the crews in severe weather, the young people have not been unmindful of their physical comfort, and so have made for them woolen wristlets, mits, yarn caps, mufflers, and socks. Four hundred and twenty-three comfort bags, well filled with useful things, have been furnished, and received with gratitude by the crews.

As we look into the future and at this great work, we are sure that all Endeavorers will continue their interest, and do what they can to forward the cause, and will rejoice together in its success.

First Presbyterian Church.

A MEETING for men only was announced for this church, Rev. W. A. Knight, the assistant pastor, presiding. The church was completely filled with an audience which listened with the deepest interest to the following address by Mr. Anthony Comstock, on "The Environment of Our Youth."

The Environment of Our Youth.

Address of Mr. Anthony Comstock.

I speak to you to-night not for the purpose of entertaining you, but to enlist you as strong Christians in a more determined and hearty warfare on behalf of our beloved youth.

They who fight for the young fight for no mean constituency. One who knew the secrets of heaven said, —

"Take heed that ye despise not one of these little ones; for I say unto you, That in heaven their angels do always behold the face of my Father which is in heaven." (Matthew xviii. 10).

Again, when remonstrance was made against the bringing of the children to Jesus, he took a little child and set him in the midst of them and said: "Of such is the kingdom of heaven."

You are the new recruits to the standing army of God upon the earth. Weapons of aggressive warfare have been placed in your hands to be used for God and humanity. Many of you are but just sworn in as soldiers. During the late war thousands volunteered by going to a recruiting station, signing the roll, and taking the oath. As soon as this was done they were soldiers. But until they were sent to the rendezvous and drilled they were soldiers but in name. They were without drill or practice, and utterly unfit to be placed in the ranks beside the veterans at the front.

The vows of God are upon you. Worthy or unworthy, feebly or efficiently drilled, lukewarm or earnest, you are each "Soldiers of the cross." You have each been mustered in. Obedience to God's commands is your highest duty; and cheerful obedience will bring you highest happiness. There is nothing that makes life so glorious as "Thy will be done" brought into daily life. The soldier who marches at the command of his general is led through brambles and marshy places, over hill and dale, by night as well as day; and the equipment he is forced to carry blisters and cuts his flesh, and causes temporary discomfort. But when victory comes all is forgotten in the triumph of conquest.

Your way will not be altogether smooth. Your trials will gall and your burdens press heavily at times, but the compensation of patient bearing and heroic doing will bring such joy that, when the peace of "Well done" comes to the soul, all clouds will take their flight.

The worst foes which we have to meet are those within. The heaviest burdens are those which we permit Satan to rivet upon us. The most wretched state is when we awaken to find ourselves fettered by the invisible chains of evil habits.

Shackles of evil habits are forged in youth, and ofttimes so insensibly formed that we scarce are aware of their existence until they are too strong to be broken by our own unaided strength.

Character is what we do and are; reputation, what people say of us. The Devil is a character wrecker. We are character builders. He gets in his finest work in infancy and youth. And many a man, like the Psalmist of old, has been forced to cry in after years, "Remember not the sins of my youth nor my transgressions."

The most pathetic wail that ever fell from mortal lips, it seems to me, fell from a gifted man, a victim of wild oats sown in youthful days, who, in his remorse and despair, said: —

"I'm in a far country where God is not." Can any condition of the soul be more pitiful and sad than such a wail, uttered despite the fact that "God is love," and, "for God so loved the world that he gave his only begotten Son, that whosoever believeth in him should not perish, but have everlasting life"?

One rainy day, while riding in the front end of a railroad car, I sat musing over the raindrops as they struck upon the front window and then ran down. Those at the top seemed at first almost stationary; little by little the motion of the car caused them to descend. They met another drop, and still another and another, gradually gaining strength and momentum, until when about half-way down the pane they plunged to the bottom of the glass and disappeared from sight. The last half of the course was swift and sure. No stops! no breaks! A lawyer of prominence came and sat in the seat beside me. I said, pointing to the drops upon the window, "Such is temptation and sin." When temptations first come we hesitate to yield. Once we yield, and another comes quickly. Uniting, they gain additional force. They carry us down lower and lower, until a certain point is reached, and we are plunged into ruin and death.

Several months afterwards I received a letter from that lawyer calling attention to this incident, and asking me to call upon him. I responded, to find him upon the brink of despair. He told me of his ancestry and early history. His ancestors were of the highest culture, and some of them had been cabinet officers. At thirty years of age he had been sent abroad as a minister to Italy to represent this government. He told of his natural endowments, his honorable course in college; and in speaking of these advantages and sins of his youth, he said, —

"God gave me a basketful of diamonds, pearls, and precious stones, but I have thrown them all away. Now I cannot feel, I cannot pray, I cannot believe. My life is a blank. Pray for me."

To-night we sit around the camp-fire. I, who have been more than twenty-two years at the front, on the skirmish line, am to speak of things which I know, and testify of things that I have seen.

According to the last census there are more than 22,400,000 youth in the institutions of learning in the United States. These youth are character building. Characters are being molded, developed, and established. In each individual it is possible to build a character so grand and sublime as to help others toward heaven and shine in glory forever. But the odds are against them. To-night we are to hold a council of war in their behalf. You shall be generals in consultation, while the scout maps out in part the situation of the enemy. Deadly foes lie athwart the pathway of each child. Character wreckers abound all along the way from earth to heaven.

The last census informs us that out of a population of about 66,000,000 inhabitants in the United States, there are 1,000,000 habitual drunkards. This is a proportion of 1 to 66 of the entire population, and less than 1 to 44 of the adult portion who are habitual drunkards.

We take up the wail of the prophet Jeremiah over the sins of the Jews, and say, "For death has come up into our windows, and is entered into our palaces to cut off, the children from without and the young men in the streets." (Jer. ix. 21.) How many children are born of these drunkards each year with tainted constitutions. The history of the world has not changed man's condition before God.

"For all have sinned."

The foes of society, church, and state, — intemperance, gambling, lust, and infidelity, — have indeed brought death into our homes and palaces; and the children and young men are cut off and slain by these terrible influences.

The defiled imagination is the most deadly, insidious, and persistent foe we have to contend with. It plants its masked batteries and trains its guns against the spiritual development of each youth. It buries sunken mines in the heart, and a line connecting the brain with them has memory's button attached, which Satan presses at his pleasure. Ruts and grooves are formed in the brain by impure thoughts, and into these the wheels of the motive power of passion, intemperance, and unhallowed living run. The flashlights of sensual pleasures and self-indulgence are turned oft times full in the face of our youth, blinding their eyes so that their feet turn aside from the strait and narrow way that leads to everlasting life.

The sloughs of secret vice are loading many down with burdens that continue to increase as old age advances, until like Ephraim they shall mourn: —

"Surely after that I was turned, I repented; and after that I was instructed, I smote upon my thighs; I was ashamed, yea, even confounded, because I did bear the reproaches of my youth."

A detachment of hell is everywhere present with fetters to bind the feet of the feeble and easily tempted — those who are brought into the world with inherited appetites and passions; and Zopher's pitiful wail concerning Job will be said of such, —

"His bones are full of the sins of his youth, which shall lie down with him in the dust."

Worse than vultures and birds of prey by day, and lions, tigers, jackals, ghouls, and beasts of prey by night, are foes overshadowing and surrounding the young men and maidens of our day.

Our Saviour marked these foes when he said, —

"For out of the heart proceedeth evil thought, murders, adulteries, fornications, thefts, false witness, blasphemies: these are the things which defile a man." (Matt. xv. 19, 20.)

In the heart of every child is a chamber of imagery — memory's storehouse. One who knew the secrets of all hearts says, —

"Behold, I stand at the door and knock."

This figure of a room or chamber in the heart is not wrong or improper. Let us treat this chamber of imagery as a room. Behind the door in each heart, unless the Holy Spirit has possession, an imp of darkness is stationed by the spirit of evil to keep the door closed, opening it only when some degrading influence is sought to be hung up as a decoration within. If the Devil can, through eye and ear, gain access for a few years only in youth, and decorate these walls according to his will, the bars within will soon be so incrusted with vanity, self-conceit, and sinful pleasures, that nothing but the grace of God can pull them back, or open the door for the entrance of the gentle messenger who stands gently pleading without the door.

Since Adam's fall the imagination has been the pilot of ruin to the human soul. It is recorded in Gen. vi. 6, that "God repented him that he had made man upon the earth."

"And God saw that the wickedness of man was great upon the earth, and that every imagination of the thought of his heart was only evil continually."

"For the imagination of man's heart is evil from his youth." (Gen. viii. 21.)

"Because that, when they knew God, they glorified him not, neither were thankful, but became vain in their imaginations, and their foolish heart was darkened." (Rom. i. 21.)

Dear brethren, comrades in the fight, you perceive that imagination is an old-time foe. It has greatly troubled God, and everywhere cursed men and women. God's chosen people of old could not escape this enemy — much less we. If there is a man in this church who can say he has never been tempted to sin through his imagination, let such a one stand up. First, however, let him give us warning, that we may all veil our faces, lest the dazzling brightness of his joyful countenance blind our eyes.

David described the waywardness of man when he said, —

"They are all gone aside, they are all together become filthy; there is none that doeth good, no, not one." (Ps. xiv. 3.)

Satan, taking advantage of man's greed for gain, has led man to open many recruiting stations for hell.

All that money can secure has been used to make their places attractive. A belt line of fire encircles our youth. Dramshops, fitted up with polished mirrors, cut glasses, carved and highly polished woods, electric lights, and walls draped and decorated with works of art, all bid for our young men. Surrounding these brokerage shops of hell are dives, brothels, and low playhouses. From the walls of saloon, dive, and brothel hang pictures where woman's fair form is denuded, and womanhood is degraded. Billboards, fences, and walls of buildings serve as finger-boards to point our youth to places where the atmosphere is fetid, and where young women are employed to divest themselves of their modest womanly apparel and disport themselves in shameless attire and in shameless manner for the entertainment of patrons of opera, theater, and low playhouses.

Concert saloons and dives are but the grading downward of these pestilential exhibitions.

When the "Black Crook" was first put before the public there was a great outcry made because of its disgusting character. The press advertised it, as it usually does; and from contempt there came toleration, and then patronage, until now the thing exists as the requirement of theater-going people.

The poet's words take new force, —

> "Vice is a monster of such hideous mien,
> That to be hated needs but to be seen;
> Yet seen too oft, familiar with its face,
> We first endure, then pity, then embrace."

Take out the unclothed parts, and the bawdy and unwomanly acting of women, from many modern plays, and there would be nothing left to attract foul-minded patrons. It is not conceivable that persons who patronize these places, or consent to be thus entertained, are clean or pure within. Only for the support of so-called reputable people many of these places could not exist.

"Be not deceived; evil communications corrupt good manners."

All these are pest-holes in society; scourges worse than the plagues of flies or locusts of old. They are slimy serpents that seek to charm the senses until the victim falls an easy prey.

Add to all these the great daily and weekly newspapers, teeming in many instances with highly sensational details of loathsome crimes and filthy details of divorce and abandonment cases in the courts; column after column of advertisements wherein the respectable editor bargains for a consideration to introduce the quack, abortionist, lottery thief, green-goods swindlers, smut dealers, race-track gamblers, tricksters, and villains of all sorts to their readers — taking, as it were, these moral lepers by the hand and leading them into bank, store, manufactory, home, and school, and introducing them with their indorsement.

The more high-toned the paper the higher price the fraud, thief, and quack are willing to pay for the privilege of advertising therein. Many and many an invalid has had his or her disease aggravated by the lies of the quack thus brought to their notice. Thousands of persons have been thus swindled and robbed each year. Thousands of youth are cursed by the stories of crimes and criminals, and wreck and ruin follow.

Then add to the above the illustrated weekly papers, devoted to stories of bloodshed, lust, and crime. Then take account of the dime novel, half-dime story-paper, and cheap books without a moral quality. These influences morally craze young people. A young man who from reading trashy books ran away from home, entered upon a life of crime, got into a fight, was wounded, and upon his deathbed, when counseled to make a fight for a new life, he replied, "'I can't. If I try to have better thoughts, the scenes of vice come right back to me like a slap in the face. They're burned in. I can't get rid of them. When you read the Bible to me I see the faces and hear the words which filled those terrible dens, and I can hear nothing else. They come, too, between me and the memory of my precious mother. How dare I think of her? Oh, I couldn't look in her dear face again! But warn all young people whom you know to let those foolish books alone. They're very silly; but they do harm to many, and they've ruined me. They take you one step on a bad road, and the rest comes quick and easy." Toward the last he was penitent; but the memory of the past haunted him and intruded upon his sacred moments.

How many Christians can testify to the same intrusion upon sacred hours of things put before the mind in youth, defilements hung up in the chamber of imagery. Many are overwhelmed and dismayed by these recurring visions. For their sake let me say, temptation is not sin. It's the devil's torture. He rings memory's bell, and as often as he does it the hated thing intrudes itself. These visions haunted this dying boy almost, if not quite, to the gates of heaven. Just before he died he said, "If through his infinite mercy I am ever forgiven, don't you think I'll cease to remember. How could I enter heaven with those polluting memories clinging to me? Oh, if I could only forget!"

Last, and worse than all, add the contagion of photographic publications, forty-seven tons weight of which have been seized and destroyed by the New York Society for the Suppression of Vice.

An equally baneful curse has arisen from the action of unscrupulous men who, for gain, have scoured the archives of ancient, Oriental, and pagan literature to find buried and forgotten indecencies to substitute for modern filth. Again, so-called reputable art and book dealers have ransacked the art galleries of the Old World with snap camera and kodak to flash out of the nude in art the indecent conceptions, where foul-minded artists have first placed woman in a lewd posture in their own minds, and then employed the hand of genius to make permanent the pictures conceived by their own disordered imagination.

Well for the community would it be if we could stop here. But no. We must add the allurements to dishonesty offered by race-track gambler, lottery, policy banking game, pool-selling, and other kindred vices, to say nothing of concert saloon, dive, brothel, and other resorts where men, led on by defiled imaginations, rush to gratify passion thus aroused.

Is there not a dire necessity, young soldiers of the cross, that each of you should put your gospel armor on and drill for the fight? We must deny ourselves, take up our cross, and follow our leader, Jesus Christ.

Professing Christians must withdraw their patronage from the brokerage shops of hell.

With corruption in high places, — statesmen turned into truckling politicians; judges and prosecuting attorneys administering laws in the interests of criminals, instead of for the protection of morals, peace, and good order; with sworn officials levying blackmail; with persons occupying positions of trust recreant to their charge, and becoming defaulters, forgers, and thieves; with newspapers every day serving up " tips " on gambling ventures; with professing Christians patronizing these swindling and dishonest schemes, and all these evil examples set before the rising generation, can we hope to save the young and build up noble characters for the future unless these evil influences are removed?

"Be not deceived; God is not mocked; for whatsoever a man soweth that shall he also reap."

Surrounded by such environments, how can our youth be saved from ruin?

A former Tammany Hall chieftain, when brought to bay by startling exposures made of his crimes, defiantly and sneeringly said, " What are you going to do about it ? "

To-night, young soldiers, I ask you with all earnestness, What are you going to do about it? The outlook is not bright. These foes are ever active and aggressive. The seed-sowing must be stopped ere the harvest of crime and ruin can be lessened.

As we contemplate the odds against us, a deeper meaning than ever before will come from the words of our great Commander when he said, "Without me ye can do nothing." Saul of Tarsus set us an example how to start. You remember that when inflated with wrath against the followers of the meek and lowly Jesus he was overtaken by the Holy Spirit. He made a full surrender of self when he cried out, " Lord, what wilt thou have me to do? " The answer came to him as it will come to every child of God who surrenders his or her will and earnestly strives to do the will of God. " Arise and go into the city, and it shall be shown thee what thou shalt do." We are to learn from this that there is something for each one to do. We are to put ourselves in the way of securing answers to our prayers. The soldier marches by authority of his commander. Each day in a regiment in the field, details are made ; some are sent on camp guard, others on picket and outpost duty, others on the skirmish line. The soldier having been detailed to a post of duty must do and dare, and die if need be. So, brethren, you and I each morning should pray Saul's prayer, " Lord, what wilt thou have me to do? " Then, not waiting for a bill of particulars, march to the post of duty, confident that it will be plainly shown us what we must do. Like some naval commander, we may be obliged to cross the ocean with sealed orders; but when the time comes for God to make known his requirements there will be no mistakes and no blunders made.

Let it not be said of us, as Ezekiel said of those of Jerusalem whose sins he mourned, " They have put no difference between the holy and the profane, neither have they shown difference between the clean and the unclean." (Ezk. xxii. 26.)

You may be detailed to some advanced field of service. Like a pioneer corps of a great army, you may be sent in advance to spy out the location of the enemy, to locate masked batteries, to fire sunken mines, to build bridges and pave the way for the advancing army. If so, whatever you build, do thoroughly. Let it not be said of you, as was said of the prophets of Jerusalem, "They daubed her with untempered mortar." Build up the hedges about you systematically. Fill every gap carefully. Let temptation's flames burn about you, but as a good soldier of the cross stand unflinchingly. Let not the Lord say of any of you, as was said of Jerusalem of old, "And I sought for a man among them, that should make up the hedge, and stand in the gap before me for the land, that I should not destroy it: but I found none. (Ezek. xxii. 30.)

The true Christian Endeavorer is a soldier of deeds, not words; character, not appearances; of faith and works, and not shiftless and listless. An old colored preacher applied the principle which I would impress upon your hearts to-night. While he did not make his illustration of that high order that becomes the servant of God, yet you can pick out the kernel and throw the broken and imperfect shell away. He is reported as saying, "Breddren, faith widout works, it am ded. If dis chile prays for a turkey and den goes to bed, dar am no turkey in de kitchen de nex' mornin'. Dat am faith widout works. But if dis chile prays for a turkey an' den goes out an' looks for it, dat am faith and works. Dar am a big fat gobbler in de kitchen de nex' mornin', suah."

Pray and wait God's coming. Put yourself in the way of receiving God's answer, as though he held in his hand his gift to you and said, "Come, my child, and receive it." So go you toward him for your answer.

This sweet lesson came to me through an attempt to assassinate me by a man whom I had arrested one Saturday night at Newark, N.J. United States Commissioner John Whitehead had committed him to jail, and the commitment had been placed in my hands to convey him to jail. As we reached the jail door, he stabbed me twice, making the wound, the scar of which mars my face. But behind this was God's way of answering prayer. For months I had been praying God to send funds to pay a debt of over $3,000. This debt had steadily increased. I had prayed for help, but no ray of light came. The work could not cease, although the debt was added to by each new effort. The heart of the people seem closed. Dark clouds of hatred and bitter opposition hung over my head. Public sentiment had been turned against me by false and malicious attacks in the newspapers. For weeks I had pleaded for help. Then the assassins's knife laid me at death's door. As I lay helpless on my bed the next morning, and alone for a few moments, the burden of debt, the thought of the exultation of my enemies over my downfall, the additions to the debt of a doctor's and nurse bills, came over me with crushing force, when all at once a still small voice speaking in silvered tones sweeter far than ever mother sang her lullaby in infant's ears, seemed to say to me, "Be still, my child, and let me work." Then light, joy, and peace flooded my soul. The burden was rolled off, as by the touch of him who has promised "to give his angels charge over thee to keep thee in all thy way." Before that wound healed, the debt was raised. The assassin's stroke was the providence which aroused the people; the token by which the treasuries of God's promises were opened and verified. That scar means "so far and no farther." Aggressive warfare means to the soldier hostile opposition. My comfort against assassins and moral assassins has for years been in the text, "No weapon that is formed against thee shall prosper; and every tongue that shall rise against thee in judgment, thou shalt condemn. This is the heritage of the servants of the Lord and their righteousness is of me, saith the Lord."

When the two-edged tongue of the gossip or the moral assassin's sword-thrusts stab you in the back, be not dismayed. These are crucial tests to many young Christians. Do not expect any better treatment in this world than our Saviour received.

Be content to accept whatever hardship comes in the same spirit of "thy will be done" which characterized his agonizing moments for you. When the burning rays of spiteful attack and bitter opposition fall upon you, seek comfort and protection under the shadow of that beautiful beatitude of our Lord Jesus Christ, when he said, "Blessed are ye when men shall revile you, and persecute you, and say all manner of evil against you, falsely, for my sake." "Rejoice and be exceeding glad; for great is your reward in heaven."

In conclusion, men and brethren, let me say our warfare is not a war to ignoble death, but a triumph of victory all the way to the eternal city. And then! then! then! —what? "Eye hath not seen, nor ear heard, neither have entered into the heart of man the things which God hath prepared for them that love him."

"Wherefore, take unto you the whole armor of God, that ye may be able to stand in the evil day, and having done all to stand."

"Stand, therefore, having your loins girt about with truth, and having on the breastplate of righteousness."

"And your feet shod with the preparation of the gospel of peace."

"Above all, taking the shield of faith, wherewith ye shall be able to quench all the fiery darts of the wicked."

"And take the helmet of salvation, and the sword of the spirit, which is the word of God."

"Praying always with all prayer and supplication in the spirit, and watching thereunto with all perseverance and supplication for all saints."

> "Arise, go forth to conquer,
> Young champions for the Lord;
> Fling out the royal standard,
> Unsheathe the mighty sword:
> The church that sword has wielded
> In many a dreadful fray
> Till Satan's army trembled,
> And, vanquished, fled away."

"Blessed be God who giveth us the victory, through our Lord Jesus Christ."

Dunham Avenue Disciple Church.

Another great audience assembled at this church, which was likewise prettily draped in honor of the Convention. The pastor, Rev. A. B. Chalmers, presided. The first speaker was Rev. H. B. Grose, professor of history in Chicago University. His theme was "Christian Endeavor and Christian Citizenship."

Christian Endeavor and Christian Citizenship.

Address of Rev. H. B. Grose.

I am going to speak to you on that part of citizenship which is called politics, and the relation of Christian Endeavor thereto. Has Christian Endeavor anything to do with politics? That is the question.

There is an Arabian legend, that when the ostrich was told to carry a load it answered, "I cannot, I am a bird;" and when it was told to fly it answered, "I cannot, I am a camel." Many people consider Christianity to be in the indefinite position of the ostrich; and when there arises a question regarding Christianity's relation to the world's practical affairs, would force it to make the ostrich's ingenious reply. The reason for this is not far to find. Christianity, practically applied to business, to society, to politics, is apt to be inconvenient. Its introduction means innovation, interference. We call this a religious age in contrast to the dark ages; but religion — the religion of Christ — is yet in this age revolutionary in every circle and condition into which it penetrates. So, when the call comes for Christianity to go down into the world and bear burdens, carry the load of sin, shame, and selfishness to the cross, and bring in its stead the righteousness that exalteth men and nations, the cry arises from the sinful and selfish, who do not wish to have things disturbed, "Christianity cannot carry loads, it can only fly." It is false. Christianity is not like the ostrich, but like the eagle. It can fly, but it can also carry. Its wings are strong wings. Swooping in its divine course to the lowest surfaces of earth, plucking thence from the quagmire or quicksand of sin the struggling soul whose every effort is but a deeper sinking, bearing the rescued one aloft, it can soar to the heights of heaven. Christianity can both carry and fly, and both it must and will do — for its place in heaven would be nothing save for its mission on earth.

Christianity cannot be relegated to the air. Bad men may desire it, indifferent Christians even may deem it wiser, because easier, but it cannot be done. Christ was not a myth, not an invisible breath, not a voice out of a cloud, but a living man. The living Christ in living men — that is Christianity. Neither, therefore, can Christianity be relegated to the tomb — for Christ is not dead, but living. Troublesome as it may be to wickedness, disturbing as it may be to worldliness, try as men may to escape or confine it, or drive it out of the kingdom of practice into the wastes and solitudes of mere profession, the thing cannot be done. Christianity is in the world, in every part and permanent plan of it, and yet ever above it — and is in the world to stay, as long as the world stays.

Some one has said that "the contribution that this age is to make to Christian thought is, that practical Christianity is Christianity. It will be seen after a while that it is as much tautological and superfluous to add the epithet "practical" to Christianity as to talk of practical plumbing or hairdressing, because the whole aim of the Christ is to make men better, life richer, and the world a place in which God's will shall be done as it is in heaven. The unfulfilled task of Christianity is the application of its principles to the common life of man — the teaching of it so as to bring the inevitable and irresistible conclusion that right thinking will never save a man unless it makes him add right living to it.

But this application of the gospel, which is exactly what is proposed, and being done, by the new movement of Christian Endeavor in citizenship, arouses opposition from various sources. Dishonest business is opposed to it, the saloon power is opposed to it, the labor demagogue and monopolist are opposed to it, the ballot-box stuffer and gambler are opposed to it, and, worst of all, the church is almost afraid of it. There are multitudes of people who think religion is a good thing and enjoyable so long as it isn't applied to them and their daily affairs or pet projects. When conscience applies it they cry out with terror; for truth is like a rose, beautiful and fragrant to see and smell, but having thorns which you discover when you bring it into contact with your own flesh. All like the rose so far as beauty and fragrance go, but few are willing to have their faults and foibles pricked by the thrust of the accompanying thorns. Christianity never touches a man hard enough to let the bad blood out till its thorns prick him.

Especially is it true that the managers of politics are opposed to any interference with their plans on the part of Christianity. Let a Christian minister speak out boldly in application of the principles of Jesus to public affairs, and instantly the timid say, "Ah, now you are treading on dangerous ground. The pulpit must be careful how it touches politics." Yes, so it must be careful in this delicate and sensitive day of ours how it denounces evil in any form. Everything must be made as easy as possible for Boss Satan and his friends. What an awful shock it would give our easy-going and cautious civilization to have a John the Baptist come along preaching a plain, fearless, unsparing gospel of repentance and a return to righteousness! What amazement and alarm and anger would result were Christ himself to come, and from the pulpit send out his startling denunciations of the modern scribes and Pharisees, hypocrites. How Mr. Pompous, our Pharisee, would give up his pew if that kind of preacher had come to stay.

All the same I do not believe in the "letting alone" policy. "Let us alone." That is the watchword of the tyrant when he is bent on destroying the liberties of a people. That is all that is asked to-day by the cunning ecclesiastical plotters against our educational institutions and religious liberties. "Let us alone." That is all the thief asks of the law. That is what the demons besought of Christ in the presence of his power, and what they have desired of his disciples ever since. All that unscrupulous ambition, civic corruption, schemes of public plunder, Tweedism and Tammanyism, plots of parties, menaces of liberty and purity — all these ask is to be let alone. So, "Let us alone" is what politics demands of Christianity. Religion must be kept out of the mire of politics or be bedraggled, is the cry. But Christians must not readily grant the assumption that they have, as Christians, no distinctive work to do in politics, and in all the other departments of citizenship. The pulpit has to do with public purity as well as private. Christianity has to do with public men and measures as well as with personal faith and life.

In considering and emphasizing this point, of course, it must not be forgotten that there is a radical difference between political principles and party prejudices. It is one thing to be a party man, another to be a partisan. The pulpit certainly should not be marked by partisanship or prejudice. It as certainly should teach plainly those principles that ought to control in politics, as in every other range of activities. And the

Christianity in the pews which you in part represent should do its proper part to restrain partisanship within right and manly and decent bounds, and to muzzle prejudice in the months of a campaign with the same prudence that muzzles dogs in dog-days. A man cannot, apparently, help having prejudices; but a Christian Endeavorer can, by care and prayer, keep them from running mad with him.

With this limitation of Christian Endeavor's work to legitimate effort to apply the principles of Jesus to the whole of citizenship, let us look a little further at the assertion that Christianity has nothing to do with politics. In the same way people say that Christianity has no business with business, and act so in business. It is a most hopeful sign that the young people of our country — the great host of them represented by this unique C. E. army — are bound to inquire whether such assertions are true or false, and bound to follow the truth when they find it.

Christianity nothing to do with politics? What is politics? Is it a wild beast that will devour? Is it a leprosy fatal to all who come into contact with it? Politics in a free government like ours is simply the working machinery by which the people provide for the administration of their public affairs. Have Christian men no part in this, and no duty to see that in the administration of these affairs the Christian principles shall prevail?

Let us seek light from the founder of Christianity, Christ himself. It is true that he came to establish, not an earthly, but a heavenly kingdom, and that this kingdom was not an outer force, but an inner life. Christianity was not, like Judaism, to be the state. It was not to overcome the temporal powers by force of arms, nor to refuse rightful obedience to government. But it was to permeate politics; it was to purify and preserve by providing right principles and enjoining upon its adherents their practice. The whole tenor and spirit of Christ's life and teaching tend to the one conclusion, that the Christian is to be the best man in citizenship, in business, in every place and position in life. Christianity being a life, it must be carried into everything. Where the true Christian goes he cannot be anything but a Christian; he is to go wherever duty calls him; and duty calls him wherever there is need of the true principles which he possesses. When politics, for example, becomes so pure as not to need Christianity, then the Christian will have nothing to do with politics and may retire into cloistered contemplation, but not till then. And we shall agree that the time for retirement has not come just yet, that, so far from it, nothing but a speedy inoculation of diseased politics with the virus of gospel principles can save us from an epidemic of official corruption and a condition of civic degradation and danger.

Christianity nothing to do with politics! Then the greatest triumphs of history could not have been wrought. Then the grandest figures as well as conquests of human story must fade from sight. Then this land of ours as it is could never have been. For the basic principle of our constitution — free and equal birthright brotherhood of man — came from Christ. "Christian law," says one, "is the cornerstone of the government. Christianity in its various connections permeates the entire structure of the government, and is its underlying and informing spirit."

Christianity nothing to do with politics in America! How the times must have changed! When the Pilgrims landed at Plymouth what did it mean? Why fled they from their distant home over the sea to the privations and perils of the red man's forest lands? The reason, in their own words, was, "the great hope and inward zeal they had of laying some good foundation for the propagating and advancing the kingdom of Christ in these remote parts of the world." With them town and church were one; and however ideal was the union of the temporal and spiritual state which they undertook to establish, the result, as we view and enjoy it to-day, is the direct outcome of Christianity in politics, not through a church interference in state, but through an individual Christian citizenship. We have no church and state combined, and never will have; but our politics have ever been indebted to Christianity for preservative principles as well as foundation stones, and Christianity in the State has been the divine power unto national perpetuity and progress. Nor are there wanting prophets who foresee a day approaching when Christianity shall so predominate that the only true union of church and state shall be realized — that union in which Christians, standing shoulder to shoulder, one great host battling for righteousness, shall take possession of the state, shall be the state, and so administer its affairs as to secure justice and order, purity and peace, safe liberty and firm government. "Then it will appear that what we call the state is not less sacred than what we call the church; that all life is sacred; that the high calling of God summons us not only to the closet and the altar, but to the workshop, the kitchen, the school, the field, the forum, the court — to be in every vocation witnesses for Christ and servants of man. And this," says Dr. Bushnell, "is the true issue of that great hope and inward zeal which impelled our fathers in the migration. All kinds of progress, political and spiritual, coalesce and work together in our history, and will do so in all the race, till finally it is raised to its true summit of greatness, felicity, and glory in God and religion. And when that summit is reached it will be found, as church and state must be parted in the crumbling and disintegrating processes of freedom, so, in freedom attained, they will coalesce again, not as church and state, but in such kind of unity as well nigh removes the distinction — the peace and love and world-wide brotherhood, established under moral ideas, and the eternal truths of God's eternal kingdom."

This is a high view of what Christianity has to do in politics; but it is like a tonic to take this in offset to the common, low-level assertion that the less Christianity has to do with politics the better for Christianity.

"But," says one, "politics is so corrupt." So much the more need for Christianity. "But it brings a man into disrepute to be seen even with professional politicians." Jesus bore the stigma of eating with publicans and sinners, not because he loved either their tax-gathering or their sins, but because there was a field of labor. He went not to lower himself to their level, but to raise them to his. The Christian certainly has no place in politics unless his purpose is like that of his Lord, and his love and faith and integrity strong. The genuine Christian man with true Christian purpose will always tell on the right side. He can even touch pitch and not be defiled. Did grand John Knox lower himself by preaching politics? He raised a nation to the gospel standard. Did learned Wilberforce lower himself by putting a Christian zeal and philanthropy into politics? He elevated the political tone of all England. And in our day, what a power has Christian character proved itself to be in the politics of a nation when put there by a Christian Gladstone.

Is the political tone low? Whose fault is it? In this country the people are directly responsible for bad men in office and low standards in politics. They have nobody but themselves to blame for neglect and indifference. Those who chose their own rulers, and then complain of their character, only condemn themselves. But how are evils, where they exist, to be remedied? By leaving the bad men to rule, and the evils to go unchecked? Is it not rather by first making sure of a pure Christianity that cannot be bribed or corrupted, and then putting that into politics as the leaven for the working out of a Christian government? If we want to save the free schools, Christian citizens must take part in the election of the school-boards, or those who appoint them. If we want to shut up the saloons, Christian citizens must go to the caucus and polls, and elect anti-saloon legislatures, excise boards, and executives. In a word, if we want to remedy any of the great evils which are upon us, if we want to reform any abuses, right any wrongs, elevate our government, and advance civilization, Christian citizens must do it by combined and continuous and comprehensive Christian endeavor. Could the united power of the Christian men and women of this land once be exerted in politics, who doubts the revolution it would create? And surely this ought to be. This must be, if this nation is to be in any true sense Christian.

The Christian young men and women of this country have a mighty responsibility laid upon their shoulders. The problems which the rising generation have to face are well illustrated by the exposures of civic rottenness in New York, the recent mining troubles, which produced a condition of practical anarchy in three States in the Union, and the present railway strikes, which have revealed a spirit of lawlessness and utter defiance of judicial and governmental authority hitherto unsuspected. Christianity demands that Tammany methods must go, in order that the American liberty may stay. Election bribery and ballot-box stuffing must stop in order that free government may go on. Christian statesmen who will live their principles must be sent to our State and national legislatures in order that these may be preserved in purity by the salt of righteousness, and not be spoiled by the sugar of speculation. One dose of sugar-coated pills from its congressional factory is about all the people can stand, and a good deal more than they ought to stand.

What can Christian Endeavor do in politics? Do right and righteously. Regard this nation as a sacred heritage, not to be handed over to ignorant or vicious foreigners, not to be allowed to fall into the hands of the worst classes of citizens, but to be governed and maintained by the best. Christian Endeavor can voice a moral sentiment that shall make itself heard and respected even by the immoral. Christian Endeavor can rise to the level of Christian statesmanship and pure patriotism. Christian Endeavor can vote, and votes enough will put good men in office and keep bad men out. Christian Endeavor can see to it that saloon-keeper and alderman are not synonymous terms. Christian Endeavor can stamp out the false assumption, now made not for the first time, that the people have no right to inquire into the private character, but only as to the public fitness of their candidates. Christian Endeavor can insist that no confessed moral leper and hypocrite shall be allowed to sit in the national legislature; and if a misguided constituency send such a one there, can help in the utterance of a protest that shall be felt the world around. Christian Endeavor can preach and teach and live good citizenship. The best Christian will be the best citizen. He who is the most loyal to God's law will be most obedient to the law of the land. Christian Endeavor can inculcate the law of love that makes a good neighbor, a noble citizenship, a truly free people, a progressive civilization, a peaceful and desirable state, a world blessing church, and an incoming kingdom of Christ upon the earth.

Christian Endeavorers. God help us to be true to our trust as Christian citizens. Ours is not to withhold our influence, but to cast it with all our power of Christian principles on the side of right. We should put our Christianity down heavy in the scale for good government, from township to national domain. Not men but measures, we sometimes hear it said. Both men and measures should we look to, and see that both are right and true. In politics let us do what we can to supplant prejudices with principles, and check the tongue of denunciation, bitterness, and slander. What a blessing it would be, and not alone to politics, if the nation could only in some way get a bit of the gospel planted right at the root of the people's tongues, and that bit, "the greatest of these is love."

When Christian Endeavor and the Christian people of America unitedly do what they ought to do in citizenship — not through church organizations, but through individual Christian influence and interest — then, as Moses cast the tree into the bitter waters of Marah, so shall men cast their Christianity into the bitter waters of politics, and the bitter shall be made sweet. As the angel went down into the pool of Bethesda, so the Christian Endeavorer, in the might and spirit of his Master, shall walk boldly into the seething political pool, and the waters shall be healing for those who come after. God hasten the day and bless all Christian Endeavor in Christian citizenship.

Rev. Teunis S. Hamlin, D.D., pastor of the Church of the Covenant, Washington, D.C., next spoke upon

Christian Endeavor as a Training School.

Address of Rev. Teunis S. Hamlin, D.D.

It has come to be clearly understood that Christian Endeavor has its distinctive field midway between the Sunday-school and the church. It indeed partakes of the nature of both. It does a great work of instruction, especially in the Holy Scriptures. It has devout, uplifting, comforting worship, and a wide range of Christian and humane activities. But its peculiar function is to intercept young men and women when they begin to think that they have outgrown the Sunday-school; to lead them into the church, and to fit them to be active, consistent, and worthy church-members in adult years and throughout life.

Now, in discharging this function, it is, or should be, chiefly a training school. That is, its work is to train the young in distinction from teaching them; and to make whatever teaching it does subordinate and subservient to training.

This very real and vital distinction is not always observed in education. In fact, the introduction of it here and there, to a limited extent, is one of the greatest of modern educational reforms, while its general prevalence would almost revolutionize our schools and colleges.

About forty years ago David Snow, a celebrated educator of Glasgow, published a book entitled "The Training System," advocating practically what is now known as the normal method. He says: "Sunday-schools have done much for the Christian instruction of the young during the last thirty years; but the moral teaching of one day in seven is not an antidote to the exposed condition or positive immoral training of the other six days of the week. And he adds: "Moral instruction and moral training are usually thought to be the same, but the former is merely the imparting of knowledge, while the latter is the cultivation of the practical habit." Such cultivation he regards as essential; and his key word as to the means of securing it is "sympathy — the sympathy of numbers of persons of the same age, and having the same pursuits."

What this author calls "the cultivation of the practical habit" is just the formation of character. It is the discipline of the affections and the will as distinct from the intellect. It is the putting to use of the knowledge that the mind acquires. It is making one's life accord with his ideas and beliefs. "As he thinketh in his heart, so is he," says the scriptural proverb; i.e., the thought must get down to the roots of action before it will control character. Dr. Joseph Baldwin of the University of Texas says: "Only right doing educates conscience. Moral lectures and moral sermons are good, but they become effective only when they become ethical emotions and ethical acts."

This is just to say that the fundamental thing that we all need is the training of the will. Self-command and self-control are the two great requisites; ability, on the one hand, to marshal all our powers and make them render their very best service; ability, on the other hand, to subdue our appetites, passions, fears, selfish ambitions, and to finally "bring every thought into captivity to the obedience of Christ."

This is training, and the result of training, character. Professor Rosenkranz, of the University of Koenigsberg, says, "Nothing in the world has an absolute value except will guided by the right." And Fichte says, "He that has a bad character must absolutely create for himself a better one."

All this constitutes a great task. But it is the task of Christian Endeavor, and one from which it need not shrink since the endeavor is Christian. We feel, as profoundly as did Fichte, that we must create for ourselves better characters, and that our endeavor must be aimed directly and persistently to that end; but we are not working alone. "We are laborers together with God." We have not only cheerfully pledged our own efforts, but we have the covenanted help of our Almighty Redeemer.

Now, in casting about for means of illustrating that Christian Endeavor is a training school in the distinctive and efficient sense already defined, I have turned to the two great educational institutions in this country that make training a specialty, viz., the military academy at West Point and the naval academy of Annapolis. We are apt to think of physical training only in connection with these schools; of the manual of arms, of horsemanship and athletics. But while these have their share of attention, the emphasis is laid on training character.

In order to get the best possible information I have addressed to several exceptionally competent men these questions: What are the characteristics of West Point and Annapolis that distinguish them as specifically training schools? What valuable elements of character do they give that are not given by colleges teaching the same subjects?

General John M. Schofield, a graduate of West Point, later a teacher there, a very distinguished soldier of the late war, and now in command of the United States army, mentions especially two things:

1. Accuracy and independence of thought and expression. Each pupil must rise, and without the least aid from the teacher, must translate his French or German, demonstrate his mathematical theorem, state and explain and defend his scientific hypothesis.

2. Obedience and regard for constituted authority. Every cadet is made to comprehend that he is under orders; that in least things as well as greatest he must obey instantly and unquestionably. And this soon ceases to be a hardship for him, for he quickly recognizes that he has superiors, and respect for them as such becomes a fixed habit of thought and a fixed attitude of the will.

Col. John M. Wilson, recently superintendent at West Point, puts first the absolute equality that prevails among the cadets. The community is a pure democracy. Birth, social standing, money, political influence, have no relation to the work or discipline of the academy. Without any qualification each young man makes his own rank.

Captain James L. Lusk, a distinguished officer of the engineer corps, and now on duty at West Point, writes: "Here the value of training as differing from instruction has been fully recognized and utilized for three-quarters of a century. Everything else is subordinated to the development of character, all instruction being a means to that end.

General Francis A. Walker, not a graduate of West Point, but a very brilliant soldier of the Civil War, and since that time very successful in public life, spoke thus to the University Convocation of the State of New York at Albany, July 9, 1891: —

"There is no reason to believe that for the thirty years preceding the Civil War the young men who went to West Point were in any degree superior to those who entered Yale or Harvard. Indeed, there was at that time, at least throughout the North, a certain disinclination on the part of the more generous and ambitious of our youth to adopt the career of arms. Yet, when the war broke out, what a wealth of intellect and character was displayed by the graduates of that one small school during the terrific trial to which they were instantly and without preparation subjected! Think how many men from that single academy, which had fewer living graduates than either Amherst or Williams, led army corps and armies with distinction on the one side or the other in what was, perhaps, the greatest war of modern history. I said 'of intellect and character;' for it is character even more than intellect which enables the commander to bear the tremendous cares, responsibilities, and burdens of his office."

Turning now to the navy, we will, of course, find some of these things repeated; for in many essential qualities the training of the soldier and of the sailor is the same. Strict equality among the cadets, obedience, regard for authority, respect for superiors, prevail at Annapolis as at West Point.

Rear-Admiral Francis M. Ramsey, a graduate of the naval academy, and for five recent years its superintendent, places chief emphasis on thoroughness of instruction. He was wont to tell the cadets that the difference between other schools and this was the difference between "playing marbles for fun and playing marbles for keeps." Every subject must be mastered. Only three studies can be taken at a time, and no new one can be entered upon until its natural predecessor has been completely learned, not simply gone over in such a fashion as to squeeze through an examination on it. This means as a result a habit of thoroughness, which is one of the most precious elements of character.

Paymaster General Edwin Stewart, not a graduate of Annapolis, but with many years' naval experience, values most highly the ability that life in the navy gives to adapt one's self to circumstances, and especially to the men with whom one lives. Three years on shipboard, with four or five hundred men, where one must live at peace with all the others, must submit himself to his official superiors, and bear himself justly and courteously to his official interiors, constitute an invaluable discipline in that highest art of civilized life, the art of a genuine, hearty Christian courtesy.

Prof. Edward K. Rawson, who has been both chaplain and teacher at the naval academy, and understands it thoroughly, would add these to the elements of training already named: —

1. A definite ideal. Few boys enter college — comparatively few leave it — with a clear idea of what their calling in life is to be; but every cadet has his career sharply marked out before him. He is animated from the first by its highest possibilities, and sees himself standing on the deck of some noble ship with an admiral's flag floating above his head. As Napoleon said, "Every French soldier carries his marshal's baton in his knapsack."

2. A high sense of honor. Lying, for instance, is held in abhorrence. All things that are "becoming an officer and a gentleman" are taught to be of paramount importance.

3. Self-discipline. The subordination of the will to a sense of duty, in every respect and under all circumstances, is not only taught, but so persistently and rigidly required, that it becomes a fixed and principal element of character.

4. Minor virtues, such as accuracy, punctuality, order, neatness. These are inculcated as necessary to the carrying out of duty. But, especially, all these things are not simply taught, as they may be in any school, and widely are, but they are enforced through a period of four plastic and formative years by the training at Annapolis, and are thus so firmly fixed in mind, affections, and will that they control all the subsequent life.

Let us now see if Christian Endeavor is adapted to give young men and women that training, mental, moral, and religious, which will produce in them these individual qualities. And here we shall need to refer constantly to that charter of both our existence and our activity, the pledge.

1. Regard for authority. We are a society of Christian Endeavor. We recognize and confess first and always our loyalty to Christ. Whatever we promise to do we promise only as "trusting in the Lord Jesus Christ for strength." Whatever we omit to do is for a reason that we can "conscientiously give" to him. We are not a merely voluntary organization, come together for social pleasure, with no bond but elective affinity; into which one is free to cast as little or as much as he pleases; from which we are at liberty to withdraw on account of any trifling dissatisfaction with fellow-members. Instead, we are enlisted under the "Captain of our salvation." We have voluntarily agreed to obey his orders. We understand that withdrawal from our society would be breaking, not a promise to men, but a covenant with Christ; in a word, would be desertion. So we act under a constant sense of his authority. This is fundamental with us. Our prime question is not "What will please myself?" not "What will be popular?" not even "What will advance the interests of my society?" but "What will please Christ?" His authority is paramount; to it our likes and dislikes, our hopes and fears, our ambitions and plans, at once and cheerfully yield.

2. Respect for superiors. The very word "superiors" is distasteful to American ears. We can hardly endure to acknowledge that any one is above us in anything. Even when we might concede that another's station is higher than ours, we are ready to offset this by dwelling upon his faults and weaknesses. It is, therefore, of the highest importance that we should recognize that we have superiors, and should learn how to conduct ourselves toward them. Now, every Christian Endeavor Society is distinctly subordinate to the church in which it exists. Our motto is, "For Christ and the Church."

The pastor is *ex officio* an officer of the society, and a member of every committee. He is, or should be, present at every business meeting and every prayer meeting, and his counsel always sought and accepted. The same is true in proper proportion to all other officers of the church. Age, wisdom, experience, are thus always cheerfully deferred to by youth, ignorance, and inexperience; unless the former make the sad mistake of being jealous of the latter, and arraying themselves in opposition. Even then yielding is infinitely better than conflict. No true Christian Endeavor society fails to accept the pastor and other officers of the church as superiors, and to heartily seek their counsel and follow their direction.

3. Obedience. This is simply carrying the two former points into practical effect. We must not associate with this word "obedience" any idea of forced submission to harsh and arbitrary commands. Even our divine Lord and Master does not so use his authority. "His commandments are not grievous." There is nothing demeaning, but everything exalting, about obeying them. And the same is true of obeying human commandments, justly and lovingly given. And accordingly members of the Christian Endeavor society are trained to prompt response when the pastor, or the president, or the chairman of a committee, summons to any kind of service. We may feel ourselves incompetent; we may think that our officers could have made a wiser choice; we may especially shrink from this thing as distasteful to us; but we are loyal to lawful authority, and we say, "Yes, we will go and do the very best we can."

4. Equality. This is the offset to the three preceding points. A Christian Endeavor society is a pure democracy. It has neither king nor pope nor any hereditary ruler. But this does not mean that it is either a mob or a commune. It chooses its own officers. It changes them frequently, so that honor and responsibility may pass from hand to hand. It asks only who will make the best officers; not what parentage or money or social standing this or that candidate may have. At its social gatherings, as at its prayer meetings, all are alike welcomed, and if they are particularly timid or ill dressed or awkward, they are the objects of special attention and courtesy. Here, if in any organization within the church, piety, modesty, zeal, and efficiency fix each person's standing, regardless of the clothes he wears, the house he lives in, or the size of his father's income.

5. Accuracy, thoroughness, and independence of thought. This has abundant scope in the Christian Endeavor prayer meeting. Every active member has pledged himself to take some part aside from singing in this meeting. He may, indeed, fulfill the letter of his pledge by reading or reciting a verse of Scripture; and that the first verse on which his eye happens to rest when he opens his Bible. But no conscientious member will do this. If he is too timid to venture beyond a verse of Scripture, he will at least search

diligently for the verse most appropriate to the theme, and he will commit it to memory instead of slavishly reading it. But if he is in downright earnest he will go far beyond this. He will say in his own words how the verse fits the subject. He will meditate and pray over the theme until he has some original thought about it, not a thought that some one else has ever had, but that has come fresh from the Holy Spirit to his own mind. He will not be concerned to know whether this is the current and popular thought, but only whether it is true. He will try to put it into the fewest and best possible words, and to speak it with such conviction that it will reach the hearts and move the wills of his fellow members. Thousands of young men and women in the Christian Endeavor societies are thus learning the rare and fine art of thinking clearly and speaking sententiously; an art that will prove one of their chief sources of power and happiness as long as they live.

6. Self-discipline both in self-command and self-control. One element of self-command is the type of thinking and speaking just described. But there are many other elements. We all have precious powers unused just because we have never arrayed them in line of action. Christian Endeavor calls for them all. You say, "I fear I have no social faculty. I do not seem to be able to make friends." But you are put on the social committee. You feel it your duty to be agreeable. You simply try to do your duty. And before you know it you are one of the most popular members of your society. Or you say, "I can talk with people about everything else except personal religion." The president appoints you on the lookout committee. You are very unhappy. You appeal to your pastor. He advises you to stand. So with much fear, but with much prayer, you begin to do your duty. And soon you have the incomparable joy of having won and directed some person to the Saviour. Who can say how many young men have already thus learned in Christian Endeavor Societies that they may have the qualities that will make them useful ministers of the gospel? How many young women have found their vocation as Bible readers or city missionaries?

And as you have developed these unsuspected powers you have at the same time and in the same course of discipline acquired self-control. You have found it quite as necessary to restrain your tongue as to use your tongue; to curb your anger or resentment as to show your sympathy and affection. And in all directions Christian Endeavor has made you a self-disciplined man or woman.

7. The great moralities, such as truthfulness, honesty, honor, etc. None of us can sincerely try to live up to our pledge without developing these qualities. For instance, the pledge puts us on our honor. Some things in it the world can see whether or not we do; others are known only to ourselves and God. Do we read God's word and pray daily? Do we give excuses to our fellow members that we know Christ must count invalid? These are matters of truthfulness, of honesty, of honor. If we are sincere we will live most scrupulously in those things about which men can never call us to account. It is a maxim at West Point and at Annapolis that a cadet's word is as good as the oath of any other man. Christian Endeavor should raise every member's word to that high place.

8. Adaptability to others. The associations of a Christian Endeavor society are not so close as those of shipboard, or of a soldiers' or sailors' mess, but they are close enough to test every member's flexibility of temper. Petty jealousies will destroy the society. So will a suspicious spirit. So will gossip. So will listening to gossip. So will paying too much heed to the whims, eccentricities, infelicities, of any member or members. Infinite tact, patience, and forbearance are required. No one's prejudices, tastes, habits, or opinions must be needlessly crossed. No one must be criticised, much less laughed at, however good reason he may give. Every one's bluntness, awkwardness, boorishness, must be met with unfailing courtesy; and, what is far harder, courtesy must not fail in the presence of egotism, self-assertion, even arrogance. We must be always ready to correct our own errors, while seeming not to observe those of others. In short, we must know and practice such Scriptural commands as "Be courteous;" "Follow peace with all;" "Follow after the things that make for peace, and things wherewith one may edify another."

9. An ideal. The furnishing of this is one of the noblest services that our society renders to the young Christian, For, as a rule, he lacks an ideal definite enough to restrain, stimulate, and guide him. He is converted, confesses Christ, and joins the church. He sincerely desires and intends to be an exemplary disciple, but the whole matter is vague

to him. Beyond attending upon public worship and being at the Lord's table, little seems clear. Then Christian Endeavor meets him with its pledge. This requires nothing not already implied in church membership, only it makes plain what is implied. It sets forth the highest ideal of Christian living; viz., "To do whatever Christ would like to have him do." It sets him, upon daily study of his Bible, and daily prayer to learn what this is. It gives him the close fellowship of a group of young men and women bent on the same object. It gives him that "sympathy" which David Stow deemed essential to character building. It gives him the counsel and help of maturer Christians, especially of his pastor. It keeps his ideal ever before him, renewing it every month at the consecration meeting. He lives every day and hour under the impulse of the noblest standard, "after the power of an endless life."

10. *Esprit de corps.* Although this was not mentioned by any of the gentlemen that I have quoted, it is undoubtedly one of the finest fruits of the training at West Point and Annapolis. The devotion of every soldier to the army, of every sailor to the navy, is proverbial. Their pride in the service, their zeal for its honor, their shame if it is disgraced, are known to us all. It is this that holds them to such lofty standards of honor, of fidelity, of courage, of patriotism, of obedience. And it is this same *esprit de corps* that Christian Endeavor has so splendidly cultivated. What a rallying cry our name has become! How potent it is to gather thousands from all parts of our land and of the world! What new life it has put into many a decadent church! How it is drawing together differing, and even conflicting, denominations of God's people! We gratefully and loyally recognize that this centers in the adjective "Christian," not in the noun "Endeavor." It is the omnipotent name that animates us. It is "the name that is above every name" that gives us our *esprit de corps.* Devotion to Christ is not waning, but mightily waxing, as Christian Endeavor is every year anew demonstrating. It is a training school that can outdo the best work of West Point and Annapolis, since in it the very "dry bones arise and stand upon their feet, an exceeding great army." We rejoice in the contagious enthusiasm of our great convention, and we need it. We need also the same enthusiasm, the same *esprit de corps,* in each local society, and in the heart of every member. We may have it if we never forget that every member carries in his badge the Saviour's promise of daily strength here, and there everlasting life.

Euclid Avenue Baptist Church.

A large and enthusiastic audience gathered at this church, where an unusually attractive programme had been provided. Rev. H. C. Applegarth, D.D., pastor of the church, presided, and after the usual opening exercises introduced Miss Anna M. Edwards of Cleveland, who spoke upon "The Possibilities of Christian Endeavor."

Rev. George Dana Boardman, D.D., of Philadelphia, next spoke eloquently upon the theme,

St. Paul's Endeavor.

Address of Rev. George Dana Boardman, D.D.

"Not as though I had already attained, either were already perfect; but I follow after, if that I may apprehend that for which also I am apprehended of Christ Jesus. Brethren, I count not myself to have apprehended; but this one thing I do, forgetting those things which are behind, and reaching forth unto those which are before, I press toward the mark for the prize of the high calling of God in Christ Jesus."— PHIL. iii. 12–14.

It is St. Paul's conception of the Christian life, stated in terms of his own personal experience, purpose, and struggle. According to him, and he was the greatest of the apostles, the Christian life is a strenuous and tireless Christian endeavor. Were he to return to earth, still feeling as he did when he wrote to his dear Philippians, he would doubtless hasten to join the society of Christian Endeavor.

In trying to unfold our text, we cannot do better than to follow the apostle's own order of thoughts and words as they stand in the revised version: —

"Not that I have already obtained." The expression is suggested by the ancient stadium, or Greek course for foot-races. Indeed, our whole paragraph is terse with the quivering excitement of a desperate runner; our apostle using such athletic expressions as "pressing on," "forgetting what is behind," "stretching forward to what is before," "goal," "prize," "obtaining." The first clause of our text asserts that our apostle has not yet obtained "the prize of God's high calling in Christ Jesus." But more of this presently.

"Or am already made perfect." Our hero has just been speaking of his own mighty transformation from a persecuting Pharisee into a Christian missionary, saying: —

"But what things were gain to me, those have I counted loss for Christ. Yea verily, and I count all things to be loss for the excellency of the knowledge of Christ Jesus my Lord: for whom I suffered the loss of all things, and do count them but refuse, that I may gain Christ, and be found in him, not having a righteousness of my own, even that which is of the law, but that which is through faith in Christ, the righteousness which is from God by faith; that I may know him, and the power of his resurrection, and the fellowship of his sufferings, becoming conformed unto his death; if by any means I may attain unto the resurrection from the dead."

But this language of our apostle is so strong that he fears that his readers may misunderstand him, as though he himself had become a saint; and therefore he immediately adds — "Not that I am already made perfect." For the sense of "perfection" is a sure and sad sign of imperfection. For consider for a moment what the New Testament means by this word "perfect;" it means something vastly more and better than mere sinlessness. "Perfect" means perfected, completed, fulfilled, matured, realized. To become perfect is to be perfected in aim, in business, in character, in details, in endurance, in faith, in growth, in hope, in ideal, in love, in maturity, in outline, in patience, in quota, in realization, in symmetry, in temperance, in unity, in variety, in wholeness. Alas, how imperfect we all are — imperfect in accomplishment, in beatitudes, in conscience, in development, in entirety, in fruition, in goal, in home, in imagination, in liberty, in mission, in opportunity, in purity, in quality, in soundness, in society, in truth, in unity, in vocation, in zeal. As Emerson says, "A man is a bundle of relations, a knot of roots, whose flower and fruitage is the world." In brief, man is "a bundle of possibilities." We live in this world embryonically, incipiently, rudimentally. "It is not yet made manifest what we shall be." Here is the secret of our discontent: envy, moral famine, ill nature, restlessness. Here is also the secret of our aspiration: endeavor, hopefulness, perseverance, struggles. While "perfectionism" is a drag-chain, perfectibility is an uplift. And so we are prepared for our next point.

"But I press on." Again it is the language of the ancient stadium. How fond St. Paul is of athletic features! Take the following familiar one as a notable example: —

"Know ye not that they who run in a race run all, but one receiveth the prize? Even so run, that ye may attain. And every man that striveth in the games is temperate in all things. Now they do it to receive a corruptible crown [a fading wreath of laurel, or oak, or pine, etc.], but we an incorruptible. I therefore so run, as not uncertainly; so fight I, as not beating the air: but I buffet my body and bring it into bondage, lest by any means after that I have preached [being a herald] to others, I myself should be rejected."

Brothers, I believe in many of our athletic sports. I sincerely wish, alike for our health of body and our health of soul, that every one of us could become an accomplished gymnast. Nevertheless, there is a nobler gymnasium than any physical — a gymnasium demanding a sterner regimen, exacter discipline, firmer will, stouter muscle, defter skill, braver movement than any you shall ever see on earth's athletic grounds; it is the gymnasium of the soul, the palestra of the Ten Commandments, the stadium of the Beatitudes. God grant that in that spiritual arena, where the wrestling is not against flesh and blood, but against all powers of lawlessness, every one of us may "wax valiant in fight, turning to flight armies of aliens." With St. Paul let us press on.

"If so be." It was not the doubt of unbelief, or agnosticism, for our apostle knew him whom he had believed. But it was the doubt of self-distrust; that sense of humility which has just led him to say, "If by any means I may attain to the resurrection from the dead" (not the resurrection of the dead — touching that he had no doubt — but the resurrection from the dead, that spiritual resurrection promised to the justified in Christ — touching that his own sense of unworthiness made him feel apprehensive); "If so be." Yet there are apparently good people on earth to-day, who declare that they never have a doubt concerning their own personal salvation. May they not learn a little lesson of modesty from the greatest of the apostles?

"That I may apprehend [lay hold on, grasp, seize] that for which also I was apprehended [laid hold on, grasped, seized] by Christ Jesus." The allusion is to that memorable scene in the life of Saul of Tarsus when, on his way to Damascus, he was suddenly apprehended or laid hold on by our Lord Jesus Christ for a distinctly Christian career or vocation. That apprehension of Saul by Christ was so intensely personal, definite, complete, lasting, absolute, that it could not be expressed by any gentler word than seizure. "That I may seize that for which also Christ Jesus seized me." What though none of us may have experienced a similar seizure? Have there not been indescribable moments in the life of each one of us when we have suddenly awaked to a new conviction of duty, a new conception of life, a new sense of a career or vocation? That sudden awakening, however commonplace our surroundings, was nothing less than Christ's own personal seizure of us for a heavenly calling. For each human life — oh, that every human being understood and believed it! — is a divine call. In other words, God does have a definite work for each of us to do. I cannot do your work; you cannot do my work. God, with reverence I speak it, has projected, as Horace Bushnell has finely shown, a separate plan or scheme of life for each one of us, leaving it to our own choice, indeed, as free and therefore responsible beings, whether to adjust ourselves or not to his scheme. And life, in its truest import, is the conscious and joyous fulfilling by every human being of God's particular plan concerning himself, so that he, in his own character and work, is, so to speak, a distinct impersonation of one of the conceptions of Deity.

Believe then, friends, that each one of you has a direct call from God Most High. Don't imagine that God calls only ministers. I grant, indeed, that some persons have a special call to the ministry, but it is in the sense that they have special qualifications for that particular service. The solemn and blessed truth is that God calls every human being to become a minister, assigning him his own parish in the great diocese of his one church. The only difference between "clergy and laity" lies in the accidents of name and form and outward service. Noah was a "preacher of righteousness" as truly as was Paul, although no ordaining presbytery had ever laid hands on the patriarch's head, and the only sermon he ever preached was the ark he built. Believe me, God calls every human being to the ministry. The diaconite, the service, employment in which he is engaged being the sphere of his call. In fact, how is it that we so instinctively style a man's employment his "calling" or "vocation," if it is not that we have a kind of feeling that God, by a sort of providential arrangement of circumstances, has called this man to this particular employment? Yes, every time you style a man's business his calling, you utter, whether you realize it or not, something profound. The thoughtful man, who is in the habit of weighing his expressions, recognizes in this word "calling" man's relations as a creature and son to God as his Creator and Father. It robes all the relations of life with a sacred celestial mantle. It recognizes and formulates this great truth: God calls me to do this thing; God calls you to do that thing; God calls him to do the other thing. Believe then, I repeat, that each one of you has a vocation from God himself. Do not do yourself the injustice, or God the dishonor, of thinking that because your vocation is, as the world phrases it, a "secular" one, it is therefore not a sacred one. The art of life is to see our Lord Christ everywhere, hallowing earth's secularities with his presence and benediction. It matters not what or how humble your employment may be, provided it is useful, and you feel sure that your Father has called you to it. As George Herbert sings: —

> "A servant with this clause
> Makes drudgery divine;
> Who sweeps a room as for thy laws
> Makes that and the action fine."

And whatever your vocation be, pursue it diligently, enthusiastically, joyously, as being God's calling. Have faith in the divinity of your vocation. Believe that Christ himself has seized you for a definite purpose or goal, and you in your turn will achieve that purpose and seize that goal. It is, as we shall see, the grand sacred victory. Meanwhile, let us return to our apostle.

"Brethren, I count not myself yet to have apprehended, laid hold on, grasped, seized." Why does our apostle repeat this statement? He has just said, "Not that I have already obtained, or am already made perfect." Why does he add, "Brothers, I count not myself yet to have apprehended, seized?" Probably because, as there is strong reason for believing, there had already arisen in the Philippian church some who imagined that they themselves had already been made perfect; the prototypes of our modern perfectionism. It is as though St. Paul, with that gracious irony of which he was peculiarly a master, had said: "Brothers, you may claim for yourselves that you have reached perfection; as for myself, I disclaim it; whatever you or others may think, I do not count myself yet to have seized that goal for which Christ Jesus seized me." What a pity that St. Paul's modesty has not made a deeper impression on modern Christendom!

"But one thing I do." It recalls our blessed Lord's saying at the hospitable home of Bethany: —

"Martha, Martha, thou art anxious and troubled about many things; but one thing is needful; for Mary hath chosen the good part, which shall not be taken away from her."

It is as though the Lord had said: "Martha, Martha, you mean well; you wish to do me the utmost honor. But you are cumbered about much serving; you allow yourself to be distracted by undertaking too great a variety of hospitable services. Only one thing is really needful — singleness of aim or ideal; unity of purpose, of life; this is the good part which your sister Mary has chosen: for while your hospitalities are many they are outward, and must therefore perish; but Mary's sitting at my feet and learning from me is a single-hearted and inward service and therefore will abide forever." Not Martha's many things, but Mary's one thing. And Mary's one thing may include Martha's many things, not in the meager sense of many separate units, but in the sublime sense of one vast diversified unity. For there is no force so converging and unifying as the force of a great idea. Here is the secret of all noblest endeavor and all noblest success. Grant, Lincoln, Field, Washington, Cromwell, Columbus, Luther, Hildebrand, Paul. Each said, "But one thing I do," and therefore each conquered.

"Forgetting the things which are behind." For our hero is still in the stadium, speeding toward his goal with all his might. So strenuous is his endeavor that he has no time to glance backward, noting neither his failures nor his successes, not even the landmarks he has already passed. Brother athletes, it is a sturdy lesson for each one of us. We lose too much time in mere retrospect, not of what Christ has done for us — perish that thought — but of what we have done for Christ — perish this thought! Too much lies before us to justify us in any self-congratulation over past successes; even in any lamentation over past failures. No energy of ours can alter our past — that has forever slipped from our grasp. No remorse, not even contrition or penitence, can change our sin. We are to repent, indeed, but repentance does not look backward, it does not mean retrace; repentance looks forward, it means advance. Not retrospect, but prospect — this is the Christian runner's watchword. This brings us to our next point.

"And stretching forward to the things which are before." What though our saintly hero is now an old man, even "Paul the aged"? What though he is a helpless prisoner at Rome awaiting Nero's order of execution? He still lives in the future, as though he were still "a young man named Saul." His prize still lies before him. And so we see this aged and manacled prisoner of the cross still struggling forward as mightily as ever in the days of yore, never loitering for a single instant to glance backward at the many things which lie behind him in that long and desperate race of more than thirty years, still pauselessly struggling forward with all "the thews of Anakim, the pulses of a Titan's heart," to grasp the things which are before him. And what are some of the things which yet lie before him? Still greater faith, hope, love, meekness, patience, knowledge, righteousness, saintliness — in one word, perfection. Oh, that each of us might emulate his tireless energy, like him, by patient continuance in well-doing, seeking for glory and honor and immortality, and therefore, like him, sharing in the reward of the life eternal.

"I press on toward the goal." No uncertain runner is our Paul, feebly vacillating between various goals. His goal is definite, and therefore his aim is undeviating. That goal is the purpose for which Christ Jesus had graciously seized him, and therefore he wastes no time and labor in trying to choose his career, or in wavering between aims. For, as Lucio said to Isabella, —

> "Our doubts are traitors,
> And make us lose the good we oft might win
> By fearing to attempt."

Definiteness of goal — this is one of the secrets of success. That is our true birthday, not when we are born into the world, but when we are consciously born into a mission. For the sense of a divine seizure for a vocation specializes life, turning it from an indefinite "an" into the definite "the." This clearness of goal gives to life directness, simplicity, coherence, unity, inspiration, persistence, grandeur, victory. Be it for you and mé to accept unhesitatingly St. Paul's definition of life, — a definition as profound as it is simple, — "To me to live is Christ!" For so alone we shall find that "To die is gain."

"Unto the prize." It is the prize of the true race, the Christian stadium. Not the Isthmian garland of fading olive or parsley; but the true immortelle, "the crown of glory that fadeth not away," the glorious amaranthine crown. In other words, the prize is the goal itself. What nobler coronation than the sense of an achieved mission?

"Of the high calling of God." What higher calling than God's upward summons, God's heavenward vocation? Why, the sense of an achieved vocation is heaven itself! Then —

> "Rise, my soul, and stretch thy wings,
> Thy better portion trace;
> Rise from transitory things
> Toward heaven, thy native place:
> Sun and moon and stars decay;
> Time shall soon this earth remove
> Rise, my soul, and haste away
> To seats prepared above."

"In Christ Jesus." It is a profound expression, a favorite formula of our great apostle. According to him, to be in Christ is to live in the sphere of Christ's personality, — work, spirit, life, character, influence, etc. This whole conception of the apostle's stadium, — this pressing on, this apprehending, this forgetting, this stretching forward, this goal, this prize, this high calling, this obtaining — all this is true and great and triumphant, because all this is in the august arena of the Divine Man; in the blessed sphere of our Lord and Saviour Jesus Christ. Or, to quote a kindred expression in our same apostle's letter to the Colossians, "Perfect in Christ;" that is, perfected in the arena of Christ's own personality. We hear a great deal in our day about "Progress, Development, Evolution," and the like. Some of it is skeptically false; much of it is sublimely true. In fact, evolution is pre-eminently a Pauline idea; recall our text: "Not that I have already obtained," etc. The truth is, there is no such champion of progress as the Apostle Paul; no such philosopher of evolution as the evangel of Jesus. The difference between the evolutionism of Darwin and the evolutionism of Paul is this: Darwin busies himself with what man has been; Paul busies himself with what man can be: Darwin looks backward, and so bruteward; Paul looks forward, and so Christward: Darwin finds the issue of evolution in man; Paul finds the issue of evolution in Christ, or, as St. Paul himself says, —

"In him [Christ] dwelleth all the fulness of the Godhead bodily [body-wise]. And ye are complete in him" [made full, completed, unfolded, matured, filled full, fulfilled, etc.]. (Col. ii. 9, 10.)

What is implicit or unfolded in man becomes explicit or unfolded in Christ. In other words, Jesus Christ is the soul's true environment, the soul's true soil, air, wet, light, heat, chemical agencies, etc. For no man truly knows what is in him and what he can become till he and Christ are in touch. Jesus Christ, and he alone, is the true perfecter of human nature; the perfecter, for instance, of our faculties of duty, enthusiasm, faith, hope, love, conscience, reason, imagination, insight, justice, liberty, loyalty, order, symmetry, ideal, fidelity, truth, sympathy, unity, aspiration, communion, worship, etc. Jesus Christ is both our author and our finisher, our inaugurator and our consummator, our Alpha and our Omega, our all in all. Perfected in Christ.

Such is St. Paul's portrayal of his own mighty endeavor after the Christly perfectation. How graphically Philip Doddridge has reproduced it in his own familiar song of "The Christian Race"!

> "Awake, my soul, stretch every nerve,
> And press with vigor on;
> A heavenly race demands thy zeal,
> And an immortal crown.
>
> A cloud of witnesses around
> Hold thee in full survey;
> Forget the steps already trod,
> And onward urge thy way.
>
> 'Tis God's all-animating voice
> That calls thee from on high;
> 'Tis his own hand presents the prize
> To thine aspiring eye;
>
> That prize, with peerless glories bright,
> Which shall new luster boast,
> When victors' wreaths and monarchs' gems
> Shall blend in common dust.
>
> Blest Saviour, introduced by thee,
> Have I my race begun;
> And, crowned with victory, at thy feet
> I'll lay my honors down."

Thus it was with St. Paul himself. Listen to his own dying testimony as recorded in his second letter to his beloved son Timothy — the last letter probably he ever wrote, perhaps on the very day of his martyrdom.

"I am already being offered [poured out on the altar as a drink offering], and the time of my departure is come. I have fought the good fight [observe the tense of the verb, no longer future or contingent, as when on his way to Jerusalem he had said to the Ephesian presbyters at Miletus, "I hold not my life of any account, as dear unto myself, so that I may finish, accomplish my course, career, and the ministry which I received from the Lord Jesus to testify the gospel of the grace of God, the goal for which Christ had seized me." But now the perfect tense]. I have fought the good fight, I have finished the course [the race set for me], I have kept the faith [the trust confided me]; henceforth there is laid up for me the crown of righteousness [not a wreath of laurel, but the chaplet of perfected character], which the Lord, the righteous judge [the just arbiter, the impartial umpire], shall give to me at that day [the day of the great final awards]; and not only to me, but also to all them that have loved his appearing."

But why do I not speak of a greater than Paul, even of that Divine Master who had seized him and who, as the Eternal Word made flesh, was himself the most illustrious of the contestants in the heavenly stadium?

"Therefore [in view of the preceding muster-roll of the sons of faith] let us also, seeing we are compassed about with so great a cloud of witnesses [martyrs], lay aside every weight [all cumbrance], and the sin which doth so easily beset us [the encircling, entangling, impeding habit], and let us run with patience [patient endurance to the end] the race that is set before us, looking unto Jesus [looking away from all other things unto Jesus alone], the author and finisher [the captain and perfecter] of faith, who for the joy that was set before him [the prize of his own high calling of God] endured the cross, despising the shame, and hath sat down at the right hand of the throne of God [wearing the royal crown of divine victory]."

Indeed, so thoroughly did Jesus finish the work which God had given him to do, so completely did he accomplish the specific work for which his father had anointed him, so perfectly did he fulfill his own divine calling, that his very vocation has become his historic title. While he was still on earth, before he had finished his work on Calvary,

his name was only Jesus. When he arose from the dead and ascended on high, leading captivity captive and giving gifts unto men, his name became, and still is, Jesus the Christ. Heaven grant that when each of us in his turn shall review life's mission, each of us may also be able to exclaim with Jesus Christ on the cross, —
"It is finished!"

Second Presbyterian Church.

Secretary John Willis Baer, of the United Society, presided over the meeting here, and received a royal welcome back to his old church home — he was formerly a Cleveland boy, and attended this church. The first speaker was Mrs. Ellen J. Phinney of Cleveland, who delivered the following address upon

Golden Opportunities for Christian Endeavor.

Address of Mrs. Ellen J. Phinney.

As I look into the faces of so many of the assembled representatives of the great Christian Endeavor movement, which has in such an incredibly short space of time permeated the church activity and the church methods of work in this and other lands, I find the question continually arising, What is the secret of this marvelous growth? Why these rapid enlistments under the banner of the cross? What means this banding together in holy service? What is the inner force that impels an outward movement which might be termed a crusade for Christ? Is not the answer summed up in the single word love? We are beginning to love him who first loved us. Archimedes said, give him a fulcrum on which to rest his lever, and he would move the world. Christian Endeavor has found a fulcrum in the hearts of men; and the love of God revealed in our Lord Jesus Christ is the lever with which the world is being moved as never before. Love to God, coupled with enthusiasm in his service, is well nigh omnipotent. It is unterrified by dangers, unhindered by obstacles; it overleaps barriers to progress; bridges chasms of difficulty; tunnels mountains of opposition, or removes them to the sea.

Enthusiasm for God is not only the holiest, but the strongest and most irresistible, force men may wield; it thrills the deeper nature, and awakens a responsive echo from the nobler self; it sweeps halting souls into the current of the divine life, and impels them onward by a tidal wave of united individual effort. Hence the strength of this movement and the greater possibilities yet to be realized when all the golden opportunities for service are fully comprehended.

We pride ourselves on the advanced thought of this age, on new methods of compassing new objects, when we have simply measured up a little nearer to the standard of the old prophets.

Jeremiah says, "It is good for a man that he bear the yoke in his youth;" or, in other words, apprenticeship in service should begin early in life. The reason is self-evident, and its forcefulness is everywhere recognized. Skill in most kinds of handicraft is acquired through the early and continued training of mind and muscles in line with that particular art or industry.

Experts in any department do not become such by accidents nor by a combination of fortuitous circumstances, but as the result of earnest endeavor to attain the highest degree of perfection. The yoke is a symbol of service. It is good both for the worker and for the work that the yoke should be borne in youth; that service for God and humanity should begin in early life and continue to the end. The Christian thus trained finds service easy, natural, joyous, the overflowing of a loving heart, eager to find expression in deeds as well as words. Such workers have an efficiency not acquired in later life; and the grand aggregate of good accomplished, begun in the morning and continued to the evening of life, is immeasurable.

John says in his first epistle, second chapter, "I have written unto you, young men, because ye are strong, and the word of God abideth in you, and ye have overcome the wicked one." The word "men" in this passage is generic, and applies equally to women; or, interpreted in the language of to-day, it would read, "I have written unto you, young 'people,' because ye are strong, and the word of God abideth in you, and ye have overcome the wicked one." If you are strong and have overcome, it is because you have the word of God hidden in your hearts; and your efficiency is due in no small degree to early apprenticeship in Christian service. By these means you have been specially fitted for carrying a large measure of responsibility in the solution of stern problems; and to you we look for such re-enforcements in the battle of the home against the saloon as will insure a complete rout of the enemy. In this warfare your earnestness and persistence will yield commensurate returns, and your unbounded enthusiasm will accelerate the coming victory. It is for you to abolish in a large degree social drinking customs, not only by your example of total abstinence, but by words fitly spoken, which Solomon declared are "like apples of gold in pictures of silver." Experience has proven that the most satisfactory results are attained by beginning early, before pernicious habits are formed; and therefore temperance instruction must be interwoven with religious and secular teaching from early youth, that it may become a part of the substratum upon which good character is built up. Who shall teach these fundamental truths if not the young people of this United Society of Christian Endeavor, in whose active membership we find so many of the teachers in Sunday and week day schools? To you, then, we want to appeal as to those who have it in their power to work wondrous changes in the interest of church and home, of God and humanity, before the dawn of the twentieth century. Right at hand are these golden opportunities for Christlike service. It is for you to save in large part the children of to-day, and thereby save the men and women of to-morrow, because you have them now under your molding influence; and their future for time and eternity will depend in no small degree on the impress you leave upon the plastic minds and hearts of childhood. Nor are the open doors of opportunity confined to the home, to the school, or to the church; but a mute appeal comes up from the neglected and sometimes uncared-for children upon the streets, or in crowded tenements, breathing the foul miasma of the slums, cramped and dwarfed mentally and morally by evil environments. These are to be rescued and redeemed through Christ's saving power; and Christian Endeavorers may form the circuit for the transmission of the electric spark of divine love which is "able to save unto the uttermost."

There are young people just on the verge of manhood and womanhood who need fortifying against the allurements of strong drink. They are, perchance, where the way divides, and an inadvertent step may mar their future life. It is for you to paint the signboard that points unerringly to safety, and to keep a watchman at the angle where the roads diverge, to turn back those who are inclined to press on toward probable ruin. How easy for you to hang out a danger signal to warn those who are approaching perilous ground, that they, seeing, may heed and be saved. These duties seem incumbent upon you because you are strong, and second, because you are enthusiastic, and can bring to the work the freshness of new methods, and a courage that knows no defeat. "The old for counsel, the young for war," is a maxim that may be fittingly applied in this case. Third, many who have done valiant service for, lo, these many years, must soon put off the harness and retire from active duty. It is imperative that the ranks be filled with vigorous recruits, better able to push the line of battle, capture the enemy's strongholds, and establish beyond question the supremacy of a government founded in righteousness. Your organization is, in the very nature of things, non-partisan and non-sectarian, and therefore specially adapted to successful effort in this branch of social reform. Will you champion this cause with all the earnestness and enthusiasm of which you are capable, in the full consciousness that it is necessarily allied to the building up of Christ's kingdom, and must therefore be a part of your work? Suppose each of the 2,000,000 in the rank and file of this movement were to win even one to total abstinence during the coming year, and then again each succeeding year, together with all the new adherents to Christian Endeavor work, how long before this land and other lands would put away the foul curse, and become that happy people whose God is the Lord?

If the sails of our temperance ship might catch this favoring breeze, how lightly would she skim the sea as she moves on toward the final harbor! Your help is coveted in many fields of Christian Endeavor.

"The fruitage of past years lies mellowed at thy feet for thee to taste:
The present with fleet hours is all in haste
To open wide its fields of golden ears."

But in no field is there promise of richer, more abundant sheaves of greater good to humanity, and therefore greater service to God, than in efforts to stay the ravages of drink, to save the young from the thralldom of this curse, and to rescue the slaves to appetite from their galling bondage.

May God help you to see and seize these golden opportunities.

Rev. Dr. John H. Barrows, of Chicago, was down on the programme for the next address, but he sent word that he was detained by the strike, and in his place Rev. Maltbie D. Babcock, of Baltimore, Md., delivered an interesting address upon "Salt."

Euclid Avenue Congregational Church.

Beautiful electric designs, potted plants, and bunting in profusion decorated the auditorium of this church, where there gathered another great audience, full of enthusiasm. Rev. H. M. Ladd, D.D., pastor, presided, and President Thwing, of Adelbert University, led in prayer. Mr. W. H. Pennell, of Washington, D.C., the first signer of the original Christian Endeavor constitution, was the first speaker, his topic being "Success in Christian Endeavor."

Next came a vigorous address by Rev. H. C. Farrar, D.D., pastor of the Trinity M. E. Church, Albany, N.Y., on

Grit and Grace.

Address of Rev. H. C. Farrar, D.D.

I am to speak to you to-night concerning our possibilities. There's magic in the very word "possibility." It is compact with electric energy. It challenges every faculty of body, brain, and spirit. Man is a bundle of possibilities. How shall he best unfold? Where shall he most wisely invest? What will he become? These are suggestive questions, far-reaching and weighty.

Marvelous have been the achievements of the human mind. They excite our wonder and command our admiration. Genius has scaled the heavens, counted the stars, measured and weighed the planets, resolved the zodiac into a concentrated blaze of starry light, halted every ray of light that has come from the far distant worlds, analyzed it, and chemically read the character of the orb from whence it came. It has brought lightnings from the heavens and harnessed them to its chariots of business and pleasure. It has built massive works of art, constructed monuments of imperishable fame, and fairly reveled in the luxury of its divine gift. Never was human genius working more wisely and Titanically than to-day. What it has done and is doing is but a prophecy of greater accomplishments in the near future. The world's best work is not yet done. The greatest and grandest achievements are yet before us, inviting brain and heart and hand. The golden age is not behind us to mock us, but ahead of us to beckon us on and out and up.

As we turn the pages of history, there have been golden ages many. Egypt had hers in the days of the Pharaohs of the Fifth and Sixth Dynasties. Babylon hers in the days of the royal Nebuchadnezzar, who sent her fame through all the Eastern world. Palestine hers when the gifted Solomon ruled with such grace as to draw the *élite* of all kingdoms to his beautiful Jerusalem. Greece hers when the eloquent Pericles swayed the scepter and Phidias, the artist, built and ornamented as none have ever excelled since his day, and few have ever equaled. Rome hers when Augustus the model ruler ruled almost the known world. Italy hers when Leo X. sat in the papal chair, and guided state and church. France hers when Louis XIV. was the typical French monarch. England hers in the days of good Queen Bess and William Shakespeare. We have not reached ours yet; it is before us. It awaits our growth and progress. It beckons us on. It holds out dazzling prizes. The future is aglow with promises and prophecies and possibilities.

The world is growing better. The kingdom is surely coming. Life is lengthening and enriching. The bonds of brotherhood are strengthening. Earth and heaven are steadily approximating. Men are thinking better of God and of his Christ and of his book and of his day.

"Out of the shadow of night the world moves into light. It is daybreak everywhere."

Did you ever consider that royal promise of Jehovah to Joshua as the leader of his people? "Every place that the sole of your foot shall tread upon that have I given you."

Mark the tenses! Then he proceeds to mark in bold outlines the generous boundaries of Israel's promised territory. And Israel, even in the palmiest days of Solomon, never occupied one-third of the promised land. Is that in any way suggestive to us, or prophetic of us? God promising three-thirds, and we satisfied with less than a third; a mere fraction, and vulgar at that. Is there one of us here that is more than one-third of what he ought to be, mentally or spiritually? Mark the conditions! "Every place that the sole of your foot shall tread upon;" i.e., theirs on condition of measuring it off, walking over it, and conquering it.

Are not these the conditions of all life, — of knowledge, art, music, grace, everything? God is an economist. He gives for use. He does not avalanche his grace on a land or a church. He never gives a second blessing until the first has been thoroughly used. And never did God seem so anxious to use the individual as to-day; never so eager to take him up into the very secret chambers of his grace and glory as now; never so longed to make all his children great and good and rich and powerful as in this decade. Were there ever such open doors, wide open with golden opportunity? Were the fields ever whiter for the harvest? Were beckoning hands ever more urgent?

How the wheels of enterprise are rolling over the world to-day! Everywhere enthusiasm is commanding the wheels of industry and pleasure on to white heat. Shall the church lag and the "old packet" type its progress? No. For that is not the plan of the King. I know he said, "The children of this world are wiser than the children of light:" but he never said it ought to be so, that it was necessary. The church is God's agency for the spread of his kingdom. It ought to be the foremost agency of this world. The Divine Spirit in the plenitude of his power waits on faith and heroic endeavor.

The church is not a social club; it is not an æsthetic association; it is not an intellectual prize ring; it is not a mutual admiration society; it is not a spiritual hammock to be swung by a willing pastor. No! But a workshop in which you are a worker; do not quarrel with your tools. It is an army in which you are a soldier; do not stain your honor or trail your colors. It is a republic in which you are a citizen; do not be disloyal to her history and mission. It is a body of which you are a member; do not become paralyzed or diseased. It is a family in which the old and the young mingle with no jealousies, but in love serving each other.

Christianity is in this world to win! While in that "upper room" where he had celebrated his last passover and established that feast, by which, the world over and history through, his name and works should be forever perpetuated, among other things he said, "He that hath no sword, let him sell his garment, and buy one." Peter at once responded, "We have two swords." The reply was, "It is enough." Then in two or three hours Peter rashly used one in the garden. Jesus said, "Put up thy sword in its sheath." He had said formerly, "They that take the sword shall perish by the sword." But now, "He that hath no sword, let him sell his garment, and buy one." What is its significance? This. The long, flowing robe of the Jew was the sign and symbol of ease and dignity and luxury. His order was to part with these and possess those that symbolized the spirit of conquest. They were to assume the aggressive; they were to go into all the world and preach the gospel to every creature. Theirs was but a single, simple mission of aggressive work and warfare. There was no time for luxurious ease or professional dally. The forces of evil were confronting on every hand, sworn and hateful and determined, and theirs was to go and proclaim the gospel, sow the seed, and gather the harvest.

My friends, we are not in the church to apologize for Jesus Christ, nor for his Bible, nor for his day or spirit. The business of the church is not to take care of religion but men; not to tinker away at creeds, but create deeds; not to criticise Moses and Jonah, but to win men and women from wrong to right in country and city. The "penknife of Jehudi" is not needed in our work, but the sword of the spirit is two-edged and fiery!

God's most marvelous opportunities are now before us. What shall we do with them, accept or reject? Speculate over them and fritter away, or rouse and utilize them? These are no idle questionings, merely to fill out my speech. America is the world's speaking gallery. How shall she speak? With what speech and tone and accent? By the church or the saloon? By the spirit of inactivity or by the Christ spirit? Our position here in this "belt of power" is deeply prophetic of prosperity and responsibility. God waits for his workers. He is waiting for us to-day. He is ever ready for every forward movement. He is ever calling and urging. He withholds nothing good. Omnipotence is not enriched by the accumulations of blessings withheld from the needy. Everywhere and in every way God seeks the needy and open heart, that he may pour himself into it. But how he waits to find the men and women he can use. He waited long for Luther and Wesley and Cromwell and Washington and Lincoln. Times and causes and men must fit. Is he waiting for one whom he can use to-day? Is he waiting in your church, in your society? Is he waiting for you?

You say, "Where shall I begin?" Begin in yourselves, here and now, as I speak and you listen. This is God's hour for your opportunity. Do your nearest duty. Do it with emphasis. Your business is to operate the "wheels." God means they shall roll on, but by and through human agency.

I know not how you may take this line of thinking, but I can't afford to let God roll on his providential wheels of enterprise without in some way becoming thoroughly identified with the forward movement.

God sets aside America's trained statesmen, and commands the rail-splitter to become her emancipator. He leaves Erasmus in his scholarship and time-serving, and calls the poor singer boy Luther to emancipate Europe. He passes by the dignitaries of the church of England, and picks out the schoolboy Spurgeon to be the preacher to the masses of England and the world. What God is planning for these closing years of this last decade I know not. I know the indications are decisive and momentous. I know he will use the willing and the obedient. I know he uses the ordinary talented. Oh, that out of our hearts there may spring this thought, hot and positive, "Here am I — send me." And he will send you, not as it pleases you, but as it pleases him.

Have you heard of the Persian fable? A young Persian prince had a noted shell. By touching a single spring it would unfold and spread a canopy covering himself and companions. Touching another spring, the canopy would enlarge sufficiently to cover the royal court of the emperor and his cabinet. Another spring, and the tent would spread out over the plains and cover an army of thousands, shielding them from sun and storm. Christian truth is sure to outrun classic fable. Our Christianity is sure to spread the world over, but it must be worked. It must be touched in its secret springs, and lo! it will spread in your heart and life; touched again, and it will spread through your church; again, and it will reach out over your city; again, and it will spread over country and world. Oh, the possibilities that God is opening before the young Christian of to-day!

Calvary Presbyterian Church.

Two thousand people, including the greater portion of the Massachusetts delegation, assembled in this church at the hour of evening service. Rev. D. O. Mears, D.D., the pastor, formerly pastor at Worcester and Cambridge, Mass., welcomed the audience in a few appropriate words, and introduced, as the first speaker, Rev. M. M. Binford, pastor of the Friends' Church at Richmond, Ind. Mr. Binford took the place of Rev. Pleasant Hunter, D.D., of Minneapolis, who was unable to be present. He spoke on "The Spiritual Life of Endeavorers."

The Spiritual Life of Endeavorers.

Address of Rev. M. M. Binford.

When the young native helper of Bishop Patterson of the South Sea Islands was sorrowing over the death of his beloved leader, and seeking, like all of us, in the shock of bereavement for some explanation of the mysterious providence of God, he said: "After all, I think God cares more for character than he does for service."

The determining quality of all work for Christ is the character of the worker, and the inner essence of Christian character is spiritual life — the life of the soul in its relation to God, its union and fellowship with him. In the prophecy of Daniel it is said that "They that know their God shall be strong and do exploits," and our Lord defines eternal life as the knowledge of God and of Jesus Christ, whom he hath sent. Christian activity is the tangible, visible incarnation and outflowing of the rich, strong tides of divine life which flow into our souls through closest union with Christ our Lord. Our intellectual, social, moral, or political forms of life are but so many ships borne onward on the deep, full current of the life of the soul, and without which all must be wrecked ere they reach their ultimate destiny of the glory of God and the highest good of men.

We are all agreed as to the source of this spiritual life. It is the gift of God through faith in Jesus Christ. "To as many as received him to them gave he power to become the sons of God." No cultured blue blood, no will power of the flesh, no rich inheritance of ancestral influences, is a substitute for that flesh-humbling birth of the spirit through faith in Jesus Christ. Let us trust that this convention, like all that have preceded it, will be the time when many already interested by association will be vitalized by personal contact with Christ the Lord.

The blessed realities of fellowship with Jesus Christ require the spiritual senses of live men. The world cannot discern these realities. They are color blind and deaf in their presence. No less do the intense Christian activities of our age demand strong men. "Finally, my brethren, be strong in the Lord and in the power of his might." Otherwise the armor of the Christian warfare will be too weighty for you, and you cannot wield the sword of the spirit.

Let us notice the growth of this spiritual life. Live things grow. Dead things may aggregate, may even solidify, but life assimilates, expands, reproduces itself. Christian life originates in antecedent life. That antecedent is Christ life. Christian life seeks to conform to its type: that type is the Christ life. The grains of wheat from the mummy-cases of ancient Egypt tend to the duplication of the fields of waving grain which greeted the eyes of Joseph as he went out over all Egypt to gather the surplus into the granaries of the king. The dynamics of seeds in their persistent efforts to reproduce their pattern life are the illustration of the longing of your soul for likeness to Jesus. These spiritual proclivities are intensified by the presence of the spirit of God in the exercise of his transforming power upon your life. "We beholding as in a glass the glory of the Lord are changed into the same image from glory to glory, even as by the spirit of the Lord." The culmination of this shall be that "when he shall appear we shall be like him, for we shall see him as he is."

But growth as a law of life is dependent upon environment. Life is the power to respond to environment. The higher the life the greater the power to choose environment, utilize resources, triumph over obstacles, and make "all things work together for good." The complexity of man's life, physical, intellectual, sensuous, moral, and spiritual, coupled with his power of choice, may result in the development or perversion of one element of his nature to the neglect of others. A physical giant may be an intellectual pigmy; an intellectual prodigy a spiritual dwarf. Even apostolic ministry did not prevent some who were enriched in all utterance and knowledge from being only dwarfs in things spiritual. The Chinese are said to plant the seeds of forest trees in little earthen pots, supplying only sufficient light and moisture to preserve life, until the result is a pitiable miniature of a giant of the forest. But you and I have seen a great deal of soul life treated that way, and the result never gives the church any timber to build the temple of the Lord. Cedars of Lebanon don't grow in earthen pots. Such spiritual life is utterly selfish in its aims. It is the talent wrapped in a napkin; a sort of spiritual paid-up insurance policy against the day of evil. Such a life comes perilously near the awful condemnation of that man who thought that barns bursting with plenty could feed an immortal soul. He added his soul to the things of earth instead of seeking first the kingdom of God, to which these things could be safely added, and utilized in its promotion.

The fleshly lusts which war against the soul must be crucified. The soul life must have room to grow. Abraham's hut wasn't large enough for Ishmael after Isaac was weaned. The new life of promise must have all the inheritance of the every power of your being.

" My strength is as the strength of ten
Because my heart is pure,"

cries Sir Galahad, and the constant warfare against the uncrucified fleshly lusts, which often gain the victory over us, is the greatest hindrance to the growth of spiritual life. Such a life is full of fears — intimidated by obstacles, cowardly in the presence of foes. There is a fable of a mouse which once went to Jupiter and besought him to turn it into a cat, because its life was in constant terror from this enemy. Jupiter did so, and the cat went forth, soon to return in dismay because of danger from the dog; so Jupiter turned the cat into a dog, which went bravely forth to roam the forest. But he soon came back in terror because of the lions, and prayed for another transformation. "No," said the god. "You will always be in fear, whatever your form, so long as you have only the heart of a mouse." Let us then have done forever with this double, divided life, and pray with the Psalmist, "Unite my heart to fear thy name."

The food of the purified life is a spiritual food. Ruskin tells of a tree weighing 500 pounds planted in 200 pounds of earth, and given plenty of air and water for five years; when it weighed 169 pounds more, while the earth had lost only two ounces. Fellowship with Christ by the power of the Holy Spirit, the life of prayer, the devotional and practical study of his word, these are the means of the promotion of spiritual life.

The life of Christ on earth was conformed to the same law of growth as our own life. He lived as man. Like as his body was sustained by food as others, so his spiritual life was maintained, not by reliance upon his own all-sufficient divinity, but by communion with his Father. Now and then the curtain is lifted and we are permitted to see the all-nights of prayer when he regirded his soul for the battle, and they always were followed by signal displays of power. The hurry and rush of modern life are likely to rob us of the seasons of waiting upon God unless we are watchful. Our pledge guards carefully the season of daily prayer, yet even then the sweetness of the hour may slip away from us, our thoughts wander, the service grow cold and barren. Queen Mary feared the prayers of John Knox more than all the armies of the kingdom. Martin Luther could find time for three hours of prayer daily. The quality of our work is worth more than its quantity, and our power with men is measured by our fellowship with God. The fellowship of prayer is of equal, if not more, value than the number of definite answers which we are able to count as so many beads upon a string. We grow like those with whom we are constantly associated. "They took knowledge of them that they had been with Jesus." Vast fields of possibility, of personal growth, and increased spiritual power are here opened before us. No man has ever permanently drawn near to God wherever he went, who was not thus drawing nigh unto God himself. Our prayer life must carry us beyond asking, into listening to hear what God will speak, for he will speak peace unto his people. It carries us into the rest and love and peace of God. We have all known those who thus seemed to habitually walk in the presence of God. They live in the restfulness of God, and make us cry like the disciples of old, "Lord, teach us also how to pray." They seemed like richly blooming plants in God's conservatories, while without all is chilling blasts and winter's snow. The prayer life ever prays, "Thy will be done " — not as the last resort of a chastened, afflicted soul, but as the answer to the constraining love of Christ. Like him we can say, " My meat and drink is to do the will of God." When prayer turns into pitiful whinings for release from God's commands, to unavailing repetitions of vows to perform neglected duties, when one prays constantly up against the stonewall of the disobeyed will of God, there is need of a revival of religion in that soul very quickly. Spiritual growth is absolutely dependent upon this harmony with the divine will. In nature no dew falls under the clouded sky or on the wind-swept fields, and the divine refreshings never come to your souls while they are clouded and tempest-swept with disobedience to God. We are almost ready to suggest that there might be certain holy days in the life of every Endeavor society spent in prayer and the devotional study of the Scriptures — spent in really waiting upon God for the renewing of our strength.

Our pledge couples daily Bible-reading with daily prayer as a means of spiritual growth. Here, again, does the hurry of modern life, the intellectual cramming processes, the multiplicity of reading material, continually encroach upon the unguarded domain of meditation upon the word of God. At best we are often content to catch at second hand the illumination of the sacred page, and thus lose the blessings of our personal priestly life in holy things. It is the vision that some other man has seen behind the veil which we receive. We drink far down the stream instead of at the fountain. Hence, while these openings of truth may feed our own souls, in some measure, at least, they lose their freshness ere we pass them on to others. The brilliant flashings of the spiritual gems of another are no compensation for the manifestation of the things of Christ to us directly by the Holy Spirit. A sure test of the growth or decline of our spiritual life is found in our relation to the word of God. The cream rises upon the milk of the word when we prayerfully wait upon its pages. Reverently critical, analytical study discerns the form of the temple of divine revelation, while the Spirit of God fills the temple with his glory as we yield ourselves a living sacrifice to the will of God thus revealed. We cannot, however, dismiss this question of soul-food without emphasizing the importance of reading books of certain type. "Keep some good biography always by you," once wrote Catherine Booth to her husband; and it is true that scarcely any other class of literature has done more to form and foster high ideals of life. When the saintly David Brainerd, toiling and praying among the wild Indians on the banks of the Delaware and Susquehanna, jotted down the brief records of his spiritual experiences, with no thought of their publication, he little knew how they would quicken the life of generations of men, and set in motion the mightiest currents of modern Christian activity. But after his death Jonathan Edwards published the brief memoirs; they were carried across the sea, and fell into the hands of William Carey, and gave tone and direction to the life of the "Father of Modern Missions." They also came into the hands of Henry Martyn, and led him to that consecration of his life to missionary work in India, the record of which, more than almost any other book, has quickened missionary zeal and led hundreds to dedicate themselves to Christ for work in foreign lands. The memoirs of Brainerd's life accomplished mighty results in our own land also; for they quickened the spiritual life of Samuel Mills, who, with Judson and others, set in motion that train of events which led to the creation of our great missionary boards. Still this little book goes on its way an evangel of deepened spiritual life to thousands, a classic of religious literature. We are the heirs of the greatness and blessedness of all this antecedent life. The story of the struggles and successes of others furnishes both an inspiration and tonic for our motives, and a bulwark against discouragements which else might overwhelm us.

Once more, the advancement of our spiritual life is by the law of sacrifice. "Except the corn of wheat fall into the ground and die it abideth alone; but if it die it bringeth forth much fruit," was not truer of our Lord than of his followers, since he himself immediately adds, "If any man serve me, let him follow me;" for "He that findeth his life shall lose it, but he that loseth his life for my sake shall find it." Self-culture is a duty enjoined upon all, but not as an end in itself. It is only an endowment giving greater value to the sacrifice for others' sake. Even religious life may become self-centered and self-destructive, a stagnant "Dead Sea" of reception, from which issue no channels of living water to bless the world. The leaves of a plant minister to its own life; it is the flower and fruit that cost its life even unto death. When the Master found nothing but leaves, after having come these three years seeking fruit and finding none, he cursed the tree forever. Christ loved until he gave — until he gave himself a sacrifice for us; and he has moved a world. The powerlessness of our life is the proof of its self-love; its powerfulness the seal of its self-sacrifice. Christ was ever seeking heroic souls. Those who sought where to lay their own heads; those who had "firsts" in burying their dead, of saying farewell to their friends, could not be his disciples. He looked upon one young man and loved him, but he let him go away, probably never to return, because he could not give up all.

Oh, how greatly we need a mighty tide of life to pour forth upon this poor world, dead in pleasure and self-love while she yet liveth! Nothing else will ever move it. When we believe upon Christ we receive life; when we believe again, believe for a larger, deeper, more abundant life, then it shall flow out from us in rivers of living water to refresh and revitalize a desert, dead world.

Rev. Gilby C. Kelly, D.D., pastor of the Methodist Episcopal Church South, of Owensboro, Kentucky, next spoke on

The Deepest Thing in Christian Endeavor.

By Rev. Gilby C. Kelly, D.D.

Depth is the measure of strength and duration. Let us drop the lead into the bright stream of youthful interest that is flowing so broadly among the churches, and for a twelvemonth has set increasingly hitherward; and now, notwithstanding the hindrance of the strike, pours through the gates of Cleveland like the confluence of many waters.

The Church of God has been gladdened by a fresh stream of consecrated young life from the beginning. Samuel, the boy prophet; David, the boy minstrel; Josiah, the boy king; and the little captive maid who was a persuasive witness for the prophet of Israel in the home of Naaman the Syrian, were illustrious juniors in the Old Testament times. But we are impressed that in no preceding age of the church have her young people as a class been so separated unto Christ for service as at present.

Is it only a pleasing fancy that we are witnessing a greater than the Pentecostal fulfillment of that which was spoken by the prophet Joel, namely, "Your sons and daughters shall prophesy and your young men shall see visions"?

More than thirty thousand weekly Christian Endeavor prayer meetings, an equal number of monthly consecration meetings, and unnumbered other services in which the young people of the Protestant churches are wont to testify for Christ, are ample proof that the spirit of prophesying is ripe among them; and the sagacity and energy that thousands of splendid young men are displaying in Christian service attest that the Holy Spirit has anointed their eyes to see the vision of the kingdom of God.

The deepest thing in Christian Endeavor is the deepest thing in every sort of endeavor that calls for "patient continuance in well doing," namely, consecration. On the occasion of his installation as Dean of Westminster, the late Arthur Penrhyn Stanley preached on the fervid appeal of the apostle to the Romans, "I beseech you therefore, brethren, by the mercies of God, that ye present your bodies a living sacrifice, holy, acceptable unto God, which is your reasonable service." In the progress of the sermon he told the interesting incident that when the armies of England landed on the shores of the Crimea, this very scripture was read to one of the advancing troops by one of the officers in command. The exhortation was equally in point in the case of the great Dean as he entered upon the peaceful duties of his sacred office, and the intrepid sons of England as they drove forward into the storm of battle. Without consecration there can be no manliness, no heroism, no Christ-likeness. It accounts for the lofty patriotism of Washington and the sublime disinterestedness of Moses, the magisterial sense of duty of Wellington, and the evangelical energy of Paul; the self-denial of the latest outgoing missionary to a heathen field, and the heroism of Robert Ross, the young Scotch-American mechanic, who was shot down at the polls in Troy, New York, last March, while bravely guarding the ballot-box, the sacred ark of our liberties, from the profanation of repeaters.

The Christian Endeavor Society has brought this venerable and sacred word, that is the key to all the true and valorous lives that have been lived on the earth, that in the popular mind is associated with rare and unworldly souls that are said to have a "genius for religion," into the daily thought and practical aims of hundreds of thousands of young people in this and other lands. This is the word that glows in the motto, that is writ large in the pledge, that breathes as a refrain through the manifold operations of the Society.

An engaging aspect of the Christian Endeavor Society that is frequently remarked is its enthusiasm. There can be no enthusiasm, in the best sense, without consecration. God the Holy Spirit does not transfigure by his indwelling presence any life that is not first separated unto him. There is an evanescent play of spirits that passes for enthusiasm; real enthusiasm is the baptism of fire that descends only upon that altar whereon lies a whole burnt-offering.

It is a saying of Pascal that "man is the scandal and the glory of the creation." He is the one when he misses, the other when he fulfills, the will of God. The duty of consecration rests on the divine fact that God has a definite purpose concerning everything that he has made. He does nothing aimlessly. He often conceals his plan, but it appears in due course. He deposits in every germ a perfect model for it to follow in its unfolding. Each of us is an envoy of the King eternal, invisible. He has charged and commissioned us individually. I may sail under sealed orders, but they will be made plain as I voyage if I only have a will to obey. I have not learned anything of Christ if I have not learned that I have a divine vocation. The *alpha* of his doctrine is, " I must be about my Father's business;" his daily maxim, " I must work the works of him that sent me;" his dying witness, " It is finished."

> " Man is not God, but hath God's end to serve,
> A Master to obey, a course to take,
> Somewhat to cast off, somewhat to become, . . .
> How could man have progression otherwise ? "

I have said that consecration is the deepest thing in Christian Endeavor. It imports the most radical act of which a rational creature is capable. It lays the ax into the root of self-pleasing. It does not imply the dethronement of my will, but the superior enthronement by my will of the will of God.

Consecration is the act of the kingly faculty of the soul. There may be high and reverent thought, fancy may mount into the third heaven, sensibility as a strong current may set towards God, but one cannot reason, or imagine, or tide himself into the service of God. It is the will that covenants and consecrates. Consecration is the deepest thing in Christian Endeavor because it is the deepest thing in life. It gives character. It supplies the constructive principle. It unifies. It makes of every act a Christian act. It recognizes no distinction between things secular and things sacred. To the pure all things are pure; to the consecrated the kingdoms of this world are provinces of the kingdom of God and his Christ. The intelligently consecrated man is in sympathy with the " free, unrestrained appreciation of what we call nature, whether in the moral or the physical world," that is everywhere manifest in the Psalms. The parables of the Master have taught him that the common things of our daily handling are symbols of divine truth and as holy as the cross, and that every act that is done in Christ's name is hallowed.

Consecration means more than the getting of first-fruits and tithes. It does not enumerate fractional offerings. It means more than the giving of things; it signifies the dedication of life and limb; it presents the body a living sacrifice.

In consecrating the priests to their office, Moses took the blood of the ram of consecration and "sprinkled the right ear and the right hand and the right foot." The ear was to be ever open to receive the word of the Lord, the right hand and the right foot were to be ever ready to do his ministrations. I have read of an old barbarous chief " who when he was baptized kept his right arm out of the water that he might still work his deeds of blood." I have also read of another chief, a young Indian, who when his family were reduced almost to starvation went out to hunt, " but all game seemed to avoid him. He thought the Great Spirit must be angry with him and that he would secure his favor by an offering. So he took his blanket and laid it on a log and said, ' Here, Great Spirit, accept this blanket and bless poor Indian, that he may find food, and that his wife and family may not starve.' The offering did not suffice. A tomahawk hung in his belt. He advanced as before, and laid it upon the log, and said, ' O Great Spirit, take my tomahawk; it is all poor Indian has. He has nothing else to give; take it and bless me and give me food for my poor children.' But no answer came. There was his gun, his only means of obtaining game, his sole support, and hitherto his unfailing friend. How could he spare that? Must he part with that also? He paused, but pressed down by his forlorn condition, almost hopeless, he took the gun in his hand and laid it on the log, and sobbed out, 'O Great Spirit, take my gun too !

it is all poor Indian has; he has nothing more, take it and bless poor Indian that his wife and children may not starve.' Still the message of love came not. Almost broken-hearted, he started to his feet, a ray of light flashed through his mind. He would go to the rude altar again and offer himself up to the Great Spirit. So he sat down on the log with his blanket, his tomahawk, and his gun by his side, and said, 'Here, Great Spirit, poor Indian has given up all that he has; he has nothing more; so take poor Indian too, and bless him, that he may find food for his famishing family that they may not starve.' In a moment a change came over him. His soul was filled with peace such as he had never known before."

Christian consecration means a living sacrifice, an active, available, productive sacrifice, a sacrifice with "hands and feet." The old religious life of the East is a life of abstraction, aloofness from the life of nature; so is Western monachism. Christ went about doing good. He was anointed to preach the gospel to the poor, to heal the broken-hearted, to preach deliverance to the captive, recovering of sight to the blind, to set at liberty them that are bruised. The consecration that he inculcated and exemplified was not a cloistered virtue, but the consecration of "those practical and energetic faculties that mark the character of the Greeks, the Romans, the Germans, and the Anglo-Saxon races of mankind."

Consecration is the deepest thing in Christian Endeavor because it is the only act that is reciprocal to that which is condensed into the profound statement, "Jesus Christ and him crucified." Jesus the Christ is Jesus the Consecrated. He expresses the self-dedication of the Godhead to the service of redeeming and glorifying man. The apostle makes the mercies of God the ethical basis of his appeal to the Romans to present their bodies living victims unto God. We understand him to mean by "the mercies of God" more than the providential blessings that have fallen to us individually in the course of our respective lives; they include the whole mind and movement of God in Christ Jesus. It is a tremendous appeal that the apostle makes. He beseeches us to answer the Divine Self-Sacrifice in our behalf by our self-sacrifice in the Divine behalf. These are the poles of the moral universe. When we give ourselves to God as he has given himself to us a union is effected "that neither death, nor life, nor angels, nor principalities, nor powers, nor things present, nor things to come, nor height, nor depth, nor any other creature, shall be able to separate."

Christian Endeavor is not chiefly a sentiment, neither is it chiefly an appeal; it is a spirit — inspired resolution — not a quiescent, or a deferred, but an active resolution — a resolution based on the sovereignty of God and the grace of the Lord Jesus Christ; not an ending, but an abiding resolution that includes all time, all faculties, all acts; not a resolution to overstep my sphere and undertake what others can do better, but to serve within my appointed place; not a resolution to do some great thing, but a resolution to do whatsoever my hand finds to do, whether it be lowly or exalted, with my might and unto Christ.

When Henry V., the conqueror of Agincourt, lay dying, the ministers of religion drew nigh and chanted the Penitential Psalms. At the words, "Thou shalt build the walls of Jerusalem," he said, "If I had finished the war in France and established peace, I would have gone to Palestine to redeem the holy city from the Saracens." The historian adds, "The lost dream of glory was sanctified by the aspirations of religion." The Christian Endeavor crusade sanctifies the first dreams of glory of its young people with the aspirations of religion; it enlists them for the rescuing of every dwelling-place of men from the dominion of lust and greed and whatsoever defileth; it teaches them that the walls of Jerusalem that are a sure defense are patriotism, philanthropy, and the fear of God.

Euclid Avenue Disciple Church.

It was to be expected that a great number of the delegates would elect to attend the "preliminary meeting" at this church; for Rev. J. Z. Tyler, D.D., the popular chairman of the Committee of '94, is pastor here, and presided on this occasion.

The pretty auditorium was filled to overflowing. Mrs. Frances J. Barnes, of New York, secretary of the Young Women's Branch of the

W. C. T. U., came first on the programme, taking as the subject of address,

Joel's Prophecy.

Address of Mrs. Frances J. Barnes.

How often in our Christian experience we have reason to look up and thank God for the outspoken championship of Peter, who, although affirming to our Lord, "Though all men shall be offended because of thee, yet will I never be offended" (Matt. xxvi. 33), so quickly turned about, thrice angrily declaring, "I know him not;" yet who, when the sound from heaven as of a rushing, mighty wind filled all the house on the day of Pentecost, comprehended the manifestation, and, boldly standing forth, proclaimed, "These are not drunken, as ye suppose. . . . But this is that which was spoken by the prophet Joel," and Joel's prophecy was the prelude or text to the first recorded sermon under the immediate baptizing power of the Holy Spirit.

Brief, concise, powerful, the outline of the prophecy's fulfillment was given, "This Jesus . . . being by the right hand of God exalted, and having received of the Father the promise of the Holy Ghost, he hath shed forth this, which ye now see and hear" (Acts ii. 32-33).

Among the learned people of ancient times the Scriptures record but three wise men who are looking for the "star in the east." These the story of "Ben Hur" imagines to have been an Egyptian, a Grecian, and a Hindoo, making but one representative for each great nation, but joins them with the few humble expectants by saying, "Their faith rested upon the signs sent them by him whom we have since come to know as the Father, and they are of the kind to whom his promises were so all-sufficient that they asked nothing about his ways. Few there were who had seen the signs and heard the promises — the mother and Joseph, the shepherds, and the three wise men — yet they all believed alike."

How slowly dawned upon the human mind in the days of our Saviour's birth and ministry the truth of prophecy, when, even after his resurrection, as he walked to Emmaus, he was constrained to say, "O fools, and slow of heart to believe all that the prophets have spoken" (Luke xxiv. 25). Full of pathos and longing his voice must have been; and who of us have not thought, when we read the narrative, we should have recognized him? Oh, hearts that are cold and distant, and hearts that are burning within, be not slow to believe, be not slow to discern that which was perfected by the birth, death, and resurrection and ascension of our blessed Lord, and which now only waits reception. We are now in the days of Joel's prophecy, and let us rejoice with reverence "in the times of the Holy Ghost." Belief in this is the need of individual souls, the need of the church. A measure of the acceptance of Joel's prophecy has brought this great concourse of young Christians together; a stronger hold by faith upon this prophecy will cause the army of Endeavorers to see with clear vision the distinction between being "full of new wine," and "being filled with the Spirit;" will enable them to discern between good and evil — the great evil of intemperance — as opposed to the kingdom of God and the strong, straight dividing line. That there is a general tacit acceptance of the fulfillment of the prophecy of the outpouring of the Holy Spirit all will admit, but before continuing further with that part of the text it may be asked, Are we also to have faith in dreams and visions? And just here we turn backward in mind to the time of childhood, when for the first time we heard the old, old story of the shepherds and the angels, and how they appeared to Joseph three times "in a dream," though openly the angels spake to Mary. The wise men were warned in a dream, and Zacharias had a long vision in the temple. It was in a dream that Pilate's wife "suffered many things." Exceeding our imagination must have been the vision seen by Peter and John with Jesus on the Mount of Transfiguration. How interesting the dream of Cornelius and Peter which led to the conversion and baptism of the Gentiles by the Holy Ghost! Then we come to the vision of Saul on the journey to Damascus, and of Ananias concerning him; and what heroic thoughts are inspired when we read of Paul standing before Agrippa, declaring, "Whereupon, O king Agrippa! I was not disobedient unto the heavenly vision" (Acts xxvi. 19)! Wonderful also, and to be interpreted only by the spirit, are the visions of the beloved apostle in the isle of Patmos. While it is written, "No prophecy of the scripture is of any private interpretation" (2 Pet. i. 20), the same may be said of dreams and visions which it might be dangerous for individuals to follow, unless in perfect accordance with the written word. With the increasing belief of the immediate guidance of the Holy Spirit, always in harmony with the Bible direction, there seems to be less need for the marvelous, while more perfectly we are coming to understand what our Saviour meant when he said, "The Comforter, which is the Holy Ghost . . . he shall teach you all things, and bring all things to your remembrance, whatsoever I have said unto you" (John xiv. 26). The hearts of countless women have been comforted and cheered when, with souls stirred by the monitions of the Holy Ghost, they have recalled the prophecy of Joel, reiterated on the day of Pentecost, when the women were present "with Mary, the mother of Jesus, and his brethren." It was with the Spirit and the understanding that Miriam the prophetess sang the song of triumph. By the Spirit, Deborah judged the people, and Hulda dwelt in the college and prophesied in the days of Jonah. It was by the power of the Spirit that Esther stood before the king, for such a time as that. In the New Testament, from the time the angels said unto Mary, " Blessed art thou among women; the Holy Ghost shall come upon thee, and the power of the Highest shall overshadow thee," special blessing, direction, and ministry seem to have been given to the women. Anna the prophetess spent much time in the temple, and gave thanks, recognizing the holy Child, and spake of him to all them that looked for redemption in Israel.

The love and heed the Master gave to their requests we hear in these words: "O woman, great is thy faith, be it unto thee even as thou wilt." "Neither do I condemn thee; go thy way and sin no more." "Maiden, I say unto thee, arise." We approve the good works of the " Disciple Tabitha," and rejoice that she was brought to life again. We are thankful for Rhoda and Lydia, the house of Chloe, the grandmother Lois, and chief women not a few, being glad that St. Paul wrote: "I entreat thee also, true yoke-fellow, help these women which labored with thee in the gospel, whose names are in the book of life." He commendeth Phebe, a servant of the church at Cenchrea, to be received as becometh saints. Salutations were sent to Priscilla, Tryphena, Tryphosa, and Persis, which labored much in the Lord; also to Julia, to Nereus and his sister, concluding with the words, "The churches of Christ salute you." Surely we are in the time when the spirit is poured out upon all flesh, and well is it to recognize our need and God's purpose in the fulfillment of this prophecy. It was in 1873, in this State, which, like Virginia, has been called the "Mother of Presidents," and which also has been known to many as the "Crusade State," that, in response to the agony of many breaking hearts, — because the blight of intemperance was upon their households, — that the Spirit came down in mighty power upon the mothers and daughters, impelling them by a force they could not gainsay to go forth to rescue their loved ones. Many organizations have been inaugurated by the Spirit, but none in modern times was so copiously baptized into corporated life as the Woman's Christian Temperance Union of Ohio twenty years ago. Young women were early called, and responded, "Here am I." It was in Cleveland that the first young woman's temperance society was banded together, a vital protest to the sin of intemperance, and an energized factor for prevention. It seems to be in harmony with the mind of the Spirit that two of the great armies of the Lord should gather here in Cleveland this year, the International Christian Endeavor Society, and the National Woman's Christian Temperance Union, to convene in November.

It would not be in accordance with God's will, or in the purpose of these organizations, to assemble and depart without realizing in a greater degree than before coming together the fulfillment of the prophecy, " I will pour out my Spirit upon all flesh, and your sons and your daughters shall prophesy." We are surrounded by the great enemy of Christ, of the Church, of the State, of the home. The open vision of desecration is ever before us; the dreams of the sin-stricken are too terrible to interpret; the destruction that threatens promises to be as inevitable as when, in blindness and willful sin, the children of Israel turned away from the living God. Statistics without number, individual experiences, the effect of co-related interests, and the surging wave of sorrow, seemingly made up of the sighs and sobs of motherhood and childhood, might be detailed to verify our need of a mighty outpouring of the Holy Spirit at this time. Ought we not desire it, nay, to pray fervently for it, as with one accord? If the world is to be taken for Christ, the Christian Endeavorers of every age, the sons and daughters, the old men and the young men, servants and handmaidens, will have to slay the liquor traffic for Christ. With enduement of power from on high let us go forth in this spiritual warfare, fulfilling the further prophecy of Joel: "Beat your plowshares into swords, and your pruninghooks into spears ; let the weak say I am strong. . . Put ye in the sickle, for the harvest is ripe: come, get you down; for the press is full, the fats overflow; for their wickedness is great. Multitudes, multitudes in the valley of decision; for the day of the Lord is near in the valley of decision" (Joel iii. 10, 13, 14).

Mrs. Barnes was followed by Rev. C. A. Dickinson, pastor of Berkeley Temple, Boston, who spoke on the subject, "The Life that Tells."

Woodland Avenue Presbyterian Church.

The New York delegates were entertained by the people of this church, and consequently they made their presence felt (certainly they made it heard) at this meeting. No preliminary gathering was more enthusiastic. Conspicuous in the throng was a company of men in sailor garb, the members of the Floating Bethel Society. The pastor of the church, Rev. Charles Townsend, presided and introduced the speakers. First came Rev. James L. Hill, D.D., of Salem, Mass., who took for the subject of an inspiring address, "Things that have stirred me."

Rev. Dr. P. S. Henson, of Chicago, was unable to be present on account of the strike ; and in his place Rev. H. T. McEwen, of New York, chairman of the Committee of '92, made an earnest address upon "Power."

The meeting closed with a brief talk by Miss Antoinette P. Jones, of Falmouth, Mass., superintendent of the department of Floating Societies of Christian Endeavor, who described the progress of the work under her care as follows : —

Floating Societies of Christian Endeavor.

Address of Antoinette P. Jones, Superintendent.

Fellow Endeavorers : — Our love for "Christ and the Church" has drawn us together to-day from the four points of the compass, — Christian Endeavor on land, ay, and on the sea also, for how can "the earth be filled with the knowledge of the Lord" until all who are "afar off upon the sea" are converted unto him.

Far off on the wilderness of waters, covering three-fourths of the earth's surface, sail from three to four million seamen in the naval and commercial marine of the world. To each seaport come and go hundreds of thousands of sailors, who, having escaped the fearful "perils in the sea," may yet fall victims to "perils in the city." Who meets "Jack" first ? Beset on every hand, our sailor must have Christ enthroned within, and "take the shield of faith" to withstand all the "fiery darts of the wicked."

Is it nothing to us that these souls go hungry for the bread of life ? "Inasmuch!"

Work for seamen does not call us to neglect missions already dear to us, but adds sails, and steam-power, more hearts and hands, to go where our strength cannot carry us.

> "Waft, waft ye winds his story,
> And you ye waters roll,
> Till, like a sea of glory,
> It spreads from pole to pole.'

Thirteenth International Convention. 47

Yes, the "winds" and the "waters" may spread the story; but we want men, — seamen, Christian Endeavor seamen, — who can carry the blessed story to every clime, —

"From Greenland's icy mountains
To India's coral strand,"

and sail back into port again, still flying the ensign of "Christ and the Church" at the masthead!

The Floating Society of Christian Endeavor is a branch of the Young People's Society of Christian Endeavor adapted to use on shipboard. Not for one ocean, one grade, or service, but for all "who go down to the sea in ships, that do business in great waters," in man-of-war, ocean steamship, merchantman, coaster, or fisherman; Christian Endeavor *always* interdenominational, international, intermarine, — "floating" the world around.

The pledge, our active membership pledge, with inserted clause approved as a declaration of principles, relating to pure living, total abstinence, and non-profanity. Members carry an introduction card, and wear regulation Christian Endeavor badge pin. The constitution is arranged from Model Constitution, and includes covenant for small bands.

Originally for enlisted men, membership soon extended to sailing-vessels.

Arranged for shipboard, a society ashore in church, mission, or reading-room, composed of sailor members, officered by Christian Endeavor workers, may be called a Floating Society, though as an *organization* it does not "float."

Honor is due established seamen's missions, but missionaries realize how great the harvest, how few the laborers.

Where new work is advisable, representatives of Christian Endeavor Societies or Local Unions, in ports, form a Floating Christian Endeavor Committee from consecrated young men and women workers, who receive cordial and practical indorsement from churches and societies.

Subdivisions are necessary when local needs are varied. How work grows as you investigate!

Ship visitation, gospel services on shipboard, dock, and shore: marine hospital services; navy-yard, receiving-ship, training-ship, marine barracks, and naval prison; reading-rooms and boarding-houses. The field may require new reading-room, or launch. Marine missionary services, comfort bagmaking, collecting good reading and libraries, furnish abundant work for societies ashore.

Does the good seed grow? Try it and see! Results? Who can estimate since the little beginning four years ago, April, 1890? About two thousand seamen have signed the pledge at all points, so far as reported.

Fifty-one Floating Societies. Seventeen of these on land especially for seamen. Seven of these reported 338 services held by them on ships. Five societies reported twenty-eight of their members joined the church during the year.

Enjoy a flying visit of inspection: To Vineyard Sound, Mass., where the first pledges were signed, and first societies formed on shipboard in 1890. To Boston's Seamen's Chapel, organized 1890. To New York, West Side, 1892; East Side, 1893. November, 1892, at Navy Yard, New York. To Portland, Me. Cleveland, O., with two societies. Now to the Pacific, with organized work in Unions of San Francisco, San Diego, Oakland, and Vallejo, for naval men. Tacoma and Seattle, Washington, at gateway of the north. Chicago at work. Philadelphia Union; and society in Eastburn Mariner's Church.

On ships? Each deserves special inspection, from "Farragut" society on U. S. S. New York, through list of societies on merchant and naval vessels, with equally heroic and noble records. Think of each member an object of target practice for a crew's ridicule through a voyage of months! Christian soldiers, indeed! Do none fail to keep the pledge? The proportion is not greater than on shore. The sailor is loyal to his God and to his promise.

Numberless the testimonies from the sea to the helpfulness, inspiration, faith, the call of God to higher service, coming directly through the Christian Endeavor Society. Thank God he is working out his plan for the sailors, and has blessed Christian Endeavor on *sea* as well as on land!

Make haste! no time to waste! Six sailors go down to death each night!

Spend no time being merely saloon substitutes, but always keep in view our highest aim, — *soul winning* and *training for service;* press forward steadily, systematically, devotedly, using opportunities as sacred trusts.

"There go the ships!" Does the call come to you? Will you let your life be the human "life-line" sent out to save these perishing souls from eternal shipwreck? "One is our Master, even Christ, all ye [seamen] *are brethren.*"

Plymouth Congregational Church.

The rally in this church, which held its own with the rest in enthusiasm, was presided over by Mr. J. G. W. Cowles of Cleveland, the church being at present without a pastor.

Following the usual praise service, Rev. S. Edward Young of Asbury Park, N.J., chairman of the International Christian Endeavor Committee on Life-saving Stations, spoke on the work among the life-savers, a subject in which he is most deeply interested.

Rev Ralph W. Brokaw, of Springfield, Mass., next spoke on —

Christian Endeavor for the Times.

Address of Rev. Ralph W. Brokaw.

After speaking of the importance of these first meetings as sounding the key-notes and making the first impressions, Mr. Brokaw said, in part, that just as a young man in choosing his life-work should be influenced more and most by what the world needs of him, rather than by what he prefers, or is even, in his own judgment, capable of, so it is with the mass of young people. As young Christians, endeavor should respond to the demands of the times.

Environment is a factor in the determination of duty.

This brings me to my theme; viz., Christian Endeavorers for the Times.

What of the times? I am not a pessimist. The world is growing better; but the times is even yet a sick patient. If I diagnose his case correctly, he is a long way from robust health, no matter if he is not so sick as he once was.

Trade is sick with the fever and ague of unfraternal competition; with the merciless la grippe of trusts that crowd small concerns to the wall, and compel the public to pay them tribute.

The State is sick with the blood-poison of the spoils' system, and the cancer of a tax system whose method is a stupendous lie.

Society is sick with the *angina pectoris* of selfishness and dilettanteism.

The Church is sick with the anaemia of a subtle commercialism in management and an insatiable sensuousness in worship. Why? — the people often just settle back in their comfortable cushioned pews, and expect the preacher to throw the chocolate creams of rhetorical eloquence into their very mouths, and the choir to gently plash their ears with delicious music. The minister must make the institution pay dividends in pew rentals, or else his church will be transformed into a cross, on which he will be crucified, while the membership sits down and watches him there.

In view of all this, what kind of Christian Endeavorers should we be?

1. For one thing *we must be broad and intelligent.* Our horizon must not be narrowly circumscribed. The whole world is married now; and the wedding-ring is constituted in railroads, telegraphs, and telephones. Our duties and obligations overleap the old lines of latitude and longitude.

Breadth, though desirable, must be accompanied by direct purpose and intelligence. We must apprehend things *in their relations,* and act accordingly.

But how shall we get a broad view? Not by surveying the land from the tops of the ecclesiastical hills called Baptist or Methodist or Presbyterian or Congregationalist, but from the summit of Mt. Zion, the Pisgah of the kingdom. From this height, no single denomination monopolizes our view. We see the *one* church, with its one Lord, one faith, and one baptism, and we are soundly converted to interdenominational fellowship.

2. Again, *Christian Endeavorers for the times must be independent.* Of course we are all dependent upon the past, the present, and each other. This dependence every sensible person realizes. But I mean independent of prejudices and of exaggerated partisanship. This point Mr. Brokaw illustrated historically from the lives of Bishop Anselm and Abraham Lincoln. He pleaded for *conviction*, and said that a man with convictions was a Samson, with his sturdy arms around the pillars of Dagon's temple.

3. And more, *the Endeavorers that the times demand must be courageous.* A conviction without courage is a candle under a bushel. No finer example of courage is recorded in all history than that of our Lord under the shadow of the cross. Sneaks and cowards are beneath contempt. James Russell Lowell spoke the truth when he said, —

> " They are slaves who will not choose
> Hatred, scoffing, and abuse,
> Rather than in silence shrink
> From the truth they needs must think.
> They are slaves who dare not be
> In the right with two or three."

4. Above all, *Endeavorers for these days must be thoroughly consecrated — devoted body and soul to the Master.* Never was there so much circumstantial stress as now upon the words, " I beseech you therefore, brethren, by the mercies of God, that you present your bodies a living sacrifice, holy, acceptable unto God, which is your reasonable service." Our great national wealth argues for such self-devotion. Missions demand it. We should pay the debts of the mission boards; send out the three thousand two hundred young men and women who are willing to go into these fields white unto the harvest, and so scatter the leaves that shall be for the healing of the nations. A revival of civic righteousness demands this same quality. No better revival could come to us than this. We are degenerating because we lack for a righteousness that will throttle a Tammany, put down anarchy, and say, " Go, thou dirty devil," to the saloon. Oh, what moral earnestness is wanted ! Oh, what enthusiasm for humanity ! Oh, what power from on high ! The old prophet's words should ring in our ears, " Awake, awake, put on thy strength, O Zion ! "

When Garibaldi had been defeated at Rome, he issued his immortal appeal, " Soldiers, I have nothing to offer you but cold and hunger, rags and hardship. Let him who loves his country follow me." And instantly thousands of the youth of Italy sprang to their feet at that high appeal. And will *you*, *Endeavorers*, *you*, the trustees of posterity, will *you* turn your backs on these demands of the advancing kingdom of Christ? He says, " My kingdom is not of this world." " You shall be hated of all men for my sake." " The Son of man hath not where to lay his head." " The servant is not greater than his Lord." " But whosoever loves his fellows, whosoever loves his country, whosoever loves his God, let him deny himself and take up his cross daily and follow me."

Who of all these Endeavor hosts will fail to respond? Who will be satisfied to march only with the rear-guard? Who will selfishly and ignobly turn aside to his own ways? Not one, I hope, not one. May God give us grace to be loyal soldiers in the army of the Captain of our salvation !

The last speaker of the evening was Rev. J. T. Beckley, D.D., of New York, who took for his theme, " Christian Endeavor Achievements."

Miles Park Presbyterian Church.

This church being the headquarters of the Washington delegation, was naturally the centering point for one of the largest gatherings of the evening. Rev. A. C. Ludlow, the pastor, presided, and the opening praise service was full of enthusiasm. The first speaker was Rev. J. F.

Cowan, of Pittsburg, Pa., well known as a writer of Christian Endeavor stories. His subject was : —

Principles, Enthusiasm, Methods.

Address of Rev. J. F. Cowan.

If we would do efficient service for Jesus Christ, we should look to at least three conditions: —

1. We should be sure that we stand for some principle precious to God; that we are following convictions as to his truth, and not mere impulses of the moment, or personal whims. Sometimes a whim and a conviction look so near alike to a near-sighted person, that it is difficult to tell them apart at first sight. They are like the toad and the knot on the log, which so puzzled the boy in the uncertain twilight, that the only way he could distinguish them was by touching both with a straw. Then the toad jumped, but the knot didn't.

Your Christian Endeavorer with a crotchet or a hobby, or a personal vanity for petty leadership, in the place of deep-rooted religious convictions, may speak as glibly or appear as well in the prayer-meeting or convention as your man of principle; but he cannot be depended upon to jump when his services are needed. But touch the fellow whose sense of religious duty bulges out like warts, and whether it is hard work on a small committee as its least member, or Sunday observance, or proportionate giving, or whatever it is, he will jump every time and all the time. That is the difference between Christian Endeavor from principle, and so-called Christian Endeavor as a fad.

Now, the most fundamental and supremest principle of all to the Christian is the lordship and mastery of Jesus Christ. We stand up with the congregation and sing, —

" Bring forth the royal diadem,
And crown him Lord of all."

Oh, how rich and resounding the strains! What an abandon of exultation in the voices which thrill the hearers, as the sentiment of the song thrills the hearts of the singers! But suppose that the Lord should appear before us as the last cadence of the hymn died away. Close your eyes and imagine the scene. The head that endured the prints and pain of the thorny crown waits before us, all radiant and kingly now, for that coronation of which we have just been singing. He is still uncrowned, notwithstanding the song; for no mere melody, no bauble of tender sentiment, is a fit crown for that brow. Jesus Christ is not satisfied to be crowned with the gilt of passing emotions; he claims the solid gold of our every action. It is every-day mastery of us that he seeks; mastery of our public life as well as our private; mastery of our time and tempers; mastery of our purse-strings and heart-strings. We cruelly mock him when we come running to him to call him Master, and then turn away sorrowfully at the first requirement of his services which crosses our personal desires; not, like the young ruler, because we have much riches, but because we have much love of ease or vanity of person, or worldly ambition, or something else. Publicly calling him Master with our lips, but handing the scepter of mastery of us over to Mammon or to sense is unworthy one who subscribes to the motto: "One is your Master, even Christ." You cannot crown Jesus Christ with any other crown until you have given him the crown of your manhood and womanhood.

When we have once given self to Christ as his crown, there is nothing else which we can withhold from him. We feel that we must crown him with our possessions — the best we have. I do so long for that act by which the magi recognized the babe as their Lord and King to become an accepted part of all worship. I mean gold and silver offerings. I hope that the time is coming when we shall be ashamed to worship the Lord of lords with our small change. There is something wrong with the religion of the man who changes his trousers on Sunday morning, and forgets to change his pocketbook. I am praying that the man who thumps his biggest copper cent into the contribution-box, hoping it will make as much noise as a silver dollar, may pass away with this generation, and a class of Christians come up in his stead in whose eyes copper shall not be a fit offering for their king. It is true that the widow's mite was probably copper; but it became transmuted into gold the moment it touched the treasury, because the woman's intentions were golden. I am tired of hearing the phrase "penny collections" conned over in the Sunday-school. When the nickel-in-the-slot machine, the soda-fountain, the merry-go-round, the Punch and Judy show, and the peanut vender will look at nothing less than the nickel of our children, why should we teach them to carry their copper to Christ? Of course if the copper is the measure of ability, then the best we can do is to see that the thought of the heart is silver and gold. Bring forth the royal diadem, and not the beggar's pittance, for our Lord's crowning.

Another thing with which we must crown him is our Christian citizenship. We pray that the kingdoms of this world may become the kingdoms of our Lord and of his Christ. "Thy kingdom come" implies universal sovereignty for Christ. Which one of the kingdoms or nations of this world can we easiest help to make a kingdom of our Lord? You, and 11,999,999 other men like you, carry around under your hats the sovereignty of the greatest nation upon which the sun ever shone. Has America been given to Christ? Let the licensed saloons, let the Sunday mail trains, let judicially protected prize-fights, let municipal misrule, answer. But the question is, Have you, who sing, —

> "Bring forth the royal diadem,
> And crown him Lord of all," —

have you crowned Jesus Christ with the one twelve-millionth interest in this nation of which you are the present sovereign, by putting your vote at his disposal through the dictates of your conscience; by throwing your influence into the primaries for the selection of pure men as candidates; by asserting that he is the King of glory, and the gates of this republic must be lifted up to let him come in; or have you taken the scepter of your citizenship that, consistently with your own prayer, you should have placed in Jesus Christ's hands, and laid it instead in the smirched palm of your ward or political boss? Jesus Christ is not crowned Lord of all, sing it as lustily as we may, until the Christian voters of this country seek to serve him as assiduously in the primaries as in the prayer meetings; and any American who stays at home on election day, or pessimistically admits that the political evils of this country are incurable, before he has lifted his hand and voice and joined with other good men to try to cure them, ought to be ashamed to ever sing old "Coronation" or to pray the Lord's Prayer again.

Another of the great principles for which we stand is the brotherhood of men. "One is your master, even Christ, and all ye are brethren." Out of brotherhood grows fellowship. Some people's idea of Christian fellowship is, your own set of fellows in your own little ship. They are perfectly willing that their young people would sail up within a cable's length or so of the rest of the fleet, and that the captains should call out through their trumpets, "Boat, ahoy, there." But the communion of the saints, which is enjoyed by means of a system of nautical signals, or over a long-distance telephone, can scarcely be that for which our Lord pleaded when he prayed the Father that his flock might be one.

But Christian brotherhood must stand for more than interdenominational fellowship. It must mean the blood relationship of the whole world. The only pill which can make the sick society of our world well is the commandment, "Thou shalt love thy neighbor as thyself." There is no use calling in any other doctor to prescribe for the evils which afflict our times. The fellow who kneels in the mud of the street corner to black your shoes, the girl at the five-cent counter, the man who is tramping for work and not for tramp, the thief who is one because society did not interest itself to see that he became something other, all these have heart-strings made of the same material as ours, and capable of responding to the same touches. Christian Endeavor must mean "Comity established" between man and man. It must mean "Common sense enthroned." It must mean "Caste exterminated."

Why, only the other day a female member of the select society for the elimination of the letter R from the English language, boarded an accommodation train on a narrow gauge railroad. As she soared onto the platform, attired in a sealskin sack and an air of conscious superiority, she thus accosted the menial brakeman: "Is thayah no cayah on this wetched twain whayah one may be secluded fwom the common herd?" The brakeman looked her over, and with a wink at the traveling man in the front seat, replied that she needn't fear, the cattle train had passed by about an hour earlier. But she looked disgusted enough to doubt his statement; and he ventured the further information that the only thing that need trouble her was a refrigerator car of dressed beef, remarking in an aside to the traveling man, that as she seemed to represent the salt of the earth, it might not be a bad idea to bring the two together. "Yes," assented the traveling man; "but if the earth is going to be salted with that kind of salt, it will have to be done as they cure their pork out West." Said he, "They load a shot-gun with rock salt and shoot the hogs with it; and the load not only kills the hog, but salts the pork at the same time."

There never was a time when the world needed the salt of Christian advantages, training, and belief diffused through it so much as now. But it is not salt shot at long range from a shot-gun, but salt rubbed in with the hand — the salt of sisterliness, the salt of brotherliness — which is needed. If the unsalted about us are to be saved, they must be hand-cured. The great social questions of the day, over which statesmen and philanthropists are gravely shaking their heads, can only be settled by perforating the brick and stone walls of our churchly exclusiveness, and making our Sunday-schools, our Christian Endeavor societies, and our church social circles salt-shakers for savoring the putrefying mass around us, instead of bonded warehouses for hoarding up salt enough to corner the market. We must make that "all ye are brethren" mean just what it would mean to-day on the lips of Jesus if he came to our midst and sought the people who needed him most, without waiting to vaccinate them, or fumigate them, or search rogues' gallery for their records, or examine them in the catechism. The helping hand may wear a diamond ring while the one it seeks to grasp has the seamstress's scars; but it must have bandages and salve for humanity's sores, in the place of the schoolmaster's rod or the critic's scalpel. He is Christ's brother who makes the world feel Christ its brother.

These are some of the vital principles of the kingdom of God. He who receives them into his heart as something to be worked out into everyday life receives Jesus Christ: has Christ in him, the hope of glory. And he who has the divine indwelling through the reception of and obedience to the truth has enthusiasm for the truth; for enthusiasm is God within. That is the second great law of successful work for Christ: enthusiasm; for enthusiasm, rightly defined, is the Holy Spirit within.

2. Principles without enthusiasm for them are neither apprehended nor potent. The man who has apprehended a great religious principle has a right to grow enthusiastic over it. Indeed, he cannot help so doing. I like to fall into company with a man who believes that the town in which he lives is destined to be the commercial center of the earth; or that the firm by which he is employed stands at the head of all competitors; or that the political party to which he belongs is the greatest landmark in American history. I like to see him kindle and beam as he talks to me, and finally reaches for my button-hole with the determination in his eye to make a convert of me then and there.

When I say that a great principle must necessarily arouse a great enthusiasm, and that we never really grasp a principle over which we do not become actively interested, I do not mean by a great enthusiasm a great effervescence. I do not mean a great emotion. The right sort of enthusiasm is not so much emotion as motion. It is to principle what the stream is to the fountain. It's a very weak fountain which doesn't overflow sometimes. It won't take that fountain long to become a mere mud puddle. Jesus said: "Out of the abundance of the heart the mouth speaketh." Big principles, filling big hearts, will make busy mouths. Mind, I didn't say "big" mouths. There is such a thing as an abundance of the mouth that counts for nothing, because it is like the Indian's "Heap too much big talk."

3. A third condition for successful work is methods commensurate with the principles and enthusiasm just pictured. The method is to the worker what the gun is to the soldier. A strapping fellow, six feet tall, however willing, is far from being a soldier when recruited. Put a blue suit on him, with stripes down the trousers and brass buttons on the coat, and still you have no soldier. Teach him the difference between "hay foot" and "straw foot," and he yet lacks much to make him a soldier. Put a gun in his hand and train him to load, fire, advance, retreat, wheel right and left in unison with the rest of the army at the word of command, and you have a soldier.

The difference between a mob and an army is not so much in numbers or courage as in method. The one has no right methods or wrong methods: the other has the best method for all. The fate of the battle no longer depends upon valor of Briton or Frank, or on the leadership of a Napoleon or Wellington, so much as on the dynamic ratio of cartridges and the relative efficiency of firing guns. The great battles of the future will be fought in the brains of inventors of death-dealing apparatus and in chemists' laboratories. The old military maxim, "Trust God and keep the powder dry," has been blown to the winds by the modern proverb, "Trust God and burn your powder faster than the other fellow."

This is equally true in business. The ignoble goose-quill used to be the measure of men's progress in the literary and business world. But the goose-quill pen has lost its job along with the spinning-wheel and the street-car mule. Pansy, Samantha, Capt. King, Mary Mapes Dodge, Kate Field, Dr. James H. Worden, Sylvanus Stall, and a score or two of our favorite authors, as well as thousands of business and public men, dictate their rapidly unfolding thoughts to the Edison phonograph.

What does all this mean but that if we would do the best work for Jesus Christ we must have the best methods, as well as principles and enthusiasm? And we must have enough of them to put a weapon in the hands of every disciple of Jesus, else much enthusiasm will be frittered away and vital principles will fail of dissemination.

If you were to ask a scientist or a man of exact language for a definition of a saw he would probably tell you that it was an elongated, obtuse-angled triangle of hardened metal, serrated upon one of its edges; and having an appurtenance attached unto the base for applying the propelling power. But should you ask a boy for a definition of a saw, he would in all probability inform you that it was a thing which saws.

I have no doubt that a theological professor could furnish a subjective definition of a Christian in much the same precision of speech and elaboration of detail that characterized the first definition of a saw, and he could do it in two or three volumes octavo, half Turkey-morocco binding; but, following the analogy of the boy's definition, would it not be a fair statement to say that, objectively, a Christian is one who works at Christianity, or Christianizes? But in many cases the difference between the professed Christian who is one only nominally, and that one who is working at it, is simply the difference of knowing "how," of having a method, and having none. The one has been shown how to work, and the other has not.

We boast of our citizen soldiery. We claim not to need a large standing army, because each State has its organization of National Guards for the purpose of instructing its farmers and clerks and mechanics in the manual of arms, and the evolutions of the battle-field. It requires only the drill, the showing them how. And when emergencies arise requiring force of arms, without laying the burden of a standing army of professional soldiers upon the tax-payers, the farmer leaves his plow-handles, the blacksmith unties his leather apron, the clerk takes his pen from behind his ear, and to the music of the fife and drum our boys in blue go marching forth to do their duty. And we pray for them and trust them; for are they not our brothers and husbands, and sweethearts, and fathers, and not hired mercenaries? And I just tell you, should the occasion arise — and I pray God it never may — I believe that America could wipe up the earth with this citizen soldiery of hers.

And I believe that Jesus Christ is going to conquer the world through this citizen soldiery of his, which is now being trained in all our Christian Endeavor camps in methods of work. They have the principles of his kingdom in their hearts. They have the ardor and enthusiasm of daring soldiers kindling their eyes. We are fast arming them with methods. The bugle has already sounded. They have stood their first baptism of fire. They withstood shot and shell, jibe and sneer, on the Sunday opening question. They are rallying again and again in behalf of temperance, social purity, and good citizenship. We hear the echoes of their battle song from far and near, —

"Against the foe in vales below let all our strength be hurled;
Faith is the victory, we know, that overcomes the world."

The next speaker was Rev. M. Rhodes, D.D., pastor of St. Mark's Lutheran Church, St. Louis, who spoke on

Sources of Power.

Address of Rev. M. Rhodes, D.D.

If I were asked to name the two most important qualifications for all Christian organizations to-day, I should indicate wisdom and power. It might seem superfluous to mention these in such connection, but only the casual observer should note that we are living in a time when these need very special emphasis.

I wish to confine myself to the latter, and to deal with sources of power. Christian Endeavor has come to be one of the evangelizing forces of the world. If its opportunity is great, so is its responsibility tremendous. If its purpose is noble, so is it awful and thrilling to contemplate. If its success is phenomenal, so must the least peril be serious. What constant need there is that we be not absorbed with those elements of power which we can see and count, and that we keep ourselves in constant and conscious possession of those we cannot see, and without which we shall be helpless as an abundant field before the driving tempest. Mere power may be only weakness or desolation. It is the sources of power we want to know. "Power by itself," says an English writer, "may be the worst kind of weakness, and so mean no more than an opportunity for vindictive tyranny. When moved by love and directed by wisdom, and working for holiness, it is the mightiest thing that exists." It is God's omnipotence and our opportunity, and his glory that it achieves through a vessel of clay.

The first source of power I mention is a knowledge of Jesus Christ. I mean that profoundest, truest knowledge that ever comes to man. I take it that we agree that there is but one true gospel conception of our Lord as to his person and mission. Into this knowledge we cannot read ourselves, nor will we attain it by any process of logic or learning. It is revealed and communicated by the Holy Ghost, and in its beautiful simplicity is as readily accessible to a child as to a sage. The true character and mission of Jesus Christ — these, in both their limitation and illimitableness, profound as they are, are the source, not only of the beginning, but of the possibility of our power. What is Jesus Christ to you and to me? That is the question to which men's minds must be turned to-day, though it divert them from every other one; for this question correctly answered and applied is the solution of all, and this question rejected or perverted is the failure of all. As we know Christ, as the Son of the living God, as the propitiation for sin, as the exalted, ever-living Lord and King, in that meaning only may we hope to be men and women of power. A superficial knowledge of Christ will make no more impression on the world's need to-day than a winter's sun would make on an iceberg. Here is a subject for our serious meditation to-day. Hundreds feel where one thinks, and are content with the feeling. It is high thinking we need just now. It was not Luther's learning, nor his withering logic, nor his rushing eloquence, that made him more than a master of the formidable host that assailed him; it was his deep-rooted conviction and knowledge of Christ. Hitherto, when he was one with his adversaries, he was as weak as they were; but now, with a new life in him, he was as David with the giant at his feet. His enemies knew the Christ of the crucifix and of the imagination. Luther knew him in all the splendid power of the incarnation, of the cross, and of the resurrection — knew him as the one through whose blood we have redemption, even the forgiveness of sins. It was this that made him irresistible as a storm. This is real power. What do I personally know of the passion, love, and grace of Jesus Christ? Do I adore him as Saviour, and serve him as Lord, and joyfully anticipate him as Judge and King? Can I say, as it only should be said, "I know whom I have believed"? When I see him as he is, seated on the throne of his glory, shall I recognize in him one whom I have worshiped, and trusted, and served, and followed, and loved, and wished for? Is this commonplace? Is it this sort of speech the flippant tongue may indulge? True, but for this great organization and its work, this is the supreme source of power, the power the world is demanding now, the only power that will ever aid us in hushing its sobs, regenerating its life, and transforming it into the kingdom of God.

To this we may add very naturally the power of love. Who knows the power of love? It is the interpreting of God. "He that loveth not knoweth not God, for God is love." When Paul came to know the Lord as it has never been given to man to know him, he said, "I count all loss for the excellency of the knowledge of Christ Jesus my Lord." "The love of Christ constraineth us." Then it was that he prayed that "we might be able to comprehend with all saints what is the breadth and length and depth and height, and to know the love of Christ, which passeth knowledge." That is to say, that we might be girded with power. The life of our Lord was a brief day, often wearied, always worried. Its greatness from first to last was that it was permeated, illuminated, hallowed, immortalized, by love. "Love is the explanation of its sacrifices; love is also the moral of its duty." "Leaving us an example that we should follow in his footsteps." Men scorned his word, but quench this passion in him they never could.

Terrible as is the resistance, slow as seems his conquest, this love of Christ is the mightiest and most effective force in the world to-day. We may have what tools we like, employ what instruments we please, but until the soul is fired with this divine passion our weakness will arouse the contempt of men, and we shall fold no sheaf in our arms. "Nothing conquers like love; and there is no love under the sun so patient, so wonderful, so tender, so beautiful, as the love of the dying Jesus." The whole of God is not in creation, wonderful as it is; but it is there in the love wherewith he hath loved us. If the infinite heart could be exhausted, love would furnish the channel through which it would flow. Who can conceive its power? It is that power, my brethren, which will at once guard and assure the great mission of the society met in this city to-day. I mean, of course, the love manifested in sacrifice, beautified by humility, yearning after holiness, welcoming sorrow or loss or pain, if only it may achieve for God and the race. This, my brethren, is the mind that is to be in us. This is power.

Then will follow that power of enthusiasm and sacrifice which is so effective and yet needs to be so carefully continued and guarded. A wholesome, well-directed enthusiasm, that is the need. The spirit of indifference and worldliness has well nigh quenched it in the church. It must be recovered. Have the young people come to the kingdom for such a time as this? Surely if enthusiasm would take on the conditions of real power, it must be among you who are young. It belongs to you, as sunlight and singing birds and fragrant blossoms do to spring. The world has grown weary of boasted claims of contention and division. It does long to hear the voice, to feel the touch, and to see the face of the King.

Our weakness is more manifest than our might, our shivering indifference than our fervor. It is high time every soldier in the Lord's army came to conviction; and some one has said, "Enthusiasm is conviction on fire." We have had the logic of the head until we are bewildered; let us have the logic of the heart pulsing under the warmth of the Holy Ghost, and the revelation to us will prove regenerating to others. If religion, if holy duty, is nothing without enthusiasm, so is enthusiasm nothing without sacrifice. This makes it real power. Our Lord was enthusiastic, Paul was enthusiastic, Luther and Swartz and Judson and Wesley and Henry Martyn and Savonarola were enthusiastic, but it cost all sacrifice. In God's kingdom what so weak, so cheap, as enthusiasm without sacrifice? what so potent as enthusiasm with a crown of thorns on its brow?

"The salt of the Christian life," says a discriminating writer, "is sacrifice; and if the spirit of sacrifice die out of it, and the essence of that spirit, which is love, becomes chilled, and its activities and devotions presently decay and disappear, the salt of life is gone, and its growth paralyzed, and its influence killed, and its testimony silenced. The bane of the church of God, the dishonor of Christ, the laughing-stock of the world, is in that far too numerous body of half-alive Christians who choose their own cross, and shape their own standard, and regulate their own sacrifices, and measure their own devotions; whose cross is very unlike the Saviour's, whose sacrifices do not deprive them from one year to another of a single comfort, or even real luxury, and whose devotions never make their hearts burn with real love of Christ." Here is the pitiable weakness of multitudes to-day, the sad symptoms of forfeited discipleship. The men and women of power in the church are those who have kindled their enthusiasm at the cross and at the altar of God, and are expending it in unwearied self-sacrificing effort to bring this lost world to the feet of our conquering Lord.

And now in closing, just a few words on prayer and the Holy Spirit as sources of power. Our familiarity with these is just one reason why they should not be forgotten now. They are inclusive and pre-eminent. All I have mentioned are dependent upon these. We are as helpless to furnish any substitute for these as is the sinner to furnish an adequate righteousness to a holy God.

The men and women of power in the kingdom are those who keep the key of the closet on the inside, and who realize their dependence upon and who know the meaning of communion with the Spirit. When we speak of prayer as a source of power, we do not mean uttering a form of words, however beautiful; prayer is not so much a form of speech as a spirit within us. I mean a burning heart speaking to God, making its earnest, persistent supplication, and filling all with gratitude and praise. This is God's method, and the duty he enjoins upon us all. The divine word not only insists on the duty, but it illustrates its power. Moses and Nehemiah and Daniel achieved something. We tell the secret when we say they were men of prayer. Luther and the Wesleys, the long line of apostles, prophets, martyrs, and missionaries, how the mention of their names inspires us; they had varied and many gifts, but the power of prayer was pre-eminent with them. The century has not produced a more remarkable trinity of brothers than John, Horatius, and Andrew Bonar. Who knows anything about them must feel their touch in the lustrous cloud that hangs over us to-night. God knows them best, and they know him best at the throne of grace. Jesus taught his own to pray, and set them the most impressive example of prayer on record. The soul is always at its best in true prayer, and when the soul is at its best the scepter of the King is lifted in its behalf. The history of all successful missionary and evangelizing efforts is but the story of prayer. We mutter a good deal, my friends. Once in a while there is a flash as though the blackened coal was about to kindle to a flame; but of that earnest, trustful pleading which lays the human heart down on the heart of God, there is not much, but this is power. It is said of that humble German Lutheran pastor, Gossner, who sent more than one hundred missionaries into the field, that " he prayed mission stations into being and missionaries into faith; he prayed open the hearts of the rich, and gold from the most distant lands." What a work was that of Pastor Harms! Since the days of Paul there has been nothing like it. The work of that one man and of his congregation of poor people in Hermansburg would blush the evangelizing efforts of the richest denomination in the land. These were lowly men, mighty in prayer, and full of faith and the Holy Ghost. Their work may be written among the miracles of God. Amid the much there is to divert attention to-day, to divide our interest in the clamor of demands that come up from the good work in which you are engaged, keep distinctly before you the call of duty and prayer; and remember that he who knows its power may be feeble in learning or eloquence, but he does more than touch the hem of the garment of his glorified Lord, he lays his hand on the arm that wields the scepter of the kingdom that is to fill the whole earth and to endure forever.

Just a word. This is the dispensation of the Spirit. To blind men to that is one of the successful evils of the times. To realize and appreciate that is to have learned the source of power that includes all others. When our Lord set about the evangelizing of this world after the new order, his first and greatest gift was the gift of power. "Ye shall receive power when the Holy Ghost is come upon you." (Acts i. 8.) All our power centers right here. Our praying will only be an empty babble, our numbers will count for nothing, the enthusiasm of youth will be noise in the air, our unity and organization will prove a rope of sand, unless we maintain a conscious dependence on the Holy Ghost, and open our hearts to his indwelling. This is power. Without this we shall have none. Bishop Westcott comprehends the whole case in this short but most truthful sentence, "This is the secret of every failure; we do not believe in the Holy Ghost." Let me urge upon you earnest, believing prayer for the presence and power of the Holy Ghost, then will you know the meaning of the apostle's word, and then only will you be able to exclaim, with an exultant faith, "Now unto Him that is able to do exceeding abundantly above all that we ask or think, according to the power that worketh in us, unto him be the glory in the church and in Christ Jesus, and unto all generations for ever and ever. Amen."

First Baptist Church.

Pennsylvania's delegates at a Christian Endeavor convention always constitute a pretty big crowd taken by themselves; and as they were joined on this occasion by another crowd equally as large, all bent upon enjoying the meeting at the First Baptist Church, the Pennsylvania headquarters, it is not surprising that the audience overflowed out into the street. Rev. A. G. Upham, D.D., pastor, presided, and a splendid choir led the audience in inspiring song. The first speaker of the evening was Rev. W. H. McMillan, D.D., pastor of the United Presbyterian Church of Allegheny, Pa., whose presence and words are always welcome at a Christian Endeavor convention. He spoke on the subject, —

Christians in the Twentieth Century.

Address of Rev. W. H. McMillan, D.D.

We are nearing the end of the greatest century of the world's history. When the bells of time, six years hence, ring out the old and ring in the new, they must needs bring in something good and great, else the present then will not equal the past. When this century opened, the map of Europe was changing through the exploits of the Man of Destiny. June 14, 1800, saw the Battle of Marengo, and Dec. 3, Hohenlinden. Five years later, the same year in which Nelson won his splendid victory at Trafalgar, the invincible Corsican triumphed over the emperors of Russia and Austria at Austerlitz. Jena and Auerstadt followed the next year, and nine years later came the end of the great tragedy and its wonderful actor at Waterloo. The wars of Grecian independence were waged between 1821 and 1829. The revolution in Belgium was in 1830. Poland won her liberties between 1830 and 1832. The uprising of the Hungarians is remembered by some of us in 1848 and 1849. The constitution of the German Empire was formed in the latter year.

At home we began the century in tears. Just seventeen days before the century began, Washington breathed out his noble life at Mount Vernon, and his compeers were attempting to take up his fallen mantle to carry on the upbuilding of the nation which he had begun so well.

In the industrial world, by the beginning of the century Watt had made the steam-engine to be the mighty servant of man that it is. In 1807 Fulton taught us to apply that power to navigation; and twenty-three years later the same power was applied, in the locomotive, to travel by land. These two inventions have revolutionized the trade and traffic of the world.

But to a Christian, the most important of the strides of progress made in this great century have been the movements of the servants of God to carry his gospel throughout all lands. The missionary fire had been kindled in the soul of Carey in 1792, and the result was the formation of the Baptist Society for Propagating the Gospel. The London Missionary Society began three years later; and Wales and Scotland were not behind in the great movement to carry the gospel to the ends of the earth. In our own land that great agent for spreading the gospel, The American Board of Commissioners for Foreign Missions, was organized in 1810; and from that time on, all the churches fell into line one after another in carrying out the great commission, "Go into all the world and preach the gospel to every creature:" and the result has been that now there is not a nation of the earth that has not in some measure been reached by the light that guides the souls of the lost to the Saviour of the world. Soon this greatest of all the centuries will close, and the scroll will begin to unroll to tell us what God has in store for the world in the years ahead. It is important that these young Christians who are to take up the falling mantles of their fathers and mothers in those coming years should consider what the outlook is, and what are likely to be the special demands which will be made upon them, as the servants of the Lord, in those coming years.

Isaiah tells us, in giving the Burden of Dumah, that the watchman cried out of Seir, "Watchman, what of the night? Watchman, what of the night?" The answer was, "The morning cometh, and also the night." It appeared to the sight of the prophet that there was to be a mingled experience of joy and sadness to that people. They were to have a morning and a night also. It appears to me that the signs portend a similar experience to those who are to bear the burdens of the Lord in the times to come. There is much to encourage, and also much to fill us with alarm.

There is, first of all, the continued presence of that great power of evil, which has been a blight to the earth wherever it has held sway, — the Romish apostasy. It is cunning and aggressive, and almost omnipresent to push its secret plans for the furtherance of its interests. It is gaining a strong footing in places of power, and is laying hold of the public press to advance its interests. That is an omen of danger both to our civil and religious liberties. Some such thoughts as these were uttered last year in a Romish city; and the man who uttered them came near being mobbed, showing what the system still is when it has the power. It is true of it, as Napoleon once said of the Bourbons, "They learn nothing, and they forget nothing."

Along with this dangerous power there is a strong and defiant spirit of secularism attempting to overthrow all that is sacred in life, and release men from the dominion of conscience in all their relations with God. Last year we saw it in full play, when it trampled on the convictions of all the millions of Christian people in this land, and made the World's Fair a shame, which ought to have been a glory to this Christian republic. On the other hand, as signs for good, as promises of the coming day out of this night, we see the unwonted zeal of all the churches, and the wiser methods, and the more potent agencies constantly employed to advance the kingdom of Christ. Thus we see shadows, and we see signs of promise, as we turn our eyes to the years to come. What, then, will be the special demands which the twentieth century will make upon you who are to be the chief workers in it? These older heads will soon be sleeping on their last pillows, and it will be for you to take up the work of the Lord and carry it on to its final triumph.

1. It seems to me that the first demand which the future will make upon you will be for the exhibition of a deeper conscientiousness than is now often seen among the professed followers of the Lord. The tendencies of thought among men seem to be governed by a law like that of the pendulum; they are inclined to swing from one extreme to the other. In the early days of this country Puritanism was the prevailing type of religion, and that, you know, was a system of stern, hard legalism; it taught people that serving the Lord was walking according to a strict rule, and being impelled largely by a fear of punishment. That produced in its disciples a type of character which was indeed straight and strong, but was hard and cold. By and by the faith of God's people began to see that that was not a true interpretation of the religion of Jesus Christ. They saw that Jesus could not have been a Puritan in his character. They saw that there should be more of mercy and tenderness seen in the perfections of God, and more of the corresponding qualities in his servants, and that there should be more of brightness and joy in the Christian life. The consequence has been that there has been a revulsion from that which was so hard and severe, toward that which was more in harmony with the spirit of the gospel and its divine Founder. Since that time the swing of popular religious thought has been in the direction of looking upon the tenderness and mercy of God, to the exclusion largely of the thought of his retributive justice. The consequence is that in these days men are not much afraid to sin; they are taught to shun evil as ignoble and abhorrent, but not to shudder at the thought of it as a crime against the justice of God. People now do not have before them much of that "Fearful looking for of judgment and fiery indignation, which shall devour the adversaries of God." I am sure that the pendulum needs to swing back a long way to a reverence for the divine law, and fear of God's displeasure, before the Christians of the twentieth century can be what God would have them to be. We cannot have too much sentiment and holy affection in our religion, but we can have too little of solid conviction of duty, and reverence for law coupled with a fear of its righteous penalties.

2. Another demand which I think the coming years will make of you, who are to be the active workers in the church, is that you shall exhibit a broader catholicity of spirit, one toward another. All the movements of Providence appear to be unmistakably in the direction of the unity of the people of God. The old walls of separation, that stood a while ago so high and strong and cold between the different branches of the church of Christ, are melting away, as the sun of righteousness rises higher above the horizon of the world's faith, and its warmth permeates more and more the hearts of believers. We all see with gladness that doctrinal differences are not emphasized now as they once were. The essential unity of the body of Christ is being realized more and more. But the followers of the Lord have not yet come by any means to that point of unity for which he prayed when he asked, that they all might be one. There

are rivalries and contentions still to be seen, and there is but little of that ecclesiastical comity of which we hear so much, but see so seldom. The world still sees a little struggling church of each denomination in a town or neighborhood, and all standing apart in their differences, and all too weak in their separate efforts to cope with the forces of evil about them.

The coming years will require of you better things than that. The world needs the efforts of the servants of Christ too much for any of their strength to be wasted in maintaining denominationalism, simply as against the general interests of the cause of the Lord. To me there is no sign of the times more significant than the existence of the United Society of Christian Endeavor. It is manifestly the child of Providence, and the whole bearing of the mighty influence exerted by it is in the direction of Christian unity. It is true that our Christian Endeavor pledge binds us to be true to our own church and denomination, and for that we honor it. That means that it is not tending to promote Christian unity by any violent methods; it seeks to unite the followers of Christ only so far and so fast as they can be united on the basis of a harmonious belief. But it does melt away the cold suspicions, and promote the mutual knowledge and love which furnish the best possible basis for coming to a mutual understanding about the things of God and everlasting life. When these young Christians have been together in one of these delightful councils, the thought comes to them with great power that the motto "For Christ and the Church" means a much larger church than they had known before, and that the differences that prevent the unification of that universal church are not half so great and important as they had supposed.

You remember the Lord had a great reason to give for asking that his people might all be one; it was that the world might believe that the Father had sent him. That reason exists to-day as strongly as when the prayer of the Saviour was first offered. Yes, it exists in a far stronger sense now; for the world thinks more now than then, and is stumbled more by the argument of the divisions in the church. The world of to-day is perplexed and repelled by the existing divisions in the church of God, and especially by the absence of the spirit of unity; and the name of the Lord is blasphemed thereby. The call of the coming years to the followers of the Lord will be, Close up the gaps in the ranks of the Lord's sacramental host; let shoulder touch shoulder; let hand join with hand, and heart feel the beating of kindred hearts, that the line of attack that goes up against those mighty forces of evil that confront you in the world's final onset against the cause of God may show no point of weakness where the enemy can gain an advantage over you.

3. Another demand to be made upon you will be for a more practical and vital religion manifested in daily life. It will not do now, and it will do still less as the world grows more enlightened, for a man to sit in the house of God on Sabbath, with a devout air, engaging in the services of worship, and then go to his business on the morrow to drive sharp bargains, and utterly lay aside the "Golden Rule" in his dealings with men. That kind of religion will not pass now, and the future is going to still more sternly reject it. Let your light so shine before men, that they may see your good works, and glorify your Father in heaven, is a command for all the seven days of the week, and for all the transactions of life.

And, furthermore, the twentieth century is going to affirm that the servants of Christ have not done enough when they have merely put their names on church-rolls, but go on living as the world does in social life. "Come out from among them and be ye separate," saith the Lord; "and touch not the unclean thing, and I will receive you," is a command that needs to be especially considered just now. The Christians who will carry the burdens and fight the battles of the cause of God in the days that are before us, will not be those who doze over a Sunday paper instead of going to the house of God, except on those rare days when it is neither too wet nor too dry, nor too hot nor too cold, to go to the place of worship. They will not be those who sit as God's people sit, in the sanctuary on the Sabbath, and sit as the servants of the Devil sit, in the theater or at the card-table on other days. They will not be such as raise a loud complaint if the story of the cross is told to them for more than thirty minutes on the Sabbath, but are ready to heave a sigh of regret when they see the curtain fall on a play that has held them spell-bound for two hours on a week-night. I do not suppose that I am speaking to many of that kind of Christians, for they are not the stuff that Christian Endeavorers are made of; but I can assure you, who are ready to take up your cross and follow the Lord faithfully in the duties that will come to you in the future, that you need not expect any real assistance from that class. They cannot serve God and Mammon, and they are determined to serve Mammon; therefore the service of God is impossible.

And those coming days will require that the servants of God shall serve him in their political acts as well as in all other duties. It will not do for them to preach and profess on the side of the Lord, and vote on the side of the Devil. We are a sovereign people in this land, and we, the people, are responsible for the laws that are enacted and enforced. For all that is done or not done in civil affairs the people are responsible, for they are the governing power. We must not forget our personal responsibility in the great mass of voters; each one must look at his own share in the results of every election. There is a power at work in this land destroying a hundred thousand lives annually; who is responsible for that fearful destruction of the bodies and souls of men? We, the people, are in so far as we have aided or abetted it, or have not done all in our power to oppose it. Look around you; put your ear to the ground, and hear the rumbling of hidden forces ready to break forth into violence and bloodshed. These are days when men's hearts are failing them for fear of the things that seem to be coming on our land. What is demanded of the Christian element in this nation, which is the controlling element, or might be if it would assert itself? It is that every one should go to the primary caucus, and to the polls, and vote with this motto before him, "For Christ and the Church." The coming century will look to this Christian element in the nation to save it from anarchy and dissolution.

4. The future years will demand of you a more aggressive spirit of evangelism than has yet been seen, even in these times of spiritual progress. You are fond of singing, "Throw out the Life-line." How many are the Christian Endeavorers who are really and earnestly throwing out any life-line to those who are sinking into eternal perdition? "Lift up your eyes, and look upon the fields that are white already unto the harvest." How many are the hands that are employing the sickle to gather in the precious sheaves? It is often a mooted question as to how the masses may be reached. It should not be a hard question to answer. The masses touch the church at every point,— in the higher walks of life, and at the bottom in the humbler places; and all that is needed for the church to reach them, is just that all should reach out a hand to them. This fruit that is to be gathered into the garner of God is all to be hand-picked. There is no machinery of evangelistic agency that will do it by wholesale; it is to be done, when it is done well, by hand-to-hand personal work.

The Master has said to all, "As the Father hath sent me into the world, even so send I you." Whenever every servant of the Lord, or even the half or the fourth of them, has heard that commission as addressed to them, and proceed by divine aid to carry it out, then the time of the church's enlargement and the world's redemption will have come. Perhaps as I have been trying to set before you some of these demands which the world of the future will make upon the servants of the Lord, you have been saying in your thoughts, These are hard sayings; who can hear them? He is putting it too strong. He is placing the standard of our duties too high.

Let us be careful lest we may have been infected with the idea to which I referred at the beginning. Perhaps we have been carried along with the belief so common now, that the demands of the Lord upon his people are not great, and their burdens are not severe; that we can afford to float largely with the currents of life, and yet expect to enter the haven of rest at last. Possibly we have been disposed to go along with this easy-going and silken-slippered age in its conclusion about Christian duty. I know of but one safe guide, and that is not custom among other Christians, but the example of our divine Master. Follow me is his call to us all. If we follow in his steps, we will surely see that we need that deeper conscientiousness of which I spoke at the beginning, and that to have it we must revise our methods of Bible-study. If we follow him we must surely fall into the spirit and purpose of his last prayer for his people's unity, and will gather together around the essentials of our faith, and cease to stand apart so far on that which is non-essential. If we follow him, we will be far less conformed to the world and more transformed by the renewing of our minds. If we follow him, we must have a great burden for the perishing on our hearts; for he so loved the perishing world that he came from his high throne in heaven to the altar of the cross to redeem it. We, therefore, cannot follow him, and should not dare to bear his name, unless we are busy rescuing the perishing.

If the duties are severe, and the claims of the Master upon you in the great future to which you are moving are weighty, the achievements which the opportunities of that future will make possible to you are enough to kindle your zeal to white heat. You ought to thank God every day that you are permitted to be a Christian Endeavorer just now. What fields of opportunity has the Lord opened before you! What forces has he placed at your command! What promises of success does he hold out before you!

Some thirty-fold, some sixty-fold, and some a hundred-fold; that is, some three thousand per cent, some six thousand per cent, and some ten thousand per cent. A good investment is it not? When the Old Guard swept down the slope at Waterloo to charge the English squares, they saw at their head the proud plume of Marshal Ney. They knew that they had followed that plume to many a victory, from frozen Moscow to sunny Italy, and they followed it now with pride and supreme confidence; but the result proved that even the Old Guard with Ney at its head could be defeated: it was shattered and hurled back in utter rout. You follow into the battles of God in the years to come that crowned rider of the white horse whom John saw in vision going forth conquering and to conquer. His legions will never be hurled back in defeat. Crowns of eternal victory await you all who are faithful unto death in following that kingly leader.

Rev. Wayland Hoyt, D.D., the popular pastor of the First Baptist Church, Minneapolis, was next introduced, and spoke briefly upon " Two Temptations Special to Christian Endeavor."

Pilgrim Congregational Church.

Maryland flung out the orange and black in profusion at this church, which was prettily decorated in honor of its guests. The enthusiasm of the delegates for " Baltimore in '96 " was catching; and a great number of would-be auditors were turned away disappointed, unable to gain admission to the church, so great was the throng. The singing was led by a splendid choir, together with the Euterpean Military Band. The meeting was presided over by the pastor of the church, Rev. Charles S. Mills. After a delightful song service, the first speaker was introduced, Rev. Canon J. B. Richardson of London, Ontario, who represents the Church of England on the Board of Trustees. His subject was " Woman's Missionary Endeavor."

Rev. Dr. David James Burrell of New York was on the programme as the next speaker; but he was unavoidably detained. His place was filled by two of the trustees of the United Society. Prof. James Lewis Howe, Ph. D., of Louisville, Ky., was the first speaker, his subject being " Some Educational Influences of Christian Endeavor."

Rev. J. M. Lowden of Boston, representing the Free Baptists on the Board of Trustees, spoke in closing on " Three Things Concerning Truth and Character."

Franklin Circle Church of Christ.

Rev. S. L. Darsie, chairman of the sub-committee on music for the convention, is the pastor of this church, and presided at this meeting. This fact alone, however, does not account for the magnificent singing at this particular rally; for this church had been assigned to the Michigan delegates as their headquarters, and Michigan was present in full force. A very respectable overflow meeting could have been made up of those who were turned away from the doors, unable to find even standing-room within. Rev. Dr. Hill, who was on the programme for this meeting, had been obliged to fill an appointment at another rally; and in his stead brief remarks were made by a number of speakers, including Rev. Geo. T. Smith, a former missionary to Japan; Mr. W. H. Strong, president of the Michigan delegation; Miss Luella E. Hull, secretary of the delegation; and Rev. Mr. Bartlett, of Elyria, O.

An original story by Mrs. I. M. Alden, better known as "Pansy," was then ready.• Mrs. Alden was greeted by a little girl as she came forward, who made her a pleasant little speech, and presented her with a basket of flowers. Mrs. Alden's story was entitled "A Christian Endeavor Revenge." The story was published as a serial in the *Golden Rule*, commencing July 26.

Y. M. C. A. Building.

A large audience, consisting mainly of young men, assembled in the auditorium of the Y. M. C. A. building. Rev. R. W. Miller, of Hummelstown, Pa., presided; and the song service was led by Rev. H. H. Ennis, of Washington, D.C. Rev. J. H. Prugh, D.D., of Pittsburg, Pa., gave the opening address on "The Brotherhood of Andrew and Philip."

The next topic was "The Travelers' Union of Christian Endeavor," concerning which remarks were made by Rev. R. W. Miller and Mr. J. Howard Breed of Philadelphia.

"The Student Volunteer Movement" was the subject of the last address, the speaker being Mr. H. B. Sharman of Chicago.

THURSDAY MORNING.

Saengerfest Hall.

Only one session was planned for Thursday morning, that in Saengerfest Hall. According to the experience of past conventions it was thought this building would be ample to accommodate the audience which usually assembles at the opening session. Never before, at any convention, has the main hall been filled at the first meeting. But to the astonishment of the committee, and to the discomfiture of thousands of delegates, Saengerfest Hall was filled to its utmost capacity long before the time announced for beginning the meeting. "To the tent, O Israel!" was the cry taken up by the multitude of delegates who were barred out of the great building by the well-disposed but inflexible policemen. And to the tent they went until, in a very short time, that, too, was filled until no more could creep under the edges. Then the Epworth Memorial Church was opened up, and that was speedily filled. Then the Woodland Avenue Presbyterian Church was brought into use, and another throng gathered there. Nearly thirty thousand delegates took part, in one place or another, in the opening exercises of the great convention of 1894.

At the hall the preliminary song service began long before the appointed time, and in fact the whole programme began and was carried through considerably ahead of time. It was a magnificent audience, fully matching in quality and enthusiasm anything in the history of Christian Endeavor conventions. The singing was led by Mr. Percy S. Foster, of Washington, assisted by a splendid choir and a large orchestra, both composed of Christian Endeavor young people of Cleveland. Three of the Park sisters of New York also lent their valuable aid with their cornets. Various incidents, besides the glorious singing, enlivened the hour previous to the opening of the convention. Governor McKinley's appearance on the platform awoke a perfect storm of applause and enthusiasm. Secretary Baer and Treasurer Shaw were also accorded a most cordial welcome as they took their seats. Several State songs were tried, the most successful being the following welcome song, sung by the Clevelanders present to the tune of " Beulah Land : " —

> " Our day of Jubilee is here,
> The bannered hosts of God appear;
> With music floating on before,
> You come to meet on Erie's shore.
>
> CHORUS:
>
> To Erie's shore, fair Erie's shore,
> We bid you welcome, o'er and o'er;
> Our songs of praise with yours shall blend,
> Our prayers with yours to God ascend,
> Till heaven seems nearer than ever before,
> To waiting hearts on Erie's shore.
>
> You come with hearts aglow with hope,
> From eastern coast and western slope,
> From land of pine and land of palm,
> You come with glad thanksgiving psalm.
>
> The bannered hosts will march away,
> But holy thoughts will last for aye,
> And life be sweeter evermore
> For visions seen on Erie's shore."

Secretary Baer, as he rose to call the convention to order, was greeted with the Chautauqua salute. He said : —

Fellow Endeavorers, — It is necessary for me to make an announcement that causes me great pain. You probably anticipate it, having read the daily papers. President Clark for three or four weeks has been continually advised — ay, has been warned — to stay away from this convention, by his physician. He is suffering from nervous exhaustion, occasioned by overwork. He came to Boston on Monday from his home at Pine Point, Me., determined to come to the convention, because he had learned that the railroad strike was likely to tear our convention to pieces, and he wanted to do everything he could, as usual, to stand in the gap. He was positively forbidden to come that night, and he is not here. I want to say to you that I know something of his grief and of his disappointment. Two years ago God placed a restraining hand upon me, and I had to stay away from the New York convention. I know what it is to lose a convention. This time it is more than one man's disappointment; for you suffer this time in the absence of our leader and president, the founder of this movement. With him we suffer together. And I want to say this word further, that, knowing his temper and his spirit, he would not want any one here to feel that this convention was to be saddened or in any way disturbed by his absence. I say to you that while we are suffering much and will miss throughout this entire convention the wisdom and guidance of our leader, I feel sure, if he could send a message even at this moment, he would say to you, " Go on, good friends, make it the best yet."

The Board of Trustees have elected Rev. Charles A. Dickinson of Boston president *pro tem.* of the Board of Trustees. Mr. Dickinson is one of the original trustees, a warm personal friend of Dr. Clark, and will have charge of this convention in President Clark's absence.

Mr. Dickinson was greeted with applause as he came forward to address the convention. He said:—

Fellow Endeavorers, — In accepting the honor which the Board of Trustees have conferred upon me, it seems to me fitting that I should read to you a letter written to this convention by Dr. Clark.

"TO THE CHRISTIAN ENDEAVORERS ASSEMBLED IN CLEVELAND.

"*My dear Friends,* — It is perhaps the bitterest disappointment of my life to be obliged to stay away from the international convention. For months I have looked forward to it with the keenest anticipation, and for the last few days I have hoped against hope that I might be able to go; and especially since the great strike threatened to disarrange our plans and reduce our numbers, I have been more than ever desirous and determined to go. But my physician (an eminent authority) at the last moment forbids my going, and assures me that I could go only at the risk of months of inability to work for the cause of Christian Endeavor, but that a few weeks of rest now will enable me to take up my work with full vigor, a kind Providence permitting. My illness is simply the result of the overstrain of the past few years. But enough of personal matters. The convention will not suffer by my absence; for my associates, wise and devoted men, will fill my place and do all that I could do. I shall pray that every hour of the convention may be a blessed hour, an hour of the felt presence of the Saviour, and of inspiration to every Endeavorer. My special thought concerning our work for the coming year is found in the president's annual address. My love to every one of you. 'God be with you till we meet again.' Your friend.

F. E. CLARK."

Because Dr. Clark cannot be with you to-day the trustees have been disposed to elect me to fill his place temporarily. In accepting this honor I do it with feelings which cannot well be expressed. I have a deep personal feeling of sorrow because he whom all love and honor cannot be with us and participate in this convention, which has been in his heart and mind for the last twelve months, but withal a feeling of satisfaction that he was persuaded to forego the excitement of this assembly and to attend at once to his immediate recovery. I have also a feeling of apprehension lest I may not be able to discharge the duties which you have imposed upon me; and still again, I have a feeling of expectation that, despite all of the disappointments which have attended this convention thus far, it will nevertheless be one of the grandest conventions of the whole series. With this hope, and with the earnest request that all the members of this convention will co-operate with the trustees and officers in making it a success, I accept the position and will do the best I can to fill it.

Mr. Brokaw moved that the ordinary committees be appointed by the chair in the regular way. The motion was carried, and the chair announced that the committees would be appointed later.

Dr. Wayland Hoyt then led in prayer, remembering especially President Clark in his illness.

MR. DICKINSON: Much of the success of the Christian Endeavor movement, especially at its great annual conventions, has depended on the local committees. We have been especially happy in the selection of these committees in the years past, but never, it seems to me, more happy than in the selection of the Committee of '94. We shall therefore be glad to give that committee a hearty welcome to-day as they appear before us through their chairman, Rev. J. Z. Tyler, D.D.

Dr. Tyler was accorded a hearty welcome, indeed, as he came forward to give the address of welcome on behalf of the Committee of '94. He spoke as follows:—

Committee of '94.

5. Rev. S. L. Darsie, Music. 6. F. Melville Lewis, Printing. 7. Norman E. Hills, Entertainment. 9. J. E. Cheesman, Hall.
4. A. E. Roblee, Treasurer, Finance. 1. Miriam C. Smith, Secretary. 3. A. W. Neale, Reception. 11. Rev. R. A. George, Ex-officio.
2. Rev. J. Z. Tyler, Chairman. 8. R. B. Hamilton, Press. 10. J. V. Hitchcock, Auditor.

Address of Welcome by Rev. J. Z. Tyler.

Fellow Endeavorers, — When, a few months ago, I visited the Governor of our beloved State, to bear the request that he should speak the welcome of Ohio to this great gathering to-day, I said to him that it might be necessary to have his address repeated in the tent. Governor McKinley is familiar with great gatherings, and is himself a master of assemblies; but he shook his head doubtingly, and said, "That can scarcely be possible. I know something of the size of Saengerfest Hall, and I shall be surprised if you are able to fill that." [*Laughter.*] But we have to-day broken all previous records. [*Applause.*] Never before in the history of these magnificent gatherings have we been able, at the opening session, to fill the main hall. As I passed the tent a while ago — a tent capable of seating from ten to twelve thousand persons — it was full, and the broad avenue leading from this hall to that tent was crowded from curb to curb. [*Applause.*] Epworth Memorial Church has been opened and is full, and we are now opening the Woodland Avenue Presbyterian Church. [*Loud applause.*] All this, too, in the face of the financial depression which we have all felt for more than a year, and in the face of the great railroad strike, which came near scaring some people to death. [*Laughter.*]

I have been asked to speak a word of welcome from the committee of '94. Your worth is warrant of your welcome. The preparations which have been made in anticipation of your coming surround you to-day as a cloud of witnesses, bearing manifold testimony to the forethought of many loving hearts. As the thought of your coming has been the inspiration of all this preparation, so now the joy of greeting you is an abundant reward for all our labor. As we extend the arms of our hospitality to welcome you, we would also, after the ancient and apostolic custom, salute each of you with a holy kiss. However, as I look upon this vast assembly, I recognize that this would be too large an undertaking for the committee of '94, a committee composed of only eleven members. [*Laughter.*] But as it has been our method, in making preparations for this convention, to distribute the work to our numerous sub-committees, so now we would assign to the 2,662 members of these sub-committees the pleasant duty of thus saluting you. [*Laughter.*]

Our joy in greeting you is greater because of the dangers you dreaded when you left your homes to come. The great railroad strike made travel uncertain and even perilous. We gratefully recognize the fact that you were graciously preserved while on the way, and have been brought within our gates in safety. The flood of telegrams that came upon me as Chairman of the Committee of Arrangements, up to so late a date as yesterday, indicates that many thousands have been kept from coming because of grave apprehension as to the possibility of arriving in safety. Under favorable circumstances, and with open highways of public travel, who can tell what the attendance at this convention would have been? I trust you will not suspect that the enthusiasm of this glad hour has robbed me of my reason, when I say that we would this morning have enrolled not less than forty thousand delegates and visitors. [*Applause.*] Possibly the great strike should be interpreted as a gracious interposition of Providence to prevent such an overwhelming flood submerging, not only the committee of '94, but this entire city. [*Laughter and applause.*] This Christian Endeavor movement, although it numbers two millions, is yet in its infancy. A giant infant, this; but more wonderful than its size is the continued rapidity of its growth.

We welcome you, not only for what you are, but for what you represent.

First, and above all, you represent personal loyalty to the personal Christ. Every active member in this movement has made a personal pledge to Christ to strive to do whatever he would have him do. We have sworn unswerving loyalty to our living Lord. Self-surrender to the personal Christ is the bond of our great fellowship. I am glad to recognize that in the best thinking of our times the personal Christ is emerging from the battle-cloud of theological controversy, and that he stands to-day before the believer's eye in a clearer light than ever before. I am not one of those who fear that the present assaults of unbelief and of destructive criticism are destined to destroy the foundations of Christian faith. Some outposts have been surrendered, and others may fall; but the surrender of these only drives us back to the citadel of our faith. We fall back from philosophical creeds and traditional theories to the personal Christ.

[*Applause.*] You who are gathered here to-day represent a magnificent army of consecrated youth who, as with uplifted hands before the crowned Christ, have solemnly made a pledge to be obedient in all things to him. We hail you, we greet you, we welcome you as the sworn soldiers of the Captain of our common salvation. [*Applause.*]

We welcome you because you represent a fellowship that is broader and deeper than denominational lines. There was a time when denominational lines did not exist. May we not cherish the hope that the time shall yet come when denominational lines, as barriers between believers, shall cease to exist? [*Applause.*] May we not look for the time when all hearts shall be bound in loyalty to our common Lord, when all wills shall be bowed to his will as supreme, when all hands that have clasped his shall be joined together in every field of service for him? Shall not we labor for the fulfillment of his prayer that all may be one in him, and that this union may be made so manifest to men that the world shall receive him? The motto given by our beloved president at the close of his St. Louis address in '90 still stands as our permanent motto: "One is your Master, even Christ; and all ye are brethren." [*Applause.*] Because Christ is our Master, we are brethren. [*Applause.*]

We welcome you because you represent applied Christianity. We have had dogmatic Christianity in the schools; we have had the theory of Christianity set forth in books. The purpose of this movement is to incarnate the will of Christ in daily service. By the terms of our pledge we are to strive to do, everywhere and always, whatever the Christ would have us do — not simply whatever he would have us do in ecclesiastical matters, not simply whatever he would have us to do in matters that are distinctively acts of worship, but whatever he would have us do in the home and in the school, in the office and in the workshop, in every place of responsibility and in every relationship in which we may be called to stand. This movement is in harmony with that larger view of the mission of Christ into which the church is slowly but surely coming. As we read the record of his perfect life, we find that he manifested his spirit in daily service, and that he came to be a quickening power in the hearts of men, that they too should work in daily life for the good of their fellows, and thus for the glory of God. A Christian is simply Christ continued. The purpose and the principles which guided and governed him are to guide and govern us. The mind that was in him should be in us. The spirit of self-sacrifice that led him to the cross should lead us to take up our cross of self-denial and follow him in daily service in ministering to others. [*Applause.*] The teachings of his gospel are to be translated and illustrated through our lives. We are to be living gospels. Each in his place is to be a miniature Christ. Because we believe you are possessed by this spirit of the Christ, and that you feel yourselves called to manifest this spirit in the practical affairs of life, we bid you a most cordial welcome.

We welcome you because you have come into such hearty and enthusiastic sympathy and co-operation with the great missionary enterprises of the church. [*Applause.*] To-day the masses of the heathen world are brought within easy reach of the gospel artillery. The way of approach is open; the armor is ready; and I believe that as we are passing out of the nineteenth into the twentieth century, God is gathering in this movement a great army that shall go forth to the conquest of the world. I cherish the hope that before this convention shall come to a close, steps shall be taken to harness the great missionary spirit of this movement to the missionary machinery of our churches for the evangelization of the world. [*Applause.*]

We pray that this convention may be to every one of us a time of heavenly vision on the Mount of Transfiguration. May there hover over us the heavenly Father! May there be transfigured before us the divine Christ! May there be heard the voice of the Father saying, "This is my beloved Son; hear ye him." As we wait together in this heavenly place, even in the midst of the great throng, may the uplifted eye of faith see no man, but Christ only. I pray that it may be such a mount of vision and transfiguration, that when we shall go down from its summit, we shall be clothed with a divine strength to cast out the demons that torment man in the valley below. In a recent letter concerning this gathering, Dr. Clark said that he thought it would be a convention characterized by service; that the reports presented would indicate a vast amount of work done through the various channels of our churches. I believe that this prediction will be verified. I cherish the hope, also, that this convention may prove to be the preparation for yet larger service in the year to come. [*Applause.*]

In the midst of this lavish display of the colors of our Local Union, we welcome you, and we beg that you take the lessons they are meant to teach. We mingle the white with the gold. The white for ages has been the fit symbol of purity; the yellow is the recognized symbol of courage. As we glance over the planes of history, among the world's heroes, our eye catches the waving white plume of Henry of Navarre, and the yellow plume of William of Orange. May these colors impress upon you the lessons of purity and courage, — personal purity, and purity of purpose; the courage of Christian conviction in every conflict of life! With these, victory is sure. [*Loud applause.*]

MR. DICKINSON: We all admire and honor the grand old State of Ohio [*applause*], one of the brightest stars in Columbia's coronet. She has done a great deal for the United States. She has given to her country two presidents, one of whom to-day wears the martyr's crown; and I presume that her presidential timber is not yet exhausted. [*Applause.*] Ohio has had a magnificent procession of able and brilliant governors; and one of the ablest and most brilliant, one whose name is a household word in America, honors us with his presence here to-day. It gives me great pleasure to introduce to a Christian Endeavor audience his excellency, Gov. William McKinley.

Governor McKinley was received with a demonstration of applause and enthusiasm which continued several moments. The Chautauqua salute was repeated again and again; and not until the great audience had risen and united in three rousing cheers for the speaker was he able to proceed.

Address of Welcome by Governor William McKinley.

Mr. President, Members of the Society of Christian Endeavor, Ladies and Gentlemen, —

It is a mighty cause that could convene in any city of any State in the Union the splendid assemblages of people gathering in so many places this morning, in this city by the lake. No cause but one could have brought together these noble, earnest people; and that is the cause of the Master, and the cause of man. [*Applause.*] It is fitting that the largest convention of Christian Endeavorers ever held should be in the State of Ohio. [*Applause.*] I bring you the welcome of the State which you have honored with your presence, — a State, the opening words of whose Constitution make grateful acknowledgment to Almighty God for our freedom; and it declares that religion, morality, and knowledge are essential to good government, and the law-making powers shall therefore protect every religious denomination in the peaceful enjoyment of its own mode of public worship, and encourage schools and means of education.

I bring you the warm greetings of more than four million people of the State of Ohio who subscribe to that Constitution, and who were glad to have this representation of young, vigorous Christians of the United States. Your coming is hailed with satisfaction. Your stay will be to us a benediction. Your going will be to us the occasion of sincere regret. You are not strangers to us. The young men and women of Ohio are your associates in the great work in which you are engaged. The whole world knows you, for it has felt and profited by your influence and example. [*Applause.*] I can conceive of no more beautiful employment than that of Christian Endeavor, the habitual effort to be better and to do better, and to make those around us better. The more faithful the endeavor, the more certain the realization; the more constant the effort, the more sublime the end. We cannot try to be good without doing good. There is good, great good, in the honest striving to do good. It is quite as easy, ladies and gentlemen, to do good as to do evil; and it is incomparably better for the moment, and for all eternity, to do right than to do wrong. [*Applause.*] Wrong doing is never profitable. Its ultimate reward is failure. Right doing brings the rich reward of a peaceful conscience and a cheerful disposition and a faithful heart.

Mr. President, there is very much in habit. A bad habit is easy to make and hard to break. This is just as true of a good habit. But bad habits ought to be broken, hard as it may be. Not so with a good habit. It must not be broken, but kept. No one can know better than you, who have tried it, how easy it is to get into the habit of doing good. Every good act makes the next one easier; every duty performed makes the next which follows lighter. The habit of doing good expels the temptation to do wrong. If the world around you knows that you are fixed in your Christian habits, and settled in

WELL-GROUNDED MORAL PRINCIPLES,

it will let you alone. [*Applause.*] It will not present you with temptations; it will not pursue you with allurements to tempt you from the paths of righteousness. If I have observed your organization rightly in its principles, its business is to form in the lives of your members this habit of being good and of doing good. [*Applause.*] It is a noble and inspiring work which engages you. It is the link that connects right living with good morals and good citizenship. It serves as the armor against evil doing and evil doers. It gives confidence and encouragement alike. The soldier gets confidence and encouragement after he has been in the field of conflict.

Mr. President, I have been peculiarly impressed with the significance and suggestiveness of the name of one of your committees, the lookout committee, or the committee on lookout. [*Applause.*] That is the most essential committee in human civilization. That is the most important committee that was ever raised, and every Christian Endeavorer, every citizen of the country, should be on that committee, and chairman of it. It is a useful and essential committee to all mankind. It ought to be adopted by everybody. "Look out." "Look out for breakers." "Look out for temptations." "Look out for sin." "Look out for pitfalls." "Look out for the enemy." "Look out for your associations." "Look out for yourselves." Keep on

THE TOWER OF OBSERVATION

always. Let no danger signal escape you. If you will keep this committee alive in every heart and alert in every life, looking out all the time, you will escape many of the discouragements to Christian living. You will avoid many severe temptations which now beset you. You will defeat many machinations of enemies of right-doing, and they are everywhere thrusting themselves across the pathway of human life. Then this committee you have organized not only looks out for yourselves, but it looks out for others. It smooths many rough places for the weak. It removes many obstacles from the footsteps of your companions. It gives strength to the weak, and courage to those who are almost led to give up the battle. It brings to all that confidence and courage that comes from contact and comradeship, unity in the holiest of all causes, the cause of God and mankind.

If I may be permitted, I would give the Christian Endeavorers an addition to their motto, and would make it "Look out. Look in. Look up." [*Applause.*] I wish, ladies and gentlemen, for your deliberations the fullest measure of success. I am proud to be with you. [*Applause.*] I wish I might remain here until the end of your sessions, but that is impossible. [*Applause.*] I am personally glad; and I am sure it is the universal sentiment of the State, that I should make acknowledgment to your association for the splendid work you are doing for conscience and Christianity, and for citizenship and the country. [*Applause.*] Remember they are all tied up together. Piety and patriotism should go hand in hand [*Applause*]; should be joined in indissoluble union; and when the voice of God and the voices of the people are in harmony, such union is invincible. [*Prolonged applause.*]

As Governor McKinley resumed his seat the audience joined in singing two stanzas of "America;" and they were sung right heartily. President Dickinson then announced that Rev. E. R. Dille, D.D., who had been appointed to respond on behalf of the trustees and delegates, was blockaded by the strike in San Francisco, and could not be present. He introduced, as the speaker appointed by the trustees to represent them, Rev. William Patterson of Toronto.

Response to the Addresses of Welcome by Rev. William Patterson.

I am not responsible for being here at this time. Mr. Baer is the man that is responsible; and you know that when a Baer gets hold of a man he may just as well give in. [*Laughter.*] We have all listened with interest to the welcome which we have received from Cleveland, and from the State of Ohio. Is there a man living in a region so remote that he has not heard of Ohio, of Cleveland, and of McKinley? We have received from you a right royal welcome, and we are now to respond to those words of welcome. You know, sometimes when people are invited to any place the invitation does not always mean what it says. Sometimes the invitation will say, "Mr. and Mrs. So-and-so request the pleasure of your company to tea at such an hour;" but the invitation really means, "We hope you will not come." [*Laughter.*] But we know that when the Christian Endeavorers of any community or city or State give an invitation to the Society to hold a meeting there, they always mean it. I am sure no one could have listened, as the trustees did yesterday, to the speeches delivered by representatives of the great cities that want the convention in '95 and '96, without being struck by the wonderful enthusiasm displayed, and without coming to the conclusion that these men meant every word they said, and far more than they said. So, when the invitation came from Cleveland, we realized that you meant what you said,—that you wanted us to come to Cleveland; and so we came. We have often heard of Cleveland; but when we reached the city we came to the same conclusion that the Queen of Sheba came to,—that, though we had heard a great deal, the half had not been told us. [*Applause.*]

Some one has said that the proof of the pudding is in the eating of it; but if I had been writing that proverb I should have said, the proof of the pudding is in the digesting of it. [*Laughter.*] We have come to prove the invitation; and I am sure that every Christian Endeavorer who is present here this morning, and who has come to Cleveland, realizes that we have received a right royal welcome, and that the citizens have put themselves to great trouble and to great expense to show us that they wanted us, and that they wanted to make us at home. Last night after the meeting I thought I would take a dander through some of the streets [*laughter*], and so I did. I went down by the monument, and looked up and saw those great arches of flags; I saw the schools illuminated, and the city beautified; and I said, "These people of Cleveland mean this thing; they want us to come! they are glad we have come!" And we are glad that we came.

Then there is another thing about it. You know, sometimes when people are invited to a place they try to make some excuse not to come. But we who have come to this convention show you how much we appreciate your invitation, because we have come, strike or no strike, railways or no railways. [*Applause.*] I say that is enough to prove positively that we appreciate your invitation.

Of course I am here not only to represent the Trustees, but to represent the Christian Endeavorers, because I am a Christian Endeavorer, a member of a Christian Endeavor Society, and I take my part in the meeting just as the other members of the society do. [*Applause.*] If I consider it an honor to be a member of the Board of Trustees, I consider it a greater honor to be a member of the Christian Endeavor Society of Cooke Church, Toronto. We all want to realize that it is an honor to be a Christian Endeavorer, an honor to represent any society and any Christian community. Now, I am here to-day not only to represent the Trustees, but to represent all the Christian Endeavor Societies, and to tender to you our thanks for the reception given us.

I am also here as a Canadian. [*Applause from Canada.*] I came across the line. You know it was said that they were going to get the people to strike in Buffalo, but the men would not strike. They said, "That will not do. How can the Canadians get over? We cannot get along without the Canadians" [*laughter*]; and so they would not strike. I see there are two old flags here on this platform. It did my heart good when I saw the governor stand beside these flags, one of his legs up against the one flag, and the other against the other. [*Laughter and applause.*]

And I am here not only to represent Canada, but to represent the British Isles, because I am a subject of Great Britain. So, in the name of any here from Great Britain, and in the name of the many societies at present in Great Britain, I thank you for the reception that you have given to Christian Endeavor; for when you say, "We are glad to receive you," you mean not only those from the States and from Canada, but from the British Isles and from the islands beyond. [*Applause.*] There is a little country that perhaps some in the audience have heard of,—a little country called Ireland. [*Laughter.*] In Ireland the people have got wide awake; they have started Christian Endeavor Societies there, and last summer I had the pleasure of speaking at one of their meetings. There are some Irish in America. I suppose you sometimes meet some of them. [*Laughter.*] I am here to represent them; and so, you see, in a certain sense, I am a kind of representative man. [*Laughter.*]

Now, I say we are glad to be here. We are glad to have all these nationalities and States and Provinces represented; because the way to break down all prejudice, all denominational barriers, all national barriers, is to get men together, and get them to know one another. [*Applause.*] Do you know, the greatest scare I ever got was from a sheep. That may seem strange; but when I was a boy there were no sheep in the country where I lived. One day a neighbor brought home a sheep, and when I saw that thing coming towards me, I ran away and howled. [*Laughter.*] I tell you, I was more scared of that sheep than I would be now of a tiger. Why was I so scared? Because I didn't know what sheep were. When I came to know sheep, I came to love them. So, as denominations, we have been scared of one another; as nations, we have been scared of one another; but we will come together and realize that of one blood God hath made all nations; that the same impulses and desires and aspirations are beating in all our hearts. Then, when we have come to know one another, we shall realize that we are brothers; and, instead of being afraid of one another, we will clasp hands and go forth, shoulder to shoulder, in the common fight against a common devil and under a common Leader. [*Loud applause.*]

Now, I have just one word more to say. In the name of all these institutions I have mentioned, I thank Ohio, grand old Ohio, and Cleveland, — I suppose it was called for the President, or the President called for it, I am not sure which. [*Laughter.*] We thank you for the right royal reception you have given us. We know you will be helpful to us. We are strangers here, in a sense. A little boy was once asked what he would like to be. He said, "I would like to be a stranger." "What do you mean?" "Why, you know the strangers get all the good things." [*Laughter.*] So we are, as strangers, getting all your good things. We appreciate it, and we trust you will do us good. We came here to get fresh inspiration and enthusiasm to carry back with us to our different States and countries and denominations, to advance the cause of our common Master. I can assure you that we shall never forget Cleveland and this convention. [*Loud applause.*]

MR. DICKINSON: Next to President Clark, we depend upon our general secretary for the prosecution of the Christian Endeavor movement. He is our general lookout committee. He stands at the forefront and tells us what he sees. He is here to-day; we are all glad to have him with us, and he will now make his report. [*Loud applause and the Chautauqua salute.*]

Annual Report of General Secretary John Willis Baer.

Another mile-stone is reached. The thirteenth! Let us halt and review the forces on this our field-day. Indeed, the Christian Endeavor army invites inspection, and, figuratively speaking, for to-day becomes a standing corps on dress parade. The commanding officer finds that this host is not a mere wave of foamy, youthful enthusiasm, a part of it cast up upon the shores of Lake Erie, to ebb as rapidly as it has flowed. On the contrary, it is an army "as strong as steel and as flexible as ribbon." It is a *God-given, God-protected, God-advanced army.*

It is said that one-half of the world does not know how the other half lives. That ought not to be true of those of us that belong to the various regiments in this grand army of Christian Endeavor; and we are thankful for the opportunity that this field-day presents to exchange reports, to burnish our arms, and to bring words of cheer from "the stay-at-homes," our comrades less fortunate than we, who to-day constitute the "home-guard."

Look about you. "Salute one another." Indeed, it can be said, "These that have turned the world upside down are come hither." It is an ever-lengthening procession that marches by each succeeding mile-stone. Last year at Montreal our numbers had been increased in a year by 5,276 local companies; and out of the fullness of our hearts we sung, "Praise God from whom all blessings flow." Another year — what would it bring forth? The largest number of recruits since the march of Christian Endeavor was begun, thirteen years ago. Look along our lines to-day, and appreciate the fact that there are now 7,395 more companies of Christian Endeavor than there were one year ago. In other words, our ranks have increased the past year more than they increased in the entire first eight years of the army's history.

Listen! The order is sounded to fall into line. The procession moves. Left, left,

left! Tramp, tramp, tramp. England in the van, and fairly entitled to that recognition, having made the largest absolute gain in number of local companies of any of the many brigades in the last year. Count them as they march by; you will find that there are now 1,453 regularly enrolled companies. These figures include the 58 companies in Scotland, and 38 in Ireland. Lead on, valiant soldiers from Victoria's home, fresh from your annual field-day in the Metropolitan Tabernacle. In 1888 you had but 18 companies in line, and this year you have a mighty brigade of 75,000 "pledged" soldiers. Three cheers for the British section!

Before the United States "troops" fall in, ay, before England's fellow-subjects of the Queen from Canada take their places, the American division will "mark time" as the brigade from under the Southern Cross follow into line their comrades from the "old" country. We have been told that in Australia the eagles are white and the swans black. The principal quadruped there, the kangaroo, is elsewhere unknown; and, though he has four legs, he runs upon two. When the days are longest with us in America, they are shortest there. With us the seed or stone of the cherry forms the center of the fruit; in Australia, the stone grows on the outside. When it is day with us, it is night with them. Their Christmas comes in midsummer, ours in midwinter. Bituminous and anthracite coal are with us only one color, black — black as Erebus; but they have white bituminous coal there, white as chalk.

True, then, it is that Australia in many ways, when compared with our own country, is a land of curious contradictions; but Christian Endeavor there stands for the same grasp upon simple, evangelical, evangelistic gospel truth that it stands for in the land of its nativity. Praise God for that! Give their 834 enrolled companies from several colonial battalions a cheer of encouragement as they pass the lines. Comrades from the Island Continent, we salute you!

India, of the regiments from foreign lands, marches next, with 72 well-organized and fully equipped companies of Christian Endeavor. Japan's 59 companies are at this hour enjoying their second national field-day; do you not feel the sympathetic thrill of their consecrated enthusiasm? Here are more whose faces are of a different color from ours, whose language is not ours. Encourage them as they salute you, the 44 companies from the West Indies. Turkey, poor downtrodden Turkey, keeps step with 38 companies. And here, fast crowding upon them, are our 23 companies from China, — cheer their "colors," and their newly organized United Society of Christian Endeavor, — and a dozen more companies of their own comrades in this our country, for whom the Geary law has no terror. The next battalion of warriors are from among the natives in the diamond and gold fields of South Africa, and from other points on that continent. They have 25 companies. Christian Endeavor has become a bright torch, and in the hands of these soldiers will do much, under God's guidance, for the lighting up of the Dark Continent. And now this division moves on the "double-quick." Here come 30 companies from Madagascar; other companies from the islands of the sea, and from every missionary camp, and from France, Spain, Mexico, Brazil, Chile, and other countries in every continent, making, in all, from foreign and missionary lands, the grand total of 2,740 companies in the several regiments and brigades of our first division.

The second division, the Canadian, now swings into line, and is separated from us by only an imaginary line. At our last field-day, which was held within their borders, they marshaled 1,882 companies. This year their ranks are increased, and they have on their roster 2,243 companies, with an individual membership of 134,580. Ontario still leads, with 1,281 companies; Nova Scotia comes next, with 391; Quebec has evidently felt some of the benefits of our camp in their midst last year at Montreal, for they report a gain of 80 companies, and now have a total of 215; Manitoba has 127; New Brunswick, 115; Prince Edward Island, 46; British Columbia, 31; Assiniboia, 17; Alberta, 13; Newfoundland, 5; and Saskatchewan, 2.

Mark their step. They have the swing of veterans, and they are veterans, for many of them are fresh from a victorious battle with his Satanic majesty's chief butler, King Alcohol.

At last the third division moves. It is a solid phalanx, with regiments from Hell Gate to the Golden Gate, from Hudson Bay on the north to the Gulf of Mexico on the south. New York State for twelve years has marched in the van when we have been on dress parade, and for the first time will give the "right of line" to Pennsylvania and her 3,458 enrolled companies. New York is next, with 3,320. Ohio takes the third place this year, with 2,274; Illinois is fourth, with 2,260; and Indiana fifth, with 1,534 societies. In all, there are now 28,696 companies in the United States. This figure includes 6 Senior societies (an advance guard), 9 Mothers' societies (a splendid movement, first started in Kansas), 30 Intermediate companies; and it includes the companies in our schools, in our colleges, in public institutions of various kinds, in prisons and schools of reform, to the number of 144. It includes that noble regiment of 200 companies known as the North American Union of German Christian Endeavor. It includes the 6 companies among the "boys in blue" in the regular army of the United States. It includes the company among the policemen and patrolmen. It includes the companies among the Indians of the West and in Canada. It includes our comrades enlisted in work among the life-saving crews, lighthouses and light-ships. It includes the Travelers' Union of Christian Endeavor, an enterprising company. It includes a regiment of 6,471 Junior companies.

And now make way for those cadets, the Juniors. In March, 1884, the first Junior company of Christian Endeavor was organized in Tabor, Io., by Rev. J. W. Cowan. And to-day there are hundreds of city battalions of Junior companies, some of which are large in numbers. Three years ago, 855 companies had reported. This year great progress has been made. Junior superintendents of State, Territorial, and Provincial brigades, and of local companies, your work has been wonderfully blessed of God!

Illinois has from the start marched first, and at Montreal had 433 companies enrolled. This year Pennsylvania has passed Illinois, and now is the banner Junior State, having 717 companies. Illinois is next, with 678; and New York a close third, with 673; Ohio next, with 415; and California fifth, with 320. With the 91 Junior companies enrolled from foreign lands, and the 247 Junior companies in Canada, there is now a brigade of 6,809 Junior companies in the world, with an enlistment of 365,000. Make way for the boys and girls!

And now the whole army is under way. The 2,740 companies from foreign lands, then the 2,243 from Canada, and then 28,696 from the United States, making an army of 33,679 companies, — and still there are more that we have not reviewed. Let me, therefore, remind the land forces that Christian Endeavor, like a famous soap, floats; and we now have not less than 51 floating companies of Christian Endeavor, the largest of which is the one in the Brooklyn Navy Yard, numbering over 350 marines, and they and all mariners and seamen on fresh and salt waters are one with us in presenting a united front against the hosts of sin on land and sea.

I have read that three natives of India once happened to come together from quite different states, and, being unable to speak one another's languages, found themselves at a mission station. At last one of them looked up to heaven, and repeated the word (which was substantially the same in every dialect throughout India), "Jesus." The second brother said, "Amen," and that was the same in every tongue; and the third added, looking and pointing upwards, "Hallelujah," which was the same everywhere. We, too, are unable to speak one another's native language. We come from every clime, from every land; our skins vary in color, — 460 are red, 18,700 are yellow, 97,020 are black, and 1,907,620 are white, making in all an interracial and international army of over two millions. The actual enrollment, including active and associate members in this thirteenth year of our history, is 2,023,800; and yet there is one common rallying-name for us all, and above that the Name above every name.

Our good friend, Mr. Dickinson, has said: "Christian Endeavor is interdenominational, interurban, interstate, international, interracial; and, if it be true that there are other worlds than this, we shall find that it is interplanetary, simply because [and now note his reasoning] — simply because it is based upon God's universal law of progress through self-denying endeavor and ministration." That is good reasoning. Our dress parade has proved that Christian Endeavor is interracial and international; and, while it will not prove beyond a doubt that it is interplanetary, another look at the moving host, and our interdenominational fellowship is easily recognized and applauded, and is ever widening. Praise God for that!

We each march in our several divisions, wearing uniforms differing, bearing banners of various hues. If any one thing is made clear by this field-day of the army of Christian Endeavor, it is God's design to bring the young people of all evangelical denominations together, not for the sake of denouncing denominations or decrying creeds, but in a common fellowship that respects differences and believes in diversity. Our army makes every young person more loyal to his own denomination, at the same time that it makes him more generous toward others. Look sharp, and you will see that thirty evangelical denominations are represented in our marching columns. In the United States the denominational representation is as follows: The Presbyterians still lead, with 6,652 companies; the Congregationalists have 5,488; the Baptists, 3,203; the Disciples of Christ and Christians, 2,895; Methodist Episcopal, 1,287; Methodist Protestants, 963; Lutherans, 851; Cumberland Presbyterians, 744; and so on through a long list. In Canada the Presbyterians lead with 842; the Methodists are next, with 812; the Baptists have 159; the Congregationalists, 128. In England the Baptists are in the van, with 391 companies; the Congregationalists have 353; the various Methodist bodies, 221; the Presbyterians, 85.

Standing, as we do, upon the earthworks thrown up by this army during the past year, and viewing the marching columns, with the aid of a field-glass we see displayed familiar badge-banners. Enthusiastically are they carrried, as they have been each field-day. But what changes! The banners are not in possession of the battalions that rallied around them at our last field-day in Montreal.

You will remember that at St. Louis, four years ago, a badge-banner, made up of badges from hundreds of companies, was displayed amidst much enthusiasm. According to a suggestion made by a comrade from Minnesota, it was decided to place that banner for one year in the custody of the State, Territory, or Province that should show the greatest *proportionate* increase in its number of local companies during the year. Oklahoma carried that banner away from Minneapolis, brought it to New York, and there turned it over to Manitoba. Manitoba triumphantly carried her banner, after a year's possession, to Montreal, and passed it back across the imaginary line to the wide-awake brigade from New Mexico. After a year's possession, New Mexico has relinquished all claims, and we now rejoice to see it in the front ranks of the lively brigade from West Virginia.

At St. Louis four years ago, it was also decided that another badge-banner should be made and given on the next field-day to the State, Territory, or Province that should show the greatest absolute gain in one year. Pennsylvania captured that banner. She too, two years ago, relinquished her possession, and started the banner upon its international pilgrimage, turning it over to Ontario. Ontario, after holding the banner a year, had the great privilege of returning it last year to the Keystone State, and it was received within Pennsylvania's borders with song and rejoicing. This year that banner, continuing its international travels, is flung to the breezes by England's brigade in their great advance. For the first time one of our badge-banners crosses the "briny deep." Guard it well, comrades, for it will certainly be captured again another year by our forces on this side of the Atlantic.

But our field-glass discovers other banners that are being cheered by our cadets, the Juniors. Illinois for three years has carried the first Junior badge-banner at the head of her regiments; but this year the cadets of Pennsylvania have followed closely in the footsteps of her older soldiers, and now valiantly shout as they display the long-coveted Junior banner. Enthusiasm runs high in all Pennsylvania's ranks; and well it may, for with that original Junior banner, side by side, is another Junior badge-banner, which New York last year carried away from Montreal for the greatest *absolute* gain in number of societies. Indeed, Pennsylvania's forces are showing to the world that pig iron is not her only product.

But why that confident tread on the part of the battalions from "little" Delaware? Look again. See you not that she proudly carries the Junior badge-banner for the largest *proportionate* increase in number of companies? The banner has been gracefully turned over by the District of Columbia after one year's possession. West Virginia, England, Pennsylvania, Delaware, yours has been a successful year; and the "colors" you display show not only a spirit of friendly rivalry, but that Christian Endeavor is not decadent within your borders. Your efforts were put forth, not for the banners, — we know there is no real value in them, — but for the blessings that come to those that valiantly fight "on the Lord's side."

New York, true it is, is no longer the "banner" State, and has surrendered her Junior banner also to Pennsylvania; still, our brigade from the Empire State is marching hopefully, with determined tread, heads erect, and "eyes front," and proudly points to a silken, richly embroidered "umbrella of state" from China, which is carried high aloft, though there is not a cloud on the horizon. Yes, our field-glass tells us that New York has the largest number of companies that have adopted Rev. A. A. Fulton's suggestion, and are giving systematically "two cents a week" to missions. The umbrella of state is a peculiarly Oriental object, and is usually presented by the Chinese to high officials that have faithfully performed their duty. This "umbrella of state" comes across the water from our brigade in China, and New York State is to guard it for at least a year. May her record for giving systematically to missions another year be even better than the generous showing this year.

And that leads me to make mention at this time of the magnificent "roll of honor" which is displayed here in Camp Cleveland. It is, indeed, a polyglot girdle, which again unites our forces east, north, south, and west. Upon it are the names of 5,552 companies from 35 States, 7 Territories, 7 Provinces, 4 foreign lands. Each company has given not less than ten dollars to its own denominational home or foreign missionary board for the cause of missions. The total amount as reported on this roll of honor is $138,205.93. In addition to this amount of money which has been given by these 5,552 societies that we have enrolled upon the roll of honor, we find that $185,512.00 has been given by these same societies for "Christ and the Church" in other ways. So much for the roll of honor, which measures 465 feet if we use a yardstick, but who can measure its real length and breadth but He that guides us all in our endeavor? But only a part of the companies asked to be enrolled upon the "roll of honor," though really entitled to a place upon it.

After careful gathering of other statistics and information, and from advices received from the representatives of missionary boards, home and foreign, we find that the third division (United States and Canada) has contributed from its companies not less than $225,000 for *missions at home and abroad*.

At our "camp-fire" talks we can rehearse the victories of the past year. Our three forward movements, which were suggested to us by President Clark, and which were adopted as our marching orders at Montreal, have been successfully conducted.

These suggestions were, that, as societies and individuals, we pay more attention during the year (1), to our duty as Christian citizens; (2), to proportionate and systematic giving to missions, at home and abroad, through our own denominational boards; and (3), to the enlargement of our interdenominational fellowship on the Christian Endeavor basis.

To stimulate interest in these methods of enlarging our work, the United Society decided to present one hundred diplomas to companies for loyal service.

Twenty-five diplomas will be awarded to societies that have been instrumental in forming the largest number of other Endeavor societies, Young People's, Senior, and Junior.

Our dress parade to-day has demonstrated how gloriously God has blessed our advance steps for a larger brotherhood.

Twenty-five more diplomas will be given to the societies that, in proportion to their ability, report the most work done for the introduction of good literature; and right royally has war been waged against corrupt literature, and for it has been substituted good literature of every kind.

Twenty-five more will be given to the societies that have reported the largest number of systematic and proportionate givers.

Our crusade for a revival of proportionate and systematic beneficence, too, means much for the cause of Christ in the coming days.

Later in this convention twenty-five of these diplomas will be given to the societies that, in the judgment of a competent committee, have reported the most done to promote the interests of Christian citizenship.

Our good-citizenship campaign has cultivated a greater and more intelligent spirit of patriotism and Christian citizenship everywhere, and has been fearlessly waged, even to the sacrifice of the life of one of our own comrades. But Bat Shea's victim, Robert Ross of Troy, cruelly murdered at the voting-booth, doing his duty, still lives; and we press on over his body to catch his spirit, determined in the right to put to flight Bat Sheas everywhere, whether it be in Troy, Boston, Chicago, New York, or in the remotest hamlets over which the Stars and Stripes or the Union Jack swing their peaceful folds. God save America! God save England! God save the world!

But who are these commanding our attention for their very worth's sake? Their marching and maneuvering attract our attention. Subordinate battalions in their respective brigades, it is true; nevertheless, upon them falls much of the fighting that has protected the lines. Many are sharp-shooters and scouts, and all are high privates, but not in the rear ranks. They are the local city battalions of Christian Endeavor, and doing practical Christian work through their missionary, executive, correspondence, lookout, press, and visiting squads. Here are some that, according to the enrollment, have more than one hundred companies, including the Juniors, in their borders: Philadelphia, 409; Chicago, 364; New York, 203; London, England, 165; Cleveland, 156; Baltimore, 131; Brooklyn, 137; Boston, 107; St. Louis, 105.

Three of these magnificent city battalions are entitled each to a banner. Soon after our last field-day it was announced that three banners would be presented at Camp Cleveland, one to the local city battalion that should report the most work done as a battalion in the interests of good citizenship. The committee, after much deliberation and much thought, have decided that that banner belongs to Chicago.

Another banner is to be presented to the city battalion that enlarged their comradeship by bringing into their ranks the largest number of local companies of Christian Endeavor. Philadelphia will receive that banner later.

A third banner is to be given to the city battalion that reported the largest number of systematic and proportionate givers to God. That banner is awarded to Cleveland.

Another cheer for the city battalions as they march by. God guide them every one!

One of our English Endeavorers tells of a man that was awakened one night by a vigorous knocking at his door. Throwing up the window and looking out, he saw a man plying his knocker below. "What do you want?" he asked, in wonder. "I want to wake the people next door," was the answer. "They haven't a knocker, so I'm using yours." Thank God, there has been a good deal of that kind of awakening done throughout our lines. One after another our soldiers have been awakened to a sense of their duty, and the doors of their hearts have rung with the knockings of God's hand; and, best of all, our brothers and sisters in the associate ranks, too, have heard the noise of battle, and have many of them been fully awakened by our having first been aroused.

Drop the field-glass; we need it no longer. What is this our eyes behold? What glad song of praise is this that is growing louder and louder, until it seems a surging sea, as billow after billow of song rises higher and higher? Listen! Catch its inspiration. Understand its meaning. Praise God for its testimony.

"At the cross, at the cross, where I first saw the light,
And the burden of my heart rolled away."

These are the new recruits. They have taken the "next step" during the past year. They are now enlisted for the whole war. Give them welcome. Raise high the banners! Strike palms with them again, for they have "come out on the Lord's side." Thousands of them. You cannot see them all. Their numbers are legion. Put your ear to the ground. The tramp of their feet, now turned into the "right way," is like sweet music to a troubled heart. *In all 183,650 have joined the churches during the past twelve months.* Yea, verily, "Praise God from whom all blessings flow." At St. Louis, 70,000; at Minneapolis, 82,500; at New York, 120,000; at Montreal, 158,000; and now at Cleveland, 183,650. What a ransomed host! How much or how little our individual work or that of the army has gained this blessed victory we know not; sufficiently happy and thankful are we to know that these recruits to the number of 614,150 have come from our ranks in five years. Again I say, "Praise God from whom all blessings flow."

Hear that burst of enthusiasm from the entire line as it belts the earth. The foundations shall be moved, for here is an army of more than two million *enthusiasts*. Ay, enthusiasts, Christian enthusiasts!

Oscar Wilde's definition of a cynic is, "A man who knows the price of everything, but the worth of nothing." And one of our prominent English enthusiasts says, "Then the enthusiast is the opposite of the cynic, and must be defined as one who knows the worth of something and the price of nothing." This Christian Endeavor army has seen much worth doing, cost what it might. Give us more enthusiasm for God!

Such a one as Carey, as Wesley, as Luther, as Spurgeon, as our own Bishop Brooks! Ay, such a one as Paul, that enthusiastic field-marshal of our Lord who fought the good fight! More Christian enthusiasts are needed. Christ, our Commander-in-chief, was one; give us more enthusiasm for him, cost what it may!

"Finally, my brethren, be strong in the Lord, and in the power of his might. Put on the whole armor of God! Stand, therefore, having your loins girt about with truth, and having on the breastplate of righteousness, taking the shield of faith, the helmet of salvation, and the sword of the Spirit." Press forward with glad praises, singing, as no other army can sing, the battle-hymn of the republic of God.

> "Like a mighty army
> Moves the church of God.
> Brothers we are treading
> Where the saints have trod;
> We are not divided,
> All one body we,
> One in faith and doctrine,
> One in charity."

At the conclusion of Secretary Baer's report, which was many times interrupted by applause, the audience united in singing the favorite hymn, "Onward, Christian Soldiers." As some of the banners to be presented had not arrived, the next item on the programme was deferred until a later hour; and after the giving of a number of notices, the audience was dismissed with the benediction, pronounced by Rev. J. M. Lowden of Boston.

THE TENT.

By 9.30 o'clock this great auditorium was filled to its utmost limits. Many were standing, and others were on the outside waiting to get in. Christian Endeavor songs arose from every part of the tent while the programme was being arranged. Quite an interesting feature of the gathering were the songs of Baltimore and Washington, attempting to show why the Convention of '96 should be held in each of these cities. The Washington delegation sang their hymn to the tune of "Tramp, Tramp, Tramp;" and the Baltimoreans, just as the last notes of Washington died away, took up the Baltimore song to the air of "Hold the Fort;" then all joined in singing "Blest be the Tie that Binds." The Cleveland Chorus sang Ohio's welcome song, "Welcome to Erie's Shore." The singing in the tent was led by Mr. J. G. Warren of Cleveland, and Mr. H. C. Lincoln of Philadelphia.

Treasurer William Shaw said at the opening of the tent meeting that on account of the strike a few days ago they hardly thought they could have a convention in the city of Cleveland; but as he came from Saengerfest Hall, where they were besieging the doors, and thousands unable to get in, and then saw outside the tent about five thousand more, he thought that the strike had not seriously affected the attendance at the Convention. "Why," said Treasurer Shaw, "if the Endeavorers were turned loose, I believe they would fill nearly every church in Cleveland.

"The meeting was opened with the reading of the Twenty-third Psalm in concert, under the leadership of Rev. R. V. Hunter of Terra Haute, Ind. Then followed a series of prayers for President F. E. Clark and the success of the Convention, by Dr. Leonard of Cincinnati, and Rev. W. F. McCauley of Dayton. At the close of the hymn that followed, Dr. J. Z. Tyler, chairman of the '94 Committee, amid cheers and

applause, made his way to the platform. His remarks were much the
same as those at Saengerfest Hall a few moments before. Governor
McKinley next appeared, and was received with renewed applause.
Several times did he try to close; but loud cries of "Go on," "Go on,"
intercepted all his attempts. At the conclusion of his address he was
given three cheers by the twelve thousand enthusiastic Endeavorers
present. Mr. Shaw then introduced Rev. Dr. Farrar of Albany, N.Y.,
who made a short address on loyalty to Christ and the Christian Endeavor movement. Prof. Graham Taylor of Chicago made a brief
address, using the labor troubles of recent times as themes on which he
showed the possibilities of the Christian Endeavor movement. Rev.
Gilbert Reid of China made a short but stirring address. Secretary
Baer's Annual Report was read by Mr. Shaw. He was frequently interrupted by applause; and when England's record for forming new societies was read, the assemblage gave three rousing cheers for the Union
Jack.

The meeting for the morning closed with "Blest Be the Tie That
Binds," and the Mizpah benediction.

The Business Men's Prayer-meeting was held in the First Presbyterian Church, and was conducted by Mr. C. N. Hunt of Minneapolis.
There was a good attendance.

THURSDAY AFTERNOON.

The afternoon was wholly devoted to denominational rallies, no session of the Convention being held in either the hall or the tent. As
these rallies were afterwards reported in the main meetings of the Convention, there is no need to give an account of them here.

THURSDAY EVENING.

SAENGERFEST HALL.

The programme announced that the exercises at the hall would begin
at 7.15 with a praise service. Instead of that they began at six o'clock,
at which time the auditorium was pretty well filled. The "service" was
not exactly after the usual order of a praise service. There was an
abundance of hymn-singing, but there was a good deal else. The Baltimore and Washington delegations were out in full force, and took seats
on opposite sides of the center aisle, up near the front. They gave vent
to their good-natured rivalries in various ways, singing their State songs,
waving their banners, etc., in all of which they were joined, more or
less, by the gathering audience. When Mr. Foster took the platform
things went a little more coherently, and the praise service was a
genuine feast of song.

President Charles F. Thwing, D.D., of Adelbert College, Cleveland, was the presiding officer of the evening, and at 7.40 o'clock he took up the formal programme of the evening.

DR. THWING: We now come to the beginning of our formal and happy service. We have but one note of sadness, and that is occasioned by the absence of our president, Rev. Dr. Francis E. Clark. We are sorry for his absence, and more sorry for its cause. In his absence we shall have the pleasure of hearing his annual address read by one who has been appointed for the purpose, and who has been for the time being chosen president, Rev. Charles A. Dickinson of Boston. To know Mr. Dickinson is to love him, and I have known him and loved him for many years.

Mr. Dickinson then came forward and read Dr. Clark's address, as follows: —

Strike! Strike! Strike!

Annual Address of President Francis E. Clark, D.D.

A picturesque scene is that which the Scriptures record as occurring near the close of the life of the prophet Elisha. The dying seer places his hands upon the hands of King Joash, which hold the royal bow and arrow, and he tells him to shoot. The king obeys, and out of the open window the arrow speeds, while the prophet cries out, "The arrow of the Lord's deliverance, and the arrow of deliverance from Syria."

Then said the prophet, "Take the arrows" and "smite upon the ground. And he smote thrice, and stayed. And the man of God was wroth with him, and said, Thou shouldst have smitten five or six times; then hadst thou smitten Syria till thou hadst consumed it, whereas now thou shalt smite Syria but thrice."

Some such message comes to us, Christian Endeavorers, on the occasion of this our thirteenth convention.

Strike. Strike in the name of the Lord.

Strike again for the principles that have made you strong.

Strike once more for converted loyalty and outspoken devotion and definite service.

"Strike again for Christian citizenship, and for the extension of the kingdom in all lands, and for your world-wide fellowship."

Do not be content with one, two, or three blows for the right. Strike, and strike, and strike again until the day is won.

If I can read aright the times, this is the message for to-day.

1. Strike once more for the principles that have made Christian Endeavor strong.

As an organization becomes popular and vigorous, it sometimes forgets the principles that gave it strength and vigor.

Let that never be said of the society of Christian Endeavor.

What are our principles? If I know anything about them, they are the ideas involved in the pledge, the consecration meeting, and the committees.

We have struck with these arrows three times, but let us not excite the just wrath of God's prophet by staying our hands. Four, five, six, perhaps sixty-six times, do we need to reiterate the truth involved in our pledge, — that it is reasonable to vow and to pay unto God our vows, that there is nothing in the Christian Endeavor pledge that the weakest and obscurest young Christian cannot fulfill; that this, more than all other things, gives lasting power to our society, and that without it, in its substance, no Endeavor society is worthy of the name.

So for the consecration meeting. This is our land of Florida, where we not only seek, but find, the fountain of perpetual youth. Our hour of consecration is our hour of rejuvenation. Antæus touched earth with but one foot or one finger, and was revived and quickened for a stronger fight. At the monthly roll-call meeting we touch heaven, and are revived for a farther journey and conflict in the world.

So with the committees. They are essential. They mean Christian work. They stand for individual service. All these are not mere methods or crutches or helps over hard places; they involve principles that go with the name "Christian Endeavor," and with which the name should always go. Upon the maintenance of these principles depends, I am confident, the future success of Christian Endeavor. Do not think that the time has come when we can ignore these ideas or treat them lightly.

Do not suppose that the public has so fully accepted them that they can be safely dropped out of sight.

At union meetings and conventions, in your own society, and in more public gatherings, by print and by speech, let us strike not three times, but five or six times, until all the world knows for what Christian Endeavor stands.

May I suggest that more of the money raised in our State conventions might be profitably spent in circulating this fundamental literature rather than in any other way? Sow broadcast this seed. Show that Christian Endeavor has principles — definite, reasonable, workable principles; principles in which we believe, principles that we can defend, principles that constitute the strength of the movement.

2. Again, Christian Endeavorers, strike once more for good citizenship. Right nobly have you rallied around this standard during the past year.

From East and West and North and South has come the good news, — Christian Endeavor stands for the election of good men, for the enactment of good laws, for sturdy and steady opposition to the saloon, the gambling-hell, the lottery, the violation of the Sabbath.

It stands by such men as Charles H. Parkhurst, and every kindred spirit in every political party that seeks to purify politics and to make this Immanuel's land. It remembers Robert Ross, the Troy martyr to the cause of Good Citizenship.

I congratulate you that none of you have been cajoled into making our organization the tail of any political kite. To be a Christian Endeavorer does not mean that one is necessarily a Republican, or a Democrat, or a Populist, or a Third Party man, a Blue or a Grit, a Tory or a Liberal.

It does mean that he is necessarily a good citizen, and that he will exert every ounce of his influence, to whichever sex he belongs (if the young men will excuse the generic pronoun), for the right.

While Tammany flourishes in New York, and open gambling in Chicago, and licensed prostitution in New Orleans, and the Louisiana Lottery has moved only across the street to Honduras, the outlook is dark.

It is dark, but not hopeless.

The last year has seen Boss McKane sent to Sing Sing, and Brooklyn redeemed. It has seen Croker fly to Europe. It has heard Woolley speak in Chicago and Indianapolis, and Murphy in Boston, and has witnessed a score of other good-citizenship campaigns. It has seen thousands of Endeavorers go to the primaries who never went before. It has seen a splendid verdict pronounced against the saloon in Canada, — a verdict that Endeavorers have made emphatic in a hundred towns.

Thank God for the year's work! But you have only struck once, Endeavorers. Strike again, and again, and again, until, if Christ should come to Chicago, or New York, or Toronto, or San Francisco, he would find clean streets, and clean city halls, and clean men in them, with never a brothel or a dive to pollute the air that he should breathe.

3. For missions, too, more has been done during the past year than ever before. That eloquent Roll of Honor tells us that tens of thousands of dollars have been given.

The Missionary Extension Course, with that "son of thunder" at its head, has kindled a genuine missionary prairie fire wherever it has swept, — through Illinois, into Indiana and Wisconsin and Kansas, south into Tennessee, and east into New York.

But it is a kindled *nation*, and not merely blazing patches of missionary enthusiasm, that we desire to see; and Christian Endeavor bears the torch that can kindle this fire.

Millions should be given where now are given thousands. A very moderate calculation puts the earnings of active Christian Endeavorers at $150,000,000 for the last twelve months. One-tenth of that, $15,000,000, would be nearly twice as much as all the Christians of America gave to home and foreign missions within that time.

We rejoice profoundly and humbly in this year of missionary work. That splendid roll of honor, these banners, the diplomas, which will mean so much to those who win them, are significant chiefly because they mean the beginning of larger and better things in missionary giving and missionary enterprise.

Listen to the sound of the missionary arrows as they strike the earth. It is a faint and feeble reverberation compared with the wail of the unsaved multitude whom we should rescue.

Strike again, Christian Endeavorers! and again, and again, and again, and then once more!

It is not the stern voice of a chiding prophet that speaks to you, but the conscious need of our own beloved land, English-speaking America, and the unconscious needs of hundreds of millions of the non-Christian world, that call upon you for a constantly larger effort.

A year ago at Montreal three advanced steps were proposed, — Christian Citizenship, Proportionate and Systematic Giving to Missions, and the Enlargement of our Christian Endeavor Fellowship.

4. All these steps you have taken with quickened pace and flying banners. As never before has Christian Endeavor advanced in numbers and in widespread fellowship. In hospitable Australia, in Mother England, in progressive Japan, in conservative China, in awakening India, as well as in the great republic and the great Dominion of North America (which in Christian Endeavor always has been, and I trust always will be, one), our fellowship has grown as in no previous year.

This year has been notable beyond every other year for its wonderful interdenominational Christian Endeavor conventions in all parts of the world.

What a royal Endeavor convention was that in London last May, when the representatives of more than seventy-five thousand brothers and sisters of Great Britain gathered their hosts in the Metropolitan Tabernacle! Our love and greetings to you, brothers and sisters of the motherland!

And what good news constantly comes from Australia! God bless you, brothers that live under the Southern Cross, who stand with us for pledged consecration and zealous Christian Endeavor work.

India already speaks for Christian Endeavor in seven languages, the vernacular of tens of millions of her people.

China sends word of overflowing rallies and of constantly increasing enthusiasm for Christian Endeavor.

In oppressed Turkey, Christian Endeavor still lives and grows; while in Japan, the advance-guard nation of the Orient, at this moment our Endeavor brothers are holding their second convention. Can you not feel the beating of their pulse to-night?

The girls and boys in the Junior societies, too, have come marching on, keeping step with their older brothers and sisters. The Mothers' societies and the Intermediate societies have been peculiar, natural, and most helpful developments of our fellowship during the past year.

Still, we need not sigh for worlds to conquer. They are all around us.

Still there is sectarian prejudice to overcome, not so much by arguments as by lives, by showing how true and loyal and faithful Christian Endeavorers always are.

Still there are slanders against Christian Endeavor, not to talk down, but to live down; for though we may belong to the church militant, we do not belong to the church termagant.

I rejoice to say that in the northern Dominion there is scarcely a division; almost all the young people's societies are either Christian Endeavor, or Epworth Leagues of Christian Endeavor.

In Australia the Methodists lead in numbers; in England, the Baptists; in the United States, the Presbyterians; but these are matters of little moment compared with the demonstrated fact that here we can all stand together. These thirteen years — particularly this past year — have proved that Baptists, and Methodists, and Presbyterians, and Lutherans, and Disciples of Christ, and Friends, and Congregationalists, and Moravians, and every variety of these denominations, can find a common meeting-place in Christian Endeavor. No creed separates us, no form of polity disrupts us, no question of disloyalty exists to terrify us; for we have come together for service, for Endeavor.

In the late war, while the soldiers were in camp, there might be rivalry between the different regiments and corps; but when they came to march against the enemy, regimental rivalry and corps jealousies were sent to the rear in double-quick time, and touching elbows (oh, the thrill of that "elbow-touch" as old soldiers have described it to me!) they stood together, and marched together, and fought together, and died together.

There is no North or South in Christian Endeavor. Thank God that, however our fathers have been divided, the hearts of a multitude of young Christians on both sides of Mason and Dixon's line are joined in Christian Endeavor. Of what incalculable benefit may such conventions as this prove in promoting true patriotism and national unity! Ours is no fratricidal contest. Our enemy is the enemy of all righteousness. Oh, why should all young people not be united against him?

Has not the time come for a still longer stride?

The suggestion has come from Australia, and has been seconded by England and China and India and Japan, of a World's Christian Endeavor Union, made up of individuals in all lands that believe in the Christian Endeavor ideas, and will stand with us on the broad platform of Endeavor principles, a platform of thorough loyalty to our own churches and of hearty co-operation one with another.

In my opinion the time has come for such an alliance, which will link many Christians of many nations together in ties of fellowship that they have never before known.

O brothers, let us cultivate every bond of fellowship. Let us strengthen every tie that binds our hearts in Christian love. Enough causes, at the best, distract and weaken and divide Christian forces. If Christian Endeavor, while maintaining and guaranteeing the loyalty of every one of us to the truth as God gives us to see the truth, should be the blessed instrument in the hands of Providence for bringing earnest Christians nearer together, the world around, our cup of happiness would be full.

And there are signs of it!

Already we may claim a Christian Endeavor spiritual federation of two millions of English-speaking Christians. In London, last Whitsuntide, they had the same kind of a convention that we are holding here in Cleveland. In Melbourne and Sydney, in Manchester and Liverpool, in their local unions they discuss the same topics, and employ the very same methods, and draw inspiration from the same sources, that we do in New York and Boston and San Francisco and Toronto.

A union of English-speaking Christians is good to contemplate; but we will not stop with those who speak our mother tongue; for in Shanghai and Tokyo, in Bombay and in Calcutta, in San Sebastian and in Paris, are earnest souls not a few, who spiritually link hands with us in an ever-growing circle that begins to belt the globe.

In substance and essence we have a world's union now; its more formal establishment would but make plain that to oppose the common enemy, to work for our common Lord, we stand together in Christian Endeavor.

Weak bands of our fellow-Christians would be strengthened; isolated companies of young believers would gain courage to persevere; and the world would understand that, so far as Endeavorers are concerned, it is not an empty boast, and not merely a pleasant song, —

"We are not divided,
All one body we."

In this world's union we may better answer our Lord's Prayer. In this world-wide fellowship we may, I believe, better obey the prophet's injunction to strike not thrice, but five or six times, until the Syrians of selfishness and prejudice and unbrotherliness shall have been slain by the nineteenth century knight errant who stands for fellowship as well as fidelity, for brotherhood as well as for loyalty.

Then in this world's Endeavor union will our yearly motto, which we cannot yet exchange for another, mean more than ever before, as we remember that in America and England, in Australia and India, in China and Japan, in France and Spain, in Mexico and South America, in Africa and Madagascar, and the islands of the sea, "One is your Master, even Christ; and all ye are brethren."

Dr. Clark's address was listened to with great interest, and many times its appeals were responded to with applause. Rev. J. L. Hill, D.D., of the Board of Trustees, who had been appointed to make the announcement concerning the conventions of '95 and '96, was introduced.

Announcement of Conventions.

DR. HILL: I have a very simple announcement to make. Every convention of the Society of Christian Endeavor has been connected with a great idea. I do not need to review them. Any one can see what they are as he looks back upon them. When we reached Montreal last year, we had a convention that stood for international fellowship. We were then under the Queen's flag, that flag under which Dr. Clark was born. It is the Trustees' endeavor always to so appoint the convention that it shall still represent some progressive idea.

"Westward the star of empire takes its way;
Time's noblest offspring is the last."

If I were asked which has been the greatest of the Christian Endeavor Conventions, I should reply in the words of Daniel Webster, who said, when he was once asked which one of the plays of Shakespeare he liked best, "The one I read last." So if I were asked which convention I liked best, I should say, "The one I am attending last." [*Applause.*]

Our idea is to take no backward step in this matter. It is the sincere desire of the trustees to go to the far West with the next convention. There is the Golden Gate. The next thing beyond the seas is Japan, the empire island. There are the Chinamen. There is the Orient. There is world-around Endeavor. We are, however, met with this obstacle. We always have appointed definitely our convention a year in advance, but the railway rates to San Francisco are not yet settled. It is the wish of the people of San Francisco that we shall not come to their fair city unless we can bring all of you, without an exception [*applause*]; and we want you to go home and get your sisters and your cousins and your aunts. We want you all to be there. To this end we want a cheaper railroad rate; and if we do not secure a better rate than is now offered, we shall not go to San Francisco next year. The matter, therefore, is held in abeyance.

I come now to speak of the convention of '96. Every convention stands for a great idea. The tendency has been, first, to go West, then to partake of the hospitality of the South. [*Applause.*] We have set our faces in that direction. Some persons, when they go South, behold some scenes which are to them very suggestive of our most precious American history. I was entertained a few days ago in a most royal and sumptuous fashion by the young men of Baltimore. [*Great applause from Maryland.*] As I was going along the Baltimore and Ohio railroad I looked out of the car window and saw Fort McHenry. I remembered that on the 13th day of September, 1814, a young lawyer launched himself out in a little boat and made his way to the British commander's vessel. He was going, under a flag of truce, to liberate a friend, if so be he could bring enough influence to bear. You remember how the little boat was swung behind the commander's vessel, and the young lawyer and his friend were both kept on board during the attack on Fort McHenry. You remember, at night the flag was still flying on Fort McHenry. The question was how it would be in the morning. So when he came out on deck, through the early light of the morning he saw the fort. Is the flag still there?

"Oh say, can you see, by the dawn's early light,
What so proudly we hailed at the twilight's last gleaming?
Whose broad stripes and bright stars through the perilous night,
From the ramparts we watched were so gallantly streaming,
And the rockets' red glare, the bombs bursting in air,
Gave proof through the night that our flag was still there.
O say, can you see" —

Just at this moment all the electric lights in the hall went suddenly out, and the hall was left in complete darkness. The audience recognized the ludicrous situation, in connection with the speaker's last words, and shouted, "No, no! we can't see!" There was a good deal of amusement over the incident; but somebody in the audience started up "The Star Spangled Banner," and it was carried through with enthusiasm. The lights, which had been turned off just to get a flashlight photograph of the Convention for the *Golden Rule*, were turned on again, and Dr. Hill proceeded.

DR. HILL: After hearing the very remarkable address sent to the convention by Dr. Clark — whom God preserve — I want to say that if we have any more strikes at the supremacy of our government we will sing the last verse, written by Dr. Oliver Wendell Holmes: —

"And the Star Spangled Banner in triumph shall wave,
While the land of the free is the home of the brave."
[*Loud applause.*]

There is one thing I always associate with Baltimore. I remember, as a boy, to have heard the singing of a bird called the Baltimore oriole, which was remarkably distinguished for its plumage. His first attraction was his beauty; his next, his very sweet song. Now, Baltimore is a city of hospitality. [*Applause.*] It is famed throughout the country as the monumental city. It put up the first monument to Washington; it is always raising up some memorial of the gratitude and patriotism of its citizens. It every way symbolizes Southern hospitality. It has the kind of manhood and womanhood in it that we like to meet. If you are thinking of hospitality, if you are thinking of personal attraction, if you are thinking of an urgent invitation, look towards Baltimore. Niobe of cities, there she stands! [*Applause.*]

But there is another city [*great applause from Washington*] that has asked for the convention. A great deal is being made in these passing days of the item of good-citizenship. The Trustees have turned their thought toward this consideration; in view of the fact that nearly all of our more than two millions of young people have had their attention drawn toward good-citizenship, should we not, so far as America is concerned, take our young people to Washington and show them the operations of our government? We are all to be understood, as first of all, and last of all, and midst of all, loyal to the United States Government. [*Loud applause.*] It is believed that we can make arrangements that will enable us to go to Washington and have there a convention that shall stand for all of the Y. P. S. C. E. principles, and at the same time get a mighty inspiration along the lines of good-citizenship. [*Applause.*] We want every young man and every young woman to stand in his place, having thought of good-citizenship, and say, "Thank God, I am an American." [*Applause.*] The trustees of the United Society of Christian Endeavor have decided that the convention of 1896 shall be held in the capital of our country.

Upon this announcement there came a scene. The Washington delegates broke loose in their enthusiasm. They shouted, leaped upon chairs, waved their flags, and cheered. Then they sang once more, but with a new meaning, the "Washington Song," hundreds of printed copies being thrown out over the audience.

WASHINGTON, '96.

(*Air* — "Tramp, Tramp, Tramp!")

From Potomac's lovely shores the historic hosts have gone,
  Leaving tales of deeds so noble, great, and grand,
But once more we hear the watchword of "On to Washington!"
  From the great Endeavor Army of our land.

CHORUS: Washington in '96! Washington in '96!
  We will bid you welcome there,
  To the Nation's home so fair,
Come to Washington, Endeavorers, '96.

Many thousands they will come, like an army to the fight,
  From the prairies, from the mountains, and the sea,
To reclaim our dear homeland for the Master and the Right;
  Welcome, noble host of Y. P. S. C. E!

CHORUS: Washington in '96! Washington in '96!
  From the hill-tops come the cry,
  From the valleys the reply,
We are coming Washington, in '96!

The song was sung twice over, the audience joining in the second time. During the singing the Baltimore delegates rose and joined in the song, and at its conclusion they proposed three cheers for Washington, which were given with a will. The Washington delegates responded with three rousing cheers for Baltimore. Mr. Foster, from the platform, then started the hymn, "Blest be the tie that binds," and the whole audience rose and joined in the hymn. This quieted the excitement; and after the audience had resumed their seats Miss Nellie Sabin Hyde, of Cleveland, rendered a beautiful vocal solo, and was followed by Miss Anna Parks, who gave "Palm Branches" as a cornet solo. Both ladies were loudly applauded. Then came the presentation of banners by Secretary Baer.

Presentation of Banners.

MR. BAER: Washington delegates have a great reason to be happy to-night, but I assure you that they will have to give up something as well as take something away. The District of Columbia has had for one year the Junior badge-banner for the largest proportionate increase in the number of Junior societies in one year. I will ask Mr. McArthur, president of that union, to come forward and present this banner, as gracefully and happily as he can, to the Delaware union, represented by Miss Lincoln.

MR. MCARTHUR: The Endeavorers of the District of Columbia succeeded last year at Montreal in winning this Junior banner. It has been a great inspiration and help to us during the year. It has been in all of our rallies and conventions, constituting a standard around which we have rallied, receiving greater enthusiasm in the work for the Master. The District of Columbia includes the city of Washington, and the conditions were such that it was impossible for us to hold this banner another year. We were glad to hold it for even one year. There is no other State to which we could give this banner so willingly as to Delaware, for in size she is not much larger than we are. [*Laughter.*] We give this banner to little Delaware very willingly. We do not want everything, and we think that the convention for 1896 is a very fair exchange for this banner. [*Laughter.*]

MISS LINCOLN: Delaware is very small, but she went home last year making up her mind to take home this Junior banner this year. That is what a woman does when she makes up her mind. [*Laughter and applause.*]

MR. BAER: In view of the fact that New Mexico, which has held this next banner during the year, is not represented in the convention, — though she is represented in the city, and right royally too, — I will myself take the pleasure of presenting this banner for the largest proportionate increase of young people's societies in one year to one of the States that we term the Southern States. Some one has said that the idea of Christian Endeavor was going slow in the Southern States. I want to tell you that when we can assign this banner to West Virginia, that statement must be discounted. We shall be glad to welcome the president of the West Virginia union, Rev. S. H. Doyle of Moundsville. [*Applause.*]

MR. DOYLE: Some people have the idea that West Virginia only produces mountains and hills, but I want to tell you now that it also produces Christian Endeavorers; and as the world is just beginning to hear of the mountains and hills of West Virginia, so also the Endeavor world is going to hear from the Endeavorers of West Virginia. West Virginia Endeavorers are workers; they do not have very much to say, but all the same they are always working. One year ago at Montreal we decided that when we went home from this convention at Cleveland we would take the Senior banner home with us, and we would also try to take the Junior banner with us, but we are glad to give that to Delaware. Now, we believe in beginning in time; so to-day at noon we decided that next year we would take home the Chinese umbrella from New York, and we serve notice on New York to-night that one year from this time that umbrella will go to West Virginia. [*Applause, the delegates from West Virginia rising and singing one verse of their State song.*]

MR. BAER: The State of Pennsylvania has been said to be noted for its pig iron, and I believe that it is also true that their pig iron is of a good quality. Christian

Endeavor in Pennsylvania is of a very high standard; its principles are well maintained. Pennsylvania has had for one year the banner for the largest absolute increase of societies during the year, taking it from Ontario. Last year they had a song, "Home Again," when that banner came back to them from Canada's shore. I wonder what their song is to-night; for the banner goes — not to Canada, but across the briny deep to our friends in England. [*Applause.*] England, I believe, has no representative on this platform; and indeed, that banner is already boxed, and, if my suggestions have been carried out, is started on its way. But Pennsylvania, I think, can part with that banner, for she has been something of a pig — iron — in her endeavor to secure the banner. [*Laughter.*] Pennsylvania, giving up that banner, takes, however, from New York State the banner for the greatest absolute gain in number of Junior societies. Pennsylvania also takes from Illinois the banner for the largest number of societies. Illinois, you know, has had that banner from the start. Rev. Dr. Taylor of New York is to present the first banner to Pennsylvania.

DR. TAYLOR: It becomes my duty, as president of the Christian Endeavor Union of New York State, to present to you, sir, this banner. I will not pretend that it is a pleasure for us to do so, for the Empire State is not used to being beaten. It is told of Mr. Lincoln that he was once met by a man who threatened to kill him, because he had made a vow that if he ever met a man homelier than himself, he would shoot him. After the future president had looked him over carefully, he said, "Well, shoot away. If I am any homelier than you are, I don't want to live." [*Laughter.*] During the past twelve years we have had all sorts of banners in New York State, and we have felt perhaps a little too secure; but we stand ready to deliver to any State which does better than we. And I may say that there is no State in the Union to which we would rather surrender this banner than Pennsylvania. [*Applause.*] The question was propounded in New York City as to what was the greatest possible difference in time between any two cities of the United States; and a New Yorker said, "The greatest possible difference in time between any two cities in the United States is that between New York and Philadelphia — about one hundred years!" [*Laughter.*] I shall have to go back and correct that impression. With all the pleasure that is possible under the circumstances, Mr. President, I give you this banner. [*Applause.*]

REV. MR. ROADS: Pennsylvania could only be beaten for the banner for the greatest absolute increase of societies by a whole country on the other side of the water. [*Applause.*] Everything on this side we had beaten entirely out of sight, but we had not calculated on Old England. When we found that England and Scotland and Wales and Ireland were thrown in against us, then, of course, we had to give up that banner. But we are the Keystone State of Christian Endeavor just as much as we are the Keystone State of the Union. Mr. Baer speaks about pig iron as if that were the only product of Pennsylvania. If he could see our broad farms, if he could see our coal mines, if he could see our manufactories in that slow city of Philadelphia, — which in Christian Endeavor manages to get ahead of all the rest of the world, Old England and all the rest thrown in, — then I am sure he would remember that Pennsylvania has a variety of products; and that of which we are most proud to-night is not our coal mines, nor our mines of iron ore, nor our fertile farms, but of our young men and women who have taken the pledge of loyalty to the Lord Jesus Christ and who are living accordingly. [*Applause.*] I tell you, we have the finest crop of Christian Endeavorers in Pennsylvania that was raised this year. [*Applause.*] Now, I give notice that we are going to take every banner next year. We are in that sense determined to conquer for Christ and his church. But do not imagine that in Pennsylvania we are aiming simply at an increase of numbers; for if you could dig into our societies as men dig into our mines, you would find there iron — the strongest steadfastness to Christian Endeavor principles; you would find there coal — that which burns with a fervor and zeal for Christ and his church as no other fire can burn, for we have anthracite coal in Pennsylvania, that which gives the hottest flame and burns the longest of any coal on the earth; you would find there gold, for we have gold in Pennsylvania, and almost every metal known. We are glad to give this banner to Old England because William Penn came from England, and he never would have left England if there had been Christian Endeavor societies in England to beat Pennsylvania. [*Laughter.*]

MR. BAER: Illinois is represented by one of her State directors, Mr. Willden, who will present the Junior banner to Pennsylvania.

Mr. Willden: Illinois, this will break poor Tom Wainwright's heart. He has fought hard for this banner, and has held it in the State for lo, these many years. But we feel that by our earnest efforts and our zeal in Illinois, and with such a leader in the Junior cause as Tom Wainwright, we have stirred up the entire country, Pennsylvania especially, to greater efforts than were ever dreamed of before. In presenting this banner to-night, with great reluctance and regret on the part of Illinois, to the State of Pennsylvania, I simply want to illustrate how we lost it. You all remember the story of the man and the bear. The man had the bear down, and he let go just a moment to spit on his hands to get a fresh grip, and the bear downed him. That is our case. [*Laughter.*] We have come to this convention eight hundred strong, in spite of railroad strikes. [*Applause.*] We were to have come fifteen hundred strong, but through the courtesy of the strikers we got through with eight hundred. I promise you, my friends, on behalf of Illinois, that, as we downed anarchy, so we will put down this strike [*cheers*], and we will take back this banner in 1895. [*Applause.*]

Mr. Roads: I want you to remember that we have no anarchy in Pennsylvania. [*Applause.*] So long as we hold this Junior banner, and keep on training our boys and girls in the principles of Christian Endeavor, we shall never have a Chicago, and we shall never have any anarchy in Pennsylvania. [*Applause.*]

Mr. Baer: I would like to have the president of the New York State Union come here a moment. I want him to look in the direction of that peculiar object (pointing to the Chinese "umbrella of state"). I want you all at the same time to look. I don't know as you know what it is. I would not know if I had not seen the directions that go with it. It is called in China an umbrella of state, and it is given to an official when he has carried on his duties, as I understand it, faithfully and well. At the suggestion of the Rev. A. A. Fulton, whom we all know as the originator of the plan of giving two cents a week per member to missions, home or foreign, through the denominational board, the Chinese Christian Endeavor Societies have sent this banner here, and it was to have been presented by Rev. Mr. Swan, but he is not here to-night. This banner goes to New York State for having within her borders the greatest number of societies reporting to us which have adopted Mr. Fulton's pledge. New York will hold this Chinese umbrella of state, rain or shine, for one year. [*Laughter and applause.*]

Dr. Taylor: "He laughs best who laughs last." Where's Pennsylvania now? [*Laughter.*] We will take that banner home with us, and I should not wonder if we built a palace car for it, and took it around the State, so as to ensure its remaining forever in the Empire State. [*Applause.*]

Dr. Thwing then introduced, as the closing speaker of the evening, Rev. Maltbie D. Babcock of Baltimore. Mr. Babcock was received with much applause, the Maryland delegates uniting in their State song, and a lot of Syracuse students present saluting the speaker with their college "yell."

Glorifying God.

Address of Rev. Maltbie D. Babcock.

"Whether, therefore, ye eat or drink, or whatsoever ye do, do all to the glory of God."

Children ask questions, for it is their nature to, and God is back of their nature. The everlasting "why" is as philosophical as the everlasting "yes" and "no." There is a purpose in everything — nothing is for nothing. Children know this, and should be dealt with as fairly as possible, and never snubbed with the reply an old lady used to make to me when I asked "why" to this and that, "To make little folks ask questions." A man may not ask a question; but he interrogates a new piece of machinery with his eyes, and catechizes it with his mind, which amounts to the same thing. He knows that it is meant for something. It is only a fair thing for us to do, to keep on asking questions, finding out what this is for and that, until we reach ourselves. "What am I for?" is as sensible and solemn a question as any one can ask. "What is my aim in life?" Have you ever deliberately asked yourself the question? There is one higher than all others, including all others, outlasting all others; it is the glory of God. Carlyle said, "The older I grow, and I am standing now on the brink of the grave, the fuller and deeper seem the words to me I learned as a child, 'Man's chief end is to glorify God.'" How can I glorify God? I cannot beautify that which is already supremely beautiful; I cannot paint the lily nor adorn the rose; how can I glorify God? I cannot, if you mean add glory to God, make him more glorious than he is. But if I cannot make God more glorious in himself, I can so live that I shall make him more glorious in the eyes of others. Can I add light to the sun? No; but I may lift the shade and add light to this room. Can I add manliness to the character of my friend? No; but I may remove an aspersion from his reputation that his character may be known as it is. I may make God glorious by revealing him, that he may be known as he is.

The glory of God, then, is the revealed character of God. There can be no higher end of living than to make this known, since the self-revelation of God is his highest glory and the greatest good of all created beings. "For this is life eternal, that they might know thee." Creation is for the glory of God, for it partly reveals him. "The heavens declare the glory of God." All nature shows his greatness, his wisdom, his "eternal power and Godhead." God is a great God. History, too, reveals his glory, in the holiness of his character, in his justice and righteousness. Disobedience means disintegration and death. That which is built out of plumb will fall. The character, personal or national, that is off the true must go to the ground. God is a holy God. But in redemption, in Christ, God makes the fullest revelation of himself, and so most fully unveils his glory. God, who at sundry times and in divers manners had spoken in the past, reveals himself most fully in Jesus Christ, who is the brightness of his glory and the express image of his person. Well may angels have sung, "Glory to God in the highest," when God was manifest in the flesh, and Jesus Christ became the visible transcript of his nature.

Can God still be revealed? Is the glory of God still to be seen? Yes, in us and through us is God yet and now to be known. "Through the church" he speaks. "Ye are my witnesses" is the recognition that we are still to show the glory of God. "As the Father hath sent me, even so send I you." He who said, "I have made known thy name," commissions us to make known God's name, and, "whether we eat, or drink, or whatever we do, to do all to the glory of God," — to reveal God, to make him glorious in the eyes of men.

Taine said, "Art is concentration in manifestation," an idea truthfully and beautifully embodied, an ideal made real. What is the art of Christian living, what is my vocation, my "high calling in Christ Jesus"? "That they might know thee," that in me the divine life might be seen, that in my mortal body God should be made glorious. Here is the aim of life for us all. There can be no classes or distinction, for, whether I am rich or poor, learned or ignorant, I can reveal God; sick or well, at home or abroad, I can be a divine message to men from God. Can you find another motive for all, everywhere and always? Other motives touch us like spheres that come in contact at but one point, or at different times; the glory of God touches me everywhere and always. Whether I eat, or drink, or whatever I do, I may so live as to glorify God.

See the power of this motive in the time of temptation. Do I belong to God? Am I here to represent him? I must cry out then like Joseph, "How can I do this great wickedness and sin against God?" In the matter of doubtful things, what motive can teach me so well how to decide? To choose selfishly, thoughtlessly, shortsightedly — is this to reveal the character of God? To say under the law of liberty all things are lawful; to say under the law of life, "Eating flesh, drinking wine, does not hurt me," and then to decide that I can do as I please — is this to reveal the character of God — when the law of love, as in the life of him who most fully revealed God, who pleased not himself, would lead me to say with Paul, "It is good neither to eat flesh, nor to drink wine, nor anything whereby thy brother stumbleth, or is offended, or is made weak"? Whether, therefore, I eat, or drink, or whatever I do, I am to do it so that God will be made glorious. How, then, can I stand on the selfish, loveless, Christless side of doubtful questions?

And when we turn to our work in life, what motive so operates to cover its every motion and moment? There is a constant struggle in life between the real and the ideal, between dead monotony on the one hand and dreamy visions on the other; but is not the solution found in the ideal doing of the real? Does God reveal his glory alone in that which to the eyes of men seems worthy and noble? Do the heavens alone declare the glory of God? Is not God as truly revealed in the flower, in the wing of the insect, in the gleam of the dewdrop, as in the solar system? Let me, then, bring the glory of God as a motive to bear upon the most common and casual things of life. We cannot divide ourselves up, as the New York *Observer* does, into a religious department and a secular department. We are to do all unto the glory of God, to show his character as well in devotion to our work on Monday as in the devoutness of our worship on Sunday. The Christian architect, who designs the noble temple to the glory of God, is swayed by no higher motive than that which makes a man thoroughly dust its darkest corner.

> "The hand that rounded Peter's dome,
> And groined the aisles of sacred Rome,
> Wrought in a sad sincerity;
> Himself from God he could not free."

> "And so a servant with this clause
> Makes drudgery divine;
> Who sweeps a room as for thy laws,
> Makes that and the action fine."

If I work for the glory of God I must do everything well, whether the work be personally agreeable or not. If I live for pleasure, why be conscientious in that which is not pleasant to me? If for money, in what does not pay me? If for ambition, in that which is not popular nor profitable? But if for the glory of God, whatever my hand finds to do shall be done as a word of explanation of the divine nature.

But what if a man succeeds in his work, how shall he be kept from pride? The danger of most men is their conceit. But how can a successful man be kept from the foolishness of Nebuchadnezzar as he paced his walls and said, "Is not this great Babylon that I have built?" Let him live for God's glory. Then he welcomes success, blesses God for usefulness and accomplishment, acknowledges that he is but a tool in the Master's hands, a servant in the Master's house; cries, "Not unto us, not unto us, but unto thy name give glory!" My brother, if you succeed you have an opportunity of revealing the God who can keep a man sensible in success, and level-headed on high places.

But what if failure has come, if a great hope is lost, and horse and rider are in the dust? Am I living for the glory of God? For his glory I can fail. I will spell disappointment with another first letter and make it read his appointment. Did not men count Christ a failure? But was it not in the hour of his crucifixion that the centurion glorified God, saying, "Truly this man is the Son of God!" I will not speak of the blessings of failure, of its correction of our false estimates of ourselves, of its showing us how we may on stepping-stones of our dead selves rise to higher things; but I will say that it is one of the magnificent opportunities of the Christian to reveal his God. The light that seems so dim in the daytime shines with a fine radiance in the dark. The ship that weathers the storm is strong proof of her builder's skill, whose praise untroubled seas had left unsung. To bear up, and steer right onward; to faint not in the day of adversity; to cry with Jesus, "Father, glorify thyself;" to say with the apostle, "Christ shall be magnified in my body," whether by life or death, — is to give a proof of the reality of the Christian life, is to unveil God before the eyes of men in a way not to be doubted or denied.

And when at last we face the inevitable, when death brings us to things as they are, then the question comes with a power never before realized, What have I been living for? If for money or for fame, if for power or pleasure, how death pricks the bubble! What earthly motive can survive this test? But if I have been living for the glory of God, I can die for his glory, and show how he who helped a Christian to live can help a Christian to die. It is but another opportunity, another phase of life, in which to reveal God; as a recent writer said of a noble woman's death, "She gave to death the same large and generous welcome which she accorded to all the other great experiences of her life." And death past, the last earthly test endured, I begin to live beyond as I have tried to live here—still for the glory of God; I will try to do his will cheerfully and exactly; having been faithful in a little, be glad to be trusted with more; finding that the reward of one duty was the power to do another and a higher, I will try in any way he says or in any place he sends me still to reveal my God, knowing him and showing him. What a magnificent outlook — to glorify God and enjoy him forever! Beloved Christians, let us feel the power of this endless life-motive now. Let it strengthen us for victory in temptation. Let it be wisdom to us in moments of hard decisions. Let it call us to our best work, steady us in success, exalt us in failure, give triumph in death, and sway us for eternity. The scope and swing of life depend upon the length of its radius. If earth is the pivot of our thought and activity, how little a sphere bounds us; but if the far distant sun is the center, then through what mighty spaces is our life carried!

Living for self — how limited, how little, how unworthy my life! Living for God, living to make him glorious — how surely must infinity be the scope of my being, and eternity its endless sweep! Beloved, "Whether therefore ye eat, or drink, or whatever ye do, do all to the glory of God."

At the close of Mr. Babcock's address, which was many times interrupted by applause, a number of notices and telegrams were read, after which the benediction was pronounced by Rev. Mr. Townsend.

THE TENT.

The evening programme drew out an immense audience, which completely filled the large tent. The song service was inspiring. Rev. Henry T. McEwen, Ph.D., New York City, presided. The exercises of the evening began with the hymn, "My Country, 'tis of Thee," at the conclusion of which the Canadian delegation sang "God save the Queen," and were applauded vigorously by the sons and daughters of Uncle Sam.

At the conclusion of the song service Dr. McEwen said that he was confident that if all in the audience were permitted to give expression as to the way in which the devotional exercises should be conducted this evening, they would ask, with one heart and one voice, for a season of silent prayer, when every heart could give utterance to its earnest supplication for the restoration of health and strength to Dr. Clark. The audience then joined in repeating the Twenty-third Psalm, and then with bowed heads prayed silently.

DR. McEWEN: One of the most pleasant features of our great International Conventions has always been the annual address by our President, Dr. Clark. I presume that if we had been asked, in our great human wisdom, a few days ago, whether it were possible for us to stand two things, one a railway strike which would extend nearly over the United States, and the other the absence of our beloved leader, we would have said, "No; we must at least have Dr. Clark with us." [*Applause.*] The absence of this beloved brother and friend permits me to say a word which perhaps in his presence he would not like to have me say. I have come very close to this good brother again and again. In the days when, like our brother Dr. Tyler, we were arranging for the Convention, we learned to appreciate his level head, his consecrated spirit, his earnest, honest, and sturdy humility. We owe a debt to Dr. Clark which we can hardly pay. So, then, to-night in his absence I have asked for your prayers for his complete restoration. Some of our friends have been saying that without his presence Christian Endeavor must fail. If that be true, it is simply the work of man. If, as Dr. Clark believes, and as thousands of others of us believe, it is a work of God, then the work will and can go on. Instead of listening to the familiar voice and seeing the splendid presence of our friend, we shall listen to his address read by his friend, his esteemed co-worker, and our friend and helper, Mr. William Shaw, Treasurer of the United Society. [*Applause.*]

As Mr. Shaw stepped to the platform he was greeted with the Chautauqua salute.

MR. SHAW: For eleven years I have been working with Dr. Clark; for nine years it has been my privilege to be officially associated with him; and those of you here who know Dr. Clark, know what it means to me to attempt to stand in his place to-night. The only thing that we are grateful for — those of us who know him best — is that he has been willing at this late hour to take the advice of his physician and remain at home and rest. For six months or more he has been working beyond his strength. We have urged him to stop, but he has felt the pressure of the work upon him to such an extent that he could not stop; so to-night we rejoice in the fact that his physician assures us that rest now for a few months will mean many years more of service under our beloved leader [*Applause*]; while we were also assured that if he persisted in coming to this Convention it might mean a complete break-down. We cannot think of such a thing in connection with Dr. Clark. And so we rejoice to-night that he can be with us in spirit, and that we can feel that he is preparing for a larger and a grander service in the years that are to come. I feel, as I stand here to-night in my own weakness, that I am borne up by his spirit and his prayers; and may God so move upon our hearts and so impress upon our lives his spirit of consecration, of utter self-abnegation to the work, that we may go from this Convention filled with Dr. Clark's spirit, even as he is filled with the Spirit of Christ. That is our prayer to-night.

Mr. Shaw then read Dr. Clark's address, at the conclusion of which there was a storm of applause, followed by the singing of "Blest be the Tie that binds."

MR. MCEWEN: The question of good citizenship, I am glad to say, has stirred your hearts. A large part of Christian Endeavor belongs to the sex that just now does not vote, but the question is being agitated. Meanwhile, young ladies and older ladies, that you be not unoccupied, remember that your mothers and aunts during the time of the war stirred up their husbands and sweethearts, so that they were braver men than they ever thought of being. The stuff was not in them to have made such heroes as they did develop, had it not been for your mothers and your aunts at home on both sides of Mason's and Dixon's line.

Now, the good citizen, like the highest type of being, adapts himself to the needs of the hour. You do not have to stir up your husbands to go to the front to war; but I will tell you what mean tricks some of them are doing. They are moving out of our great cities to avoid personal taxation on their large property. Traitors, aren't they? See that they do not do it. [*Applause*.] Again I will tell you what some of them are doing; they are afraid to tell you, but I will tell you. They do not register their names, otherwise they would appear for jury duty; and, in order to avoid the dreadful task of jury duty in our cities, they are refusing to register; for a little bit of comfort they are sacrificing the duties of a citizen, who is also a steward. Hiss them out of it; it is a shame, a disgrace.

Dr. McEwen then introduced Rev. J. T. Beckley, D.D., who announced that the Convention of '95 would be held in San Francisco, providing satisfactory railroad rates can be secured; and that the Convention of '96 would be held in Washington City, which announcement was followed by general applause.

MR. MCEWEN: When we were in convention at New York, there was a brother there who was one of the most peculiarly difficult fellows to locate I ever saw. One time we wanted a greeting from the Tar Heel State, and up jumped this fellow, and gave us a rousing greeting. Pretty soon we wanted to know something about what Maryland was doing, and this same genius arose again. [*Laughter.*] We thought we had heard the last of him, until by and by we wanted to know something about the city just across the river, greater New York, where municipal reform has set in, otherwise known as Brooklyn, and the same individual, with the same placid face and sublime assurance, arose again. I have the pleasure of introducing this same brother from many States, Rev. A. C. Dixon, D.D., pastor of the Hanson Place Baptist Church, Brooklyn.

Heroes of Faith.

Address of Rev. A. C. Dixon, D.D.

Paul pressed "toward the mark for the prize of the high calling of God in Christ Jesus." Many run; one receives the prize. Paul was religiously ambitious. He desired to be first in faith and hope and works. His pet horror was that, after having preached to others, he himself might come out second best. He might have written: —

> "In the Christian field of battle,
> In the bivouac of life,
> Be not like dumb, driven cattle,
> Be a hero in the strife."

Paul's standard of heroism was very high; the basis of it was faith. Faith is the basis of all great endeavor. Men believe, and therefore speak and act. Martyrs never die for their doubts.

Whoever wrote the eleventh chapter of Hebrews gives us the standard of that heroism. Photographers make a composite picture, many features formed into one face. It is my purpose now, for a few minutes, just to bring the camera before that eleventh chapter of Hebrews, and form out of a few features there the face of the true hero of faith. Whether theologians or scientists, we all believe that by the Word of God the worlds were created. It takes a man of faith to be a good orthodox scientist. We study in the schools what we know as the nebular hypothesis. What does that mean? Mr. Kant tells us that away back in the misty past all created matter was in a rarefied, homogeneous state, so rare that it took millions of cubic miles to weigh a grain. Didn't it get thin? [*Laughter*.] Just shut your eyes and try to think how thin. LaPlace says, "Mr. Kant, your theory is entirely too thin." [*Laughter*.] You must have a central sun with revolving gas about it before you can make a planetary system like this. And Herbert Spencer accepts the theory of LaPlace, but Sir William Thompson says it is still too thin. We must have, he says, in the revolving mist stones and earth. My question is, How do you know? Were you there when it was so thin? [*Laughter*.] Did you ever see anybody who was there? Did you ever hear of anybody who saw anybody who was there? Did you ever see anybody who heard of anybody who saw anybody who heard of anybody who was there? [*Laughter*.] I believe in the nebular hypothesis; it is a good working theory; and, therefore, I accept it. When you come to the modern theory of evolution it takes faith "Simon pure." [*Laughter*.] The doctrine of the "survival of the fittest" and "natural selection" cannot be accepted without a large amount of faith. I am not abusing the scientist, but it takes more faith to be a good orthodox scientist to-day than it does to believe in Jonah and the whale. I repeat: whether theologians or scientists, "by faith we understand that the worlds were framed by the Word of God."

The first feature in the face of our hero is sacrifice; "By faith Abel offered unto God." It takes very little heroism to receive from God something in answer to prayer. Any beggar can do that. All you have to do is to sit and ask and take. No heroism especially about that. "By faith Abel offered unto God." An old Baptist deacon down South said he was perfectly willing to confess that his contractile muscles were stronger than his extensile; he could hold during collection better than he could give. [*Laughter*.] And some people exercise their contractile muscles until their extensile become withered. They are all hands to take and no hands to give. Like the devilfish, with a score of hands to fill himself, but not a hand to give off to others. The offering becomes noble when the motive is unto God. "What are you doing there?" said a man to an old blacksmith, as he found him ringing the sparks from his anvil. Continuing his heavy blows, he said, "Sir, I am preaching the gospel to the regions beyond." [*Laughter*.] That man's muscle was a good deal better than the tongues of some people I have heard wag. [*Applause*.] Muscle was offered unto God.

Abel offered the sacrifice that pleased God. There was blood in it. Cain brought the fruits of his fields; he needed no atonement. Sin he could not, for he believed in industry, in character, in a man's doing something and being something. Abel was heroic enough to see himself as he was; Cain refused to see himself thus, but simply looked at himself as he wanted to be. He brought his fruits as amends for sinning; he believed that fruit would atone for fault; he brought the result of his industry to make amends for sin. "Didn't you know, Johnny," said a mother to her boy, "that you were doing wrong while eating those preserves?" "Yes, mamma," he said, "I did, and all the time I was eating I prayed God to forgive me." [*Laughter.*] Prayer to him was an amends for sin. He didn't give it up and quit, but kept on, and prayed to make amends to God for the iniquity of his act. I thank God that Christian Endeavor emphasizes the blood, stands by the altar and offers sacrifice first, and then brings the fruit cleansed by the blood of Jesus Christ.

Such men never die. "For he, being dead, yet speaketh." The thrones of this earth are in the cemeteries; the power of England is not at Windsor palace, but in Westminster Abbey. The men that live are the men that die; and like Abel, sometimes they live long because they die soon. Dead and yet speaking. Be such a Christian, such a man, such a woman, that the world can afford to let you live after you have died. The world builds monuments to the men of sacrifice. I stood the other day in New York in front of the monument of Nathan Hale, and on the pedestal are written these words: "I regret that I have only one life to lose for my country." Why is it that men will not let his memory die? Self-sacrifice has been molded into bronze. An æsthetic, cultured young man said to me the other day, "I never partake of the Lord's Supper, because it savors of blood and torn flesh." I said, "Friend, did you ever stand by Bunker Hill monument?" "Yes," said he. "Does not that suggest blood and torn flesh; and yet in that case you look beneath the surface, under the rough, and finding there the spirit that is noble, you build the monument to self-sacrifice, and the climax of that spirit is on Calvary, where the Master and Leader of all Christian Endeavor died, the hero of self-sacrifice." [*Loud applause.*]

The second feature in the face of our hero is persistence in right doing. "By faith Enoch walked with God." He did not try to get God to walk with him; he simply fell in with God's way and will and work, and kept step with Jehovah. What we need to learn is, What is God doing? Which way is he moving? Some one came to Abraham Lincoln, that hero of common-sense, and said, "Mr. President, appoint a day of fasting and prayer, in order that the Lord may be on our side." "Never mind about the Lord," said Lincoln; "you get on his side; he is all right now." [*Applause.*] What we need is to get on God's side.

Whatever may be said about President Cleveland, he has the genius for vetoing bills; he has taken the prize along that line. One trouble with Cleveland is that Congress passes the bills without consulting him, and they send them up to him for approval, and he vetoes about nine-tenths of them. In our little Congressional halls of selfishness, and sometimes of sin, we decide what we want God to do, and then we pass the bill up for his signature in our prayers, and no wonder he vetoes about nine-tenths of them. [*Laughter.*] Good for us that he does. We had better consult him first. Enoch was an every-day hero. "They that wait upon the Lord shall renew their strength, they shall mount up on wings as eagles, they shall run and not grow weary, they shall walk and faint not." The climax is in the last clause. It is harder to walk than to fly or run. There is an appeal to the heroic in us when we think about mounting up like the eagle. I tell you that is different from just walking through the dust, month by month, week by week, day by day, hour by hour, moment by moment walking with God. Elijah was a hero on Mount Carmel; Elijah whimpering under the juniper-tree was made of common stuff. Jonah was a hero in Nineveh; Jonah complaining of the withered gourd-vine came down from his pedestal. Paul was a hero on Mars' Hill and before Felix; and, Paul, if you had kept your temper a little better in talking with Barnabas about John Mark, you might have kept it up. It is easier to be a hero on Mount Carmel than it is to be a hero under the juniper-trees of life. [*Applause.*] The men and women we meet every day struggling with annoyances and pain are the true heroes of life's battle. I would rather fight a lion, if I had a Winchester rifle and behind a tree, than to fight through the night three Jersey mosquitoes. [*Laughter.*] Napoleon charging across the bridge at Lodi was a hero, but Napoleon could not stand the presence of a cat. That is authenticated. It would make him sick at his stomach. If the Russians had just known that, the victory would have been easy. [*Laughter.*]

In the Turko-German war a village was besieged by Turks. They broke down the gates, and were marching up the narrow streets, when some German young women, taking in the situation, went in the back yard, and each got a beehive full of bees, and flung them over among the Turkish soldiers. These did in five minutes what German bayonets could not accomplish. [*Laughter.*] The soldiers knew how to shoot the enemy, but they did not know how to fight bees. The best picture Murillo ever made was one in which he represented a kitchen scene, in the midst of which are angelic forms sent of God to minister to his lowly servants.

The heroes of the kitchen and the needle and the workshop are more noble, frequently, than the men that charge in battle under the gaze of their country. [*Applause.*]

The principal feature of Enoch's heroism was that he walked with God while everybody else walked the other way. He lived just before the Flood, and the most of them that went the other way got drowned. [*Laughter.*] I would rather walk alone with God than be under the flood with a crowd. It is easy to walk with a surging multitude; it is quite hard to make your way against them. There are two books we ought to study: one of them is the Bible, written by the Spirit of God; the other is the spirit of the times, written to a large extent by the other side. The Bible is authority. What we call the trend of the times may have precious little authority. *Vox populi* may be *vox diaboli*. It is not always *vox Dei*, or Christ had not been crucified. A colored man down South was brought before the court for stealing a chicken; and the judge said, "What defense have you, John?" John replied, "I have a book at home, sir, which they keep in the kitchen, and I turned to that book, and I saw this written, 'Take one chicken.' [*Laughter.*] It didn't say whose chicken and whar to git it, so I just struck out and got the fust I laid my hands on." [*Laughter.*] The cook-book, even if interpreted correctly, was not authority in court, and John was sent to jail. The spirit of the times is the cook-book of the day; and when the spirit of the times is against the Spirit of God, let God be true and every man a liar. [*Applause, Amen, Amen.*] I believe that in the hearts of the people instructed aright there is a conscientiousness, but God's way and walk we need to consult and follow if we would be true heroes. A part of Enoch's creed that helped him to walk with God, we are told, was that he believed that "God is, and that he is a rewarder of them that diligently seek him." Some of us have a religion in the past tense. We believe that God was with the prophets and with Paul and the rest of them; but we need to bring it down to date, that God is in the person of his Spirit with his people every day, and that "he is a rewarder of them that seek him," not his. The true hero, like Enoch walking with God, does not seek the things of God so much as God himself. His delight is in Christ, in his love and presence; and that is better than the approval of all the multitude that may be going the other way.

The third feature of this face of our lives is fear. "By faith Noah, warned of God, moved with fear, prepared an ark." Fear makes cowards or heroes. Fear to do right makes a coward; fear to do wrong makes a hero. Fear of God makes a hero; fear of men makes a coward. "Noah, moved with fear, prepared an ark." And just let me say — I do not know whether this is with the trend of the times or not, and care as little as I know — what we want is an emphasis of law. [*Applause.*] The law of our country, if you please. The only sovereign that wears a crown and holds a scepter and sits on a throne in the United States is law. [*Applause.*] Presidents, governors, congressmen, and mayors are simply servants of this king; and what we need is to preach the sacredness of law, for our rulers as well as the people. [*Loud applause.*] If the president or governor or mayor fails to enforce the law he ought to be impeached for the good of the rising generation. [*Great applause.*] Men need to fear the penitentiary and the jail and the gallows and Hell spelled with a capital letter. We need to preach no less the glories of heaven, but he who speaks of those glories speaks also of the "worm that dieth not and the fire that is not quenched." I hate Puritanicalism; I love Puritanism. God save us from being Puritanical; God make us Puritan by giving us some backbone. [*Applause.*] What we need is vertebræ made out of Plymouth Rock. [*Loud applause.*] Vertebræ for officials in state, and for the pulpit, and for the pew, men that stand for something. No man has a right to sit on the fence. Every fence should be made of barbed wire. [*Laughter and applause.*] We need men who are Christians; men that worship Christ as King. We need men that believe something and are willing to die for their faith. That is the need of this age.

Down South, where I came from, a teacher was asked by the Board of Examiners what school of astronomy and geography he proposed to teach; and his reply was that he would teach the round or flat theory, according to the wishes of the patrons. [*Laughter.*] We have a trifle too much of that sort of thing in our Christian work. "But," said a man to me, "you know the Christian ought not to vote, his citizenship is in heaven." I am afraid if he does not do his duty here that is about all he will get there. "What you need," say these pious men, "is not to bother with mundane things, but just sit and sing yourself away to everlasting bliss. Be gentle, and kind, and sweet, and considerate, and loving, and tender, and compassionate to the poor sinners in office or out of office." Well, I submit that the gospel is dew; but the same Scripture that compares it to dew, tells us that the Lord is like a lion with tooth and claw. The gospel is light; but when God dealt with a certain individual, he flung him out of heaven like lightning. The need is light for the sinner, and lightning for his sin. [*Applause.*] We need not less light, but more lightning. The great iniquities that are thriving in our soil, iniquities such as Anthony Comstock suppresses, iniquities such as Parkhurst suppresses, iniquities such as every good citizen ought to suppress, not by maudlin whimperings of sentimentalism, but by the flashing lightning from God's Sinai. You remember that the Lord led Israel by a gentle angel. That is true about Israel, but I beg leave to observe that he dealt with the Canaanites through hornets Now, you know a hornet does not take a man on his bayonet and fling him out of the country; it just makes him willing to get out. [*Laughter and applause.*] I would like to be an angel leading God's hosts; but I want to be hornets for the Canaanites, and make it so hot for them that they will have to get out, every one.

"Moved with fear." You notice that Noah's fear propelled him; he went forward. There is quite a difference between the fear that makes a man stand, and the fear that makes him run. John, we are told, at the battle of Fredericksburg, ran at the first fire, and came back after the battle. The master said, "John, what made you run, you miserable coward, at the most critical point?" John replied, "Master, the difference between you and me is that I am afraid to fight and you are afraid to run." The fear that makes a man run is cowardice, and the fear that makes a man stand may be heroism. Of all heroes, I like best the cowardly hero, the man who trembles from head to foot but stands; the man who is scared, and will not run. [*Applause.*] The man who has a chicken heart but a lion's liver. [*Laughter.*] Napoleon said the difference between Marshal Ney and Marshal Brune was that Ney was never conscious of danger, and Brune was frightened at the first gun, and trembled from head to foot, but he stood. We need young men and young women that stand for the true and the pure, conscious of danger, but willing to stand, nevertheless. [*Applause.*]

The next feature in the face of our hero is obedience. Abraham obeyed God in spite of his promise. A promise frequently helps us to obey God. But in Abraham's case the command was in direct conflict with the promise. God promised that in Isaac all nations should be blessed, and then he commanded him to sacrifice Isaac. We are told that Abraham believed that God was able to raise Isaac from the dead, and so fulfill the promise. My friend, it is ours to obey the command; God will look after the promise. Walk with God and obey him, and, though the promise may contradict the command, you will come out all right. [*Applause.*] Everything you have put upon the altar will come back improved under the touch of God.

The last feature in the face of our hero is self-denial. "Moses, when he came to years, refused to be called the son of Pharaoh's daughter, choosing rather to suffer affliction with the people of God than to enjoy the pleasures of sin for a season, esteeming the reproach of Christ greater riches than the treasures of Egypt; for he had respect unto the recompense of the reward." In every young person's life there comes the crisis when he must decide what he will do and what he will not do. Moses refused pleasure because it was associated with Egypt, not because pleasure was sinful. Moses refused honor because it was associated with Egypt; Moses refused wealth because it was linked with Egypt and not with God's people. He stands out through all ages as the hero of self-denial. Henry Clay was a hero when he said, "I would rather be right than be President." The young find it difficult to refuse sinful or doubtful pleasure. "I don't drink wine; I don't dance; I don't go to the theater." And why? Because those things are wrong *per se?* Not at all; but because every one of them is associated with a great evil Egyptian institution. When I go to the innocent play I am not associated with that, but with the black institution of the theater. I might drink wine and not get drunk; but I don't do it because the wine-glass links me with a great evil Egyptian institution. When I dance innocently I am not associated with that innocent performance *per se*, but I am linking myself with that great evil institution. [*Applause.*] I don't play cards, because the very sight of a card in my hands links me with a great evil institution. [*Applause.*] When people see me they think not of Canaan, but of Egypt, and I want to keep them thinking about Canaan all the time. [*Applause.*] We Americans are always ready to die for liberty. Great is this Diana of America! A drunken man was going down the street in Baltimore flinging his hands right and left, when one of his arms came across the nose of a passer-by. The passer-by instinctively clenched his fist and sent the intruder sprawling to the ground. He got up, rubbing the place where he was hit, and said, "I would like to know if this is not a land of liberty." "It is," said the other fellow; "but I want you to understand that your liberty ends just where my nose begins." [*Laughter and Applause.*] Everybody, capitalist, laboring-man, striker, listen! your liberty ends right where the good of the next man begins. [*Applause.*] Paul said, "I can drink wine and eat flesh offered to idols, but if it may cause my weaker brother to stumble, I will not do it." There is something higher than defending one's rights, higher even than dying for one's rights, and that is the right to give up one's rights for the good of other people. [*Applause.*] That ought to be the principle in politics, in commerce, and in the family, — self-denial for the good of other people, and refusing to give or to take what brings honor or pleasure or wealth, when it injures the next man.

Let me in just two minutes close where I began. Young people, it is a noble ambition to want to live after you have died, not in heaven but on earth, making it better.

"The period of life is brief;
It is the red in the red rose leaf,
It is the gold in the sunset sky,
It is the flight of a bird on high;
But one may fill the space
With such an infinite grace,
That the red shall vein all time,
And the gold through the ages shine,
And the bird fly swift and straight
To the portals of God's own gate."

"Build a little fence of trust
   Around to-day;
Fill the space with loving deeds
   And therein stay;
Look not through the sheltering bars
   Upon to-morrow;
God will help thee bear what comes,
   Of joy or sorrow."

Faith, unswerving faith, in God and his word will help you do it.

A telegram from the Congo Regions, Africa, sending greetings, was read, announcing that a new society was formed in the dark continent.

The meeting of the evening was closed with "God be with You till We meet again," and the Mizpah benediction.

FRIDAY MORNING.

Early morning prayer meetings were held at 6.30 o'clock in twelve different churches throughout the city. The attendance was large, and the spiritual interest of the meetings reached a high level. The convention programme began, as usual, with meetings at the hall and the tent, beginning with a praise service at 9.30.

Saengerfest Hall.

The hall was filled some time before the opening hour; and the singing, which was led by Mr. E. O. Excell, who happened to be present, was grandly inspiring. A feature of the preliminary services which met with much favor was the singing of the Cleveland Christian Endeavor Male Quartette, led by Mr. Darsie. The four voices blended finely, and the words of the hymns sung were heard easily throughout the hall.

The session was presided over by Rev. M. L. Haines, D.D., of Indianapolis. Mr. Baer first read the committees appointed by President Dickinson, as follows:—

RESOLUTIONS COMMITTEE:— Rev. W. H. McMillian, D.D., Alleghany City, Pa.; Judge L. J. Kirkpatrick, Kokomo, Ind.; Rev. Canon J. B. Richardson, London, Ont.; Miss Luella E. Holt, Saginaw, Mich.; Rev. R. E. Dunpal, Seattle, Wash.; Rev. Burt Estes Howard, Los Angeles, Cal.; Mr. W. G. Bell, Austin, Tex.

BUSINESS COMMITTEE:— Secretary, John Willis Baer; Rev. A. B. Christy, Albuquerque, N.M.; Prof. Ralph Barnes, Portland, Or.; Mr. John Josten, Denver, Col.; Mr. A. E. Dewhurst, Utica, N.Y.; Mr. W. H. Knapp, Rochester, Minn.; Mr. H. H. Spooner, Chicago, Ill.

Rev. John Becket of Baltimore, a colored brother, then sang without accompaniment a plaintive negro hymn which was received with much applause.

Dr. Haines called on the audience to read the Twenty-fourth Psalm responsively, the choir and ministers' platform alternating with the floor. Rev. William Patterson of Toronto offered prayer.

Dr. Haines announced that Rev. G. H. Simmons of Louisville, Ky., who was upon the programme to conduct an open parliament on "The Pledge," was sick and unable to be present. In his place Rev. R. V. Hunter of Terra Haute, Ind., conducted the parliament.

Open Parliament.—"The Pledge."

MR. HUNTER: It does not matter, my friends, whether we are conscripts or whether we are volunteers, or whether we are drafted, just so we are in the ranks of this great Christian Endeavor army. It seems to me that that is about the best work in which we can be engaged. Dr. Haines says that our sympathies go out to this brother in Louisville who is sick. It strikes me that I need your sympathies more than he does. A few moments ago I was asked to take charge of this parliament. Now, if its success depends upon the leader, it is going to be a failure: but if you will take hold of it and make it go, it will be a success. This pledge is a magnificent instrument. We could not get on without it. It is the very heart of the Endeavor movement. It is that around which all gathers. Some one has said that the pledge enables the young people to stand without hitching. I believe that is true. It gives the young people backbone. It makes their religion mean something. Now, I would like to have you this morning tell what the pledge has done for you, what it means in your society. Has it been a help? Could you get on without it? I am going to divide the time into three parts, considering first the question, Do the young people keep the pledge? Second, What are your methods for impressing the pledge upon your young people? and thirdly, I want you to give the strong points of the pledge, in your judgment.

Now, as to the first question, Do the young people keep the pledge? We are going to allow each speaker to take just sixty seconds and no more.

REPLIES: "Ninety-seven per cent keep it."

"Yes and no. They keep the pledge in a measure, and yet it seems to me that the great difficulty before our Christian Endeavor societies is that our members do not fully keep the pledge."

Mr. Hunter: Can anybody suggest how to get them to keep it better?
"Give them a deeper conception of the truth of God's word." "A cultivated conscience." "Personal work is what counts."
"Get them into the conventions." [Applause.] "Get the conventions into them." "Personal work with the delinquents." "The promises of God are conditioned on our being faithful." "More consecration to Christ; more concentration in work." "Full of the spirit of the Lord." "All for Christ and none for self." "Teach them the sense of obligation of the pledge."

Mr. Hunter: Is the pledge being kept as well as it ought to be?
"No."

Mr. Hunter: "What can we do to bring about a more faithful keeping of the pledge?" "I would like to testify that my keeping of the pledge has drawn me into a closer relation with the word of God, and led me into a daily and more systematic reading of it." "The young people do not keep the pledge perfectly, but they keep it better than any other pledge which they have ever taken." [Applause.] "If you can make them understand the pledge, they will keep it." "The Juniors keep it better than the Seniors." [Applause.] "Impress upon them the fact that the pledge is to God, and not to man or to the society." "Begin to cultivate faithfulness in the Junior Society." "The Seniors keep the pledge better than the church-members keep their church covenant." "Have the lookout committee less anxious to hurry members into the society without knowing their motives for joining."

Mr. Hunter: "How many in the building this morning have signed the pledge?" (Nearly the entire audience rose.)

A delegate: "I would like to know by what right we make any distinction in the keeping of the pledge and our church-membership vows." [Applause.] "The best way to get others to keep the pledge is to keep it ourselves."

Mr. Hunter: "We must now pass to the second point: What are your methods for impressing the pledge?" "We do it through a consecrated prayer-meeting committee." "Have the members read the pledge in concert." "Repeat the pledge in concert every time you receive a new member." "Commit the pledge to memory, and repeat it to yourself every hour of prayer." "Not only repeat the pledge in concert, but have plenty of talks explaining it just after you have repeated it." "The pastor has a great deal to do with the keeping of the pledge on the part of the young people. Pastors should cultivate the conscience of the young people on this point."

Dr. Tyler: "I desire to say simply a word to my brethren in the pastorate concerning this matter. I have found that it is profitable to preach a series of sermons on the Christian Endeavor Pledge. [Applause.] Give them a sermon on trusting in Christ, another on striving to please Christ, another on daily Bible-reading, another on daily prayer, another on helping the church, another on the Christian life, reaching a climax with a sermon on entire consecration to Jesus." [Applause.] "Get a great big copy of the pledge and hang it on the assembly wall."

A pastor: "I have taken the same course that Dr. Tyler suggests with marked success." "Set the pledge to music; make a chant of it, and give it a place on the evening programme."

A pastor: "My young people always say amen to every truth I utter from my pulpit, and when I keep that pledge they keep it too." "Let greater care be used in selecting the lookout committee." "Let the lookout committee examine each candidate, and see if he understands the pledge before he is admitted into the society." "Have a special pledge meeting." "Preach to them the doctrine of complete sanctification as found in the nineteenth chapter of Acts, first nine verses." "Impress upon them the personal nature of the pledge. It is not what 'we promise, but what 'I' promise." "Preach the sweet reasonableness of the pledge."

A delegate: "Should we drop the names of those who fail to take part in the meetings?" "No, no." "Educate them and help them." "Get the spirit of this convention into their hearts, and they have got to keep it."

Mr. Hunter: "We must now pass to the third point: What are the strong points of the pledge? This will give opportunity to eight or ten preachers to preach a sermon; but we don't want any of your sermons. [Laughter and applause.] We want you to simply state what you consider the strong points in this pledge, what have been the most helpful to you and to your society." "The first word, 'Trusting,' is the strongest point." "The personal responsibility of every member to Christ." "Taking part in the meeting." "Prayer and reading the Bible every day." "The words, ' Whatever he would like to have me do, I promise him I will strive to do.' We do not say we will do it every time; we will strive to do our best." "Loyalty to Christ, our church, our creed, our country, and society." "Entire consecration in the words ' I promise.'" "The main thing is in the first clause, ' Trusting in the Lord Jesus Christ for strength.' We talk about breaking the pledge, and not keeping it. Why? Because we have not the strength; we are weak. But ' trusting in the Lord Jesus Christ for strength;' if that is kept, all the rest will follow."

The time having arrived for closing the parliament, Mr. Hunter called on Bishop Fallows of Chicago to offer prayer. After prayer a hymn was sung, Mr. Excell leading.

DR. HAINES: We are making history fast in these modern days. Certainly no crusade of the Middle Ages ever had the importance and the lasting influence that the crusade under Christian Endeavor leadership possesses. We are organizing and creating public sentiment, and preparing to drive that sentiment against the great organized evils of society. One of the leaders in this Christian Endeavor movement of creating a right public sentiment, and giving it right direction, is the next speaker whom we are privileged to hear. I, for one, believe that if this movement goes on as it now bids fair to go on, the time will come when this monstrous iniquity of the saloon in America will be buried as the good Welsh woman wanted the Devil to be buried — first killed, and then buried with his face downward, so that if by any chance he should come to life and try to dig his way out, he would only go the deeper. [*Laughter and applause.*] When that result is reached, Mr. John G. Woolley, who is now to speak to us, will be acknowledged as one of the leaders in that magnificent movement.

Mr. Woolley was received with loud applause and the waving of handkerchiefs. He spoke as follows, —

Christian Endeavor vs. The Saloon.

Address of Mr. John G. Woolley.

Three years ago at Minneapolis I spoke to you about gospel temperance. Rarely is a man insane enough to fancy *himself* responsible for such a scene as took place then. Fifteen thousand of you stood up and cheered. One delegation sprang into the aisle, and marched to the platform rail waving a banner with the inscription "Iowa. A schoolhouse on every hilltop and no saloon in the valley!"

The orator was obliterated in an instant, like the first flake of an avalanche; and for one breathless, inexplicable moment our lives fused into one tremendous impulse as we felt the Spirit of God come into the midst, and in the brightness of his presence recognized the divinity of our own humanity, and uttered a fiat.

From that time, every day the liquor traffic lawfully lives concerns the innocence, the honor, and the plighted word of these societies. For we declared, — I have the official record, —

"Since the liquor traffic is the implacable enemy of righteousness and purity, of Christ and his church,

"*Resolved*, That we condemn intemperance in every form; that we stand for total abstinence, for the suppression of the saloon, and for the annihilation of the power of the ' whiskey ring ' in the politics of this nation."

And we meant what we said. We shall make our word good. We *are* making it good.

Albeit none too rapidly. Each house of Congress still has a saloon. Our "Soldiers' Homes" are still institutional drink shops. At our military posts to-day enlisted men in uniform are detailed to do *Federal duty* serving drinks at the canteen bar. In consideration of the payment by it of about one-third of the public revenue, the liquor traffic remains our sovereign industry, censor of our press, controller of our finances, and moderator of our politics. Christian commerce still lights darkest Africa with the blue hell-fire of alcohol, and uses the brain of a race for a wick.

Where is Iowa's silk and golden hallelujah of three years ago? Look for it among the banners. There is Iowa, but that flag has gone down. Moths eat it. The school still stands on the hill, but the valleys of the Western Massachusetts have been quit-claimed back to the saloon. And in nearly all the land the rampant havoc of it riots on.

Try to realize what that means. If the ordinary staple death business of it, since the Minneapolis convention, had been wrought in this most beautiful of cities, Cleveland would be as destitute of human life to-day as the heart of an iceberg. If all the waste of these three fiscal saloon years had fallen within the borders of this State, Ohio would be to-day one vast ash-heap, as desolate as Herculaneum. If the three liquor years last past had focused and culminated here last night in one stupendous homicidal carnival, the Cuyahoga River would to-day flow blood to the bank rim, and crimson Lake Erie to the outer bar.

But much has been done. In party-cursed Indiana, Charles E. Newlin has opened a Quaker cannonade of non-partisan gospel truth, and storms the commonwealth town by town. Edwin D. Wheelock has set the plumed and bladed prairie forests of Illinois whispering from hill to hill a wonderful new gospel of salvation from Peoria, the hell of corn. Herbert B. Ames and a devoted company of praying boys have taken a Montreal election between their knees and scoured it, and made a literature and working plans by which, altered to fit local needs, any Endeavor union can become a wisp of hyssop in God's hand to purge the city clean. Yonder, beyond the lake, Ontario, already the whitest, fairest, cleanest daughter of the great mother land, has forged ahead, with Manitoba, Newfoundland, Nova Scotia, and Prince Edward Island to lead the epoch. The plebiscite has spoken; and the Provincial liquor traffic packs its *lares* and *penates*, its movable plunder, and comes to be annexed to the States, *the land of liberty*, where even to *suggest* a plebiscite is politically infamous. The mayor of Toronto, invited recently to deliver a brief address of welcome to the assembled liquor dealers of the Province, moved the previous question, held it undebatable, decided that the main question should be now put, put it, carried it, and declared that *no enemy of Canada was welcome to Toronto*. And the work goes on, and *will* go on until no license law beslimes the fame of any Christian country.

Two years ago, at New York City, I spoke to you again from a heart that had in that great hour nothing meaner in it than tears and prayers for tempted men and anguished women. And the man is on this platform who has dared to say, *I sold you to a party*. May God, whose truth I spoke and he insulted, forgive him and enlarge him to the size of comprehending that there are experiences in life through which, if a man comes sane, he comes too big for party-lugging, party cowardice, private slander, or personal fear.

I speak to-day upon a topic chosen by the International committee: "THE YOUNG PEOPLE'S SOCIETY OF CHRISTIAN ENDEAVOR *versus* THE SALOON."

Take what road you may of Christian Endeavor, it will lead you to a screened and painted door, back of which *a good man*, so certified by the authorities and thereunto expressly authorized by statute, despite the Word of God and the organic law and reason of the government, pumps the putrid blood of murdered harvests into the veins of the body politic, and gangrene into the hearts and homes of men. That is the saloon, the third person of a despicable trinity, of which the other two are the partisan city and the politic church — this society versus *that*.

I am continually receiving letters asking, "What shall Christian young peple *do* against the saloon?" The question is its own perfect answer, and I can only give it back expanded, as one may blow a rosebud into bloom.

The candid, honest, modest way for one to publish an idea is to exhibit a sample of its operation; and so I answer by a simple showing of my own position, which may, of course, be wrong. The question is, what shall I — a "Christian — man — do — against the saloon?"

First of all *I will be a Christian*. I will keep *myself* pure. I will, as to this thing, abolish the word "temperance." It is the Pharisee of grammar, the arch hypocrite of the vocabulary of this reform, the blood-guiltiest common noun in the language, a quagmire of definition not to be trusted by the foot of reason, or crossed by any but an empty vehicle of thought.

What is "temperance"? A claret cup, a drop of sherry, a glass of ale, a pint of wine, a bottle of whisky, a shameful night, a blank day, debt, dishonor, disease, despair, delirium, death. I have inflected it in all its attributes and languages, from the whisper of the dainty delicious lust of ruby wine moving itself aright, to the adder hiss of the sodden, passionless adultery of drunkenness at the last, and am here alive, but on the way have passed a million men rotting unburied, and though living, lost until the judgment day.

I will be a *Christian*. Henceforth I'll stand upon the mountain top of Paul's great verse, of which the familiar version is: "If meat make my brother to offend, I will not eat meat enough to hurt *myself* though the world perish," but which *is written*, " I will eat *no meat* while the world stands." And drinking wine *does* cause my brother to offend. From the first, the strong, clean, moderate drinker has been, and is to-day, the weak man's schoolmaster to lead him to the gutter.

Am I saying that one who drinks is not a Christian? No; but he is not *such* a Christian as can help in this endeavor. A drinking church cannot rebuke the drinking world. A tippling Christian is a teacher of tippling, a decoy self-anchored in the slough of animalism, luring prey for the saloon, a corrupter of youth, for which offense, merely alleged and guessed at, Socrates was condemned to swallow hemlock for his country's good in the twilight of reform, two thousand years ago. They who would lend a hand to this endeavor must have a *clean* hand to lend. For *this* surgery there must be aseptic fingers and ballots sterilized by the very health of God.

In the perplexing movements of patriotic service I will keep faith with Jesus Christ, though it cost peace, pride, prestige, pulpit, or party. I will confess him *before people*, and on election day, which in this land of equal rights is *man's* day; I will show myself a *Christian* voter, fit to represent unfranchised womanhood at the *polls*. I will go to him, hear his words, and whatsoever he says unto *me*, I will do it. Upon that rock I will build my politics, and the gates of hell shall not prevail against it.

I will take up my cross *daily*, — not semi-weekly, — and will *follow* him up the long Calvary of criticism, suspicion, uncharity, and persecution, to the skull-shaped dome at the land's end of Christian Endeavor, and abide the issue there. Cross or coronation, loss or gain, pleasure or pain, glory or disgrace, life or death, in my person, in my property and politics, I will be a Christian.

I will be a man, an active, definite, persistent, self-respecting and respect-compelling *man ;* no flunky to a party or a sect; no toady to a majority; no trimmer to the popular breeze; no lisping baby-talker to committees, no whimpering petitioner of my own servants; no whispering, apologetic preacher, with a gag; no wire-puller's Punch and Judy penny puppet annex to a party show; no straddling, small, and easy reformer; no driveling camp follower of the world's forward march; no dreary spouter of the Concordance; no Christian whose convictions require editing; no sniveling, moral coward* trembling at a politician's sneer; no pastor whose politics are queer; no crawfish pietist backing under a creed at the approach of a new thought. *I will be intelligent*. I will take a prohibition newspaper and read it. I will have an opinion, and express it. *I will be consistent*. I will let no man despise me. I will not despise myself; if I keep political company where saloon-keepers feel at home, I will be man enough not to pray, "Thy kingdom come on earth." I will be too much of a man to talk of taking the world for Christ while I am consenting to farm out the highways of my own country to saloons and live on the rentals. I will hold no politician's coat while he stones a prophet or denies full citizenship to a woman. By the grace of God I will be a Christian Christian and a manly man.

I will be "against the saloon" and anything that favors, fears, or ignores it. The liquor traffic is the foot-rot of civilization. Saloons are the progeny of cities betrayed by party politics. I will renounce utterly and forever all allegiance to any political party in municipal government. I will not be bound by a caucus. But when a citizen's meeting conflicts with my prayer-meeting I will miss the prayer-meeting. I will count any man the city's enemy who drags his party into its affairs. I will trust no man in city politics who winks at the saloon in national politics.

I will not be cajoled, frightened, nor jeered into the stupid wickedness of trying to secure good men to enforce bad laws. *Any man* is good enough to grant or sign a license. The men who levy, collect, and disburse the price of the city's shame shall never be *my* representatives. The uniformed supervisor of a stipendiary public virtue shall never wear *my* star. While the law is wrong I will not touch it. Let shrewdness, greed, and party policy look out for themselves; I am for Christ and the church.

In national affairs I will belong to a party, and be true to it, so true that when it goes wrong, I will leave it and go straight ahead until it catches up. I will scratch the wickedness out of its ticket, and then throw the ticket away, unless I can stand with it upon a clean, brave, open platform. A man who is false to himself cannot be true to *anything;* and a party that asks a man to belie himself and *speak easy* his convictions, will in time betray both him and the country. A coward is potentially a traitor. I will square my politics to my church, or leave the church. The man, the ticket, or the party that expects or desires votes from the saloon shall have no vote from me.

Two great political parties strive for pre-eminence in our national affairs. It was so from the beginning; it will be so to the end. Their names change, and the lines of their cleavage, but not their general character. The resultant of their contending power records the progress of this country. The problem of our Christian civilization is to diminish the angle of their drawing apart, until in some great day, *a clean church* shall slip the yoke of Jesus Christ upon their mighty necks and make them pull together for a thousand years. Do you say the saloon will persist? What if it does? A clean church will win its customers and keepers, to a man. Even two hundred and fifty thousand saloons would be an infinitesimal trifle in the race for power against a clean church. Let who will win this election, sell the licenses, and administer the all-pervasive paltry-treason of the spoils; when the clean church comes, whose right it is, she will take, without a rival or a question, the scepter of the world, and reign, I will be for *that*. These hands are hers, only two of millions, but I will wash *them*, by the grace of God, and keep them clean for her. *No sales, no spoils, no saloon votes, in Christian Endeavor!*

Great men have said to me, the humblest locust-eater in the wilderness, with fine, high admonition in their voice and mien, "Preach the old gospel!" I do. I did for six clean years. God helping me, I will to-day. I have it from the mouth of its first minister, fresh from the secret place of the Most High, unshopworn, unseminaried, uncoached by doctors of divinity, uncriticisable, ineligible for a salary, incorrigibly clear, smelling of wild honey, "a man *sent from God* whose name was John."

I will maintain to-day that he lifts most the Son of God who exalts mankind the most. No man cometh unto the Father but by *being* a son, and no man becomes a son of God but by being a *man*. To *live* is Christ; to preach or to "belong to church" is anything or nothing — Paul, Barnabas, or Cephas; Peter, who denied his Lord at the election; Eutychus, who slept while Paul spoke; Ananias, who lied about his taxes; or you or I, who do all three or neither.

I preach the gospel according to John. Listen: "*Prepare ye* the *way* of the Lord; make his paths *straight*. Every valley *shall be filled*, and every mountain and hill *shall be brought low*, and the crooked *shall be made straight*, and the rough places *shall be made smooth*. O generation of vipers! O crawling, slippery, sinuous, stealthy, wriggling Pharisees, who hath advised you to *flee?* How can cause escape effect? What authority do you find for *running away* from the consequences of your own sin or your own neglect? Wrath is the whole 'afterward' of unforgiven wrong. Whither can we fly from that? Turn about! Face the foe! Repent! Stand up and meet the results of your doings — then live so worthily as to make wrath itself repent! *Let go* of Abraham. Be men on your own account. Trust no old respectability or ancestry or history. Let the dead past bury its dead. Divine wrath pursues nobody, but men are burning other men for fuel *now*. Take an ax! Strike at the root of the Upas tree that breathes out poison to the world, nor rest until the very wood is burned to ashes; — *so* get forgiveness for *yourself, and give all flesh a chance to see salvation.*"

When Jesus Christ heard *that*, he said, "Baptize me!" and when the preacher hesitated, added, "Come on, my brother John; we will show that courtesy to the past, and by this simple seeming useless link couple the ages together," and then walked straight away dripping from the water of ceremony into a wilderness of temptation and the hot heart of the world; and the rigid old ceremonial heaven split like a chrysalis, and men saw that the spirit of God was no abstraction infinitely distant, but a thing of the earth, as real, plain-tinted, and timid as a dove. Seeing which John prophesied, "*Preaching* is at a discount hereafter, *Messiah is a doer.*"

And Jesus "took the road," to *live* John's gospel, and prepare a way for the world's weary feet Godward; and at the end of it was spiked upon a guide-post where heaven, earth, and hell cornered, and after he was dead still preached, with bleeding hands outstretched, in awful pantomime, " *Prepare ye the way of the Lord!* "

So, and yet not so, labor laid a human body down, they say, for every railroad tie across the Isthmus. They died, but they prepared a way for commerce through Panama to India's wealth and California's gold; and every train that draws this world along is lifted up on *labor crucified.*

"*Prepare* the way;" it means *build a road beforehand.* Jesus abbreviated it as *pr-a-y*, expanded it in the Lord's Prayer, and expounded it, saying, "When ye pray," remember that the infinite and gracious Providence has left nothing unprovided for; your prayer, if it be anything a father ought to grant a child, is answered from the foundation of the world; therefore, "believe, rest assured, ye *have* the thing ye pray for;" pray about what ye *have*, and not for what ye have not. Take possession in your Father's name of everything in sight; hold it up and say, "Father, see what I have found, or thought, or made!" and he will say, — has said, — " Whatsoever ye discover, invent, or work out, *filially*, ye shall *have.* For this is the law, and, *therefore*, the prophecy. Filial labor is prevailing prayer. Faith is honesty toward God. Fidelity is omnipotence — a filial son cannot fail until his father does.

A city is famine stricken; the people pray for rain. The heavens are brass; the roofs curl and crackle in the heat, and the leaves writhe from the stems in pulseless air; a spark of fire would mean a holocaust. Some morning they lift their eyes to the hills, cease saying prayers, and *lay down pipes*, press through the crowd of difficulties until they touch the folded granite of his garment's hem; and the virtue, blessing, health, coolness, and safety of the mountain's heart come into the city and abide. The rain they prayed for had fallen years before; the lack was not the water, but the *way.* "Prepare ye the way of the Lord!"

"*Make his paths straight!*" God is not limited, but like his own lightning comes the shortest way, responds to facilities. Take out the curves, undo the snarls of custom and of law, let us have straight work for his appearing, no easy, zigzag compromise to indolence; straight, level, smooth for him.

But the valley! Fill it with mountain tops! Mix lowliest earth with crystal summit rock; advance upon the submerged by the exalted; muster the hills in squadrons, march them to the heart of the abyss and break it! You scholar of the diamond-pointed intellect, set it against the cliff! You statesman, turn on power! You preacher, "rightly dividing the word of truth," follow where science excavates, charge the caverns with fulminate, and lay down your own life for fuse! Now, voter, thrust in ballots, the clay of civil faith! Now, teacher, tamp it home! All ready! Truth and faith and human life *versus* the black basalt of error! Now pray for fire; and it shall come to pass that some consecrated child of God, whose feet are planted on the crushed and pent up truth, shall stretch up his hands in the night of one of earth's Gethsemanes, groping, dead beat with agony, and at random clutch one of Heaven's low-swinging electrodes, and "THE LORD SHALL DESCEND FROM HEAVEN WITH A SHOUT."

Now, while the mountains smoke, you with a pick, clear away, and you shovelers and those with hammers, all together; open it for teams and trams; lay on loam, walk on it, roll on it, fertilize it, plant it. On into the forest, — fell trees, train vines, hew logs, set fires, scoop out cups for the springs. "The kingdom of heaven is *at hand.*" "*Go through, go through the gates; prepare ye the way of the people*" — TO FOLLOW. "*Cast up, cast up the highway; gather out the stones; lift up a standard for the people.*" " *And all flesh — prince, peasant, beggar, thief, horse, dog — shall SEE Salvation.*" The rest is in their own hands.

The American desert gasped in a drought ages long, yearning up to lakes and rivers of mirage that ever tantalized in mocking splendor. Each individual cactus hoarded its bright drops, poised its defensive javelins, lit its scarlet danger-signals, and gloried in *its own;* but still the plain languished in the hot simoom from year to year, and saw no hope. One day a band of laborers, directed by a scholar and ordered by the law, came and trenched the fevered sand and set the river's heart a-beating through the panting waste; and to-day vine and wheat and flax and corn wave a doxology together for multiplying homes.

I am tired of hearing so much about " *my personal* Saviour." O poor, small soul, of course he *is* your personal Saviour; but not because you have said or done or believed something, nor because you are *you*, but because you are a *man*, — one of a *lot* swept from the cross-trees of hell when Jesus Christ ran her down. God so loved *the world* that he sent his *every* begotten Son to hunt selfishness, slavery, and superstition out of it; to level it for weary feet, straighten it for the haste of the King's business, drain it against miasma, dyke it against flood, pipe it against fire, wire it for light and power, mine it for gems and gold, and farm it into universal brotherhood.

There is an American desert more bleak and desolate and famished than ever western wind or ravening wolf howled over. Across its arid ridges Capital puffs its flabby jowls in deadly peril, and jibbers like an idiot about the scenery and the sunset; and Labor gasps and yelps and staggers, and, with dry tongue protruding, snaps at friend and foe like a mad dog. It reeks with the blood of millions who would else have been stars in the crown of Jesus Christ. It whitens with the bones of innocent women and little children, dragged thither from our very altars by the greedy, red-mouthed pack of two hundred and fifty thousand saloons protected by the law. It is drunkenness, the *mauvaise terre* — the scourge, the pestilence, the perdition of living men, the wrath of God for violated harvests and mercenary public virtue. And we have been fleeing from it, or dancing about ridiculous incantation fires, or drinking wine and praising the gods of license gold. The hand of Jehovah writes upon the wall of the world in burning letters : *"Prepare ye the way of the Lord!"* *The liquor traffic ought to die; and any politics or any religion that postpones or ignores that ought to die too, and be buried with it in the middle of the king's highway. AND IT WILL.*

Mr. Woolley's address aroused very great enthusiasm, his fervid rhetoric and eloquent utterance commanding the closest attention, and frequently awakening loud applause. After the address the audience were favored with a sacred solo, "Calvary," sung very beautifully by Miss Minnie O'Connor of Cleveland. After a number of announcements were made by Mr. Baer, the banner for good citizenship was presented.

Presentation of Banner for Best Work in Good Citizenship.

MR. BAER: The United Society of Christian Endeavor is pleased to present a banner to the Local Union of Christian Endeavor that, in the estimate of a competent committee, has done the most work for good citizenship during the year. The committee have based their estimate, as was advertised and suggested, upon the reports that came in. I have asked Rev. W. R. Taylor, D.D., president of the New York Union, to present this banner to Mr. Frank E. Page, president of the Chicago Union. [*Loud Applause.*]

DR. TAYLOR: My dear brother, on behalf of the United Society of Christian Endeavor, it becomes my very pleasant duty to present to you this banner. I desire to say that no more honorable testimonial has ever been borne away from an International Christian Endeavor Convention than this which is awarded to the Chicago Local Union. Professor Fiske, in his admirable book, "The Beginnings of New England," has shown that there have been three great methods of nation-building; first, the Oriental method of conquest without incorporation. A great military genius would sweep over country after country, reducing the inhabitants practically to a state of slavery, but conferring upon them none of the benefits of citizenship. That type of nation having proved itself wanting, the Roman idea of nation-making came into play; namely, that of conquest with incorporation, but without representation. As you know, for centuries that idea was dominant in Europe. That type also showed itself insufficient, and there came the Teutonic idea of government based upon representation. We do not know where the Teutonic tribes got that idea, but they brought it with them. Wherever they went throughout Europe, there went the principle of representative government. In England that idea came to its most perfect development, and for two reasons: first, because the Saxons were almost the only ones of the Teutonic tribes that had not been reached by Christian missionaries when they came and made the conquest of England; and in the second place, carrying their ideas of government, they drove out the former inhabitants of the land; and there, in a virgin soil, these ideas had a chance to grow for a century and a half. A few centuries afterward this principle of government by representation was contending with the old Roman idea of government without representation; and we all know that English liberty and American liberty came as the result of that struggle. But we should not forget that our liberty is due to something more than the English love of liberty. Its preservation and its triumph in the world to-day are due to the Puritan zeal for religion, the Puritan zeal for the kingdom of God. Professor Fiske is authority for the statement that, had it not been for Cromwell and his Puritan followers, there is no reason to believe that the cause of popular liberty would not have perished from the earth in the seventeenth century. And so liberty and religion have gone hand in hand, and so they must go hand in hand, if we are to come to the perfect state of the kingdom of God upon the earth. We have come to realize in the Church of Christ that piety and patriotism go together, and that the good Christian must be a good citizen. I take all the more pleasure in presenting this banner, Mr. President, because we have done something in New York State in this direction, and because the first martyr to the cause of good citizenship, as promulgated by the Christian Endeavor, was a New York man. It may not be known to all the members of this Convention that it was a Christian Endeavorer, a member of one of the Presbyterian churches of Troy, who fell under Bat Shea's bullet at Troy, being the first martyr in the cause of good citizenship. [*Applause.*] I understand that one determining reason for the awarding of this banner to the Chicago Union is not only the fact that it has done such good work in its own city, but that it has done pioneer work in determining methods to be followed by other societies. With great pleasure, therefore, Mr. President, I hand to you this most honorable trophy for your year's work. [*Applause.*]

MR. PAGE: You may be sure it is to me a great joy, and it will be to my friends at home, to take back this banner to our city union. It is a surprise to me, my first notice of it having been when Secretary Baer called for me to come forward. I can only say that we have tried to do a little; we have tried to do our best. I feel that it will be an inspiration to our people to take this banner to them. Just now, when our beloved city is crushed and bleeding in this great industrial struggle, mobs upon her streets and soldiers parading her highways and guarding her interests, we shall feel a new desire, a new inspiration, to go forth as a band of Christian soldiers marching as to war under the banner of our Lord and Saviour, Jesus Christ, working and fighting to the end for Christ, for the church, and for our country. [*Applause.*]

DR. HAINES: Mr. Baer thinks he knows all about this programme, but he is greatly mistaken. He knows a great deal, but he doesn't know it all. Your attention is now asked to the next item on the programme. It is not on the programme as printed, but it is really on the programme, and it will meet, I am sure, with the approval of everybody in this great hall.

At this announcement Mr. J. E. Cheesman, Chairman of the Hall Committee, stepped forward with a magnificent basket of flowers in white and gold.

MR. CHEESMAN: It is with great pleasure that the Cleveland Union of Christian Endeavor societies recognize in our general secretary a Cleveland boy. [*Applause.*] He knows all about our city. He knows its homes, he knows its beauty, he knows its smoke, he knows the genial character of its citizens. He knows its hospitality — and so do you, don't you? [*Loud applause.*] He knows the salubrious breezes that you have heard about, and which have fanned our heated brows for the last few hours — some of them. It is with very great pleasure that I, as president of the Christian Endeavor Union of Cleveland, give to Secretary Baer, as a gentle reminder of the love it bears to him, this basket of flowers. [*Loud applause.*]

MR. BAER: Friends of the Cleveland Union, this expression is one that I feel very much. I have not forgotten, I assure you, the first eighteen years of my life — except the first two months of it [*laughter*] — for when I was a boy, two months old, I decided to move to Cleveland. [*Laughter.*] I lived the first eighteen years of my life in this beautiful city, and I have always enjoyed the thought of knowing that when I should come to this convention it would be a home coming. As I have ridden back and forth from the hotel to this building, I have passed familiar churches — my old church home among them. Together with my father on this platform to-day, who is a visitor again to this city, we are enjoying the hospitality of our old home. I assure you that it is best for me to sit down and simply thank you heartily. From the bottom of my heart I appreciate honestly and sincerely this token that you have chosen to extend to me. [*Applause.*]

After singing the hymn, "Onward, Christian Soldiers," Dr. Haines introduced Rev. Smith Baker, D.D., pastor of the Maverick Congregational Church of East Boston, as the next speaker. Dr. Baker was given a cordial welcome by the audience.

Christian Citizenship.

Address of Rev. Smith Baker, D.D.

God seems to have made of our country a general mess-pot, into which he is bringing of all peoples, and out of which he is to bring a larger Christian civilization. Those of you who have been abroad and mingled with the common people in England, Germany, France, or Italy, securing to a moderate degree their confidence, have learned that their ears are upon the ground listening to every report which comes from America, and their eyes are intently watching the results of our democracy. You know, also, with what eagerness they listen to every story told them by some friend who returns after a few years' residence in our land, and how they drink in all his accounts of the freedom and the prosperity of the common people among us. It is this listening by the masses of the old world, and their thinking and talking among themselves, which is shaking every throne in Europe, and which, before another century is gone, will make the old world democratic in its governments. Thus our country is the world's great object lesson, to which humanity is looking for a solution of the people's rights and the people's destinies. We are not responsible simply for our own government, but we are responsible for the leadership of the world.

The question with us is, how can we transform the millions who come to us in ignorance of the principles of our politics and make them Americans; for it is not only democracy, but American democracy, and not only American democracy, but Christian democracy, which is the hope of our land and of the world. In order to perpetuate the principles which we have inherited from our fathers, in order to truly represent pure democracy to the world, in order to transform and mold into sympathy with us those who come to us, our democracy must be Christian; hence the importance of the subject, "Christian Citizenship."

In what does Christian citizenship consist?

1. Christian citizenship must be intelligent. It may do in a monarchical form of government for only the rulers to be intelligent, or for a few select minds to be cultured; but in a democracy, where every man is the peer of every other man in rights and in responsibilities, there can be no strength, no permanent growth, only in the universal intelligence of its citizens. Hence the principles of our government and the fundamental truths of political economy should be taught, not only in our colleges and universities, but in our common schools, to the common boys and girls who are to live in the humble walks of life. It should be one of the required studies that every boy and girl should know the Constitution of the United States, and the fundamental facts in the history of our land, that in the remotest hamlet every voter shall be an intelligent voter.

Politics is a Christian duty in the United States, and every man by the necessity of his birthright is a politician; and he is recreant to himself, to his home, and to his country, unless to a greater or less extent he is conversant with political questions. This was one of the safeguards of old New England, that, though the majority of her citizens were not educated men, they were intelligent men upon all the common questions of the day. Her farmers and mechanics had three books which they read, and from which they discussed local and national questions of interest; and these three books were the Bible, the revised statutes, and the dictionary. Hence the New England farmer and the New England mechanic voted intelligently. He discussed with his neighbor during the long winter evenings, he discussed in his family at all times questions of religion and politics, and the country store and the country shoeshop were debating places, where the honest men of old New England quickened each other's minds on all public questions. The New England farmer also educated his children in politics.

If you will allow a personal reference, I shall never cease to be grateful for the example of my own father, who, though a New England countryman, was a New England politician, with his farm and his store. He provided himself with the political newspaper and the religious newspaper; and when I was only a lad just entering my teens he would have me read to him daily the political news, and discuss with him the questions of the day. I did not understand the old gentleman's motives; but I now see it was his wise way of educating his boy in the politics of the times, so that at the age of fifteen I was more conversant with the particulars of political questions than I am at the present time, and thus the boys of New England and the young men of New England were intelligent voters. They had convictions, they thought for themselves, they voted for themselves, and their votes were honest votes. This intelligence should be required of all.

A man should be required to reside in this country long enough to read its language, to understand the meanings of its institutions, to begin to be Americanized in his intelligence and his character, before he should be permitted to vote. This requiring American boys to go to school twenty-one years before they can exercise the right of franchise, and allowing the foreigner, who knows nothing of our language or of our institutions, to vote within one month after he has landed upon our shores, is not only a disgrace, but a peril. No other nation does it. We cannot long continue to do it with safety to ourselves. If men are dissatisfied with their native land, if they wish the freer air of our land, let them come; but let them stay here long enough to know something of the difference between our government and the government they have left.

2. The second qualification of Christian citizenship is impartiality.

This is the glory of democracy, that it honors no man for his wealth, for his birth, or for his culture, but that it recognizes the manhood of every man, be he poor or rich, learned or ignorant, white or black, who is seeking to be a man. This is the justice and the equality which give the poor man the same vote as the rich man, and the laboring man the same vote as the educated man, and the black man the same vote as the white man. It must be understood that in a Christian land every man shall have his rights, not only of freedom of speech, but of freedom of ballot, no matter who he is, where he is, or how he votes. Any intimidation at the polls is a crime against democracy, whether it be in Boston, in Cleveland, or in New Orleans.

This is not only liberty, but this is justice; and liberty without justice is constant peril. Yea, liberty only is liberty as it is just, and it is only just as it is impartial; and here is one of the dark clouds, even now larger than a man's hand, which is the next great peril we are to meet.

As a Christian democracy our fathers made and revealed to the world their right and power to be an independent nation and to gain their independence. As a Christian democracy they revealed afterwards their power to defend themselves from a foreign foe. As a Christian democracy they, later still, revealed their power to conquer another nation and to extend their territory by aggression. As a Christian democracy they, later still, in the greatest conflict which the world has ever known, revealed their power to suppress rebellion within their borders. And now the last great test which is to reveal the power of democracy to live is the test of universal suffrage — the most fearful experiment a nation ever tried, and in the midst of which we are now at work. And the test is only commenced. It will be a failure unless it is maintained, unless the ballot-box is kept pure and honest, free and fair, every time, everywhere.

I do not wish to sound alarm; but the peril of our country is not in Socialism, not in Romanism. We shall Americanize the Roman Church. But the peril of our country is the denial of the honest exercise of the ballot-box. So long as in any part of our land at any time any man cannot vote as he pleases without fear of any other man, just so long our nation is in peril. There is a patient race among us; a race whom we have lifted out of bondage; a race to whom we have promised political rights; a race who have suffered more and borne more than any other race; a race who, since their emancipation, have grown in their intelligence and in their wealth faster than any other race in the history of the world; a race who are increasing in their intelligence and their property, but increasing in their numbers still faster; a race who, in a short time, will be a vast majority in many portions of our domain; a race who fought our battles for us, and were heroic to the last drop of their blood in the defense of our land; a race who, by every right of sacrifice, every right for wrong done upon them, every right of manhood, can claim the unmolested ballot. It is no secret that they have it not; but as sure as human nature is human nature, as sure as justice is justice, as sure as liberty is liberty, as sure as God is on the side of the oppressed, just so sure they must and will have it. Their patience will come to an end; and that is the awful, the fearful thing, which is the darkest cloud in our horizon, that the patience of this race will become exhausted, and then woe to that part of the land in which they are found when that race rises, as it will rise in the inevitable laws of God's providence, unless their rights are given them. Then a more awful scene of bloodshed than this country ever saw will have come to pass.

We might have, years ago, for a good deal less money, by wise legislation, freed every slave in our land, in peace, without the shedding of a drop of blood, without the loss of a single life. But we refused to be just, and God compelled us to give the negro freedom at the cost of billions of money, and rivers of blood, and thousands of lives, and the wrecking of thousands of homes.

Let us not tempt Providence to another scourge. Let us by wise and firm justice to the thousands to whom we have given liberty secure to them their rights, and avert the inevitable deluge of blood and suffering which must otherwise come. These words may seem harsh words, but they are prophetic words, which some of the children here may live to sadly witness unless our suffrage becomes impartial, and the colored man can vote as freely as the white man.

Then, again, impartial suffrage means not only impartial as between the races, but it means impartial as between the sexes. In the gospel there is neither male nor female, in the church of God there is neither male nor female, and in a Christian democracy there should not be. What justice is there in forbidding an intelligent, cultured woman, possessed of property, who is conversant with the history of her land, paying taxes to support the schools of her land, the right to vote? what justice is there in allowing a poor, penniless, illiterate foreigner to vote, when such a woman is not permitted to do so? I do not propose to discuss this question; but when the woman who is capable of being president of a college, when the woman who is capable of presiding over business affairs, when the woman who is capable of teaching boys and girls the principles of our Constitution, when the woman who is capable of taking care of a home and children, and oftentimes her husband also, shall have justice done her, she will have the right to vote. These are truths which Christian democracy and which Christian citizenship must recognize.

Christian citizenship includes impartiality in its administration, that it shall not favor in any way, directly or indirectly, one nationality, one class, one sect, or one religion more than another. Christian citizenship means the ruling of the land upon Christian principles, not the ruling of the land by any church or by all the churches. Christian citizenship makes the spirit of Christianity a living power, which shall permeate all parts of government.

Christian citizenship includes no organic connection between church and state. As the Christian man in his Christian life is above any organization, so the church in its spiritual power is above all government. And while the church in its spiritual life is to be superior to all government, it is to be absolutely free from all government, and the government to be free from it, only as it shall protect its members in their rights. Hence it is understood with the spirit of Christian citizenship that no church or sect should in any way, directly or indirectly, receive any support from the government. Not only must the ordinances of the church be free from any governmental control, and the officers of the church be free from governmental control, and the institutions of the church be free from governmental control, but all its schools, colleges, and societies are to be absolutely beyond any aid from the government in any way. This is the logical and absolutely necessary condition of Christian citizenship, that every man in a Christian democracy, that every sect in a Christian democracy, shall be religiously free and independent of the government under which they live. The Protestant shall receive no help. The Romanist shall receive no help. The Jew shall receive no help. The Agnostic shall receive no help. But every one shall be free from all connection with the government, other than that of protection. This must be insisted upon — the absolute impartiality of the government, without which the little wedge of peril will constantly be entering into our political life. And this is fair; it is fair for the Jew, and fair for the Romanist, and fair for the Protestant, and fair for everybody; and the opposite is unfair. They tell us, you know, that it is unfair to compel the Romanist to support his parochial school and also be taxed for the public school; but it is only unfair as the Romanist taxes himself. It would be unfair for the government to release the Romanist from his school tax, or the Methodist from his school tax, or the Baptist from his school tax, or the Agnostic from his school tax; yea, such would be confusion confused. The Romanist has the same opportunity to teach his children the faith of his church outside of the public schools that the Jew or the Protestant or any other sect has; and for them to claim more than the others claim is unfair on the part of the Romanist, and not unfair on the part of the government.

3. A Christian democracy must be ethical in its character. It cannot be confined to questions of roads and bridges and telegraphs or public schools, or the mere administration of justice, or the mere protection of the citizen from physical ills; but the Christian democracy must be interested in every question which pertains to the elevation of the community in its moral character, and the defense of the community from immoral influences. You cannot banish moral questions from national politics any more than you can banish moral questions from the home. As the family is but a collection of individuals, and the town but a collection of families, and the State but a collection of towns, and the nation but a collection of States, so questions which interest the homes must enter into the interests of the town, of the State, and of the nation. Whatsoever has an evil influence in a family, and tempts the boys in that family to ruin, fathers are in duty bound to oppose and to prohibit. He is recreant to his fatherhood who fails to do this; and thus whatsoever in a town imperils its youth and its young men, and tempts them from their manhood, that town is recreant to itself unless it prohibits. And whatsoever in the commonwealth is working disease and death and leading men away into dishonesty and ruin, that State is recreant to itself unless it prohibits. And so with the whole land, whatsoever imperils the welfare of the nation must be put away; and the Christian democracy cannot be silent and inactive upon moral questions any more than can a father in his home. Hence all questions of reform which pertain to the questions of intemperance or impurity or to gambling cannot be kept out of politics; for politics is the science of government, and government must protect its citizens. A Christian democracy must protect itself from that which will corrupt its people.

Ethical questions, as Christianity advances, intelligence rises, and civilization increases, will more and more come to the front. Yea, the time will come when what now seems to be purely material questions, like the building of railroads or the drainage of a city, will be considered from an ethical standpoint rather than from the physical.

More and more the political parties of our land are to become representatives of moral ideas. More and more every party is to be known by the moral tendency of its platform. More and more every citizen must choose his party by the ethical questions which it represents, and more and more ethical questions are to enter into the character of the men who represent us. There is no sentiment more pernicious, more deadly in every way, than that which is sometimes spoken in high places: No matter what a man's private character is if he only has right political principles. A nation of corrupt men will become a corrupt nation; and a man's character is more and more to decide whether he shall be chosen a leader; for a corrupt man, even though his politics may be right, is always an unsafe man. Away, then, with the pernicious sentiment that no matter what a man's character is if his political sentiments are correct. Such teachers are baneful teachers; they poison our young men. More and more let it be seen that the parties must be represented by good men in order to have the suffrage of good men.

4. Christian citizenship means independent citizenship. In a democracy, where every man is the peer of every other man in his rights, every man should be an independent man, untrammeled by any other man or by any party. In this dignity every Christian is to stand. He is to read for himself, to think for himself, to act for himself. He who does not is a slave. The too common sentiment that we must go with our party, whether the party be right or not, is the bane of modern politics. Every man should have his party convictions. Every man should be a Republican, if he wishes to be, or a Democrat, or a Prohibitionist, or a third party man. It is his right to belong to any party where his convictions lead him; but every man should stand in his dignity above any party, and no party should be sure of any man's vote simply because they ask it. Every party should feel that the humblest man is superior to their lash; that

they cannot buy him; that they cannot frighten him; that, unless they give him the right man, he is free and will vote for some other man. Only thus are parties to be kept pure. As long as any party feels sure of our votes because we have gone with that party, just so long we have no power in that party, but are simply the tools of its leaders. Just as long as any party feels that it must respect our wishes, just so long every man is its master, and not the party master of him. If you are a Democrat, when it is understood that you will not vote the Democratic ticket unless it gives you a man who is honorable, then they will be careful to give you honorable men. If you are a Republican in sentiment, when it is understood that you will not vote the Republican ticket unless they give you an honorable man to vote for, then they will give you honorable men. Thus the purity of every party is to be maintained only by the personal independence of each man in the party. Every American citizen is to be superior to all parties; and if his party asks him to vote for a man whom he personally condemns, then let him vote for the man of his convictions, and let him stand up in the personal dignity of his conscience. The liberty of scratching the ballot, and thus maintaining the right of voting for just so much of the ticket as you please, and rejecting just so much as you please, is the only position that a self-respecting man can take, and, as I have already said, this is the only safeguard from political corruption.

We sometimes complain that politicians are seeking the achievement of some selfish plans. This is doubtless too true. But the leaders can only lead those who will be led. The leaders are the very quickest men to become servants when common voters stand up in their dignity and in their independence.

5. Christian citizenship means a conscientious responsibility.

In a monarchical government the common man may pursue his private interests, and feel that he has no responsibility in the government under which he lives; but in a republic every public question is of private interest, and is every man's concern. We are not mere servants in the firm, we are partners of the firm; hence, we cannot roll off the responsibility of any public question from our hearts. Every American citizen is in duty bound to be a politician. He is one by birthright, and he cannot avoid it, and the responsibility of the government rests upon him as truly as upon the President himself. The United States senator who neglects his vote when some important measure is pending in the Senate, who stays away from the place to which he is sent by his constituents, is no more recreant to his duty than any American citizen who stays away from the polls on election day. For every town or ward voting-place is the first meeting of the American congress of which every voter is a member, and any man who stays away from the polls and refuses to vote refuses to discharge his duty as a citizen. He is recreant to himself, to his country, to his God. Voting is a religious duty in Christian citizenship, a responsibility which we cannot throw off upon another. And though my vote does not change results, that does not change my responsibility to vote.

Yea, they tell us that the elections at the ballot-box are decided mostly by the previous caucus. Very well, so let it be. Then the responsibility of Christian citizenship goes back into the caucus; and no man has a right to stay away from the primary caucus of the party to which he belongs, and then complain that only unworthy men were given him to vote for. It is an obligation to be at the primary caucus and help decide what men's names shall be presented before their fellow-citizens; and if this caucus meet on prayer-meeting night, then let the deacons of my church go to the caucus and leave the women to pray. Let them see to it in the beginning that the start is right, and that only good and true men are presented to the community.

When Christian men and women shall rise up, and in their dignity of Christian citizenship claim and exercise their rights and obligations, then our parties will be purer and our public men better.

These, then, are the five conditions of Christian citizenship, — intelligence, impartiality, righteousness, independence, and conscientiousness. As these five principles are pressed to the front, our ship of state will stand any waters through which she shall be called to pass. She can meet foes without and she can conquer foes within. With these she shall be to the world the vanguard of civilization. With these she may welcome to herself all the world can send her, from the highest to the lowest. With these she will boil down and bring out into Christian civilization all nations and all peoples.

The session closed with the benediction by Rev. Dr. B. B. Tyler.

THE TENT.

Long before the hour for opening the exercises of the morning the tent was crowded. All over the audience different delegations were singing their favorite hymns. Sometimes four or five hymns resounded through the tent simultaneously.

The preliminary song service was led by Mr. J. G. Warren. Rev. C. A. Dickinson of Boston presided.

The programme opened with the hymn, "Scatter the Sunshine." All then united in repeating the Twenty-third Psalm. Prayer was offered by Rev. Richard L. Swain of Massachusetts.

Mr. Edwin D. Wheelock of Chicago then conducted the open parliament, which had for its subject, "What has Your Society done to Promote Good Citizenship?"

OPEN PARLIAMENT.

What has Your Society done to Promote Good Citizenship?

MR. WHEELOCK: In this blessed land of ours few gifts are greater and few more abused than that of citizenship. To be a citizen is to be a ruler; to be a righteous ruler is to be the direct ambassador of the Most High God; and therefore no present question is of greater importance to the progress of the kingdom of God than that of Christian Citizenship. The future welfare of our nation, yea, its very existence, depends less upon labor questions, tariffs and silver bills, than upon loyalty to Jesus Christ on the part of its citizens. Professor Herron has said in a recent letter, "I can see but two ways in which the course of our nation's history may move in the next twenty years; one way leads to anarchy, and the other leads straight to the recognition of the kingship of Jesus." Righteousness exalteth a nation. The wages of sin is death to a state as well as to a man. Men are often Christians in their business, their homes, their private life, and absolutely atheistic in their politics, in their citizenship, denying allegiance to God by casting their ballots for things which are hateful in his sight, at the bequest of some political party. As a result, political rings and the saloons rule our country; crime and corruption are upon every hand; votes are sold to the highest bidder, from the Senate to the ward caucus, and anarchy hovers as a vulture over us. No government can long exist under such a state of affairs.

We must have a pacific revolution or we must go to destruction. Either Jesus Christ must rule or we are lost. The whole nation groaneth and travaileth in pain, waiting for redemption from the curse of a competitive system which makes every man the lawful prey of his brother; from the curse of the saloon, which daily crucifies our Lord afresh; and from the curse of the professional politician, who has said in his heart, "There is no God."

That redemption can come only through Jesus Christ, the Saviour of nations as well as men; and to you, Christian men and Christian women, are given the power and the privilege to lead out of this horrible pit, upward and onward to victory in his name.

In the next ten years a million Juniors will become voters. If across their ballots and across your ballots is written, "Loyalty to Jesus Christ," instead of "Loyalty to Party," the coming of the kingdom of Christ among men will be greatly hastened, and the will of God shall be done upon earth. [*Applause.*]

Never before has there been so perfect a reproduction of that scene which took place in the Valley of Elah nearly three thousand years ago. Now, as then, the hosts of the Philistines are arrayed against the army of the Lord. Chief among them all stands the organized liquor traffic, the giant evil of the nineteenth century, insolent and defiant as the Goliath of old; he laughs in disdain at the weak, hesitating attitude of the church, and openly defies Jehovah and his people. Following him are a great host of public evils, created, fostered, and protected by the saloon.

But mark you! There came out from the ranks of the Israelites a youth, a stripling, who, by the power of his faith in God, slew the giant and scattered the Philistines. I ask you, Where is the deliverer for to-day? Is there a David for this Goliath and his vile host? Who will come up to the help of the Lord against the mighty? I say to you that David has already come. The first great manifestations of his power were seen in the great convention at Minneapolis. He sat in the great meetings at New York and Montreal. He sits in this convention to-day. The David of this battle is the organized Christian youth. [*Applause.*] And on the authority of the Word of God, I say to you, O soldiers of the Cross! that if you go forth against the Philistines of to-day with faith in God and perfect loyalty to Christ, not one of them can stand before you; and that is Christian citizenship. [*Applause.*]

One year ago Dr. Clark, whose absence we mourn to-day, asked for a great advance step along citizenship lines. I believe that request was a call from God. It was not a call to form a new political party; it was not a call to bring the church into politics; it was not a call to combine church and state, or do any other foolish thing; but a call for Christian men and women to put their loyalty to Jesus Christ into their politics and citizenship, to talk and pray and vote as Jesus Christ would have them do.

Now, the question is, How have you answered this call? What have you done? Have you been loyal to your great leader, Jesus Christ? Have you voted as your Master would have you vote? Have you, in your societies, in your conventions, and in your committees, taught your fellows to stand as Daniel did against things unapproved of God? What has your society or union done to promote the cause of Christian citizenship and the reforms for which it stands?

Mr. Wheelock then announced that in twenty-five minutes fifty speeches were wanted.

AKRON (OHIO) Christian Endeavor Union reported that out of eighteen candidates last spring, they elected fourteen Christian men.

AN IOWA DELEGATE said that in his town the young men were being led astray, but religious men came to the rescue, and that town has not had a saloon for seven years.

PHILADELPHIA has appointed a superintendent and committee of good citizenship.

CHICAGO reports that in connection with a good citizenship campaign, the church is trying to do what it can in the way of disseminating information, and for the enforcement of the Sunday saloon-closing law, and in efforts to send the right men to the Legislature, that they may, in other words, vote "for Christ and the Church" intelligently.

A DELEGATE FROM IOWA reported a bill passed last year prohibiting the sale of liquor and tobacco to minors. This originated in the mind and heart of the temperance committee of a society in Shenandoah, Ia.

A SOCIETY IN PHILADELPHIA has done helpful work in making good citizens by furnishing free breakfasts every Sunday morning, and working amongst those they feed.

ALLEGHENY COUNTY, PA., reported a twenty-five dollar penalty for Sabbath violators, — the only county in the State that has a penalty of that amount.

NORTH MISSOURI: "Through the influences of good citizenship we are throwing aside the banners of high license, and declaring Missouri for Christ."

A DELEGATE FROM CHICAGO reports that the primaries are being attended by Christian men, and they are trying to see that men are nominated such as Christians can vote for.

INDIANA reported that that State has sent President Clark's recommendations to the State Legislature, and has a new pledge which includes the clause, "I will vote as Christ would have me vote."

TORONTO, ONT., reported eighty thousand majority for prohibition. Every city in Ontario went for prohibition with the exception of one.

A TROY, N.Y., DELEGATE SAID: New York State has given the world the martyr, Robert Ross, and his blood is going to wipe out the infamy of our State." [*Applause.*]

WASHINGTON, PA.: We have held three great rallies for good citizenship. The saloons for retail were afraid to apply, and we downed every one for wholesale license.

A COLORED DELEGATE FROM PHILADELPHIA SPOKE AS FOLLOWS: I am here to give color to this meeting. [*Laughter.*] We are with you in the Christian Endeavor movement and every other good movement. The young men of my race are coming up as good citizens. [*Applause.*] We were not with you in the Coxey movement; we were not with you in the railway strike; but we are with you in the work of Christianity. [*Applause.*]

The Montreal Christian Endeavor Union has taken up an active campaign against the liquor traffic in that city.

Many more delegates were on their feet, anxious to tell of the work they had been doing in the past year to promote good citizenship; but the time being limited, they were deprived of telling many more good things. A rising vote of all those engaged in the good citizenship movement was called for, and nearly the entire audience arose to their feet.

MR. WHEELOCK: If we need anything in this work it is practical methods, and there is a man here from Chicago who knows all about it, Prof. Graham Taylor.

PROF. TAYLOR: The purpose of the church is Christ for the world. The method of bringing the kingdom of God to the earth, the church to society, is, educate, educate, educate! Now, to educate we have to have a popular sociological literature. How can you get on the track of that literature? Wm. Howe Tolman, secretary of the City Vigilance League of the City of New York, has published a pamphlet, telling you what books to get on the subject of citizenship. We need organization. An institute of Christian sociology has been organized, and Josiah Strong has been elected president. They organized for the study of these subjects. We need more light, but no less do we need heat.

Now, we must have co-operation, — co-operation between the Endeavor Societies. Every Endeavor Society, or group of Endeavor Societies, should have a school of citizenship. Then there should be good citizenship rallies.

We have had in Chicago for the last thirty-five weeks a meeting on social economics. Every seat was occupied by laboring-men. There was a man to open the subject, and then several questions and answers and discussions. Men who had not been to a Christian meeting for years were there; anarchists have been there; men who have never thought Christianity had anything to do with such things.

Friends, we are on the crest of a tremendous tidal wave, and it remains for Christian Endeavorers and church people to say whether that tidal wave shall be Christian or atheistic. We need Christian education.

It is to be hoped that good citizenship will soon be considered an essential quality of Christianity. If this solution is ever to be brought about it will be through the organized church and organized labor. And when the cross is taken in the brawny hands of toil the victory will be ours.

The Cleveland Christian Endeavor male quartette sang, "What will the Harvest be?" and were applauded loudly. The Park sisters then gave a beautiful cornet selection.

Rev. E. B. Chappell, D.D., pastor Methodist-Episcopal Church South, of St. Louis, was then introduced to speak on the subject of "Christian Citizenship."

Christian Citizenship.

Address of Rev. E. B. Chappell, D.D.

Every age has its peculiar perils. Those that confront us in the United States just now are largely due to the new forces which have, during the last one hundred years, been introduced into our civilization. Great forces always contain within them elements of great danger as well as large possibilities of good. They become curses or blessings according to the use we make of them, just as the sails of a ship, which, manipulated by a skillful boatman, carry the vessel to her port in safety, in the hands of an inexperienced bungler may become the means of her destruction. I wish to speak briefly of at least two of these forces, and the dangers that result from them.

1. The nineteenth century is distinguished above all others for its material discoveries and inventions. The vast resources of nature have been brought into the service of man. Wondrously contrived machines impelled by steam or electricity carry his bur-

dens and accomplish with ease and rapidity the work which his hands formerly did slowly and with difficulty. This larger use of natural forces and commodities has already brought about results of profound and far-reaching importance.

Consider first the almost incalculable increase in the power of production, making possible the rapid multiplication of material wealth. The financial resources of the civilized world have increased during the last fifty years to an extent that seems almost incredible; and America is the richest country on earth. The fabulous wealth of such splendid ancient capitals as Babylon and Rome would be insignificant in comparison with that of New York or Chicago. And almost all of this wealth accumulated within a single century! Immense fortunes are built up by great financiers or shrewd manipulators with an ease and rapidity which remind us of the magical power of Aladdin's lamp. It is not uncommon to see the small tradesman transformed within a few years into the distinguished money baron, and the humble cottage with its simple belongings into the splendid palace with its ostentatious and luxurious furnishings.

This multiplication of wealth has already exerted a marked influence upon our natural tastes, ideals, and habits. Our thoughts have been so taken up with making new machines, building new railroads, developing new industries, and accumulating big fortunes, that we have, in large measure, lost sight of the ideal and the spiritual. Excessive devotion to the material has become one of our characteristics. We have our Napoleons of finance; but where are the poets, philosophers, and statesmen that rank with Lowell, Holmes, Whittier, Bryant, Longfellow, Emerson, Thoreau, Franklin, Jefferson, Hamilton, and Webster? The truth is, the men of genius among us are turning their attention chiefly to money-getting. And what wonder? Is not this the shortest and surest way to honor and power? Are we not agreed that the "Sorrow crown of sorrows" is being poor? that the one absolute essential of success in life is to be rich? What cares your ambitious youth for being a poet or a philosopher, if he cannot live in a palace and own a yacht? The Goulds, Astors, and Vanderbilts are the heroes of his fancy. All his neighbors talk about them and envy them. The newspapers advertise them from one year's end to another. The names of our successful financiers and stock gamblers are familiar household words in thousands of families in the United States that never heard of Emerson or Lowell. Is it strange that the young man who wants to command the admiration of his fellow-citizens, and to wield the largest possible power among them, should adopt these as his models? A distinguished railroad magnate, in a fit of confidence, told the public a while ago how he narrowly escaped being a lawyer. What a piece of luck! But for that fortunate circumstance he would now, in all probability, be but a plain, ordinary citizen, eking out a poor existence on a contemptible $20,000 or $30,000 a year, and hardly known beyond his native State, instead of a jolly millionaire, not only honored by his untitled countrymen, but respected by the nobles, popes, and Cæsars beyond the seas. How the story of such a life thrills the heart of the gifted and ambitious boy! Such a career fulfills his ideal of success. What are lawyers, scholars, poets, and statesmen compared with men like this? Why bother about statesmanship, anyway, when political preferment goes rather to the highest bidder than to the wisest leader? What wonder that under such circumstances the young man too often sets out to reach the coveted goal by the shortest possible route, leaving behind him such impedimenta as honesty, justice, and humanity? He is sure that success in this one thing will, in the estimation of the public, atone for all other failures, and his worth at last be measured in terms of the coin of the realm.

Thus we are confronted with a danger which, of all others in a republic, is most serious, — the danger of degrading manhood, and building up a vast and monstrous material civilization that must erelong fall of its own weight. A despotism may be maintained by brute force; but a democracy must have men and patriots, or it cannot stand. If our scientific triumphs are to make us the victims of a dense, damning, practical materialism, to cause us to lose our hold upon the unseen and spiritual, and to think less of truth, beauty, and righteousness, then must all wise men look upon them as curses instead of blessings. We are already face to face with this danger. The accursed selfishness which is a never-failing characteristic of the worshiper of mammon is destroying patriotism. Politics is a game played for the stakes. Its motto, "To the victor belong the spoils;" and by the spoils is generally meant everything that the victor can manage to appropriate without incurring the risk of being sent to the penitentiary. Our cities are governed by rings of unprincipled ruffians organized for public plunder, and some of these rings have carried on their business so successfully that they have become potent factors in our State and national elections. Thus they have thrust into places of honor and responsibility brainless demagogues and contemptible and ignorant "bosses," who have more affinity with the state prison than with the capital of the freest nation in the world.

In ancient Athens a wealthy citizen deemed that the highest honor was conferred upon him when he was elected to expend a large part of his fortune in having the tragedies of the Greek poets enacted for the edification and pleasure of his native city. But in Christian America the average rich man is dead as a stone to such considerations of noble patriotism. He takes no interest in social problems, labor problems, or any other great human problems, except as they seem directly related to his financial interests. A few months ago, when it was evident that our country must pass through a period of almost unparalleled financial depression, with its consequent danger and suffering, the papers told us how one of the most distinguished representatives of our American plutocracy locked up his three magnificent palaces, and, fitting up his handsome yacht, sailed away for a year's cruise in foreign waters, leaving his afflicted land to wrestle with her difficulties as best she could.

What shall we be profited if we gain unlimited wealth and lose our manhood and patriotism?

Still another danger has come from the use of the forces of nature in the arts of production. The entire industrial system of the civilized world has been revolutionized. Individualism has given place to combination and corporate control. Instead of the small shop owned and operated by a single independent workingman, we have the vast factory owned by a powerful corporation and operated by an army of dependent "hands." As consequences of these changes, we have our social and labor problems. These problems are real, and not, as some would have us believe, imaginary. The changed conditions demand a radical readjustment of industrial relations, which we have not yet been able to bring about. And so we are called upon to-day, in this the closing decade of the nineteenth century of the Christian era, to witness the spectacle of a great Christian republic divided into two hostile and contending classes. On the one hand organized labor, restless, dissatisfied, chafing under a sense of intolerable dependence; on the other, organized capital, haughty, determined, powerful. Between these two distrust, growing enmity, and perpetual warfare. Strikes, lockouts, and riots have become so common that we take them as matters of course; and yet it must be evident to every thoughtful observer that the relations between these conflicting classes are fast becoming intolerable, and that the danger of serious collision is every year becoming more imminent. Already we hear the mutterings of the tempest that will burst upon us if we do not learn so to use these new forces as that they shall bring to all larger freedom and opportunity.

Another source of danger lies in the experiment of universal manhood suffrage which we have adopted. This would be an occasion of danger even under the most favorable circumstances. Unfortunately, however, there are many things that complicate the situation and increase the peril. We use the word "manhood" in quite an accommodated sense. Everything in pants over twenty-one years old we count as a man; and so, within the memory of persons still living, the voting population of our country has been more than doubled. How? In the first place, by a vast influx of foreigners, many of whom come from the worst elements of the overcrowded cities of the Old World, and almost all of whom are to a large extent ignorant of our language and institutions, and utterly incapable of assuming the duties of citizenship in a free republic. In the second place, by the emancipation and enfranchisement of 6,000,000 slaves whose culture and previous training, to put it in the most moderate way, were hardly calculated to fit them for a wise and intelligent use of the ballot. And all this comes along with the industrial transformation, and the excessive devotion to the material of which I have spoken. As a result we have the reign of corruptionists and "bosses." In our elections the arts of the demagogue count for more than the wisdom of the statesman. Men are marched to the polls in herds, and voted by party dictators who are destitute both of honor and patriotism.

Doubtless you are ready to say that this is a dark picture; but you will please understand that it is not in any spirit of pessimism that I have called attention to these perils. I am an optimist, because I am a Christian. But I believe an optimism that is blind to facts is both irrational and dangerous. It is best always to know the truth; and I have spoken of these things in order to emphasize the responsibilities which rest upon the

Christian citizens of this republic. Let us face the facts. Our democracy is on trial. We are passing through a period of peril hardly less severe than that of our bloody Civil War. What the issue is to be depends upon the loyalty and fidelity of those who have learned of Christ. It is a time when every true American should arouse himself and do his full duty. The need of patriot heroes is not altogether past. We call this an age of piping peace; in truth, it is an age of tremendous strife, wherein the armed civilian is called to be soldier and hero.

1. First of all, the Christian citizen should be an earnest and intelligent student of current conditions and problems. For such a crisis we need men who, like the children of Issachar, have "understanding of the times to know what Israel ought to do." I verily believe that Christianity contains the remedy for the social ills that imperil our national life; but we must understand the disease before we can apply the remedy. I fear that we have been kept from taking such profound and intelligent interest in these things as we should by an irrational conservatism. There is a certain noble conservatism in which I believe. We have grown out of the past, are rooted in it, and should conscientiously conserve whatever good it has left to us. But as we trust in God we should not be afraid of growth. It is natural, beautiful, and healthful. It is foolish to curse the reformers, and sigh for the return of the good old days. Nothing gone ever returns except as a vital force in the life of the new, for which it has helped to prepare the way. Let us rather welcome such natural changes as time brings, recognizing the fact that the fault is ours if these changes are not healthful and beneficial.

2. For it is not only our duty to study and try to understand the new forces that are at work among us and the new conditions that surround us, but also to endeavor so to control these forces and modify these conditions, as that they shall result in the largest good to our country. The doctrine of *Laissez faire*, growing out of a false materialistic philosophy, has already served too long as an excuse for sinful indifference. There is a sense, I know, in which society is a living organism, and grows by natural processes and according to fixed and unchangeable laws. But there is an element that enters into the growth of the social organism of which materialism takes no account, — the voluntary activity of the units of social life. We are to take hold of and so direct the movements now in progress as to aid in bringing about the most beneficent and happy results. God can overrule even a French Revolution so as to bring out of it ultimate good; but no one who carefully studies the social and political movements of the eighteenth century can doubt that, had the ruling classes of France understood these movements and known how to direct them according to the spirit of the gospel, the cause of "liberty, equality, and fraternity" might to-day be a full century in advance of what it actually is.

The Christian citizen in an emergency like the present cannot afford to let things alone. It is his duty to preach and exemplify among his neighbors, both rich and poor, the gospel of purity, justice, and brotherhood; to try to make them understand that, in spite of hate and warfare, they are one body, that the good of one is the good of all, and the hurt of one is the hurt of all. He should teach the strong that the only way to make their strength a blessing to themselves is to use it for the good of the weak and needy, and that selfishness and injustice always result in disaster and sorrow. He should teach the poor also, who clamor for recognition, that he sympathizes with all their noble aspirations, and at the same time recognizes the fact that there is no way by which ignorant, thriftless, and rum-enslaved idlers can be legislated into a condition of independence and respectability; that what we need more than anything else is not more money nor more laws, but more men, and a juster and more adequate recognition among all classes of the worth and dignity of manhood, and the meaning of human brotherhood. So long as rich and poor alike regard honest poverty as one of the greatest misfortunes, and are alike animated by the all-absorbing ambition to get rich, there is not much prospect of any wise and permanent adjustment of our social problems. No one, I think, can be more anxious than I for that social amelioration about which, just now, we hear so much. But I fear we are in danger of being brought into serious difficulty by the undue haste of hot-headed visionaries, who dream of an immediate millennium to be brought about by legislation. Such a hope is vain. Social amelioration must go hand in hand with the growth of the kingdom of God on earth; and this kingdom is like unto a grain of mustard-seed, or the fruit which the earth bringeth forth of herself, "first the blade, then the ear, after that the full corn in the ear."

Let us love, and scatter the fruit, and practice the Golden Rule, and we shall do more to solve our perplexing social and political problems than all the legislatures and senates combined.

3. Do not understand me, however, as meaning that I do not believe in legislation as one of the means by which we are to seek to promote our national welfare. Bad laws are a sore hindrance to progress, and bad men in office are a menace and a curse to the land. Good laws, on the other hand, administered by wise and patriotic men, help to conserve that which is good and to hasten the natural processes of growth. The Christian citizen ought, therefore, to take an active interest in practical politics. The fact that so many do not is one of the most disheartening features in our present national life. There is scarcely a city in the United States in the government of which the saloons do not have more influence than all the churches combined. Stanch and intelligent citizens stay at home, and leave the elections to "boodlers" and "ward-heelers," excusing themselves for their criminal neglect by claiming that they are too busy, or that they have no taste for such matters. Such excuses are selfish and ignoble. Interpreted they mean that "the country may get along as best it can, so long as our homes are reasonably secure and our business reasonably prosperous."

Others declare frankly that they stand aloof because they regard all efforts to reform our politics as utterly vain. The very mention of such a thing in many quarters provokes a smile of derision. Either the honest men, they seem to think, are in a hopeless minority, or else the rascals have most of the wit.

Away with such pessimism. The trouble is with us. We have never seriously tried to do what we all know should be done. Occasionally we become aroused by the exposure of some very flagrant abuse, and take hold as though we were going to reform everything at once. But such fits of pious enthusiasm only amuse the practical politician. He knows they will last but for a little while, and that by and by the preachers, bankers, merchants, and farmers will return to their work and leave him in charge as before. This matter of conscientious voting and standing for integrity of the ballot and the enforcement of law needs to be brought home to the consciences of the Christian citizens of these United States to-day. Continued neglect means the rule of scoundrels and the reign of anarchy. Let us not be deterred from doing our duty by the wretched "*bête noire*" raised by the demagogue's nonsense about mixing politics and religion. Let us go to the primaries and polls like men and patriots, and vote for honest men and just measures. I can think of nothing that would be more wholesome just now than the infusion of some downright, earnest religion into our politics. I dare not say that a Christian citizen should have no party affiliation; but I do declare that he prostitutes his manhood and dishonors his Lord when he consents to consort with thieves and tricksters, and to condone their villainy for the sake of partisan triumph. The standard of morality which, according to all accounts, prevails at present among our public officials, municipal, State and national, is a fearful commentary upon the partisan blindness and moral apathy of men who profess to be followers of Jesus Christ. If the Christian citizens of this country should let it be understood that they mean to vote in the next elections, and to vote only for men of sterling honesty and sound morals, no party would dare to hazard its chances of success by nominating gamblers, libertines, and all sorts of nondescript rascals.

4. I regard it as one of the hopeful indications of our time that the leaders of this great young people's movement are emphasizing the duties of Christian citizenship. We have but little to hope from the older men who are already confirmed in their selfish indifference, or their slavish allegiance to party. We must, before any great reforms are brought about, train a generation of intelligent patriots, who value country above party, and are willing to forsake their ease to serve their responsibilities; and I trust that this society, under the blessing of God and the guidance of its honored president, may become one of the chief agencies in accomplishing this important and difficult work.

5. One thing more: your banners and badges tell me that you come from every section of our land. Representatives from the East and West, from North and South, meet here upon a common level of Christian brotherhood. Do we not read, in the beautiful spirit of harmony and good will which pervades this vast convention, a prophecy of the sure and speedy termination of that sectionalism which has so long disturbed the peace and hindered the progress of our country? I am a native of the South, as my fathers have been for almost two centuries. Of course that sunny land is peculiarly dear to me.

I love her vine-clad hills, her green savannas, and her clear blue sky. I love her chivalrous sons and her queenly daughters. I am not blind to their faults; but I know their virtues also, and for these I love them. But while I am a patriotic son of the South, I am a loyal citizen of the United States. I claim kinship with you all, and feel that I have personal interest and ownership in every section of my beloved native land. Massachusetts as well as Tennessee belongs to me. I feel a patriotic and loyal pride in all the noble achievements both of New England Puritan and Virginia Cavalier.

I am glad that one flag waves over us all, and that our destinies are inseparably linked together; and I long to see the time when the good men of the South and the good men of the North shall stand shoulder to shoulder against the foes of freedom and righteousness. May God help this society in its noble efforts to bring about this consummation so devoutly to be wished!

After all that I have said about the difficulties and dangers that confront us, I must tell you that I look forward to our future with unwavering hope. I believe in the destiny of our democratic government, because I believe in God and humanity. At the entrance of New York harbor stands Bartholdi's magnificent Statue of Liberty, holding aloft the symbolic light that greets strangers from every clime and country as they approach our shores.

So I think this republic has been raised up in the order of divine Providence to stand for justice and brotherhood, and to hold aloft the beacon light of freedom for the benighted and oppressed of all lands. The responsibility of maintaining and developing her free institutions is left with her own redeemed children.

I cannot be persuaded that they will betray this sacred trust; that democracy is to prove a failure, and that the hands upon the dial of time are to be turned back for a century.

If Jesus could intrust his earthly kingdom to the fidelity of his disciples, and die in the calm assurance that the gates of hell should not prevail against it, cannot the cause of freedom be intrusted to her sons? Out of that confidence in man taught me by my Lord, I answer yes. Through dangers and conflicts our country shall be guided safely, until she shall come ere long to a serener and a more blessed peace than she has ever known, and in a nobler sense than our fathers dreamed, shall become "the land of the free and the home of the brave."

DR. DICKINSON: A good Cleveland friend said to me yesterday, "I think that all the Christian Endeavorers must be here." "Oh, no," I said, "you are mistaken, there are about two millions of them at home." Now, we want to remember to-day the two millions who could not come with us; and it is fitting that here in convention assembled, we should lift our hearts in prayer in behalf of those who could not come with us.

Rev. Dr. Dixon of New York, and Rev. Dr. Kelly of Kentucky, then led in prayer.

Presentation of Diplomas.

The presentation of diplomas, awarded by the United Society of Christian Endeavor for the best work reported in the promotion of good citizenship and the circulation of good literature, followed, Mr. Shaw conducting the exercise.

MR. SHAW (stepping forward with diplomas): What do those look like? They look like a Gatling gun. Do you see them? I want to tell you that they represent twenty-five Gatling guns, and probably twenty-five hundred more that in the name of good citizenship have been turned upon the enemies of God and our country and our homes. [*Applause.*] We have in these tubes the diplomas that have been awarded to the twenty-five societies that have reported the best work done in the line of good citizenship and of good literature. Perhaps your society did better work than any named here; but you did not let us know about it, and that is the reason you will not receive a diploma this morning. Next year perhaps you will be more zealous in making your reports.

Diplomas were awarded to the following unions and societies : —

GOOD CITIZENSHIP.

Christian Endeavor Union, Wilmington, Del.
Christian Endeavor Union, Syracuse, N.Y.
Christian Endeavor Union, Denver, Col.
Christian Endeavor Union, Kansas City, Mo.
Christian Endeavor Union, Boston, Mass.
Christian Endeavor Union, Indianapolis, Ind.
Oakwood Avenue Presbyterian Y. P. S. C. E., Troy, N.Y.
Christian Y. P. S. C. E., Fairview, Ind.
Union Park Congregational Y. P. S. C. E., Chicago, Ill.
First Presbyterian Y. P. S. C. E., Truro, N.S.
Grove Y. P. S. C. E., Halifax, N.S.
American Presbyterian Y. P. S. C. E., Montreal, P.Q.
Fourth Methodist Protestant Y. P. S. C. E., Pittsburg, Penn.
Central Christian Y. P. S. C. E., Cleveland, O.
Mount Morris Baptist Y. P. S. C. E., New York, N.Y.
Clyde Congregational Y. P. S. C. E., Kansas City, Mo.
First Presbyterian Y. P. S. C. E., Shenandoah, Ia.
Cooke's Presbyterian Y. P. S. C. E., Toronto, Ont.
Congregational Y. P. S. C. E., Greenwich, Conn.
Christ Evangelical Y. P. S. C. E., Philadelphia, Penn.
First Presbyterian Y. P. S. C. E., Wichita, Kan.
Central Presbyterian Y. P. S. C. E., Detroit, Mich.
Presbyterian Y. P. S. C. E., Sac City, Ia.
Sunday Breakfast Association Y. P. S. C. E., Philadelphia, Penn.
Olivet Baptist Y. P. S. C. E., Montreal, P.Q.

GOOD LITERATURE.

Maryland Ave. Presbyterian Y. P. S. C. E., Baltimore, Md.
Ebenezer Evangelical Y. P. S. C. E., Allentown, Penn.
Methodist Y. P. S. C. E., Portadown, Ireland.
First Presbyterian Y. P. S. C. E., Kansas City, Kan.
First Congregational Y. P. S. C. E., Spokane, Wash.
Irish Grove Cumberland Presbyterian Y. P. S. C. E., Middletown, Ill.
St. James Square Presbyterian Y. P. S. C. E., Toronto, Ont.
Congregational Y. P. S. C. E., Central Falls, R.I.
Dawson Street Baptist Y. P. S. C. E., Ballarat, Australia.
First Presbyterian Y. P. S. C. E., Honesdale, Penn.
St. Andrew's Presbyterian Y. P. S. C. E., London, Ont.
Presbyterian Y. P. S. C. E., Frankfort, Ind.
Union Y. P. S. C. E., Big Flats, N.Y.
American Presbyterian Y. P. S. C. E., Montreal, P.Q.
Trinity Presbyterian Y. P. S. C. E., Berwyn, Penn.
Plymouth Y. P. S. C. E., Worcester, Mass.
Onward Presbyterian Y. P. S. C. E., Chicago, Ill.
First Presbyterian Y. P. S. C. E., Muscatine, Ia.
Presbyterian Y. P. S. C. E., Monticello, N.Y.
Baptist Y. P. S. C. E., Hammonton, N.J.
Bethel Congregational Y. P. S. C. E., Kingston, Ont.
Corn Hill Methodist Episcopal Y. P. S. C. E., Rochester, N.Y.
Presbyterian Y. P. S. C. E., Paola, Kan.
Central Congregational Y. P. S. C. E., Forest, Ont.
Congregational Y. P. S. C. E., Brighton, Mass.

After the presentation of the diplomas the audience sang one verse of " America."

Mr. Dickinson: We have with us to-day a master of assemblies and a prince of reformers, one who has spoken a good many times to Christian Endeavor audiences, and always to their satisfaction and delight. I am glad to introduce to you Mr. John G. Woolley. [*Prolonged applause and Chautauqua salute.*]

Mr. Woolley then proceeded to repeat the address already delivered at the hall.

When he finished, the audience arose to their feet and applauded enthusiastically.

"Onward, Christian Soldiers," and the benediction by Rev. M. M. Binford, closed the session.

The Business Men's Prayer-Meeting, conducted by Mr. C. N. Hunt, was full of interest and largely attended.

FRIDAY AFTERNOON.

No session of the Convention was held in the hall or tent, the afternoon being devoted to committee conferences for the discussion of practical methods of work. The following conferences were held : —

Lookout Committee.

The Euclid Avenue Baptist Church was completely filled with a large audience, which gathered to attend the session of this conference, Mr. W. H. Lewis of Seattle, Wash., presiding. After introductory exercises of song and prayer, Mr. Lewis defined briefly the work of the lookout committee, and then called for suggestions as to how its work could best be done. Responses came rapidly and in large numbers. Some discussion ensued as to the method of taking in new members, the treatment of church-members who say they cannot keep the pledge, the best way to keep members faithful, work for new members, and various other practical topics. The meeting proved a highly profitable and interesting one.

Social Committee.

About eight hundred of the delegates met in the Sunday-school room of Plymouth Church to discuss the social committee's work. Mr. W. E. Sweet of Denver, Col., presided. The modern church social was the chief subject of discussion, and many practical ideas were brought out. The raising of money through social meetings was emphatically discouraged by a resolution adopted by the delegates present, the thought being that an appeal should rather be made to the hearts of the people on the ground of its being a privilege to give directly to the work of the Lord without compensation.

Sunday-School Committee.

The session was held in the First M. E. Church, Mr. W. G. Bell of Austin, Tex., presiding. There was a large attendance, and the meeting was decidedly animated in interest and replete with helpful suggestions. Among the topics discussed were the use of cards and pamphlets, substitute teachers, systematic Bible study, lesson helps, absent scholars, methods for winning new scholars, etc. Mr. Bell addressed the delegates on the Christian Endeavor Society as the re-enforcing power of the Sunday-school.

Missionary Committee Conference.

The conference on the work of the missionary committee was held in the Central High School building Hall, which was crowded to its utmost capacity by more than a thousand enthusiastic Endeavorers.

The meeting was opened with a song service, followed by a number of brief prayers.

Rev. C. J. Landrith of Tennessee presided. The entire meeting was of an informal character, every one taking part freely in the questions under discussion. In his preliminary remarks Mr. Landrith said the whole work of missions was comprised in the words "explanation," "exhortation," and "exportation," and that it was the duty of the Christian Endeavor Society to attend to all three.

Mr. W. Henry Grant then led a twenty minutes' conference on "The Committee and Its Organization." Reciting the story of a famous archer of India, he insisted that every society should have at least one member who could see only one thing, — Missions. This great army of Christian Endeavor has thrown out its skirmish-line of missionary committees. These committees, during the past year, have been discovering the lay of the land and where the difficulties and obstacles exist, and have opened up the way for advance of the main army. A show of hands proved that a large proportion of those present at the conference actually served on this committee. In answer to questions, it was evident that the greatest success in securing missionary meetings was where the work was divided between sub-committee on meetings, literature, systematic giving, etc. It was strongly emphasized that there should be two meetings of the missionary committee for every missionary meeting of the society, and that a record be kept by the chairman of the work assigned to each member of the committee, with the reports of progress made.

Miss Elizabeth M. Wishard then conducted an open discussion on "The Meeting of the Society." The questions were discussed under the heads, "How Often to Meet," "How to Plan a Programme," "The Way to Make Members Participate," and "Missionary Literature."

Mr. Thornton B. Penfield continued the discussion, and said that all societies should be in direct communication with the missionaries on the field through their denominational Boards.

The discussion of the subject of "Systematic Giving" was opened by Mr. W. L. Amerman, who said that systematic giving consisted in giving regularly and from principle, rather than spasmodically and from impulse. He then showed what had been done in one society by securing a pledged offering from each member, and making each member a collector to get nine others to give also. Societies where there was a specific object, or where the members were contributing toward the support of a missionary on the field, showed the greatest result.

Mr. S. L. Mershon spoke for a few minutes on the Missionary Extension Course and its practical results in developing missionary enthusiasm.

Mr. D. Willard Lyon, Secretary of the Student Volunteer Movement, gave a stirring address on the "Watchword" of the movement, "The Evangelization of the World in This Generation," defining the relation of Christian Endeavor to the Student Volunteers. He was followed by Mr. Rains on the subject, "Ought I to go?" Upon asking how many persons were ready, God willing, to go to the foreign field, over one hundred rose, some of whom have already been accepted by their Boards. All those who were going to the field were invited to meet missionaries in the audience at the platform.

Good Literature Committee.

This conference met in the Sunday-school room of the Euclid Avenue Baptist Church, Mr. E. G. Routzahn of Dayton, Ohio, presiding. Rev. H. W. Pope spoke on "Results in Literature Work," and Rev. W. G. Hubbard described the work of the American Railway Literary Union. A question-box, followed by general discussion, brought out many practical hints. It was shown how lack of interest and ignorance of methods in Christian Endeavor work may be removed through the committee's work, and how the committee may render efficient service to every other committee of the society.

Temperance and Good Citizenship Committees.

The auditorium of Plymouth Church held a magnificent audience which assembled at the united conference of these two committees. Mr. George W. Coleman of Boston presided; and inspiring addresses were delivered by Dr. Clara Shaw of Chicago on scientific temperance in the schools, by Mr. Francis Murphy and his son, Thomas E. Murphy, and by Mr. John G. Woolley. Much enthusiasm was awakened by these addresses, and there were besides a number of practical testimonies as to actual results accomplished in good citizenship work.

PRAYER-MEETING COMMITTEE.

No conference, perhaps, was more largely attended or more helpful than the one which gathered in the Old Stone Church, under the auspices of the prayer-meeting committee. Rev. M. H. Appleby, Wingate, Ind., presided. There were no formal addresses, but the time was fully occupied with general discussion as to methods of committee work. The duties of leaders, cottage prayer-meetings, conduct of the meetings, how to avoid pauses, ways to secure the best spiritual results, etc., were among the subjects considered.

SENIOR AND MOTHERS' SOCIETY CONFERENCE.

Rev. H. N. Kinney of Syracuse, N.Y., presided at the session of this conference, which was held in the lecture-room of the Y. M. C. A. building. While the attendance was not large, the meeting was full of interest. Mr. Kinney and Mr. P. F. Chase of Chicago spoke upon the scope and objects of the Senior societies, and Miss Bonney of Norwich, Conn., spoke briefly on the home department. Rev. F. F. Lewis of Hardwick, Vt., told how two churches in Vermont had been very successful in adopting and carrying out the Christian Endeavor constitution as their own. The Mothers' society was represented by Mrs. Alice P. Thompson of Chicago, and Miss Wilson of Topeka, Kan., who described how successful these societies had been in enlisting the interest of mothers whose children belong to Junior societies.

CORRESPONDING SECRETARIES' CONFERENCE.

The auditorium of the Euclid Avenue Presbyterian Church was well filled at this conference, Mr. J. Howard Breed of Philadelphia presiding. Only about one in thirty of the corresponding secretaries of the country were represented, but the meeting proved very helpful. The time was occupied with a general discussion of the duties of the corresponding secretary, the difficulties he has to contend with, etc.

SYSTEMATIC AND PROPORTIONATE GIVING CONFERENCE.

The delegates who attended this gathering did not hesitate to declare themselves the most important conference of the afternoon. They were not so many in number as attended some of the other conferences, but they were by no means lacking in enthusiasm and devoted spirit. The session was held in the Sunday-school room of the Euclid Avenue Presbyterian Church, Mr. F. C. Brittain of Allegheny City, Pa., presiding. Various methods and suggestions as to giving were advanced, and testimonies as to the value of systematic benevolence were numerous. The conference adopted a resolution advocating the appointment of a committee on proportionate giving in every Christian Endeavor society "for the purpose of promoting the practice of giving among God's people."

LOCAL UNION OFFICERS' AND DISTRICT SECRETARIES' CONFERENCE.

About two hundred local union officers and district secretaries assembled in the primary department room of the Woodland Avenue Presbyterian Church, where, led by Mr. W. O. Atwood of Baltimore, Md., they kept up a running fire of questions and answers as to plans and methods, relating to their special fields of work.

STATE, TERRITORIAL, AND PROVINCIAL OFFICERS' CONFERENCE.

This conference was held in the intermediate room of the same building, and was presided over by Mr. W. H. Strong of Detroit, Mich. The meeting, though naturally small in attendance, was full of interest. The practical experience of the delegates was drawn upon for helpful methods of conducting State organizations. Missionary extension, finances, denominational secretaries, the good citizenship campaign, temperance, Sabbath observance, and other subjects were reported upon and discussed.

Junior Societies' Superintendents' Conference.

About eight hundred of the Junior workers present at the convention assembled in the auditorium of the Y. M. C. A. building, led by Mr. C. J. Atkinson, of Mimico, Ont. The meeting was one of the most enthusiastic and helpful of the afternoon. No set speeches were made, but practical testimonies as to actual work were given in great number. Sometimes as many as twenty delegates would be on their feet at once in their enthusiasm to contribute to the discussion.

At the close of this conference the State, Territorial, and Provincial Union Junior superintendents gathered in an upper room in the same building, where for an hour they discussed State organization, the extension of Junior societies, Junior rallies, means for promoting healthy interest and securing spiritual results, etc. A recommendation to the United Society was adopted, to the effect that hereafter the Junior work be made a distinct department of the general work of the Boston office. A number of reports of the work in several States were given.

Reception and Tea.

At five o'clock the executive committee of the Cleveland Union gave a delightful reception and lunch to the Committee of '94, the officers of the various State and Provincial unions, and to the officers and trustees of the United Society. After enjoying the hospitalities of the dining-room the company assembled up-stairs, where brief addresses were made by Rev. C. A. Dickinson, Secretary Baer, Rev. W. F. McCauley, president of the Ohio union, and Dr. J. Z. Tyler. Mr. J. E. Cheesman presided.

FRIDAY EVENING.

Saengerfest Hall.

ANOTHER immense audience gathered at the hall long before the time of commencing the meeting. The waiting hour was spent as usual in impromptu singing. Mr. H. C. Lincoln of Philadelphia had charge of the praise service. The male quartette gave a pleasing variety to the programme by their quartette singing. Promptly at 7.45, Mr. Dickinson, who presided, introduced Rev. D. O. Mears, D.D., of Cleveland, who conducted the devotional service. At his request the audience rose and repeated together the One Hundredth Psalm, after which Dr. Mears led in prayer.

MR. DICKINSON: This convention is full of surprises to most of us. Many of us were surprised to get here, and we are all surprised to find so many other people here. We have been surprised again and again with the rich feast of good things provided for us; and, indeed, this Committee of '94 has been constantly surprising us by their ability to manage a mammoth convention like this, and by the provision which they have made for our comfort. Now a few of us propose to turn the tables on this committee and surprise them a little, and if you will wait a moment we will let you into the secret.

MR. BAER (bringing forward a beautiful banner): You have met the chairman of the Committee of '94, Rev. Dr. J. Z. Tyler. We also want you to see with him those faithful soldiers who so nobly prepared for this convention, and so I have been asked to introduce these friends to you. In recognition of their fidelity the United Society of Christian Endeavor has prepared this banner. It reads: " Presented to the Cleveland Christian Endeavor Union by the United Society of Christian Endeavor at the thirteenth international convention for faithful service." [*Applause.*] This banner is to be presented to the Cleveland Union through the Committee of '94; for it was the Cleveland

Union that invited this large family to this glorious city, and placed in the hands of Dr. Tyler and his associates the honorable duty of providing for us after they had invited us. So I take great pleasure in standing aside and asking Dr. Tyler and all his associates to come forward.

Dr. Tyler and the other members of the Committee of '94 then came forward, and were introduced severally to the audience: Miss Miriam C. Smith, secretary; Mr. A. E. Roblee, finance and treasurer; Mr. J. E. Cheesman, hall; Mr. N. E. Hills, entertainment; Mr. F. Melville Lewis, printing; Rev. S. L. Darsie, music; Mr. R. B. Hamilton, press; Mr. A. W. Neale, reception; Mr. J. V. Hitchcock, auditing; and Rev. R. A. George, *ex-officio*.

MR. BAER: Dr. Tyler, we want you to keep this banner in Cleveland. We are going to leave it here. I do not suppose you will forget us very soon, and I am sure we never shall forget you. We shall hope to leave an atmosphere in this city which even the salubrious breezes which have blown upon the circulars that you have sent out will not dispel. [*Loud applause.*]

DR. TYLER: Mr. Baer, and members of the Board of Trustees of the United Society of Christian Endeavor, in behalf of the Committee of '94, a committee appointed by the local union of this city, I accept with expressions of profoundest appreciation this token of your appreciation of our efforts in your behalf. We have not been insensible, fellow-Endeavorers, to the expressions which have come to us from all sides of your appreciation of the homes in which you have been placed and the general reception that has been accorded to you; but I can assure you that, in the midst of the experiences of this Convention, so full of joy that our cup has been running over, we have experienced nothing that has been sweeter than the labor of our hands, and the hands of the almost three thousand members of sub-committees in preparing for your reception, and then at last having the joy of greeting you in these magnificent assemblies. I wish to say that the affairs of the Committee of '94 have from the beginning been conducted on strictly business principles. We have selected the men who have been chairmen of committees, because of their fitness for the work to be done; and I wish to say, concerning the members of the Committee of '94 who are the chairmen of the principal sub-committees, that each one has undertaken to make his work the very best, and I stand in this presence to bear witness to the fact that each one has succeeded. [*Applause.*] In addition to this I wish to say that the preparations which have been made have been so conducted that we have been enabled to do all this at an expense of almost $4,000 less than the expense which has fallen on previous committees. [*Applause.*] Our business affairs have been conducted according to such business methods that we know to-day just where we are, and we stand ready to pay 100 cents on every dollar of just obligation. [*Applause.*] And I take very great pleasure in saying that at the meeting of our committee held after this morning's session, I was authorized to say to the Board of Trustees of the United Society, that, in addition to paying all these just obligations here in local arrangements, we are also able to meet an obligation that rests upon us to assist the United Society of Christian Endeavor in bearing the expense incident to bringing these speakers into our midst to perform the excellent service they have rendered. [*Applause.*] And so, in the name of the Committee of '94, we shall present to the trustees of the United Society one thousand dollars [*loud applause*] — this not so much as a present as a legitimate expense, as we conceive it, which we should bear in connection with this magnificent gathering. I wish again to thank you for this banner; and now, being but a sub-committee among many committees in this the best union I have ever seen [*applause*], I shall perform the duty of a servant simply as I shall take this beautiful banner and present it to the chairman of our hall committee, who is also the president of our local union, Mr. J. E. Cheesman [*applause*], that he may receive it for the union, and keep it among our most cherished treasures. [*Mr. Cheesman came forward.*] As president of the local union of Christian Endeavor in the city of Cleveland, I present to you, coming from the Board of Trustees of the United Society, this beautiful banner. Accept it, and may it ever be treasured as among the most precious of all our treasures! [*Applause.*]

Mr. Cheesman: I am sure, Dr. Tyler, officers and trustees of the United Society, that I voice the sentiment of every member of the Cleveland Christian Endeavor Union when I say that we accept this banner with our hearts overflowing with gratitude and love in return for the best wishes that you have given us. We will try to keep this in our hearts and before our eyes as a motto of earnestness and faithfulness for Christ and the church. [*Applause and three cheers for the Committee of '94.*]

Mr. Baer: When the officers and trustees thought it would be wise to leave a memento of our visit here, we had no idea of making it so expensive for those to whom we were giving it. You never thought that this would cost you one thousand dollars. [*Laughter.*] But speaking seriously, I know the Board of Trustees are grateful, and I am sure that President Clark would, if he only knew it, be very grateful indeed to the Christian Endeavor Union and to the Cleveland Committee for bearing a part of the expenses that we naturally take in a convention of this kind. But the best announcement that you have made, sir — I am quite sure the members of the Board will agree with me — is that this magnificent convention, which is the largest convention I believe that we have held yet, magnificently conducted, nothing out of order, homes perfect, everybody delighted and everybody enthusiastic, and probably everybody would like to stay with you forever — that this whole convention has been carried on at an expense of $4,000 less than any recent international convention. God bless you for your careful economy! [*Loud applause.*]

After singing the hymn, "Christian Soldiers All," Mr. Dickinson introduced Pres. W. J. Tucker, D.D., of Dartmouth College, as one of the warmest friends of Christian Endeavor. Dr. Tucker was warmly greeted, and read his address, as follows: —

The Claims of an Educated Life.

Address of Pres. W. J. Tucker, D.D.

Mr. Chairman, Members of the Christian Endeavor Societies, — The claims of an educated life, upon whom do they rest to-day? Answering that question in your presence, I say upon those who have consecrated their lives to Christ and to his service. A Christian is one who has consecrated himself, not only as he is, but as he may be, to Christ. A Christian is one who has consecrated not only what he has, but what he may have, to Christ. Christian consecration is the converting of the increase of life to God. It is the pledging of the possibilities of our being to him. "Thou oughtest to have put my money to the exchangers," Jesus said to the slothful servant in the parable, "and at my coming I should have received my own with usury." What we are is God's gift to us; what we make of ourselves is our gift to God.

This idea of consecration as concerned so largely with the future of life shows us at once the tremendous meaning of all movements which lay hold upon the early years of life. Very much of the moral progress of the world has been due to young men working singly or in groups. Why? Not simply because they were more in earnest or had more enthusiasm than their elders, but chiefly because they had time on their side, time to plan, and time to execute their plans. They could count upon a whole generation of working years in advance. Take a series of moral movements issuing from a single center — the University of Oxford. First John Wesley and his young friends starting the great evangelical revival of England, then John Henry Newman and his friends striving to infuse into the church of their day something of the spirit of the Christian Fathers. And then Arnold Toynbee and his friends, taking the culture of Oxford into the slums of London to live Christianity in the midst of its shame; a series of movements which has a parallel in our own country, beginning with the campaign of Samuel J. Mills at Williams College for foreign missions. "We ought," he said to his classmates, "we ought to carry the gospel to dark and heathen lands, and we can do it if we will. I would that we might break out on the heathen like the Irish Rebellion, forty thousand strong."

Here is the significance in good part of the Christian Endeavor movement. Consecration has time in which to plan and work. Over against the pastors, of all workers whose cry is "Give us twenty, ten, five years more of work," is the strong, exultant power of your rejoicing: "The years are ours, we will fill them with results; we will write a new chapter in the history of the kingdom of God." But we may be disappointed. We shall be disappointed unless we rightly use the agencies which insure success. Consecration will not succeed of itself. Character, goodness, piety, must be re-enforced and equipped with those powers through which Christianity does its work in our age. Hence my plea to-night for an educated life. I do not speak of it as a source of personal culture, however helpful that may be toward personal influence. I speak of it as a means of Christian power. Multiply into the consecration, the enthusiasm, the endeavor of this movement, the power of great intelligence, and who can calculate the result? There are, as any one can see, three great agencies through which results are gained in our time. In themselves they are purely secular. Christianize them, and you make them of rightful effect anywhere. They are the power of money, the power of organization, and the power of education. I venture no mean prophecy when I say that the great agency of the immediate future is education. The day of quick and easy fortune is drawing to a close. A smaller and smaller number will be able to act through money; and this great agency, and their power, will come under increasing restrictions. When Peter Cooper went to New York as a young man, he determined upon two things: First, that he would make a fortune, and then, that he would devote it to the good of the young men and women of the city; and Cooper Institute is the lasting proof that he kept faith with himself. But a like purpose is not so easily carried out to-day, albeit we have institutes springing up in our great cities. Beyond the difficulty of making a fortune to-day is the difficulty of holding it till it can accomplish its moral purpose. It is no longer true that a man is the master of his fortune for many years. Money has its larger place, even in the kingdom of God. But I doubt if it will appeal as strongly to the Christian imagination of the next generation as it has to this. Money will always have its place and its uses in the kingdom, and its uses will widen rather than diminish. There are signs that the purely commercial spirit which has dominated the country since the war is beginning to yield to the passion for education. The power of organization, which has brought about such quick and startling results within the past years, has entirely failed to bring about permanent results to the degree in which it has been arbitrary or hasty. Organization seems a short and easy way of reaching the desired end. There is no short and easy method of reaching a sufficient end. Organization is effective to the precise degree in which it has a reason, and to the degree in which those organized can be made worthy of the ends proposed. I am heartily in favor of the principle of organization as applied to labor. I believe in the justice of it, and in the worth of it. But I believe that every arbitrary and every unconsidered or reckless use of any labor organizations only goes to show the insufficiency of the principle when too much reliance is placed upon it. The greater leaders of organized bodies are discarding all forced methods, all mere massing of men, and are falling back upon what they wisely term a campaign of education. Organization is stronger as a power in reserve than as a power in action.

By common consent, as it seems to me, we are now entering upon the great educational epoch of our country. Money will have a permanent place and power; organization will have a permanent place and power. Relatively, the power of education will increase more and more. I am concerned that the church of God should recognize this fact. I am concerned that Christianity should avail itself of the coming agency as thoroughly as it has proved those which are still at work. I am especially concerned that this Christian movement, which has gathered up into itself so much of the choice life of the land, which has been guided with such consummate skill and wisdom, should take a commanding part in the commanding influences of the times before us.

Let me, then, go on to speak briefly, but in more detail, of the part which an educated life is to have in the Christian movements of the immediate future. These movements wait on the power which can come only from a sufficient education. You will remember that I am assuming in all that I say a Christian purpose. That granted, I contend that it is to the power which lies in a broad and ennobling education that we must look for results.

True, in the first place, we have outgrown all the methods of Christian work which lie within the range of mere charity or of mere activity, except as they are informed by the clearest and most authoritative knowledge. Our common Christian activity without this clearer knowledge is little better than running to and fro. Conscience no longer tells us just what we ought to do in many cases of right and wrong; for conscience uninformed cannot tell us what is right and what is wrong. Society is becoming so complicated that it is not a very simple thing for a man who means to do right in his business to be sure that he is doing right.

Every day's business begins in the assumption that every man is doing his duty. But a great many are not doing their duty; and every one who is false or neglectful makes it harder for every other one to be honest. An honest man makes the appeal to his conscience when he is perplexed. But back of his conscience is the conscience of his trade, his profession, his party, his church, — and the answers he gets from them are sometimes very confusing. How to do right, how to be honest in some circumstance, is the question which troubles many a man of natural rectitude. It sometimes seems to me that the most careful men at this point in every community are not our ministers, but men of every calling who are teaching their fellows how to make their callings more honorable, — politicians who are making politics purer; manufacturers and traders who are making and selling goods up to the standard, and making it profitable; and capitalists and agents who are putting souls into corporations. And besides these and beyond these, men who are determined, at all cost, upon the necessary reforms of society. One of the most terrible fallacies into which we fall is that of assuming in the midst of so much prosperity that things are about right. Things are not about right because they are better than they were. Let us not deify progress. Progress is nothing but the intelligent, patient, persistent action of the wise and better men working in harmony with the purpose of God. To-day the theory, the hope, the struggle, — to-morrow the fact. Somebody must think, and keep right on thinking, if the world is to grow better. At times I feel that this is the one word to say to our generation, with its abounding and not always effective activity. Nothing is more painful than the helplessness of mere charity or mere energy before the more serious problems of our age. The most dangerous men in the field of reform are those most in earnest who have the least intelligence. I do not expect that we can all become competent leaders; but next to competent leadership is intelligent support — and this means two things. It means that we will not be misled on public questions of moral significance, and it means that we will follow without flinching when the leadership is brave and intelligent.

But more even than we need the larger knowledge, we need the larger sympathy, the sympathy which comes from the power to put one's self in another's place; deeper even than this, the power to interpret men to themselves. The beggar at your door asks an alms. You give him an alms; you leave him still a beggar. What does the man want, the man within the beggar? His cry to you, if you have any ear to hear, is the cry of the man's mind, the cry of his soul. It is the province of an educated life to interpret the deeper wants of humanity, wants which are unintelligible, it may be, to the great hungering and thirsting mass. We have no right to accept the opinions of society about men until we have been able to verify its opinion. If it is wrong we ought to be able to disprove it. The saddest words in literature are the words attributed to Lord Byron: "Men took me to be what I said I was, and I came to be what I thought I was." I do not wonder that Dr. Lyman Beecher used to say, "If I could have got hold of Byron I could have saved him." I believe that he could, because he believed in him, believed in him against himself.

I cannot overestimate the moral, the Christian power which comes from the clear interpretation of human life. It is infinitely beyond and above mere sentiment. Christ loved men because he respected them. There is no love for any man that is worth anything, which is not preceded by respect. But to have respect one must have insight, — the power to see the hidden worth, the value that is almost effaced, the soul in a man that is almost worn out by sin. And beyond this power of interpretation, which belongs to a truly educated life, lies the self-respecting quality, which enables one to do in person what other men might be ashamed to do. The most instructive act in the life of our Lord was his washing the disciples' feet. The secret of the act is told in the opening words of the story: "Jesus, knowing that the Father had put all things into his hands, and that he was come from God and went to God, he riseth from supper and took a towel and girded himself; after that he poureth water into a basin and began to wash the disciples' feet." Why should not our Lord have stooped to wash the disciples' feet? Other men might have hesitated whether they could afford to do such a thing; but as for him, knowing what he knew of himself, that he was come from God and was on his way back to God, what was it which he could not afford to stop to do by the way? It is the office of a generous and ennobling education to make one not ashamed to do some things which ought to be done, but which most people are ashamed to do. Wealth works by proxy. It patronizes. Education, if it is true and genuine, teaches that self-respect which allows the doing of things which are least and lowest. It dares to stoop, if need be, to drudgery. Society needs this class of self-respecting workers more than anybody else. If we are to save the lowest in our cities, we must save them in person. We must supplement the mission by the settlement. It is a very significant fact that the people who actually live among those with whom they work in the cities, with the direct view of establishing social relations, are the graduates of our colleges and universities.

And then, more than knowledge, more than sympathy, we want that inspiration and motive which ought to be the special contribution of an educated life. The educated man is the man plus the fact he knows, the idea he cherishes, the truth he believes. No, that is not the full statement of it. Facts, ideas, the truth, are made a part of an educated life. The personal influence of such a life is thus far more than that of the life in itself. It is representative of the principle which masters it, of the truth which informs and quickens it. I cannot dwell upon this power of inspiration which comes from one who has really gotten hold of a supreme fact or truth, but I want to make an application of it. When our president, Dr. Clark, asked me to speak on this subject, he thought at first that he would like to put it, The claims of the Christian ministry. I was glad to take the wider subject; but everything that I have said, or can say, culminates in the thought of the ministry as a source of Christian power. Who is the Christian minister? He is, above all else, the man possessed of the truth of the gospel of Christ, and able to impress that truth upon men. The last part of my definition is a very essential part. Not every one possessed of the truth, or possessed by it, can gain a hearing for it among men. To accomplish that requires the utmost training and study. One of the best definitions of preaching I ever heard runs, " Preaching is making men think, and feel as they think, and act as they feel." That is it. It is the business of the minister to carry the truth in hand through the whole nation, and not leave one power untouched, — mind, heart, will, everything subdued and quickened and enlarged. Then a man is a Christian. And the Christian ministry stands for all this power of persuasion and mastery. And then, it opens the magnificent field of constructive and aggressive work. For years we listened to the cry from the far West, constantly receding till it reached at last the Pacific, "Give us men to shape and mold the States that are to be." That cry is still urgent; but more urgent, if it be possible, is the cry that comes up from all our cities, "Give us men to recover and save the multitude." And for this work, as for the other, we want leaders of men, men whose hearts burn with the love of humanity, but who are as clear and sure in their plans as a general in the field. The religious problem of every city is a part of the problem of good citizenship, clean government, honest employment, social purity, — in short, of applied Christianity. And in this work the Christian ministry is to-day at the front.

And beyond these calls from every part of our growing land, there comes still the long, patient, unsatisfied cry of the nations like the moan of the sea, the weak calling for the strong, the ignorant for the enlightened, the oppressed for the free, the world in its sin for those who know that it has been redeemed. This is the opportunity. I do not care to urge the necessity. I do not call for volunteers for a forlorn hope. What I want to impress upon your minds is the power for good which awaits you if you may be persuaded to enter the ministry. As a wise teacher once said to his students, " Gentlemen, the ministry is power all round. There is a power for righteousness in every calling, if a man will use it. I cannot find a clean and honest business in which a Christian is out of place. Neither can I find one in which an educated life will not count for more than one undisciplined and uninformed. But in the Christian ministry, with its wide possibilities, its varied openings, its constant and unchanging power, I find a claim upon you which is urgent and inspiring. To every young man among you who feels the kindling of his mind toward the truth, and the kindling of his heart toward men, to every such a one I say, you have your call to the ministry in yourself. Make yourself worthy of it. Spare no time, no discipline, no sacrifice, to qualify yourself to take advantage of the privilege and the honor, in this day of service, of the Christian ministry.

And so I leave with you all my plea for an educated life. There are two excuses which are utterly inefficient, whenever we are challenged by any high duty. One excuse runs: "I am not worthy of it; I am not good enough to attempt it." Consecration takes away that excuse. In place of the "I am not good enough," it puts your own motto: "I will try; I can do all things through Christ which strengtheneth me." The other excuse runs: "I am not competent to do it; I do not know enough." Education takes away that excuse. It offers to give the sufficient knowledge, the needful sympathy, the inspiring motive.

I return to the thought with which I began. It is not what we are, but what we may become, which makes us of great value to our common Master. It is the increase of our lives which he wants. What if there could come upon this convention, and upon all whom it represents, the supreme gift of a great intelligence? What if we could go hence with the insight to discern and apply the exact remedies for our social ills? What if we could settle the questions which vex the state and the church? What if such a wisdom were to-day one of the immediate gifts of the spirit to be received rather than to be earned? Wisdom is always the gift of the Spirit of God; but blessed be that process through which the Spirit disciplines and informs the mind, and purifies and ennobles the nature, to make us co-workers with him toward so great an end. Education is the chief process through which God is shaping and forging men as the instruments for his designs. Of old the word of the Lord came to a man, saying: "I will take thee, and I will make thee as a signet." "I will use thee to set my seal, to stamp my purpose on men and on events." The ancient word still sounds in the ears of him who will hear it. It is the call to-day of an educated life for Christ and his service: "I will take thee, and I will make thee as a signet."

After Dr. Tucker had concluded his address, the favorite hymn, "Onward, Christian Soldiers," was sung. Mr. Baer made several announcements, among which was one referring to the Roll of Honor upon which were inscribed the names of over five thousand societies which had contributed over ten dollars each to missions through their own denominational boards during the year. This roll was 465 feet long, and was draped along the front of the gallery. The hymn, "Scatter the Sunshine," was then sung with splendid effect, after which Mr. Dickinson introduced Rev. John Potts, D.D., of Toronto, Ont., Secretary of Education of the Methodist Church of Canada, who delivered an eloquent and inspiring address as follows: —

Christ the Worker: a Model for All Endeavorers.

Address of Rev. John Potts, D.D.

Those in this audience will not object if, in the treatment of my subject, I shall be guided by the words of the Great Worker in the New Testament record of his incarnate life.

I want to speak of a threefold picture of the working Christ, and a threefold lesson from the working Christ, founded upon Luke ii. 49, "Wist ye not that I must be about my Father's business?" John ix. 4, "I must work the works of him that sent me while it is day; the night cometh when no man can work;" and John xvii. 4, "I have finished the work which thou gavest me to do."

It seems fitting that at a convention of the Christian Endeavor Society the example of Christ as the model worker for all disciples should be made prominent, and especially as the Sunday-school world has begun a year of study of the life of Christ, this July should begin a great year in the study of the life of our blessed Lord. The study of the life of Christ should enlarge our knowledge of Christ, our faith in Christ, and our resemblance to Christ. This should be a year of such concentrated contemplation of the Saviour, as revealed in the Gospel narratives, that the words of Paul should be translated into the experience of all devout disciples of the Christ. "But we all, with open face beholding as in a glass the glory of the Lord, are changed into the same image from glory to glory, even as by the Spirit of the Lord."

The life of Christ is inexhaustible, as the words of Christ are inexhaustible. The New Testament presents Christ in a great variety of aspects, from the Bethlehem scene of angel song and shepherd wonder and magi worship, along the three and thirty years, until the tragic event of Calvary astonished the universe, glorified God, and redeemed mankind.

It is proper to think of the Christ in his divinity and incarnation as taught in the first chapter of John's Gospel, verses 1 and 14: "In the beginning was the Word, and the Word was with God, and the Word was God." "And the Word was made flesh." It is proper to think of his nativity as taught in the second chapter of Matthew and in the second chapter of Luke.

It is proper to think of the teaching, compassion, sympathy, suffering, and dying, and also of the monarch miracle of Christianity, the resurrection of Jesus Christ from the dead.

The church rejoices in a living Christ who can say, "I am he that liveth and was dead; and, behold, I am alive for evermore, Amen."

But to-day let us rather contemplate Christ in his working character.

The working Christ would have working disciples; and, therefore, he says to the loiterers: "Why stand ye here all the day idle?" "Son, go work to-day in my vineyard," and to all disciples, "Let your light so shine before men, that they may see your good works, and glorify your Father which is in heaven."

The gospel of work must be preached. Christ and his disciples lived it and preached it. In extolling the doctrine of justification by faith we seem to have belittled works — works the fruit of faith. Paul and James are reconcilable. Christian work is Christ's way of saving sinners. Work is Christ's way of blessing the church. It is by work that Christ makes the church healthy and strong and happy. Christ's greatest apostle was constantly exhorting disciples of Christ to consecrated service, saying, "Let us not be weary in well doing, for in due season we shall reap, if we faint not." How many there are who call Christ Master and yet do little or no work for him — in the church, and yet living selfish lives — professing to believe the Word of God, and yet doing nothing to save men from impending ruin.

How refreshing to contemplate Christ the worker as a model for all Christian workers. An inspired apostle afterwards gave that brief but beautiful description of Christ, "Who went about doing good." That was the every-day description of the man, Christ Jesus. It is something worth remembering that Christian work can be done anywhere, everywhere, and always. If we would imitate Christ the worker, we must have his spirit of prayerfulness and of zeal for the glory of God.

And now let us study "A Threefold Picture of the Working Christ."

The first scene is recorded in the second chapter of Luke's Gospel. It carries us back to Christ's first passover. The celebration is over, and the visitors are starting for their distant homes. The company from Nazareth has started on the return journey. Soon it is known that one is absent — Jesus, the son of Mary, is not with them. Mary and Joseph return to the city and search for the missing boy. Jesus was found in the temple. Many have found Jesus in the temple since then.

What a picture — Jesus in the midst of the doctors, both hearing them and asking them questions. It would be good for the teaching doctors now to have Jesus in the midst — Jesus in the midst of our theological schools, Sunday-schools, Endeavor societies, and in the midst of all church work. What questions did he propose? How interesting it would be to know the questions asked by Christ! Did he expound the law, the prophets, or the psalms? Was it then that the great mission of his life dawned upon him? Did the feast, with its historic reminiscences, its typical lamb, and its sprinkled blood, open up to him anything extraordinary as to a greater redemption?

In the midst of this scene, which commanded and captivated the venerable doctors as they gazed upon the lad in their midst, being astonished at his understanding and answers, Mary appears. To her word of almost seeming reproof Jesus said, "Wist ye not that I must be about my Father's business?" And by those words he would remind her of the mysterious past. Thus early do we find Christ working at his Father's business.

The second picture is presented to us in John ix. 4: "I must work the works of him that sent me while it is day; the night cometh when no man can work."

Twenty years have passed away since the picture referred to in Luke took place. Since then there was the wonderful baptism in Jordan, when the Holy Ghost, in form like a dove, descended upon him, who said to the Baptist, "Suffer it to be so now; for thus it becometh us to fulfill all righteousness." The Christ had entered upon his great life work, saying in the Nazareth synagogue, "The Spirit of the Lord is upon me, because he hath anointed me to preach the gospel." This passage fully represents him as the working Christ — working in teaching, working in miracles, and working in that every-day exemplarship which left us an example that we should walk in his steps. Hear the solemn and emphatic words of the working Christ, "I must work."

Scene third, John xvii. 4: "I have glorified thee on the earth; I have finished the work which thou gavest me to do."

The first picture presented Christ to us at his first passover; now we see him at his last passover and at the last passover. Since then passover ceremonies have no significance. The feast has been partaken of, the farewell address has been spoken, contained in the fourteenth, fifteenth, and sixteenth chapters of John's Gospel, which may well be designated the holy of holies of Christ's teaching. The Christ turns from speaking to his disciples to speak to his Father in the language of the seventeenth chapter, which should be called the Lord's Prayer, rather than the prayer usually called the Lord's Prayer.

I have often wondered if this prayer of the seventeenth chapter of John might not be regarded as a specimen of the intercession of Christ in heaven itself.

The shadow of the cross has fallen upon Christ; and we hear him say, "Father, the hour is come," that hour to which all lines of Messianic prophecy converged. Mark his testimony: "I have glorified thee on the earth; I have finished the work which thou gavest me to do." Here is a perfect life with its work finished.

Now we turn to consider a threefold lesson from the threefold picture of the working Christ.

First, a lesson on the desirableness and beauty of early consecration. Recall the temple scene in the second chapter of Luke. Who is that in the midst of the doctors? Who is that whom we hear saying to Mary, "I must be about my Father's business"? It is Jesus at the age of twelve years.

Take Christ's thought of religion. How impressive it is! Religion a business — religion the business of life. Let young people get this Jesus idea of religion — that it is a business. It should be a lifelong business — no retiring from it. In the ordinary affairs of life it is well for a man, when able to do so, to lessen the business cares and burdens, and take life more quietly in old age than in early and middle manhood; but in the great business of religion he should cease at once to work and live. His knowledge and experience should be of great value to the cause of God and to the young people.

Contemplate religion as the great business of life. Let me ask, When should a business be learned? When should a musician learn music, or an artist painting, or a lawyer law, or a doctor medicine, or a merchant commerce? Is it in old age? Is it in middle life? Is it not rather in the days of youth? So of the great business of religion. It should be begun in the days of childhood. Remember Jesus and his declaration of consecration to his Father's business. How beautiful is this early consecration! How desirable it is in the light of prevention! With a young person it is not religion or nothing; it is plants of vice or weeds of sin. It is habits of godliness or habits of sinfulness. How desirable in the light of usefulness! Two men — one begins Christian life at fifty and works till he reaches fourscore years; the other begins Christian life at twenty and works till eighty. The one has thirty years of service for Christ, the other has twice thirty.

How desirable in the light of happiness is this early consecration! What precious memories of work done for Jesus! What sweet communion with the Master in all that work! How often has that whisper come as the earnest of the final "Well done, good and faithful servant," the assurance of the Master's approval!

How desirable is early consecration in the light of heaven! "One star differeth from another star in glory; so also is the resurrection from the dead." Degrees of glory in heaven; and those degrees are effected by practical Christian service here. An ideal life of consecrated service would be to begin in childhood and to render an uninterrupted, a Holy Spirit directed service, until, at the close of life's long day, the whisper is heard from the Master, "Come up hither."

Young people, learn the lesson of early consecration to the work of God from the childhood consecration of Jesus. Begin early and be about your Father's business until the end shall come. Let parents and teachers give all diligence to win the children for the service of the Lord.

Shall Christianity or infidelity have the young people? Infidelity is catering for the young. In the sugar-coated but poisonous periodical literature of the age, there is the most persistent determination to alienate the intelligent and educated young people away from the Bible and from the salvation therein revealed. Infidelity cares little for gray hairs and old age; it is after the brainy young people of the nineteenth century. Let the Church of Christ, and all societies in harmony with the Church of Christ, give unceasing attention to the shepherding of the lambs and to the spiritual care of the young people.

Second, a lesson on the importance of manhood activity in the work of God.

Recall the scene of the ninth chapter of John. The disciple should be as his Master. How did the Master live and work? Hear what Jesus said, "I must work." If so in his case, can there be exemption in our case? There was a redemptional necessity resting upon the man Christ to work the works of him that sent him. Why? How? Because no one else could do his work. In the work of redemption Christ was alone. "He trod the winepress alone, and of the people there was none with him." But in salvation his people are co-workers with him. In a subordinate sense it is true of each of us that there is a work for us to do. "To every man his work." No one can do it as well as ourselves. "The night cometh when no man can work," — the night which means the end of life's working-day. That night, ever approaching, should intensify our earnestness. It seems to have effected the mind even of Christ. The counsel of Solomon is pertinent in view of the example of the working Christ: "Whatsoever thy hand findeth to do, do it with thy might; for there is no work, nor device, nor knowledge, nor wisdom, in the grave, whither thou goest."

Work is the law of life, — of all kinds of life, from the insect to the archangel.

Work is the law of success. This is true in all departments of life, in professional and commercial life. Take the eminently successful men, and in every instance work has been the royal road to success. Great lawyers are great workers; great doctors are great workers; great merchants are great workers.

Christian work is the law of spiritual life, and it is the law of spiritual prosperity. Christian work is the law of Christian character, and Christian work shall be the test of the judgment day. In the final and supreme assize, as described in the twenty-fifth chapter of Matthew, service for Christ, which means service for humanity, shall be the test of the judgment: "I was an hungred, and ye gave me meat: I was thirsty, and ye gave me drink: I was a stranger, and ye took me in: naked, and ye clothed me: I was sick, and ye visited me: I was in prison, and ye came unto me. Then shall the righteous answer him, saying, Lord, when saw we thee an hungred, and fed thee? or thirsty, and gave thee drink? When saw we thee a stranger, and took thee in? or naked, and clothed thee? Or when saw we thee sick, or in prison, and came unto thee? And the King shall answer and say unto them, Verily I say unto you, Inasmuch as ye have done it unto one of the least of these, my brethren, ye have done it unto me."

Excuses are made by men who are members of the church, and who doubtless are Christians — Cannot spare time to engage in Christian work, is a very familiar kind of excuse. No Christian man has any right to be so busy as to be unable to work for God and his fellows. There is a rule of proportion to be observed — time for business and also time for Christ. "Not slothful in business, fervent in spirit, serving the Lord."

Let Christ's motive to work influence each of us, all of us. "The night cometh when no man can work."

There is work to be done in our spiritual life and character. "Work out your own salvation with fear and trembling; for it is God that worketh in you to will and to do of his own good pleasure." Surely the temple palace of character is deserving of painstaking care and culture.

There is work to be done in our families. How shall we stand in the presence of God with that neglected?

There is work to be done in our places of business, if employers or employed.

There is work to be done in the circle of our influence in the community. There is work at hand and all around. Lift up your eyes — lift up your eyes from the counter, from the desk, from the bench. Lift up your eyes and look on the fields — on the family field, on the Sunday-school field, on the temperance field, on the home mission rescue field, and on the foreign missionary field, for they are white unto harvest. "Say not there are four months and then cometh harvest." The devil is as well pleased with a four months' postponement of work as with a four years' postponement, as long as Christian work is postponed.

Then let us hear Jesus say, and let us say it for ourselves, "I must work, the night cometh." It is nearer than ever, nearer than when you were converted, nearer than when you joined the church, nearer than when you left home for this service. How near?

Thirdly, a lesson on the blessedness of reviewing a life spent in the service of the Lord.

Recall the third scene in the life of the working Christ, John xvii. 4. The end came to Christ, and how did it find him? "I have glorified thee on the earth; I have finished the work which thou gavest me to do."

The end comes to all. The end of opportunity, the end of work, the end of life, of probationary life, itself. How different is the end of a Christian compared with that of others? There is all the difference between success and abject failure, between victory and appalling defeat. To the faithful worker, the "well done, good and faithful servant," shall be addressed. Concerning such, the words may be spoken of them, "I heard a voice from heaven saying unto me, Write, Blessed are the dead which die in the Lord from henceforth: Yea, saith the Spirit, that they may rest from their labours; and their works do follow them." The working Christian can say in a subordinate sense, as the end is at hand: "I have glorified thee on the earth; I have finished the work which thou gavest me to do."

Life must not be measured by years, but by character in Christ Jesus, and by work done for God and humanity. Paul felt that his had been a life of work in imitation of Christ, and therefore from the Roman dungeon he could write thus grandly to Timothy, "I am now ready to be offered, and the time of my departure is at hand. I have fought a good fight, I have finished my course, I have kept the faith."

Working for Christ — working like Christ — is the way to save the world. Christ put great value on one soul. All Christian workers should remember that. You may remember how he taught Nicodemus the way into the kingdom; and how he dealt with the woman of Samaria at Jacob's well; and how he emphasized the importance of the repentance of one sinner in the fifteenth chapter of Luke; and you remember that, when on the way to Jerusalem to redeem the world, Jesus heard the cry of a poor, blind beggar, and he paused and saved him.

Let us all engage in the work of the Lord afresh, and in the spirit of Miss Havergal's consecrated hymn, —

> "Take my life, and let it be
> Consecrated, Lord, to thee.
> Take my moments and my days,
> Let them flow in ceaseless praise."

When John Wesley was asked on one occasion as to what his religious experience was, he replied, "You will find it in such a hymn, written by my brother Charles, and in the third and fourth verses: —

> "Jesus, confirm my heart's desire
> To work and speak and think for thee;
> Still let me guard the holy fire,
> And still stir up thy gift in me.
>
> Ready for all thy perfect will,
> My acts of faith and love repeat;
> Till death thy endless mercies seal,
> And make the sacrifice complete."

Where are we in relation to Christian work?

Have we, each of us, some definite work on hand? and are we imbued with the Christ Spirit, impelling us to say, "I must work, for the night cometh, when no man can work"?

The great qualifier for Christian work is the Holy Spirit. This vital truth cannot be too often repeated. "Not by might, nor by power, but by my spirit," saith the Lord.

The man Christ Jesus was thus qualified: "The spirit of the Lord is upon me."

Each disciple of Christ may have the same spirit, and be able to say of all kinds of service, "The spirit of the Lord is upon me, because he hath anointed me to preach the gospel; because he hath anointed me to teach in the Sunday-school; because he hath anointed me to testify of the inward blessed life; because he hath anointed me to pray the prayer of intercession for others; because he hath anointed me to persuade sinners to be reconciled to God; and because he hath anointed me to be a winner of souls for Christ and salvation and heaven."

To one and all workers, let me say in the comprehensive exhortation of Paul the apostle, "Therefore, my beloved brethren, be ye steadfast, unmovable, always abounding in the work of the Lord, forasmuch as ye know that your labor is not in vain in the Lord."

Dr. Potts was frequently interrupted by storms of applause. At the close of the address the audience joined in singing, "Work, for the Night is Coming." This was followed by a beautiful rendering of "The Lost Chord" by the three Park sisters; and an *encore* being demanded, they played "Down on the Suwanee River." The benediction was then pronounced by Rev. Dr. H. C. Farrar.

THE TENT.

The gathering of the delegates was characterized by the usual good fellowship and impromptu singing, a little variety being afforded by selections from the brass band stationed on the platform.

Treasurer Shaw presided over the session. Immediately after calling the assembly to order he introduced the following resolution, which was adopted by a rising vote: —

"*Resolved*, that we send to our president the expression of our deep and abiding love, assuring him how keenly we have missed his presence, which has always been one of the benedictions of these great conventions, and how sincerely we pray and fervently hope that he may be speedily restored to the most vigorous health. Thankful to the heavenly Father that he has used him to inspire one of the mightiest movements of modern Christendom, we invoke upon him utmost blessings."

The Park sisters then captured the audience by rendering a cornet selection very beautifully; but there was no time for the *encore* which the audience persistently demanded.

Rev. H. M. Ladd, D.D., of Cleveland, next led the assembly in prayer.

Bishop Arnett was the first speaker on the programme, but he was detained at home by illness. Mr. Shaw stated this fact to the audience, and then introduced Rev. W. D. Johnson, D.D., of Atlanta, Ga., a colored preacher, who spoke as follows: —

The Negro and the Endeavorer.

Address of Rev. W. D. Johnson, D.D.

I am very sorry that the great representative of our people does not stand before you to-night. I refer to Bishop Benjamin W. Arnett, who is detained by sickness. Recognizing the mighty task before me, I can only ask your sympathy and the help of our heavenly Father.

The great commandment of Jesus is: "Go ye therefore and teach all nations, baptizing them in the name of the Father and of the Son and of the Holy Ghost. While thus you follow my commandment I am with you until the world shall end. All power is intrusted in my hand; I can destroy and can defend."

It seems but, fair to say: Africa for the black man; Asia for the yellow man; Europe for the white man; America for all men, and all men for God. [*Applause.*]

It is a strange fact that while all other races came here of their own accord, the black race came by special invitation. [*Laughter and applause.*] And, to make sure that we would come, some ships were fitted up in style and sent to bring us over.

It is a favorite notion with some that all nations must contribute some great idea for the benefit of the world. With the Hebrews it was religion; with the Greeks it was beauty; with the Romans it was law; with the Saxons it was liberty; but with the negro it was love. [*Applause.*]

When Bishop Asbury came to America great crowds flocked to hear him. The bishop had to wait on him a colored preacher named Black Harry; and sometimes, if the bishop was not well, Harry would preach in his place. On this occasion one man started from his home happy, for in those times white people used to get happy just as we do [*laughter and applause*]; and when this man got near the church he began to shout, and as he heard the sound of the multitude he cried, "Glory." He shouted, and by and by rolled in the dirt and had a good time, and then picking himself up, walked around, exclaiming, "Oh, what a glorious sermon the bishop preached to-day!" By and by some one said: "Why, my dear sir, that was not the bishop that preached to-day, that was Black Harry." "Oh, well," said the man, "then I had my shout all for nothing." [*Laughter.*]

The black man has always stood close to God. Homer speaks of the blameless Ethiopians, the favorites of the gods; and Africa opened her arms to receive the Christ child when Herod sought his life; and a man from the same country, on his great black shoulders, carried the cross up Mount Calvary when Jesus fainted beneath the load. [*Applause.*] The cross was not popular in those days; but now, as the electric cars are bearing their thousands to this tent and to the great Saengerfest Hall, the happy Endeavorers, with the refrain echoing around the world, are singing:—

> "Must Jesus bear the cross alone,
> And all the world go free?
> No, there's a cross for every one,
> And there's a cross for me."
> [*Applause.*]

Mr. Moody tells: "During a shipwreck the mate stood with two pistols guarding a lifeboat, when the cook, a stout black fellow, came to the rail with a great bundle in his arms. The mate said to him, 'You will either have to leave that bundle or stay out yourself.' Seeing there was no other way, he uncovered the bundle and there lay two beautiful white babes. He kissed them, and handing them into a lifeboat, said, 'Tell master that I saved the babes, but I went down with the ship.'" [*Applause.*]

There is hope for anything that young people will take hold of. A father once prayed for a hungry man and bade him good-by, when his little boy said, "Father, you ought to answer that prayer yourself by giving that man a bushel of those potatoes down in the cellar." It was done, and all three were made happy.

The scientific spirit looks at all the facts and the work to be done. We cannot pray "Our Father, who art in heaven," in such a way as to be helpful to us, without remembering at the same time all other needy creatures. Another fact is, if the saints shall inherit the earth, who are the saints? Turn to the Gospel of St. John, in the first chapter, and you will find that they are those who are born, not of blood, nor the will of the flesh, nor the will of man, but of God.

I always had hope for my people, because they are men loyal to Christ. I knew our white brethren would either have to admit us as full Christians, or else Christ would forsake them, and we would have him all to ourselves. [*Applause.*]

I believe right now that, as the Jews went into slavery to receive Christ at his first coming, so we negroes went into slavery that we might receive him at his second coming. [*Applause.*]

And in this I seem to be borne out by Psalm xviii., which says: "Princes shall come out of Egypt, and Ethiopia shall soon stretch out her hands to God." Even so amen, come Lord Jesus. Then will come up to the pearly gates the great and final muster of the hosts of the Christian Endeavor, from the east and from the west, from the north and from the south, out of every nation and kindred and tribe and tongue and people, with the voice of a great multitude, with the voice as the sound of many waters, with the voice as a mighty thundering, saying, Hallelujah, for the Lord God Omnipotent reigneth. [*Applause.*]

Rev. John W. Beckett, a colored singer, next gave a vocal selection, without accompaniment, which was received with prolonged applause.

MR. SHAW: I have now the pleasure of introducing Rev. Dr. C. F. Smith, secretary of the A. M. E. Sunday-school Union of Nashville, Tenn.

DR. SMITH: *Mr. Chairman, Ladies and Gentlemen,* — I regard the Thirteenth Convention of the United Society of Christian Endeavor as the most marvelous accomplishment of this century. It has been my pleasure at other times and in other places to mingle in large assemblies. Last year I was permitted to attend the World's Parliament of Religions, and a great many complimentary things have been said about the World's Parliament of Religions. Some one has said that it was the second Pentecost. Well, if that was the second Pentecost, this, the Thirteenth International Convention of the United Society of Christian Endeavor, in my opinion, is the first pentecostal Pentecost. [*Applause.*] For, after the Parliament, the delegates found that they could rally under no single ensign or banner; in fact, they came together to find out, not how near they were together, but how far they were apart.

There are two million of you who are marching under one banner, with one purpose. There was never such an army before in times of war or peace. If God called Martin Luther to awaken the inert conscience of the Catholic Church, if he called John Wesley to give earnestness to Christianity, then he called Francis E. Clark to put Christianity in motion. And this society stands out before us to-night a Luther, a Wesley, and a Clark. If you are faithful and active, your results will show that, of all the movements, there is none greater than that inaugurated by Francis E. Clark.

The Park sisters rendered "The Suwanee River" exquisitely, and it was with great reluctance that the audience was compelled to desist in its efforts for an *encore*.

MR. SHAW: Now we will have something that is not on our programme. I have been asking almost every delegate that I have met if they are having a good time in Cleveland, and everybody says "Yes." [*Applause.*] Every one that I have met is being entertained at the best house in Cleveland. [*Applause.*] We never have had a better convention than the Thirteenth International Convention, and I want to introduce to this audience at this point the lady and gentlemen who are responsible for this.

The Committee of '94 then stepped upon the platform, and were individually introduced. Great applause followed the introduction of each one, and they were all given a hearty Chautauqua salute.

Mr. Shaw then introduced Rev. Jos. K. Dixon, D.D., of Philadelphia, who spoke on the subject of "Common Sense in Church Life and Work."

Common-Sense in Church Life and Work.

Address of Rev. Joseph K. Dixon, D.D.

The lily needs no paint. A smile is eloquent without the lips of oratory. Forgiveness is sublime when measured by the standard of mountains, sea, and sky. The soul's roses never fade. The lily, the smile, the word of reconciliation, the flower of the heart, are all numbered among the simple things, but they are angels always on the wing. They are like the passion of a great thought which throbs on with the tides of ocean.

The nine digits are simple, but out of them we frame the table of multiplication and the higher mathematics. Without them science would limp along on crutches, and we could not weigh and measure the moon. The alphabet is simple, but it is the basis of all vocabularies and the proudest and profoundest attainment of all literature. The octave runs the simple scale — one to eight — but it is the fountain of inspiration for all the masterpieces of music that have gone, —

"Sounding down the ringing grooves of change."

A fire and a perfume will advance even against a head wind. There is something about an apple blossom that steals over the high board fences and saturates the atmosphere beyond. This opens the door for me to say that common-sense, according to Sir William Hamilton, is "the complement of those cognitions or convictions which we receive from nature, which all men possess in common, and by which we test the truth of knowledge and the morality of actions. When the substantive is emphasized it is native practical intelligence, mother wit, tact in behavior, acuteness in the observation of character, in contrast to habits of acquired learning or of speculation."

On this foundation, then, all action of a high and worthy sort is builded. Here is the groundwork for the largest and broadest Christian Endeavor. We all start with this attainment, whatever altitude we reach. Our ability to build high and broad and massive and grand will depend upon how much common-sense we mix in the mortar.

Two frogs fell into a pan of milk; after struggling for a long time to get out, ending in failure, one of the frogs said to the other: "This is such a novel experience that I don't know what to do about it. I can't stand it much longer." Finally he said: "There is nothing left for me to do but to go to the bottom and die; I can fight no longer." His mate said: "You can go to the bottom and die if you will, but I am going to hold on a little." He did. Shortly the cream began to rise, his paddling churned it into butter, and he walked off. Common-sense frog.

In church life and work there is too little consideration of what may be done with the cream. We are too apt to drown in the buttermilk. It makes a mountainous difference which is on top, the cream or the frog; it is all the difference between life and death — lack of sense and common-sense.

I am not here to hang my harp on the willows, nor to pronounce the strain of those dear old people who are all the time croaking because they cannot be their own grandfathers; neither will I strike the key of that old hymn so many of us like to sing: "Hark from the tomb a doleful sound" The dead marches of the world belong to the powers of darkness; the song of triumph, the army with banners, belong to the kingdom of Christ.

In the study of a Western pastor I saw an artist at work on a painting designed for use in a temperance lecture. In the foreground was the sweep of a mighty river; the current was wild and swift. A rope of huge dimensions was strung from bank to bank; fastened to the strands of the rope were great hooks of steel on which were caught the voluptuaries of sin. The gambler was there with the print of the cards and dice on his brow; the profligate was there, his face stamped with the stain of sin; the drunkard, bearing the marks of debauchery. Sitting on the bank was a beautiful female figure, clad in white with wings half folded, watching men and women becoming snared by the hooks in the stream. Behind the woman there crouched the fiend of darkness, with traditional horns and tail, and the awful, ghastly grin of triumph which betokened his victory.

The artist had just struck in the ship Zion in an arm of the river where the water was peaceful; the ship was coming to rescue the fallen and the falling, but it was a dismantled old thing; the masts were splintered, the sails were torn; it looked as though it had weathered a thousand storms and would soon find the fate of the Kearsarge. The pastor asked me if I had any suggestions to make. I said, "Yes; take a brush and dash that ship from the canvas; go up the river and paint a ship with sails at fullest sweep, cordage strung to hardest tension, masts proudly erect. Paint the old ship Zion stanch and swift, bearing down upon the tempted and overborne for their safety and rescue."

The church of God is in the world, not wrecked by the world, but proudly conscious of her glorious and divine mission; she is here to sweep every sea, and spread her sails to every breeze of heaven.

It is easy to criticise; any little child can pull a rose in pieces and throw it down upon the summer breeze in fragments of parted beauty. It took a God to make that flower. Any fool can find fault with the church; but we have a right to ask if we are living in the valley, on the table-lands, or far up the mountain sides, with reference to our methods of church life and work.

The problem of living grows more intense. We must shorten our creeds and lengthen our deeds. "The pure in heart shall see God" is more than all catechisms. It is the epitome of all theologies. With this spirit we shall triumph. Christ said to John, when islanded away yonder from the green hills of his own Galilee, "Be of good cheer, for I have overcome the world." The whole glorious spirit of the New Testament is a call to victory. Yet victory the third day means that there must be a second and a first day's challenge of the enemy.

When the Master went into that chamber of death he took the little girl by the hand and said unto her, "Damsel, I say unto thee arise!" But he had no sooner sent the new life-current surging through her veins than he said to the parents, "Give her something to eat." When he bade the five thousand sit down on the grassy slopes overlooking the sacred sea, after he had broken the bread and given thanks, he said to his disciples, "Give ye them to eat." Our miracle of feeding the multitude is quite as necessary as the divine power applied to the loaves and fishes which wrought such increase.

The church is the institution established to represent Christ. Christ fed every want of man. Poor little Simon rose to a point of order and said, "What are these among so many?" Christ said there was no need that any go away. Insomuch as the church falters, hesitates, fails, by that much she loses her place in the shining ranks of those who do the bidding of their Lord. By so much is she a partial representative of her great Head.

1. Common-sense in church life and work prepares for the multitude in the character of its workshop.

A church is largely what its building is. Church life is known by its architecture, as an age is known by its ideas. The books are full of inspiring accounts of how the ancient builders wrought. We are told of the somber Egyptian, the graceful Grecian, and the forestlike Gothic. Those were the days when the old builders carved the granite into poems, and the marble into prayers.

In the days to come the people's architecture must take the place of the arch and architrave, the long-drawn aisle and the fretted vault. The stones may be molded into prayers and poems, but they must contain ideas as well. Architects are sticklers for ecclesiastical lines. Into the structure they build, there must be imported somewhere a cathedral feature. Some churches ought to have a Westminster Abbey attachment, a place where they may bury their dead.

The architecture for coming days must construct for a larger spiritual life and an ampler outreach for the people. There must be something besides the confessional-box, and a chapel for masses and petitions looking towards purgatory.

Two preaching services on Sunday, Sunday-school, and a midweek prayer-meeting is a programme that belongs with the days of the stage-coach and the tallow dip. Church buildings must be reared no longer with the idea that architecture is frozen music, with an ice-palace attachment, or as an ornament to the neighborhood, or for the glory and praise of the architect.

If the church is to lay her hand on this mighty world she must become a center of beneficence; she must build to do work along many and varied lines, educational, reformatory, philanthropic, spiritual.

If I were not talking to the Christian Endeavor host, my speech would land right up against the prejudice of some hard-headed saint; and this because we advance faster in everything else than we do in the kingdom of God. There is a good deal of cold iron to bend into shape without the aid of bellows or forge. There will always be people who, like the saints of old, are afraid the ark of the Lord is going to topple over, and hasten to steady it. They ought to recall the tragedy of Old Testament times. Then I remember that Ephraim's cake was only done on one side — a crust is better than dough.

If our churches are not useful and vital, why not bar the doors? Why invest money and time and brains in the stupendous folly? What the age wants is uplifting. In order to lift the world the church must get under the world. In Switzerland I did not see a single mill-wheel up the mountain-side. They were all down in the valley where the full force of the furious mountain torrent might make its power felt. The trouble with the church is she builds too high up; she does not get down where the purposes of God are flowing in mighty tide for the healing of the world's hurt. Point me to a spot where the Caucasian has put his foot that he has not left a mark of progress. Advance is the watchword of the hour. In far too many instances the church has made advance like the colored brother, who, during the war, was with the Gray. One day after a great disaster the troops were badly used up. Tom said to his master, "Gen'l, this chile would like to go home and see de ole folks ef you have no dejection." This was a great place to get homesick. The general said, "You can't go. We can't spare you. What would you say, Tom, as an excuse for going home?" "Well," he said, "we could say that, owing to the state of the country, and the peculiar circumstances ob de case, we were advancing backwards, and the enemy was retreating on us."

The church building should have hospitality written all over it. It should be ventilated, not merely a few air-holes punctured in the ceiling. It should be flooded with light. The auditorium should be a place where everybody could see and hear. To construct an edifice on any other plan, one might as well pattern after the Mammoth Cave. The ordinary church auditorium is built more like a shooting-gallery, or a long drawn out telescope; ecclesiastical they call it; but this sort of ecclesiasticism is more concerned for the sanctity of the church than for the salvation of men.

I believe in the institutional *church*. I do not believe in the *institutional* church. It makes all the difference where we place the emphasis. Religion has to do with every part of man, — his mind, his body, his soul. I would have a place for the development of all these faculties connected with the church.

Every church should have its parish house in close proximity to the sanctuary under whose roof all these varied activities shall have largest hospitality.

This building should be the every-day gospel of the church's life. Here shall be found the art-school, the training-school for household duties, the Bible set in motion in making better bodies and better homes; here shall be the music-room, with a man of God and a man of art, who shall here spend his working-hours, a man who shall have charge of the music in school, prayer-meeting, and the services of God's house. Then the pastor can put his hand on the entire music of the church, by putting his hand on the one man who is in most vital sympathy with the work of the leader. Here, then, singers shall be trained for chorus and choir work, and the poor will have music, which is sometimes more than bread. The multitude who will be left without such training may here learn the first notes of the new song. Voices that profane the street might be consecrated to the worship and service of the King.

In this building there shall be a play-room for the children, with its nursery provisions, its flowers and its aquariums, its birds and its swings. Here, also, there shall be an entertainment hall for concerts, lectures, and receptions. The wide church, the commonsense church, holds that an evening of good pleasure is an assistance to true religion, without either a prayer or a sermon. All the philanthropic, educational, and missionary work of the church should be carried on in this parish building, reserving for the hour of worship the place dedicated to the praise of the Father Almighty.

There will always be a time and a place for churches where the sermons of Sunday will fill the horizon of church life, but many times over will coming days behold this common-sense achievement. The spirit has been aroused which pledges its victory.

2. Common-sense in church life and work prepares for the multitude in the way in which it does its work.

I want to plead for "open doors," — a church that shall always be open. Let the stream of humanity have a chance to flow through. Some of it will stop, some of it will take root. As a general thing our churches are closed from ten o'clock on Sunday night until nine o'clock the next Sunday morning. They are opened stealthily, as Nicodemus came to Christ — by night. About the only thing you can see on some of our churches is the name of the undertaker, and that he stands ready to bury you — about the last man you want to see, and the last business you care to attend to. Often there are iron fences and iron gates securely padlocked, and somewhere a sign visible, "Fifty dollars fine for any one caught trespassing on these premises." Churches that carve in stone above their doorways, "Enter thy gates with thanksgiving, and thy courts with praise," and then shut the gates and bar the courts so that you can get in but one day in seven.

You will hear it argued that we have no altar, no holy mother, no crucifix before which to kneel. True; but in the hurry and strain of life how many times the tired head and the grief-laden heart would like to go aside for a sweet moment of meditation, or under the awful pressure of temptation get under cover of the sanctuary for deliverance. The saloon is open day and night, Sundays as well as week-days.

Said an American, when traveling abroad, "Your churches and cathedrals all have such an untidy look." — "Ah," said the attendant, "that is the trouble with your churches in America; they are not dirty enough; you don't give the people a chance to get into them. Here the poor and the rich all come to worship; it is the glory of the church that it is so."

Those of us who are more favored little realize the lack of comfort and the longing for rest that fill the life of many a mother, wearied beyond her strength, the children noisy — still she must live on. It is then that the soul cries out with the psalmist, "My soul longeth, yea, even fainteth for the courts of the Lord." The temple at Jerusalem was always open. David knew it; if he could only get there he could get in without drumming up the sexton or prying open the rear door. He knew the house of prayer, with sheltering arms, would give him a place of rest.

The temple of Janus in Rome is closed in times of peace; but when the purple cloud of war hangs over the Apennines, and the safety of the mistress of the world is threatened, her doors are thrown wide open, and the people flock to her altars. A time of aggression and war is on the Christian church. Let her doors be thrown continually open and the smoke of her altars go continually up.

3. Common-sense pleads for business methods in the prosecution of church-work.

In the city of Norristown, Pa., last November the people elected a dead man to the office of justice of the peace. John Arnold, the candidate, died suddenly on Sunday; the tickets had already been printed; his name could not be replaced by another; the voters forgot to write another name in the blank column; the ward was a Republican stronghold, and Arnold, the dead man, was elected.

Far too many churches elect dead men to fill places of responsibility and power. They never did do anything. They are honored with positions with the purpose of getting something out of them; but it is the case of John Arnold over again — the man is already dead, and needs a church grave. He may have been dead when he joined the church, which is likely to be the case. In a country cemetery where there was no minister to pronounce the committal service, the undertaker thought it irreverent to lower the casket of the dead man without some simple utterance, and so he said, "This corpse joined the church nine years ago." Too many corpses join the church; and then too many churches put them in office at a later day.

The charge has often been brought that if business men managed their affairs with as little tact and skill as they manage church affairs, nothing could save them from penury and want. The same men, the same brains, the same forecast of thought, belong to the church as are used in the business world. The business progresses, why not the church? A great boot and shoe firm paid the proprietors of the *Youth's Companion* $2,500 for the first page of one issue of that paper — 500,000 copies. They expected that each paper would be read by at least two people, or 1,000,000 readers. They expected to sell every tenth person who read — or 100,000 sales, which would be a cost of $2\frac{1}{2}$ cents on each pair of boots for their advertising.

Nothing seems so unspeakably useless to the multitude of church officials as a bill for printing. They will advertise to the last limit in their own business, but to commit to paper the workings and purposes of the church seems a waste and an extravagance. The common-sense that holds sway in the commerce of the world ought to find its rightful exercise before the altar.

Representative men in all the walks of life ought to be representative men in the church. Too many men join the church only to be a fairly proportioned brother-in-law to all that goes on inside, while they devote their best strength and talents to the outside. For this reason some churches would be fuller if they were emptier. We need not so much more men, but more man. Funerals are not always an unmixed blessing.

In some of our small towns during the storm of a winter night the boys often make merry by changing the signs on the village shops; the sign of the blacksmith shop taking the place of the one over the drug-store, and the one over the gristmill finding its way over the millinery shop. Would the boys have made a mistake if they had taken the sign so often found over some great fruit-canning establishment and put it over the church, "All kinds of fruit dried here."

Dr. Eggleston tells the story of a half-witted boy who found a horse that everybody else failed to find, though there had been constant and diligent search made for the valuable creature. When asked how he came to find the animal, he said: "I just went and sat down on that 'ar stump—and I thought, if I were a horse where would I go and what would I do, and I went right off and found him." That is the "horse-sense" we need to push on the kingdom of heaven.

Expansion, not contraction, is the law of the kingdom. We are told to grow in grace. But we often imitate the Confederate soldier whom General Lee found standing under a persimmon-tree eating green persimmons. The astonished general said to the man: "Why in the world are you trying to eat that horrible, green, puckery thing?" The soldier replied that he was trying to dry up his stomach to the size of his rations. We have too much of the narrowing down and puckering up process in the Lord's army.

4. I am reaching the end of my survey chain—let me in a little word point out some common-sense kinds of work to do.

Our churches should be free churches. Not free in the sense that stingy men may line their pocketbooks—nor free in the sense that men may shirk who are walking around in order to save the expense of a shroud, but supported by the glad free-will offerings of the people. We are too almightily busy in our churches trying to raise a revenue. The money would be forthcoming if we used the same kind and degree of common-sense in church life and work that we use in trade. I wish we could do away with the strain which money makes in the church, or the strain which comes because of the lack of money. I wish we could get rid of these oppressive pew-rents. Because a pew is rented the man comes to a sense of ownership—because the pew is rented the man comes to a point of dictation in all church finance. Everybody in the church knows what the minister gets; he does not know what a single man in the congregation receives. I long for the day when I shall not touch a penny of any man's money for preaching. It is often made a humiliation to receive it. On the other hand, I deny that the gospel is ever paid for. No mathematician let loose among stored-up bullion can ever figure out payment for the blood-red pangs that drive themselves through a faithful minister's heart.

Church fairs and church follies, church races and church disgraces, all come back at last to the old pew question—when we abolish paying for church privileges, and go to giving for Christ's dear sake, the millennium doors will open in church finance. That old man in a New England town who bought a pew when they erected a house of worship, and took a deed for it, and held on to the deed, and the pew as well, is an illustration of the vices of this system. The time came for the removal of the edifice; they asked the old saint, spelled with a small "s," to give up his pew—which he sternly refused to do. They finally sold the old house subject to this deeded pew; and when the building was torn down they cut the earth away for the excavation just the length and breadth of that pew, leaving it standing high and dry in the air. The pew system stakes out our heavenly territory little beyond the boundaries of the New England sinner. It provokes to coldness, and a startling lack of hospitality—it suggests the attitude of that man who stood in the aisle trying to freeze a stranger out, then pushed inside with an austerity that might have done credit to some feature of a menagerie; then wrote on a slip of paper, "I pay $100 for this pew;" which brought back the answer, "Do you? It is worth it."

This sort of niggardliness is barren of faith and rife with infidelity. It means that the preacher of Christ's gospel must fight the mammon spirit in his church before he can get through the gates to fight the devil in the world. It is a covetousness that fattens on the meager compensation of wage-earners, that sits with folded hands behind silken draperies, while men with hell in their thoughts beg for an hour's toil. We are too much engaged about eschatology and the future state, when our hearts should be busy with benevolence and the present state.

Common-sense calls for the use of tact, and the use of the law of adaptation.

The disease of the day is superiority. There are more saints than niches. There are other people in the world besides our own dear selves and our own particular "set." We must feel the ties of kinship. We ought to be intensely human. There is a mirror in the palace at Versailles that, looked into from a certain position, puts thirteen heads on the shoulders of one man. Some churches have this sort of a mirror, and it magnifies their particular work to the exclusion of all else. The field is the world. We owe the white man, the black man, the yellow man, the red man, the pledge of brotherhood, for he bears about with him the stamp of divinity. This spirit will apply to our work, this will exhaust our resources in the mighty endeavor to win men for God. Tact consists in using the thing you have to do the thing you desire to do.

Mr. Warren A. Kelsay, paymaster in the navy during the war, and for some time on duty in the blockade before Charleston, told a friend of mine the following incident. The land forces were for a considerable time under the command of that distinguished general and engineer, Quincy A. Gillmore. General Gillmore, seeing that the destruction of Charleston largely depended upon the ability to shell the city from a distance, was anxious that this result be accomplished. It was a task of great difficulty. The one accessible place was a deep and wretched swamp. But General Gillmore determined that a gun must be placed in that swamp in such a way as to drop shells into the city. Accordingly, he sent for his engineer officer, told him of the task to be accomplished, said to him that the resources of the United States government were behind him, and that he might make a requisition for everything and anything required and it would be furnished, but the great gun must be placed in the swamp. The engineer recounted the difficulties in the way, regarded the matter as the next thing to an impossibility, and left his general in despair, but proceeded to make out the requisition, the first item of which was, "Required one hundred and fifty men eighteen feet tall to work in a swamp twelve feet deep." But the fact is, that average men of average height did locate the great gun, known in history as the "Swamp Angel," and thenceforth shells did begin to drop into Charleston, and had much to do with the reduction of the city. Is it not plain that men with average ability, but with high ideals and a willingness to adapt their powers, accomplish the great results of the world?

Common-sense will lead to the saving of the child life.

Emphasis too long and too loud cannot be placed upon the work of saving the children. In my own city a mother sat on the bedside with her sick boy. The motherheart was glad, because she thought the disease had fled and safety was assured. But it was the prelude to the end, for the home was very soon to lose out of it the shining spirit of this bright little fellow. They were talking love to each other, as only a boy and his mother can talk, when the dear little fellow said, as he clasped her about the neck, "Oh, you are just a boy's mother."

That is what the church should be, a great, loving, tender mother. The changeless beauty that glows on the canvas of a Benjamin West was put there by the kiss of his mother; for it was the pressure of her sweet Quaker face that inspired him with a genius that has made art glorious in the proudest galleries of the world.

In the storm of terror that swept over France in the days of her Revolution, one of her gifted and patriotic sons was looking out from behind prison bars, expecting every moment to hear the rattle of the death wagon, and see the flashing knife of the guillotine; but he had time and thought to say this wondrous speech: "Even at this incomprehensible moment, when mortality, enlightment, love of country, all of them only make death at the prison door, or on the scaffold, more certain, yes, on the fatal tumbril itself, with nothing free but my voice, I would still cry 'take care,' to a child that should come too near the wheel. Perhaps I may save his life; perhaps he may one day save France."

In the Old State House in Philadelphia, crowded with so many memories of the birth of our freedom, and filled with Revolutionary relics, there may be seen the headless shell of a drum. Above it you may read the words, "This drum was beaten at the battle of Germantown, 1777, by John Shoemaker, aged twelve years."

Men may load and fire the great guns, and bombard the resisting fortresses, but boys have held the drumsticks, and given the beat of the furious charge that has re-echoed in the tramp of Freedom's footsteps.

Masaniello, the son of a fisherman, became the leader of a revolt against the Duke of Arcos, Spanish viceroy of Naples, and in three days he went from the garret to the throne, — from the fishing-nets to the scepter. At the head of fifty thousand insurgents he compelled the duke to abolish a hateful tax which he had imposed upon the very necessaries of life, and out of which he was reaping a harvest of gold.

Look at his weapons of attack, simple but august! A city on the verge of riot, inflamed to the point of bloodiest passion. Masaniello began by collecting in the market-place a knot of boys. To each of these he taught a phrase of words, and gave a little cane, bearing on the top a streamer of black linen like a flag. Soon five hundred, at last two thousand, of these volunteers were going up and down the city. In the hovels of the lazzaroni, among the halls of the fruit-sellers, before the gates of the toll-house; under the windows of the Spanish nobles, everywhere their slender ensigns fluttered and the pregnant words were heard, "God be with us, and our lady, and the King of Spain; but down with the government, the fruit tax, and the Devil."

The work was done, the revolution was on; the army grew from boys to men. Naples was ruled by the fisherman, and the people were freed from the exactions of the grinding impositions of their ruler. Boys, boys, boys! Save the boys! save the girls! save the children! Enlist them in the army in whose war there is no discharge; and with fluttering banners the children will march, crying the death-knell of every tax upon virtue and righteousness, until not Masaniello the fisherman, but Jesus Christ the carpenter, shall take the throne and rule with unhindered scepter the kingdoms of this world.

My friend, the brilliant George N. McCain, one of the editors of the Philadelphia *Press*, tells in a lecture how William the Conqueror sailed from the shores of France, eight hundred years ago, to wrest the crown of England from false Harold's head; how the royal galley led the fleet. The figure-head upon its prow was a golden boy, with arm outstretched, pointing the way to England and to victory.

That golden boy on the galley of the Norman conqueror pointed to all the liberties that came with Magna Charta to be twisted from the unwilling fingers of John; pointed to the achievements of science, the song of poetry, the shining star of philanthropy; pointed to Plymouth Rock, the founding of a nation, —

> "The queen of the earth,
> The bride of the skies."

Church of God, Ship of Zion, put the living boy on the prow of thy proud craft, and the flash of more than a golden light shall spangle the waters, and that boy shall point to the destiny of races and kingdoms and tribes and tongues made for God, and finding their eternal rest in the Father's heart.

Dr. Dixon was frequently interrupted by applause, which emphasized the telling points in his address.

After a few notices had been given by Mr. Cheesman, the benediction was pronounced by Rev. Dr. Johnson of Atlanta.

SATURDAY MORNING.

The day began with the early morning prayer-meetings at 6.30 in the various places of rendezvous already noted. It was marked that, while the convention programme discussed so largely matters of practical import, its spiritual tone, especially as indicated by the attendance and interest connected with these early morning prayer-meetings, was of the highest.

Saengerfest Hall.

The hall was again thronged at an early hour. The opening praise service was conducted by Mr. J. G. Warren of Cleveland, a special feature being the singing of a number of new hymns in which the strong lead of the Park Sisters with their cornets proved a welcome help.

Ten minutes before the hour, Mr. Dickinson took up the morning's programme, and introduced Rev. A. B. Christy of Albuquerque, N.M., as the leader of the devotional exercises. These consisted of the repeating of the Beatitudes, the choir alternating with the congregation, and prayer by Mr. Christy. A new hymn of Mr. Sankey's was then sung, "Still, still, with Thee," the words being by Mrs. H. B. Stowe. A very pleasing variation was made with this hymn, the Cleveland Male Quartette singing the first verse, the choir the second, the audience the third, and the quartette closing softly with the fourth. This was followed by the old hymn, "All hail the power of Jesus' name," the audience rising and joining in the hymn with a magnificent volume of tone.

MR. DICKINSON: The hope of the Christian Endeavor movement, as we all believe, lies in this Junior department; and in no part of the work which we are doing do we find more manifest signs of God's providential leading than in this Junior work. The boys and the girls are coming up from all parts of our country to the help of the Lord against the mighty, and we are glad to emphasize this great fact here this morning by devoting this half-hour to the Junior department. I am glad to introduce to you Rev. Cornelius Brett, D.D., of Jersey City, who will have charge of the Parliament. [*Applause.*]

Open Parliament. — "The Junior Society."

DR. BRETT [*greeted with cheers from New Jersey*]: After such a greeting from my own State it will be comparatively easy to face all the States' and all the nation's assembly here to-day in the interests of our youth. We have just half an hour, friends, to consider one of the most important themes — if not the most important — that can possibly come before this or any other convention, the work of the Lord Jesus Christ among the children of the church. It would seem as if this half-hour were all insufficient for the work. A parliament of half an hour — just think of it! Over in Great Britain they would be very glad — at least, some of them would — to limit the sitting of their parliament to half an hour; and there are some people in this country who even would say that the American Congress might adjourn after half an hour's session with profit to the country. [*Laughter and applause.*] But a Christian Endeavor convention can perform astounding feats. Just think of it, friends, since last December the Congress of our nation has been wrestling with great financial issues, while here on the first day of this convention we passed the great and only and original McKinley Bill through two houses and three or four churches in a single morning! [*Great laughter and applause.*] There is one clause in that McKinley Bill — or rather in the eloquent oration of his excellency, Gov. William McKinley — which is worth our carrying away with us. He said that the only currency that would pass everywhere and at all times is character, and that he loved Christian Endeavor because Christian Endeavor made character. Now, if we believe this — and I sincerely hope we do — the place to begin character building is with the little child. Froebel, the great educator, claimed that the education of children should begin when the babe is in its mother's arms at three months old. You can purchase in some of the shops where they sell Froebel's gifts three colored balls on a rubber string. These are designed to attract the child's notice, and teach it form and color while still the little hands are feebly putting out to find something that they can lay hold upon. And we want to take these little hands as they are being stretched out, and our first gift to the child shall be the cross of our Lord and Saviour Jesus Christ. We will train them from earliest childhood in the name of our blessed Master. I saw once, not long ago, on the front page of a paper published by the Salvation Army, the picture of a long line of children dressed in the peculiar garb of the Army. The litttle girls looked very quaint with their poke-bonnets and the boys with the caps of the army. Below the picture was a banner; and on this banner was written, "We are the coming army." If your Junior Endeavorers were here in convention, they might spread this broad banner to the breeze and march before you and before the world, saying, "We are the coming army." Why, they come on very fast. There are delegates in this convention — great, strong delegates — that I have held in my arms when they were babies. It is a joyful thing to know that so soon the children will be in this convention, holding the places which the older ones now hold.

Now, there are just four reasons why I love the Junior Endeavor Society, and believe it to be the response of the modern church to the Master's command, "Feed my lambs." First, it forms a stepping-stone between the Sundays. We want to get all the influence we can over our children. The Sunday-school must not be interfered with by this movement. It will be strengthened if we can only put somewhere in that great gulf of the week a stepping-stone where the children can safely land and spend one hour out of the whole one hundred and sixty talking about Jesus Christ. Then, I believe in Junior Endeavor as a present and valuable movement, because it is a part of our system. I believe that Christian Endeavor will soon begin to wane if we do not feed it. You cannot run your Sunday-school without the infant class; you cannot run your young people's society without this Junior department. Then, I believe that the Junior idea is adaptable. You remember that sentence in Secretary Baer's report about the Young People's Society, that it is as strong as steel and flexible as ribbon. So is the Junior Society. In the next place, we want it because the children like it. It is like Pitcher's Castoria, — the children just cry for it. [*Laughter.*] Everywhere, in all parts of the land, they are asking for it, and we have only to go and give it to them.

So much for my speech; now for yours. I shall want to divide this parliament into two parts; and we must pass to the first, second, and third reading, considering it in the committee of the whole, and then pass the enacting clause on these two propositions: First, what has Junior Endeavor done for the children? second, what has Junior Endeavor through the children done for the world? Now, No. 1, What has Junior Endeavor done for the children?

Replies: "I want to say it has done a great deal for my children. I have five children; three of them are Christian Endeavorers, and the other two will be when they are old enough. They like their Christian Endeavor meeting, and they walk Sunday afternoon at least two miles and back in order to attend it."

"It has taught the children to pray."

"Junior Endeavor in Minnesota has done a great deal for the children all over the State. I believe we are more enthusiastic in regard to the Junior Endeavor movement than we are, if possible, in regard to the Young People's movement. Great additions are being made in the line of Junior Societies. Gathering up the results for the year in Minnesota, we find that the very best work is being done by the Juniors, and that the Juniors who have been graduated at the age of fourteen into the Young People's Society are considered the best members of the Society." [*Applause.*]

"A Junior Society in Toronto has adopted a very fine plan for helping the children to live Christian lives. We send to their school-teachers in the public schools and the Sunday-schools their names, and say, 'These children have taken the Junior Endeavor Pledge. Now, if they do anything to be reproved for, show them their pledge, and ask them to live like true Christian Endeavorers.'" [*Applause.*] "Out of our society of 34, 13 have united with the church since November." "Ohio Junior Endeavorers have become so strong that they have formed a Junior Union." "Nineteen out of 50 of our society have joined the church since the new year." "The Juniors are the only ones in our church who are promptly on time." "A Junior Endeavor Society was started in Tungcho, North China, within the year." "The Juniors of California are ahead of the Young People. Thirty out of the San Bernadino Society united with the church." "Our society has been engaged for three months past in saving pennies to help children along the fresh-air line."

A YOUNG GIRL: "Fourteen out of our society of 40 have joined the church since last November." [*Applause.*] "Our society raised $400 for mission work."

DR. BRETT: "Now what has the Junior Society done through the children for the church? We have been talking about how many have joined the church. Now let us tell what those who have come into the church are doing for the world in active work."

"Our society pays a regular contribution, Sunday after Sunday, into the church treasury." "Last October we had 19 members, now 72. We have contributed $42 to missions. Nine have united with the church." "A little girl nine years old brought father and mother and two sisters into the church." [*Applause.*] "Our society is supporting a missionary in Japan."

DR. BRETT: "How do the pastors view the Junior Endeavor Society? All who believe in it please rise." (All the ministers seated on the platform, and many in the audience, arose.)

"Our Juniors attend the morning service in a body." "One of our members goes five miles to attend the meeting." "Indiana Juniors are the future missionaries of the State."

A PASTOR: "My Junior Society has 14 members of the church out of 40. They have constituted a whole class of contributors for the support of the church. They recently bought for us new pulpit furniture and a communion-table." [*Applause.*]

A LADY: "The Juniors have awakened the mothers in our church, and we are trying to do our part in helping them in their daily life, and they are helping us. We take for our motto, For Christ, the Church, and the Children." [*Applause.*] "The children bring out the fathers. A few weeks ago a saloon-keeper came to church to hear his little girl recite." "The Mothers' Society of Christian Endeavor has been a wonderful blessing to me as a Junior superintendent, in knowing that daily the mothers are bringing us to the throne of grace. They are present at our meetings with helpful words, and they are especially helpful in our social work." [*Applause.*] "Our society is educating four children in Turkey." [*Applause.*] "The Topeka Juniors have so interested the mothers that they have formed a Mothers' Christian Endeavor Society." "One Junior Society in Ohio has given $17 to church extension, and pledged $50 on the new church building." "Our society has 34 members. Every one of them now belongs to the church. When the leader of the meeting is not present they carry it on alone." "There is a Junior Society in every church in Colorado Springs where a Young People's Society exists." "The Juniors in a Nebraska society collect the Sunday-school papers not used, take them down town on Saturday, and put a bundle in every farmer's wagon they find in the streets. They look up children for our Sabbath-school, and are the general every-day workers in our church." [*Applause.*]

DR. BRETT: All who are Junior delegates to this convention please rise.

(Several hundred rose in different parts of the hall.)

DR. BRETT: I promised two minutes to a representative of the Mothers' society. It is a new idea in Christian Endeavor, and I think it bids fair to carry a great deal of weight with it in the future.

MRS. F. S. THOMPSON of Chicago: I hardly hoped for this blessed privilege of speaking for the mothers to so many. Only a few of the Christian mothers have been awakened to the fact that they must help the Junior superintendents or they cannot be successful in their work for the children. After taking the Christian Endeavor pledge ourselves almost like your own — it is sent out by the United Society — with the addition that we will daily pray for the children, we feel that it has greatly blessed us. Our society has been but two or three months in working order, and there have been between twenty and thirty children brought into the church. It seemed like a direct answer to the mothers' prayers. [*Applause.*]

A PASTOR: May I just say that, as a pastor in Chicago, I have found the Mothers' society a very great help. Things have gone ever so much better among the Juniors than they did before that society was formed. There is a tendency to underrate any great thing that comes just before or just after a still greater thing. The French and Indian war is little known, important as it was, because of the Revolution. So it is that the Junior society is likely to suffer because it is so close to the greater thing, the Christian Endeavor society, and yet it is of the very highest value. I am sure it ought to be said that the Junior society and the Mothers' society are applications of the same principle to boys' and girls' meetings and to mothers' meetings that the Christian Endeavor is to the older young people's association.

A lady from Melbourne, Australia, who had tried to get an opportunity to speak, was called forward, and said a few words about the difficulty there of contending with the drink habit, and the part taken by the young people against it.

DR. BRETT: In closing, since we are a parliament, shall we not pass this resolution: that we recommend to every Christian Endeavor society to organize a Junior society by its side?

(The resolution was passed unanimously, with applause.)

The audience then united in singing the hymn, "Praise Him," all rising.

MR. DICKINSON: Christian Endeavor is not undenominational. We wish to emphasize that truth again and again. It is inter-denominational. [*Applause.*] As our worthy secretary has said so often, it is " inter, inter, inter-denominational." Christian Endeavor believes in keeping Christians within their respective denominational folds; but it also believes that they should be tall enough and lofty-minded enough to stand above the denominational fences and shake hands over them and say, " How do you do, brother?" [*Applause.*] One of the most interesting parts of the programme in Cleveland has been the denominational rallies; and now we are to listen to some echoes of those rallies. The meetings were crowded; there were overflows to many of them, and sometimes there were overflows from the overflows. Now we are just to get a word or two from each one of these denominations, so far as they are represented, in the two great congregations in the tent and in the hall to-day. We are to hear from thirteen of them here, and the other thirteen will report in the tent.

Reports from Denominational Rallies.

CUMBERLAND PRESBYTERIAN CHURCH, *Rev. Dr. W. J. Darby of Evansville, Ind.:* — With an attendance that surprised us all, we had a very delightful afternoon. The representatives on the programme came from nearly all the twenty States in which the Head of the church has ordained our denomination to do its principal work. Due attention was given to the fact that our General Assembly, the highest court in our church, has taken official cognizance of Christian Endeavor work, and that by a unanimous vote, without even a dissenting voice in the discussion preceding that vote, Christian Endeavor was recognized as the official young people's society of the denomination. [*Applause.*] Along with committees on education and publication and missions and Sabbath-schools, we are to have hereafter, at every meeting of our General Assembly, a standing committee on Christian Endeavor work. [*Applause.*] We took cognizance also of the fact that the General Assembly desires that we shall have a generation of educated young people, — educated in the history and doctrines of the church, educated in the literature of the times, educated in the great underlying principles that are to be the substratum and the power of all great movements like this; and hence that we are to read, and in doing so to read systematically, and to have an annual reading course in our societies. We are to focalize our efforts, as we decided through this rally, by direction of our General Assembly, to build this year, in one of the great cities of the West, upon the immediate Pacific Coast, a Christian Endeavor church. There were many other things which we talked about, but my time will not allow me to mention them here. [*Applause.*]

PRESBYTERIAN, CANADIAN PRESBYTERIAN, AND SOUTHERN PRESBYTERIAN, *Rev. R. V. Hunter of Terre Haute, Ind.:* — This splendid Committee of '94 has only failed in one particular, in so far as I have any knowledge; and that is, they failed to provide room enough for a Presbyterian rally. [*Laughter.*] We filled the Stone Church until Dr. Haines said he believed now in the doctrine of purgatory. We overflowed into another church, and, had the people known it, we could have filled a third church. Our discussion was around three points: first, the Endeavorers and the local church. It was said that the local church should educate the Endeavorers. They should be educated in the church, by the church, and for the church, for the purpose of serving the church. Secondly, Endeavorers and the denomination. It was said that denominational loyalty had been promoted by the Endeavor movement such as the church had never seen before. Again, the discussion centered around missions. We had missionary extension explained and discussed. The home mission cause was thoroughly presented by representatives of the various boards. The foreign mission cause was also presented; and at the close a resolution was passed something like this: " Resolved, That we have in every church an Endeavor Society and a Junior Endeavor Society, and that we work with the church along missionary lines." [*Applause.*]

MENNONITE. *Rev. Dr. N. B. Grubb, Philadelphia :* — At Montreal last year I was the only delegate from our denomination. To-day we have twenty, and ten are absent on account of the strike. These delegates came from Philadelphia on the East, Kansas on the West, Kentucky on the South, and Canada on the North. Every one of these delegates came anxious to catch the spirit of this convention, which is the spirit of Christ, endeavoring when they go home to create new societies and spread this idea over the land. The attendance at our rally was small, but there was a good spirit manifest. Eleven addresses were made by representatives of the denomination; some sent in their greetings. The society in our church has just doubled its numbers the past year, and we are going home determined to double again this coming year. We have this motto: " Contact, Co-operation, Consecration, and Service." [*Applause.*]

METHODIST OF CANADA, METHODIST EPISCOPAL SOUTH, AND METHODIST EPISCOPAL. *Rev. Charles Roads, Philadelphia :* — The rally at the Epworth Memorial Church, almost filled that large, beautiful audience-room; and throughout the meeting there was the old Methodist fire, touched, purified, and broadened by the Christian Endeavor spirit. [*Applause.*] I want you Christian Endeavorers who feel with me some humiliation that the Methodist church is not in the front rank of Christian Endeavor to have some conception of how much the name Methodist, and the old Methodist fire, mean to us. When we remember that it was first a term of reproach, and then became the badge of the highest honor, we need not wonder that Methodists love the name, and that they shrink from anything which seems to touch, or in any wise interfere with, the old Methodist fire. But we Methodist Endeavorers are learning that here is a fire that burns with even more steadfastness, that burns with a stronger and purer flame, if that can be possible, and here is a spirit which means to the close of the nineteenth century just what the John Wesley spirit meant to the close of the last century. So we are none the less loyal Methodists, but more loyal if possible, because we are Methodist Endeavorers. That was the spirit of the rally. We had magnificent addresses; we had a most delightful conference; and throughout you could have felt the same thrill and enthusiasm, the same presence and power of the Spirit, felt in these larger assemblies. I have hope of the Methodist church that she will yet wheel, with all her mighty forces, into this Christian Endeavor movement. [*Loud Applause.*]

METHODIST PROTESTANT. *Mr. William C. Perkins, Baltimore :* — The Methodist Protestant Church is strongly loyal to Christian Endeavor. We have adopted Christian Endeavor as the official young people's organization of the church. I believe we were the first denomination to take official action in this matter. We feel that a Methodist Protestant church that has not a Christian Endeavor society is simply " not in it." [*Laughter.*] Our rally yesterday was a success in every sense of the word. Our attendance was good; the interest did not flag. We shall all return to our separate fields of labor with more inspiration for the Master's service than when we came here. Our Endeavorers have undertaken the erection of a church in Kansas City, and a chapel in Nagoya, Japan. Some $2,500 have been subscribed, and we intend that these objects of our effort shall be accomplished. Along the lines of the spread of denominational literature, of our college interests, and of our missionary work, Methodist Protestants at the rally pledged their hearty support ; and all along the line of Methodist Protestant interests there shall go out, because of this convention and of this rally, a deeper interest, a more consecrated effort, and larger and fuller results. [*Applause.*]

MORAVIAN. *Rev. W. H. Vogler, Hope, Ind. :* — The first organized Moravian rally, while it did not overflow so as to repeat itself three times, gave a great impetus to Christian Endeavor work. If the Moravian church has been a little slow to lay hold of the Christian Endeavor idea, remember that August 17, 1727, a revival among the children set the whole church at work for the children, for the boys and girls, for the young men and young women. But, as one of our representatives said, we recognize in the Christian Endeavor movement an onward step; and as " Tar heels-stick when they get there," so say we all! [*Laughter.*]

REFORMED CHURCH IN AMERICA. *Rev. Dr. Cornelius Brett, Jersey City :* — The Reformed Church in America is the oldest Protestant Church in the United States. In

1628 our good old Hollander fathers, fresh from the conflicts which had bathed that spongy soil with blood, came and founded the church in the old fort at the Battery in New York. We are a small church yet; but we have this proud distinction, that we have the largest number of Christian Endeavor Societies, in proportion to our members, of any church represented in Christian Endeavor. [*Applause.*] We expected our rally to be small. We have two small churches in this city. These churches are bi-lingual. They were formed by the recent immigration from the Netherlands. Oh, I do wish the Netherlands would pour out a few more of their good people here as salt in the great fountain of America; for they come bringing their church with their Bible and their catechism. These two churches turned out to bid us welcome; and we had one of the churches packed, so that the people were looking in at the windows. We had our four synods all represented, and twenty-two out of our thirty-five classes represented. We had a missionary from Japan; we had the president of our Christian Endeavor Missionary League, and he told us that we were supporting one of the missions in India, and that we had built three churches in destitute localities through the gifts of the Christian Endeavorers. The Reformed Church is moving on. She lives in New Jersey, in New York, and in Pennsylvania, and she is going on out West to San Francisco. [*Applause.*]

REFORMED CHURCH IN THE UNITED STATES. *Mr. F. G. Hobson, Norristown, Pa.:* — Had the United Society provided a banner for that denominational rally which should show the greatest increase, that banner would have gone to us. Last year we had twelve representatives at the rally; this year we had over one thousand [*applause*], all of them under the time-honored colors of Zwingli, the founder of our church. We had fourteen speakers announced beforehand; every man was present and up to time. Our new Sunday-school secretary of the church was present, and spoke of the work of the Sunday-school, and we promised him that the Christian Endeavor society would help the Sunday-school. The Christian Endeavor societies of the church have taken an active part in missions during the past year. They have said to the board of missions, " We will support a Christian Endeavor missionary in Japan if you will appoint one." We have raised the money; and the board has now said that, as we have raised the money, we shall raise the man; and a Christian Endeavor brother from Columbiana, Ohio, has been selected to fill that position. [*Applause.*] We have also taken action that looks toward the formation of the Reformed League of Christian Endeavor in the United States. What we have done means that next year we will come up to the convention with greater results to show than we have had during this past year. [*Applause.*]

REFORMED EPISCOPAL. *Rev. A. H. Grace, Ashtabula, Ohio:* — The Reformed Dutch Church, from which we have just heard, is, it is said, the oldest church in the United States. The Reformed Episcopal, as such, is one of the youngest; but it is just as Protestant as the Reformed Dutch, or any other church; and not only is it just as Protestant, but it is just as thoroughly a Christian Endeavor church. Our denominational rally was a decided and emphatic success. Its attendance was not large — not as large as we would have been pleased to have it; but, considering the size of our church as a whole, the attendance at the rally was good. It was a representative attendance. We had at the rally addresses on the subjects of the relation of our denomination to the Christian Endeavor movement and missionary extension. The two principal things emphasized in the rally were loyalty to denomination, blended, as it always is in Christian Endeavor gatherings, with interdenominational fellowship, and the missionary work. We had with us from Chicago Miss Frances B. Patterson, probably known to some of you, who addressed us on the subject of missionary extension, explained to us the matter, and sent us away determined to carry out the principles that were there laid down. There was in the rally a great deal of consecrated spirit displayed, a manifest desire on the part of those present to reconsecrate themselves to the service of the Master; and the rally culminated in a genuine Christian Endeavor consecration meeting, led by one of the delegates present. We left the rally determined, by the grace of God, to go forward in the work for Christ, for the church in general, and for the Reformed Episcopal Church in particular. [*Applause.*]

REFORMED PRESBYTERIAN. *Rev. Dr. W. M. Glasgow, Beaver Falls, Pa.:* — The Reformed Presbyterian or Covenanter Church in America is the lineal descendant and true representative of the Church of Scotland in her purest days; and it embodies in its testimony all those priceless Scriptural principles for which its members were subjected to fierce persecution and baptism of blood, and gave to this country its principles of civil and religious liberty. The central doctrine of this church is the headship of Jesus Christ over all things. Hence, the motto of this Endeavor movement being "For Christ and the Church," the old Scotch Covenanter Church must of necessity favor it. Our supreme court has several times recommended the organization of these societies in all our congregations, and I can report that in three out of four of the congregations of our church Christian Endeavor Societies are now organized. We had a splendid rally. We did not have an overflow, but we did flow over with enthusiasm. [*Laughter.*] We had eight set speeches, and perhaps twenty others, and a grand social time. We went away determined that we would push this movement so that in all our congregations before next year these societies will be established. We believe these principles, as well as those upon which our church is founded, will fill the whole world with peace and happiness, and exalt Jesus Christ as Lord of all. [*Applause.*]

UNITED BRETHREN. *Rev. G. W. Arnold, Vandalia, O.* :— I am happy to report that the United Brethren denomination held in very many respects the greatest denominational rally ever held by that church. It was greatest in talent, greatest in the character of the addresses. Dr. Miller, of Harrisburg, Pa., spoke upon the relation and helpfulness of the Christian Endeavor movement of the United Brethren Church; Dr. Landis' spoke earnestly and eloquently on the relation of the Christian Endeavor movement to our denominational union; Rev. H. F. Shupe, editor of our new young people's paper, spoke on the relation of the movement to the young's people's paper; Dr. Bell, missionary secretary, spoke on the relation of the Christian Endeavor movement to our missionary work. They were all red-hot addresses, and received great applause. It was the greatest rally, in the third place, in divine unction, the greatest in Christian Endeavor enthusiasm. I want to illustrate that fact by a story. A party of friends stepping over from New York on the soil of New Jersey, there came up in conversation the deadly and despised New Jersey mosquito. While there was much said against him, one arose and championed him, and said, "There is one thing in his favor; some of the very best blood in New York flows through the veins of the New Jersey mosquito." [*Laughter.*] So I say that some of the very best Christian Endeavor blood in this land or any other land flows through the Christian Endeavorers of the United Brethren Church. [*Applause.*]

UNITED PRESBYTERIAN CHURCH. *Rev. M. W. Pressly, Hamilton, O.*:— The United Presbyterian Church is called the U. P. Church, which means out West, "Union Pacific;" but under the impulse and inspiration of Christian Endeavor it means simply what it says, "Up, up!" [*Applause.*] We had a very fine rally, with strong speakers, a splendid spirit, free fellowship, evangelistic earnestness, and enthusiastic endeavor. This rally made us all feel that things that live must move. I am sure that our distinctive doctrine of the Psalter will mean more to us than ever before in the ministry of song. This rally will help us henceforth to transpose our creed into deed; it will help us to mingle tolerance with truth, fellowship with fidelity. I know that for all our young United Presbyterians the letters "C. E." shall henceforth mean Consecration of Effort, Combination of Elements, Co-operation of Enterprise, Consecration of Energy, Continuation of Enthusiasm, and Conversion of Everybody. [*Applause*].

This closed the reports from the rallies. The old hymn, "I Love Thy Kingdom, Lord," was then sung, after which came an interesting exercise.

Awarding the Diplomas.

MR. DICKINSON: As a fitting climax to this part of our service, we are to award certain diplomas to those societies which have done the most toward promoting interdenominational fellowship and systematic giving; and this part of our programme will be conducted by one of our trustees, Bishop Fallows. [*Applause.*]

BISHOP FALLOWS: Mr. President and Christian Endeavor friends, I have been called upon in my life to bestow diplomas upon the graduates of the graded schools of our country, upon the graduates of normal schools and of high schools and of academies and of colleges and of universities; but I venture to say that no man in the history of the world was ever called upon to present diplomas on such an occasion as this and for such a purpose. Edward Everett said in one of his magnificent orations, "The earth moves, and the waters move, and the mighty tides of air move, and the planets move;" and if he were here to-day he would say, "The railroads move." [*Laughter.*] And the world of thought moves to bolder effects and grander generalizations; and the Christian Endeavor Society moves to sublimer ideas and more glorious, comprehensive, and effective methods for the extension of the kingdom of our Lord Jesus Christ. Let me say to these grave and reverend seniors, who represent as pastors the Christian church, and as college presidents and professors and teachers the culture of that church, that if all the colleges and universities of Christendom, from the first university of the church down to the present, could have their presidents concentrated and combined into one man, to give diplomas to represent the highest culture the world knows, it would be on this occasion, and for the presentation of these diplomas. I do not say it enthusiastically, but I say it advisedly, in giving for the first time in the history of these societies these diplomas, which represent the culture of the highest Christian thought, the culture of the highest Christian conscience, the culture of the deepest Christian heart, and the culture of the deepest Christian pocket, since time began. For these diplomas are to be given to the societies which have done the most, upon a competitive examination, for interdenominational fellowship, and for systematic and proportionate giving to God. God bless the man who thought of this means of emphasizing these three great cardinal principles of the Christian thought and the Christian life of the world!

Bishop Fallows then announced the names of those societies entitled to receive diplomas, which were as follows:—

SYSTEMATIC GIVING.

Second Presbyterian Y. P. S. C. E., Chicago, Ill.
Warren Avenue Congregational Y. P. S. C. E., Chicago, Ill.
Trinity Baptist Y. P. S. C. E., Chicago, Ill.
Central Park Presbyterian Y. P. S. C. E., Chicago Ill.
First Presbyterian Y. P. S. C. E., Huntingdon, Ind.
Clarendon Street Baptist Y. P. S. C. E., Boston, Mass.
First Congregational Y. P. S. C. E., Galesburg, Ill.
First Church Y. P. S. C. E., Galesburg, Ill.
Presbyterian Y. P. S. C. E., Galesburg, Ill.
Lutheran Y. P. S. C. E., Galesburg, Ill.
Christian Y. P. S. C. E., Galesburg, Ill.
Second Presbyterian Y. P. S. C. E., Knoxville, Tenn.
Thirteenth Street M. E. Y. P. S. C. E., Philadelphia, Penn.
Knox Y. P. S. C. E., Sapperton, New Westminster, B.C.
Presbyterian Y. P. S. C. E., Adrian, Mich.
Immanuel Presbyterian Y. P. S. C. E., Milwaukee, Wis.
First Congregational Y. P. S. C. E., Colchester, Conn.
Congregational Y. P. S. C. E., Davenport, Ia.
Central Presbyterian Y. P. S. C. E., New York, N.Y.
Presbyterian Y. P. S. C. E., McGrawville, N.Y.
Third Presbyterian Y. P. S. C. E., Toledo, Ohio.
United Presbyterian Y. P. S. C. E., Olathe, Kan.
Sunnyside Presbyterian Y. P. S. C. E., Catskill, N.Y.
Presbyterian Y. P. S. C. E., Windham, N.Y.
Friends' Y. P. S. C. E., Sweetland, Ia.

FELLOWSHIP.

Second Evangelical Y. P. S. C. E., Lancaster City, Penn.
Memorial Presbyterian Y. P. S. C. E., Rockville, Ind.
First Presbyterian Y. P. S. C. E., Bay City, Mich.
Christian Y. P. S. C. E., Valparaiso, Ind.
Memorial Chapel Y. P. S. C. E., Grafton, W. Va.

St. Paul Y. P. S. C. E., Beaumont, Tex.
Christian Y. P. S. C. E., Versailles, Ky.
First Christian Y. P. S. C. E., Waco, Tex.
Cumberland Presbyterian Y. P. S. C. E., Lebanon, Tenn.
First Congregational Y. P. S. C. E., Amherst, Mass.
Disciples of Christ Y. P. S. C. E., Lebanon, Mo.
Friends' Y. P. S. C. E., Wilmington, Ohio.
Cumberland Presbyterian Y. P. S. C. E., Union City, Tenn.
Presbyterian Y. P. S. C. E., Carrollton, Ill.
Disciples of Christ Y. P. S. C. E., Warrensburg, Mo.
First Presbyterian Y. P. S. C. E., Tracy, Minn.
First Congregational Y. P. S. C. E., Terre Haute, Ind.
First United Presbyterian Y. P. S. C. E., Baltimore, Md.
First Christian Y. P. S. C. E., Maysville, Ky.
First Baptist Y. P. S. C. E., Bacone, I.T.
Trinity Evangelical Lutheran Y. P. S. C. E., Taneytown, Md.
Cumberland Presbyterian Y. P. S. C. E., Corsicana, Tex.
Presbyterian Y. P. S. C. E., Moundsville, W. Va.
Presbyterian Y. P. S. C. E., Rockburn, P.Q.
Reformed Presbyterian Y. P. S. C. E., Sterling, Kan.

Prayer was offered by Rev. Dr. W. H. McMillan in special behalf of the boys and girls of the great Junior Endeavor army.

The next item on the programme was an address of greeting from Australia; but Mr. J. G. Thompson, who was to make the address, was blockaded in San Francisco. He sent a telegram conveying the greetings of Australia to the Convention; and at the suggestion of Mr. Dickinson the audience rose and joined in the Chautauqua salute in honor of Australia, followed by the hymn, " Blest be the Tie that Binds."

The closing address of the morning was by Rev. P. R. Danley. D.D.. pastor of the Cumberland Presbyterian Church, Springfield, Ill., who spoke on the subject, —

Interdenominational Fellowship.

Address of Rev. P. R. Danley, D.D.

Two worshipers who could neither speak the language of the other were one day seated side by side in a gospel service. In the course of the service one of them responded with a hearty "Amen!" to some sentiment uttered by the speaker. With a thrill of delight beaming on his face the other extended his hand in token of a newfound fellowship, as he shouted "Hallelujah!" To-day we clasp hands across the chasm of our differences in mutual fraternal recognition of that which is common to us all.

Mr. President, I esteem myself happy to-day to stand before this delegated throng, representing as it does the broadest and noblest spirit of Christian culture and brotherhood, and a loyalty and devotion to their one Master which are beautiful and inspiring.

As culture is the totality of all civilizing forces that work in society, so is the brotherhood of Christian fellowship among the hosts of the Lord. The Young People's Society, representing and breathing forth this spirit, is a product of the times and for the times. As a religious evolution it stands for denominational loyalty and interdenominational fellowship. It serves in the providence of God a twofold purpose, not only to bind the heart of the young people more closely and loyally to their own church, but to discover to a wondering world a new dynamic force to bind together and hold in Christian fellowship followers of the Lord in every denomination. As you concentrate the energies of life so will you conserve her forces. Never has there been found a parallel to the activity in the local church and to the warm-hearted loyalty that have been realized through the organization of the young for concentrated work; and yet the spirit of the age is interdenominational. The Christian Endeavor Society is the embodiment of this advanced thought.

The strongest influence at work to-day in the interests of Christian unity is found in the active relations of Christianity to the world. No other organization has done so much to unite the divergent forces of a divided Protestantism, because no other agency has been able to inspire an equal degree of activity in Christian service. LaPlace held that "discoveries are in the union of such ideas as fit each other, and yet have been held apart in the past." Beyond all question, the synthesis of those things which belong to each other will produce new forces and additional results not within the reach of either alone. In moral forces the strength of all the parts is multiplied, and the whole becomes greater than the sum of all the parts, as the army has a might which cannot be computed by adding together the individual forces of those composing it. The philosophy of human thought necessitates the unity of Christian activity. A German philosopher has said that "the tendency to unify all things so that they constitute one system is innate in the human mind." That no idea is isolated, and that the specialization of the day to attempt to isolate the individual members of the organism, and to treat them as complete in themselves, is a process of disintegration which destroys the unity of life. Evidently the attempt to treat any sect or denomination as complete in itself is in conflict with philosophy, with truth, and out of accord with the spirit of the times. No sect has a monopoly of the truth. The purest type of Christian fellowship is found in that spirit which cheerfully recognizes the excellencies in others. That for which we plead to-day is the law of unity in diversity. As Philip Schaff has expressed it, "The church of the future will never become wholly Greek or Roman or Protestant, but will become wholly Christian, embracing all shades of truth in endless variety and harmonious unity, Christ being all and all." The kingdom of Christ is one, — its forces are many. Its distinctive peculiarity is that it has one altar where all offerings are laid with cheerful recognition of mutual relations and obligations to one Lord. Its unity is not one of dead uniformity. Humanity is one, but its peoples are heterogeneous. Truth is a unit, though it is many sided and all sided, and reflected in all colors. The fellowship for which we stand to-day is that which makes for righteousness rather than for uniformity. Though we are nearer to interdenominational federation now than our grandfathers were to the fellowship which we so much enjoy and prize to-day, organic union is not essential for those who would combine to establish and extend the principles which have given us our splendid Christian civilization. But co-operation is an imperative command. The sinking of denominational rivalries and competition is the growing Christly thought of a world's great need. The spirit of Christian unity which is so much in the air is a part of a much larger movement, which tends at once to the conservation of effort and the concentration of power, and leads the mind away from the abstract discussions of the past to the live practical issues of the present. Society never needed a gospel of sympathy and love and power more than it needs it to-day. The perils which threaten the Christian civilization of our own land are menacing us on every hand. The united hostile forces of infidelity demand a united Christendom. Gross materialism and uncurbed greed for gain and power, together with the allied and combined forces of the saloon, the gambling evil, and the social vice, form an unbroken battle-line against the right. But the church of Christ is not a feeble, forceless body, but with its vast resources combined is fully able to preserve and develop the civilization it has created. The most potent influences at work to-day in the interests of a closer fellowship are to be found in the active relations of Christianity to the necessities of the age. In this struggle for the mastery over world forces, the maximum of help with the minimum of interference is the ultimate aim and endeavor of all who seek a closer and firmer bond of fellowship among all denominations. A kind of spiritual nerve center, the ramifications of which will penetrate the heart of every church, would wonderfully facilitate the task of bringing the knowledge of the Christ to all men.

Christian fellowship involves co-operation, as faith without works is dead; and co-operation draws men as with a twofold cord into a mutual confidence and regard for one another. Nothing gives greater emphasis to the value of Christianity than a personal religious friendship which overleaps the walls of denominational differences. The demand for a real fellowship of a helpful order among all the divergent arms of Christ's church is enforced on the grounds of principle. The kingdom of God is inclusive, conclusive, comprehensive; not exclusive and schismatic. It is broader than any or all denominations. It is a unit. Its parts are corporate and co-operative. What is helpful to the body is of value to all the parts. But if you impair or destroy the unity you weaken the body and cut off the life of the member. Fellowship among the members is a law of life and helpfulness, and the measure and the means of the largest measure of success in effort. There is no promise of triumph over the world save only to the church in its unity and integrity. A divided church can never, will never, conquer the world. A united church is a necessary witness of this truth to an unbelieving world. It is a fact of great significance that when divergent denominational hosts join their forces in contending against the wrong the world always breathes a new interest in religion. This is a tangible truth to the enemies of the gospel that the claims of Christ upon the world are valid. The most effective unity is in a common loyalty to truth and duty. Those whom the church would win scoff and ridicule, as absurdly inefficient, disassociated and unallied efforts. But if all who love the truth, and bow to one Master in a noble purpose to extend the power of truth and the reign of righteousness, shall combine their energies, then the splendor of their magnificent purpose will be recognized, and the ridicule will be turned into an approving admiration for the worker, and a glad reception of the truth he teaches.

Fellowship among all the forces of the church of Christ comes to us with an imperative command, in view of the threatened condition of our civil and religious institutions, which we are concerned to defend and preserve. Mighty and hostile forces are being organized and marshaled against them. For the church to remain divided in the presence of such tremendous organized powers arrayed against all that we cherish and hold most dear, would be the madness of insanity. It is a deep conviction — and I am not a pessimist — that these are times when men who love their country, with her Christian institutions, should speak with a courage and candor stirred by the approach of an impending conflict. It is a conviction that, if our American civilization is to abide as we prize it, co-operation must take the place of division and competition among Protestant Christians of this country. Ultramontanism has taken advantage of a divided Protestantism to banish the Bible from our public schools, and then, with the most glaring inconsistency and redoubled fury, demand their overthrow because they are Godless. But we thank God that they are not Godless. It has passed into a proverb that our free republican institutions depend upon the virtue and intelligence of the people. The one American institution which above all others is the outcome of our evangelical civilization, which is pre-eminently essential to good citizenship, is imperiled to-day to a degree beyond which we are reluctant to admit. I mean our free public schools. This noble Christian institution is not simply the foundation of good citizenship, but the bulwark of Protestantism in its struggle to emancipate the children of aliens, and strike from them the shackles of error and superstition fastened upon them by ultramontanism and propagandism of an alien power. The sinful division of Protestantism — and the division is only a local expression of the disease — have well nigh surrendered this stronghold of our Christian civilization. The perilous condition of our institutions calls loudly for such a fellowship of all Protestant communions in an undivided effort to defend and preserve our peculiar institutions, which are the safeguard and guaranty of our existence. The peculiar social and moral tendencies of our times render it imperative that the church shall front them with a strength unimpaired by a distracted purpose or contending motive. The church broken into divisions and contending forces cannot hope to secure a controlling hold upon the restless masses, impressed more forcibly with the spirit of rivalry than with its unity and integrity. More than ever before the age demands a correlated and co-ordinated unity of all the diversified forms of church life. This indispensable attainment is possible only when we recognize that which is best in all, and for that reason common to all. The recognition and co-operation of these best things is the only true Christian philosophy. Emerson puts it in this way, —

"All are united by each one;
Nothing is good or fair alone."

And interdenominational fellowship is vital in counteracting the estrangement of probably increasing multitudes from the church. The gospel was meant for the masses and is adapted to them. The church in its various sympathetic Protestant communions is well able to conserve the Christian civilization which it has created, and to turn the tide of popular thought back to the teachings and behests of the gospel, as the only sure and permanent basis of hope for a happy and prosperous humanity. But it can be done alone by bringing the scattered forces and resources, which in their dispersion are powerless, and surely inadequate to the end, into harmonious fellowship, causing them to act and interact upon each other in their combined effort to maintain the principles of our Christian civilization. The moral life and tone of the land could receive no stronger stimulus than the sight of Christians of all denominations grasping hands, not unmindful of their differences, but recognizing the importance of the magnificent end to be achieved, massing their forces shoulder to shoulder in the struggle of a common cause. Such a sight would dissipate the belief in the minds of many that the religious denominations of Christendom are hopelessly divided, and their usefulness paralyzed by a strong dislike for each other. It is for this reason largely that we are told that the churches do not touch and mold the moral life of the community as they should. The inauguration of a movement like this, massing as it does the energies of all denominations, portends great things in the moral regeneration and reconstruction of society after the divine ideal in Jesus Christ. It impresses the world as no merely sectarian enterprise could affect it. In this way men are compelled to accept the truth as a working basis of the immanence of God in the world, and the divine mission of Jesus of Nazareth as the Saviour of men. The tap-root of infidelity has been cut when you present Christ to the God-consciousness of men in the demonstration of love as their Saviour with authority and power. All the great forces of civilization are looking toward combination and co-operation for mutual protection and the accomplishment of common ends. This is the spirit of the age; and as it deepens and broadens in its hold upon the thought of the times, men more strenuously protest against the spirit of rivalry and exclusiveness in the church, which owes allegiance to one Master, and derives inspiration from a common purpose and destiny. The spirit of fellowship among denominations is a broadening of the principle of ecclesiasticism. Under its force the world field will be less studied from the standpoint of denominational opportunity. This policy aggregates an unequal and wasteful distribution of energy and means. The body of interdenominational fellowship will be co-operation, as words are the habiliment of thought. It precludes the spirit of rivalry and competition. It develops a higher order of feeling for Christians not of our own brotherhood. It lays stress on conduct rather than on creed. Under the growing, healthy spirit of the age, men are coming to feel that conduct is a much larger factor in Christian living than creed; that Christianity is rather a life than a belief; and that dead orthodoxy is destructive of the highest forms of life. Without detracting anything from doctrine, as a fundamental part of a good life, we feel like giving the following sentiment our approval, —

> "For faith let heartless zealous fight;
> That man's can't be wrong whose life is right."

We all will agree that the ground of Christian unity is broader than accord in doctrinal beliefs. That which makes a man a Christian should unite him with all who receive the same Christ. The gospel does not make Jews of Gentiles, nor Gentiles of Jews, but it does make of twain one new man in Christ Jesus. The essence of religion is not in creed distinctions, which are mostly exclusive, but in fellowship and love to God and man. This is the dove after the deluge; the olive leaf appears, and the bow of promise spans the heavens with a new hope inspired. It becomes a mighty factor in securing co-operation in all branches of missionary effort. In this way it saves expenses of a divided work, and conserves the best energies of the church. It prevents the sacrifice of Christianity on the altar of ecclesiasticism.

The weak point in Protestantism is where competition takes the place of co-operation. Much of the effort put forth in our home mission fields reminds one strikingly of the remark made by a small boy to his sister occupying a seat with him on his hobby-horse too small for two, "Daisy, if one of us would get off there would be more room for me." Even evolutionists repudiate the law of strife as ethically defective. The Young People's Society of Christian Endeavor has borne no fruit of richer and rarer flavor than the spirit of fellowship which marks the spirit of the age among denominations. Nothing else so effectively destroys the spirit of rivalry. Competition not only incurs a needless and sinful waste of energy and money, but it weakens the working-force and moral influence of Protestant Christianity among those whom it should win for Christ. The universal testimony of the representatives of the Oriental religions in the congress of religions in Chicago was that the religion of the West could not command the confidence of the East while its own divisions remained unhealed. Melanchthon illustrated the disintegrating effects of a divided and competing Christianity by his fable of the wolves and dogs. The dogs gathered in council to devise the best plans to exterminate the wolf tribe. While they deliberated, the wolves sent a mastiff to spy out and report their plans. He soon returned with the report that the woods were full of them; but that there would be no trouble in gaining a signal victory, as the dogs were of an endless variety, and were snapping and snarling at one another at a great rate. That the world may know that Thou hast sent me, states the most weighty argument for a united church. Its necessity is found in two simple and primary laws,— love of God and man, and the Golden Rule as a method of operation. Fellowship is not the compliment we pay to each other in the assembly of the gathered hosts, but a mutual recognition and appreciation of each other which will prevent us from ecclesiastically cutting each other's throats in the struggle for denominational ascendency. Sectarianism is the Pharisaism of the modern church. We rejoice to-day that there is no provision for it in this theocratic movement. The divine order of the new life is Christ, fellowship, co-operation, conquest. Broadness and intensity are cardinal principles in the Christian Endeavor movement, and of first importance in the Christian life. The Christian Endeavor Society has by virtue of its governing motive lifted the individual Christian to a higher view-point, where he can see what is fair and good in others, and at the same time has intensified his fervor and loyalty for his own church. Shakespeare tells us of the parties who exchanged eyes and got a new fondness for each other. That is exactly what interdenominational fellowship will do for the followers of the Master. When such a spirit shall pervade the heart and life of the church, we shall be ready to join in the language of one of our great poets in repeating the promised joy, —

> "Rise, crowned with life, imperial Salem, rise!
> Exalt thy towering head and lift thine eyes!
> See a long race thy spacious courts adorn!
> See future sons and daughters yet unborn!
> See barbarous nations at thy gates attend,
> Walk in thy light, and in thy temple bend!
> See thy bright altars thronged with prostrate kings,
> And heaped with products of Sabaean springs!
> No more the rising sun shall gild the morn,
> Nor evening Cynthia fill her silver horn;
> But lost, dissolved, in thy superior rays,
> One tide of glory, one unclouded blaze,
> O'erflow thy courts; the light himself shall shine
> Revealed, and God's eternal day be thine!
> The seas shall waste, the skies to smoke decay,
> Rocks fall to dust, and mountains melt away;
> But fixed his word, his sovereign power remains,
> Thy realm forever lasts — thy own Messiah reigns!"

The address was received with great enthusiasm, and frequently applauded.

The benediction was pronounced by Professor Graham Taylor, D.D., of Chicago.

THE TENT.

Some of the Endeavorers were on hand at the tent as early as 7.30 o'clock, so that they might get a comfortable seat. The weather was cooler, but not the enthusiasm of the Endeavorers who assembled at the tent. While the crowd was gathering, Chicago gave a number of yells of "Chicago! Chicago! Y. P. S. C. E. Chicago!" The Endeavorers of the Buckeye State would not be outdone by those from the Windy City, and they gave a shout of, "Hi-o-hi! Ohio! Y. P. S. C. E. Ohio!" Then the audience joined in singing "America." At the conclusion of this, several Canadians, feeling that their Queen should also be recognized in song, mounted the platform, and to the waving of the Christian Endeavor banners and Canadian flags, sang three verses of "God Save the Queen." Then a series of cheers were given for Cleveland, America, and Canada.

Rev. Dr. B. B. Tyler of New York City presided, and at the conclusion of the praise service introduced Rev. George T. Smith of Japan, who led the audience in the devotional exercises.

Dr. James Lewis Howe of Louisville, Ky., was introduced, and conducted an Open Parliament on "What are the Benefits of Interdenominational Fellowship?"

Open Parliament — "The Benefits of Interdenominational Fellowship."

DR. HOWE: What are the benefits of Interdenominational Fellowship in Christian Endeavor work? Notice the origin of the Christian Endeavor Society, and trace the growth of interdenominational fellowship. First a single society in a Congregational church on the North Atlantic coast, with principles in that society which could be applied in other churches and in other denominations. As a result such principles are adopted; and then what more natural than if you, working your way, and I, working my way, but for the same ends, that we should come together and talk it over; and then what more natural than that we should see that which we have in common, and that we should for the time set aside that in which we differ? Hence has come about, I believe, this idea of interdenominational fellowship in Christian Endeavor. We do not disbelieve in denominations, but we do not believe in sects. The denomination is that by which our method of work is named. Sects would indicate that we were cut up. We believe in denominations; we do not believe in denominationalism. We do not believe in the emphasis being laid upon those points which separate us; we believe the emphasis must be laid upon the fact that we are all working together for Christ. We need our denominations. You can work better in your way, and I can work better in mine, and yet we remember that we are all working for the same end. The illustration is old about the army; nevertheless, it is so true that it bears repeating again and again, that as the different regiments and companies have their different leaders, and all marching against the same enemy, so are we. We are one body, but that body must have its different members. We must have our Methodist voice to shout — and thank God they have taught the rest of the body to shout; we must have our Episcopalian face in order to present beautiful features to the world; we must have our Baptist feet to carry us, even if they sometimes carry us through wet places [*laughter*]; we must have our Congregational brain to think independently; we must have the ears of Friends to hear, even if the Spirit does not move us to speak; we must have the heart of the Disciples, beating with the red blood of Christ; we must have Presbyterian backbone to hold us erect; we must have our Salvation Army hands to reach down into the slums and lift men up. [*Applause.*] But we are all the body of Christ.

We come together to tell how interdenominational fellowship is benefiting us. And now we want to have just as many speakers as we can crowd into the twenty-two minutes that remain.

FIRST SPEAKER: "The greatest witness to the divinity of Christ that this time needs is the unity of Christianity."

"Interdenominational fellowship is bringing together in a focus, more nearly than any other single branch of our Christian work, the grand idea of our fatherhood in God and our brotherhood in man; and it is our earnest prayer that the church, with the new inspiration given it heretofore by this Christian Endeavor movement, shall gain such vigor in its Christian life as to swallow up the last fragment of sectarianism." [*Applause.*]

"The Presbytery of Quebec and the Methodist Conference of Quebec, the Methodists and the Presbyterians, are going to meet next month at the same place on the same day to consider how they can work together in their mission fields in the Province." [*Applause.*]

"My father is a Methodist minister, my elder brother a Baptist minister, another brother belongs to the Congregational Church, a sister belongs to the Methodist Church, and I belong to the Presbyterian Church. [*Laughter.*] I should call this congregation a Presby-congre-bapti-methodi-palian." [*Laughter.*]

"Standing under the shadow of the cross, I believe that the black hand is to clasp hands with the white, and that we are all to stand on one grand plane, working for the coming of the Lord Jesus Christ." [*Applause.*]

"The Christian Endeavor Society in the Protestant Episcopal Church in Hartford, Conn., has taken down all of the barbed wire fences, and we are shaking hands and having one of the sweetest times you ever saw. There is nothing grander than the broad plane of the love of Jesus Christ."

"The Christian Unity Association of Chicago sends greeting to this Convention. During the past eighteen months we have canvassed over six hundred English-speaking evangelical churches, and we have spoken in over one hundred of those churches. We were met cordially by the ministers and members. On an average, it takes about a quarter of a minute to become acquainted with each. We are more and more impressed with the spiritual unity of the one body of the Lord Jesus Christ. May the days of the ultimate and visible unity of the Lord Jesus Christ be hastened on!"

"I am ashamed of the man who has never discovered that he can be loyal to his own denomination in every drop of his blood, and at the same time be a broad-minded Christian." [*Applause.*]

"I just wish to bring an accusation this morning against the Presbyterian Church. Last winter in Northwest Missouri a union meeting which convened in the Presbyterian church got the Methodists and the Baptists all mixed up, and we have not been able to tell them apart since." [*Laughter.*]

"In our denominational rallies a brother made the remark, 'With Methodist fire and Baptist water we will have enough steam to run the machinery in all the other churches.'"

"In the city of Philadelphia there is a Sunday Breakfast Association composed of forty members of every evangelical church. Through that Association thousands of poor, homeless people of every conceivable religion, and those of no religion, have been brought under the influence of the gospel. Praise God for the work that that Association has done. It is interdenominational."

"Not long ago I heard this little story. Two brothers went to heaven, and one asked the other where he came from, and he said, 'From that little rolling ball called the earth.' — 'I came from the State of Connecticut.' — 'I came from there also.' — 'What part of the State of Connecticut did you come from?' — 'From Hartford.' — 'I came from there also.' — 'What church?' — 'From —— Congregational Church.' — 'I am very glad to see you. I remember you now. You sat in the seat in front of me for twelve years, and I never met you. I am very glad to meet you now.'" [*Laughter.*]

"Ontario is glad that we can all work together on one common platform, for one common cause, for Christ and the church."

"A Presbyterian church wanted to lay the corner-stone. They invited all denominations to assist them. It began to rain, and the Baptist brethren invited them down to their church, and they laid the corner-stone of the Presbyterian church in the Baptist church."

"There is no city in this Union where the pastors are bound so close together as in Cleveland. Why, we even love each other so much that we have a bicycle club in this city of about twenty-five or thirty ministers. And no man can tell by the way the other rides, by the color of his wheel, or by the headers that he takes, whether he is a Baptist, a Congregationalist, a Methodist, or a Disciple." [*Laughter.*]

"The Mennonites are all working with the rest for Christ and the Church."

A unanimous vote in favor of international fellowship was given. "Blest be the Tie that binds," was then sung, after which Mr. Shaw announced that Mr. John G. Thompson of Sydney, New South Wales, had been for ten days in San Francisco, but, owing to the strikes, was unable to reach the convention to speak. A greeting was sent to Australia expressing regret that their representative was prevented from meeting with the convention.

Dr. Tyler then introduced Rev. R. Haywood Stitt, D.D., as the representative of the A. M. E. Zion Church.

DR. STITT: I am very sure that you recognize at once that I am not a full-blooded Australian [*laughter*], and therefore cannot take Mr. Thompson's place. I am glad to take, however, my own place. But I am modest, and I am blushing now [*laughter*], like the maid, who, after long waiting and a desperate effort, came to the day of her marriage at seventy-five years of age. It was customary at that time to sing some song that the maiden desired. The pastor asked what song they should sing, and the maiden, looking with anxious face to the pastor, said: "Sing this song, 'This is the Way I long have sought.'" [*Laughter*.]

I represent the A. M. E. Zion Church, that spreads over this country, the islands of the sea, and Africa. We represent a following of 500,000 communicants and more than a hundred thousand organized Christian Endeavorers. [*Applause*.] We have no official young people's society. The Board of Bishops, who sent me here, indorse the Christian Endeavor Society [*applause*]; and allow me to say that at the next General Conference, which meets in May, 1896, in Mobile, Ala., we will adopt as our young people's official society the Christian Endeavor. [*Loud Applause*.]

Reports from Denominational Rallies.

DR. TYLER: We are now to occupy a few minutes listening to reports from the various denominational rallies that were held Thursday afternoon. We are to have thirteen reports in twenty-six minutes. This does not permit the chairman to indulge in his fondness for talk any further than to call out the representatives, reminding them that their time is limited to two minutes.

A. M. E. AND THE A. M. E. ZION CHURCHES. *Rev. R. H. Stitt:* — We had a glorious time at our rally in St. John's Church, this city. We came together knowing no difference as to denomination. We had speeches from men and women of our race represented there; and I can only say that we concluded that the Christian Endeavor Society afforded the best field of operation, not only for the young people of our churches, who, had been hitherto almost shut out, but for that fraternity and that brotherhood so much needed in the pulpits and in the pews of our denomination. [*Applause*.]

BAPTIST. *Rev. A. W. H. Hodder, N. Y.:* — We had the best rally that the Baptists have ever had in the history of the Christian Endeavor movement. It was absolutely a Christian Endeavor rally from beginning to end. It began with prayer, followed by a few words from the other side of the world, from our famous missionary, Dr. Ashmore, who has been forty-four years in China; followed by Rev. Frank Dobbins of Philadelphia, who spoke upon "Christian Endeavor and Missions;" followed by Dr. A. C. Dixon, on "Christian Endeavorers as Soul Winners;" followed by Professor Coates of Rochester Theological Seminary, on "Christian Endeavor and Higher Education;" and then Dr. Beckley, on "Christian Endeavorers and what they have done for the Denominations;" and then finally by that one we all love, Dr. Hoyt, who spoke to us of the Christian Endeavor work and its relation to our Baptist Union work. We have set a standard, and we hope to rise above the standard now set. [*Applause*.]

CHRISTIAN. *Rev. G. A. Conibear, Westerly, R. I.*. — There were two practical results from our rally held on Thursday. One of them was the arrangement for the formation of a national Christian Endeavor Union; the other was the arrangement for larger work along the line of foreign missions. We can find nowhere anything better for us than Christian Endeavor, and we love it as much as we love ourselves; and we had a grand and glorious time, and we praise the Lord for all his blessings. [*Applause*.]

CHURCH OF GOD. *Mr. W. L. Stevens:* — We met in the Y. M. C. A. building; and while the room was not full our hearts were full of the love of God, and the result of it was that we filled the room with his praise. We decided that wherever the Convention will be held next year we will have many more delegates, and we will go home and pray for the advancement of the cause of Christian Endeavor, and for the enlargement of its borders in all denominations; and we will not only pray, but go home and work for it. [*Applause.*]

CONGREGATIONAL. *Mr. F. E. Page, Chicago :* — We had a rally of twenty-five hundred Congregationalists in Plymouth Congregational Church. We had twenty-five speakers at the rally and five appointed delegates sent to us by our various denominational missionary boards. We had the secretary of the Christian Endeavor Missionary Institute and Extension Course. We had glowing reports from all over the country, from Florida, New York, New Mexico, New England, Alabama, and Canada; and a delegate who was a returned missionary from India, and a colored brother, spoke to us. We heard from Professor Graham Taylor of the Chicago Theological Seminary, a delegate from that seminary to this Convention. That seminary stands pledged to introduce Christian Endeavor methods and principles into its course of instruction. What a glorious thought that twenty-six red-hot, white-hot denominational meetings can melt themselves into such a mold as this! [*Applause.*]

DISCIPLES OF CHRIST. *Rev. Dr. B. B. Tyler, N.Y. :* — If I could persuade somebody to introduce me in fitting terms to this audience [*laughter*] — observe, fitting terms [*laughter*] — I would report for the Disciples. Think I will do so anyway. We could not find a meeting-house in Cleveland big enough to hold our rally. [*Applause.*] We filled to overflowing the Euclid Avenue Disciple Church and the Euclid Avenue Congregational Church. The rally was devoted specifically to the cause of missions. The representatives of our missionary societies and the boards connected with them reported, with the object in view of giving our young people a definite understanding of the various societies and the specific work they have in hand, the General Christian Missionary Convention, the Foreign Christian Missionary Society, the Christian Women's Board of Missions. [*Laughter.*] They lay their own plans, collect their money, employ their agents, select their missionaries, send them to the field, direct their operations, receive their reports, administer discipline, dismiss them from their service, or commend them for fidelity, and never say to the lords of creation, "By your leave, brethren." Connected with these societies are the Board of Church Extension, connected with the General Christian Missionary Convention, the Board of Negro Education and Evangelization. In addition to these we had an address by Dean H. L. Willett of the Disciples Divinity House in connection with the Chicago University, in behalf of ministerial education. [*Applause.*]

EVANGELICAL ASSOCIATION. *Rev. L. H. Seager, Akron, O. :* — I am very glad to bring to this Convention the greetings of the Evangelical Association. We believe that we had the very best rally that was held in this city. We were not so very strong, yet we filled the church. We had addresses that were spicy, addresses that were excellent, addresses that were to the point. While there we were drawn closer together than we ever were before, and we were also drawn closer to this great work of Christian Endeavor. We are now, and we always have been, identified with this movement in spirit, and we hope and joyfully look forward to the time when we shall be identified with it denominationally and officially. We had representatives from the East and the West; we had them from Canada and from England; and our hearts beat in accord with these in the great work of Christian Endeavor the wide world over. [*Applause.*]

FREE BAPTIST. *Rev. J. M. Lowden, Boston :* — I am glad to report that we had a grand meeting, a full house, and glowing enthusiasm, and the heartiest response to every reference to the essential principles of Christian Endeavor. We had fine addresses on the elements of success in Christian Endeavor work. In conference we had before us, "Thoughts on Free Baptists and Interdenominational Loyalty." We also had a conference on this subject, "Christian Endeavor serving Our Denominational Interests;" and on this we are heartily orthodox. You may remember that at one time Lady Huntingdon was listening to Whitefield as he was preaching from the text: "And I, if I be lifted up from the earth, will draw all men unto me." This noble Christian woman had in her faith seen Jesus Christ lifted up from the earth; and so glorious did he seem to her exalted spiritual vision, that even the eloquence of Whitefield failed to portray him as she saw him; and so, rising to her feet in the glow of her spiritual enthusiasm, she cried, "Oh, lift him higher! lift him higher! can you not lift him a little higher?" And this is the message of all loyal Free Baptists to this Convention, "Lift him higher in the coming year! lift him higher!" [*Applause.*]

FRIENDS. *Mr. C. E. Newlin, Indianapolis, Ind.:* — To a great extent the Friends have laid aside the broad-brimmed hat and the strait-cut coat; but they have not laid aside their broad ideas of individual worship for each member of the church, and their clear-cut thought of the leading of the Holy Spirit in everything they do. It was shown to us most admirably that George Fox, the founder of our church, was one link in the great chain that has brought down the pure religion from the Evangelical Church of the disciples. It has been brought out very distinctly that the Friends' Church has been at the front in the Christian Endeavor movement. The Friends' Church has ever recognized the right of women to speak in their public meetings. [*Applause.*]

GERMAN SOCIETIES. *Rev. G. Berner, Buffalo, N. Y.:* — I have to report that the work among the Germans is in a very prosperous condition.

KEYSTONE LEAGUE. *Rev. W. A. Fouke, Chicago:* — The Keystone League of Christian Endeavor, representing constituencies in Pennsylvania, Ohio, Illinois, Iowa, Nebraska, California, and Oregon, met in the Y.M.C.A. lecture room of this city, completely filling the room on Thursday afternoon. We were welcomed by the youngest member of this model Cleveland Christian Endeavor Union, and we had the honor of having displayed in our midst a banner awarded to them showing that they had made the largest per cent gain in the past year. We had themes discussed upon important matters connected with our denominational relation with the great Christian Endeavor movement. We had everything pressed down, shaken together, and running over. We only had ten minutes to give to each speaker. The notes of our rally were Christ, Clark, Cleveland, Country, Christian Citizenship, and Charity, all sung to the tune of Christian Endeavor. [*Applause.*]

LUTHERAN. *Rev. Leander Keyser, Springfield, Ohio:* — We Lutherans are apt to be a little conservative. A great many of us are Germans, and we have to evolve a great many things from our inner consciousness, and that, usually, is also a long process. Our rally was the most successful one that we have ever held at these international conventions. Our church was overcrowded. We took an advance step, one that has not been reported on this platform as yet; and that is, we formed a permanent organization at our rally, and we there decided to call it "The Lutheran Christian Endeavor Union," which is to include all Lutheran Christian Endeavor societies the whole world over; and if you knew as well as I do how much that means, you would say it means a great deal in our Lutheran Church. We are with the Christian Endeavor movement heart and soul, not because we feel that we are so useful to it, but because we feel we cannot allow the opportunity to go by to benefit ourselves by this great movement. The Lutheran Church, we feel, cannot afford to divorce her efforts from this great International and interracial Christian Endeavor movement.

DR. TYLER: Now we will have an address by Rev. Theo. F. John of New Albany, Ind., on

Christian Endeavor Among the Germans.

Address of Rev. Theo. F. John.

I have the honor to stand before you at this grand convention as the representative of six thousand German Endeavorers. It is the first opportunity we have to present our cause before you, and to claim recognition. We feel justified in believing that you rejoice with us over the fact that at last the Christian Endeavor movement has gained a firm foothold among the Germans of our land. This was by no means an easy task. While in the American churches the society of Christian Endeavor has been hailed everywhere as the supply of a long-felt want, it has met with much indifference, misrepresentation, and open antagonism in the German churches. Our nationality is somewhat slow in the adoption of new religious ideas and institutions, which are American in their origin and character. As Nathanael of old exclaimed, "Can there any good thing come out of Nazareth?" so many of our people are disposed to say, "Can there any good thing come out of America?" Some dislike the Endeavor idea because it aims to replace the customary passiveness at religious meetings by active participation. Others seem to fear that it will carry an undesirable foreign spirit into our churches. Again others believe that it has not yet withstood the test of time, and fails to hold the enthusiasm it at first creates. But then we German Americans have already accepted, either directly or indirectly, several valuable auxiliaries to church work from our American neighbors. For instance, the Sunday school and the Young Men's Christian Association, though both originated in England, were adopted by us only after they had proved successful in the American churches; and to-day the former is considered indispensable, and the latter highly desirable among us. I hope that in a like manner my brethren may overcome their prejudice against the cause we represent here. I trust that they may accept this good thing, no matter where it comes from, and that all may be convinced that before it came from America it came from Almighty God.

What has been said so far should not convey the idea that the Endeavor movement has had a slow progress among the people. Such is not the case. Though it has found much opposition, it has found more hearty support and approval. A brief review of its growth will show this. Just when and where the first German Endeavor Society was organized is not positively known, at least not to me. I presume it was in the church of Rev. G. Hildner in Detroit. Inquiries sent in September, 1892, brought to our knowledge 12 German societies with about 300 members. At the end of the same year there were already 38 societies; and to-day, less than two years after the introduction of the Endeavor movement into German religious circles, we have 148 societies, with an active membership of nearly 6,000. Some of these societies are quite strong, the one in my church at New Albany, for instance, numbering 184 active members. Remembering how difficult the beginning of such undertakings are, this is a phenomenal growth, exceeding even that of the American general society itself, which at the end of its third year had only 56 societies with 2,900 members. Bear also in mind that our field of operation as compared to yours is very limited, embracing as it does only a fractional portion of the foreign born and their progeny.

Of these 148 German societies, by far the greater majority, viz., 97, are found in the German Evangelical Church, 20 in the German Reformed, 16 in the German Presbyterian, 7 in the Moravian, 2 in the German Baptist, 2 in the German Congregational Church, and 1 in the Evangelical Association. The great German Lutheran and the German Methodist Church are as yet closed to us. All these societies are organized into a German general society, which is divided into fifteen districts, and holds a mass meeting once a year. The first occurred in April, 1893, at Chicago; the second, in April, 1894, at Tiffin, Ohio. At these happy occasions all denominational differences are obliterated, and we meet as Christians only, and laborers in the same vineyard. This is one of the great blessings of Christian Endeavor, that it furthers the spirit of Christian unity.

The man who was instrumental above all others in establishing the Endeavor cause among the Germans is Rev. G. Berner of Buffalo, N.Y. He might properly be called the German Dr. Clark. For a long time he noticed with deep regret the heavy loss sustained by many of our churches among their young people, resulting from the absence of a proper institution to hold them. While away from home he attended a Christian Endeavor prayer-meeting, and was touched by its spirit of devotion. Examining more closely into the nature of this institution, he found it to be the proper remedy for the evil he had so often deplored. He at once remodeled the young people's society of his church into a Christian Endeavor society. Not satisfied to have discovered a good thing for himself, he now strove to impart it to others. He accordingly published a book of some 150 pages entitled "Unsere Jugend" (Our Youth), in which he sets forth and warmly recommends the excellent qualities of the cause to which he had just been won. This book has served as a guide in the organization of many other societies. Simultaneously Mr. Berner issued a monthly paper, "Der Mitarbeiter" (The Co-Laborer), in the interest of the same work. It has gradually been enlarged to sixteen pages, with illustrations, and is edited in a bright, crisp, and entertaining manner. As our official organ it has become as indispensable to us as *The Golden Rule* to you. Other literature issued in rapid succession from the same source are a German hymn-book, constitution and by-laws, pledge and topic cards, etc. I am in a position to state that the publication of all these articles has up to date been possible only by sacrifices on the part of the author. Not only has the work of two whole years been given gratis, but there has been a considerable financial loss. We trust, however, that as the work assumes larger dimensions this will be rectified.

Let it be said in this connection that in our opinion it would greatly advance the

CONVENTION HALL.

work among the Germans if we were able to engage a reliable man to give his entire time and effort to that purpose. It is fast becoming impossible for one man to discharge the manifold duties of the general president and at the same time serve a large city congregation. There would be work enough to keep such a man busy all the year around. He would attend to the official correspondence, which even now is very heavy. He would edit our paper, which then perhaps could be enlarged, and published semi-monthly instead of monthly. He would visit the conferences of the fifteen districts and keep aflame the enthusiasm. He would aid in establishing new societies wherever his advice might be required. I am sure he would receive many such calls. There are many churches which would to-morrow start a Christian Endeavor society if only they saw their way clear. But for the present this fond wish of engaging such a person cannot be realized, because of the lack of means.

In conclusion, it may interest you to know that the Christian Endeavor idea has of late found its way to Germany. Through the literature before mentioned a young minister in Bielefeld, Blecher by name, has become an enthusiastic advocate of our cause. He is publishing a series of articles in several leading religious papers, explaining and recommending it. He of course meets with many obstacles. One clerical brother before whom he laid the matter made the characteristic reply: "It is very good, but it's American." Yet the seed is sown, and it remains to be seen what the harvest will be. Personally I am convinced that Christian Endeavor will soon have taken root in the Fatherland.

Presentation of Banners.

MR. SHAW: We wish now to recognize faithful service by our local unions in the matter of systematic and proportionate giving and interdenominational fellowship. I have the honor this morning to present these banners to the unions that, in the judgment of the committee, judging from the reports sent in, best deserve them. They mean that multitudes of our young people are practicing systematic and proportionate giving to God; they mean that multitudes of societies are striving to extend our blessed fellowship by organizing new societies.

First of all, the Union that has the largest number of systematic and proportionate givers will please come to the platform. [*Laughter.*] Why, I thought you would all be here. I know you will all be glad to hear me announce that the Union that has the largest number of systematic and proportionate givers is the Union for which we cannot say too much or do too much, the Cleveland Christian Endeavor Union. [*Applause.*] Mr. L. V. Denis will receive the banner. I am informed that those initials stand for lively and vigorous Denis. [*Laughter.*]

MR. DENIS: *Mr. Chairman,* — I think I can honestly state that the members of the Cleveland Union, including myself, are too full for utterance. And I think that if you will consider the success of this convention, for which we have labored and prayed for two years, you will agree with me that we have adequate reason for being in that condition. This has been a week of surprises. In accepting this banner in behalf of my brothers and sisters, I do not do it carelessly and thoughtlessly, or without some adequate appreciation of what it means. There has never before been a banner given for this work. This is the first, and, therefore, we hope that next year very many unions of Christian Endeavor will be far in advance of where the Cleveland Union now stands. As the recipient of this beautiful banner, as I said, we do not forget what it means; it represents a great advance movement along the line of giving to God, and we do hope that all Endeavorers will adopt this; for all who have done it, or will do it, will receive a special blessing from God. I thank you, Mr. Chairman, in behalf of the Union, for this banner.

MR. SHAW: And now the question comes, What other great union in the country shall receive the banner for having organized and received into its union the largest number of new societies? I do not know whether the representative of this union is present here this morning. I hope so. If he is here we will give him a welcome. This banner stands for the extension of Christian Endeavor fellowship. I suppose that there are a great many unions here that would like to have this beautiful white-and-gold banner, because it will remind them of Cleveland — white and gold. But then we always like to remember our friends ; and as the headquarters of the Friends is Philadel-

INTERIOR OF THE CONVENTION HALL, LOOKING TOWARD THE PLATFORM.

phia, Philadelphia will have to take the banner. I have the pleasure of introducing Mr. J. Burns Allen, President of the Philadelphia Union.

MR. ALLEN: *Mr. Chairman, Fellow Endeavorers,* — The Pennsylvania delegation has great reason to rejoice at this time, not because we have taken the banner from New York, for the largest union, but because we have gained it. The second reason is that within the borders of that grand old State of Pennsylvania is the largest local Christian Endeavor Union in the world. [*Applause.*] If it were not for some of the characteristics which are assigned to Philadelphians, I think that the Philadelphia delegation would have to buy new hats to go on their journey home; but you know we are a quiet and modest people, and therefore we are not susceptible to the undue influence of this great excitement; but I tell you, my friends, I believe that these things that are so often said about Philadelphia have no foundation whatever, because I believe that if there is any city under the sun that stands for hospitality, for patriotism, for progress, and for Christian Endeavor, it is this grand old municipality located in Pennsylvania, known as the City of Brotherly Love, Philadelphia — to us the best in the world. [The Pennsylvanians then sang their State song.] Therefore, Mr. Treasurer, on behalf of the Philadelphia Union we most gladly accept this most beautiful banner which has been presented to us for the cause mentioned. We will guard it carefully, and ever cherish the memories that it must always bring to us of this Thirteenth International Christian Endeavor Convention at Cleveland, Ohio.

DR. TYLER: Since I came to Cleveland I have heard over and over, again and again and again, something about a person whom you call the Rev. J. Z. Tyler, D.D., I don't know anything about him, but I have the privilege now of introducing to this audience my little brother, Joseph Zechariah Tyler. [*Laughter.*]

Dr. J. Z. Tyler announced the excursions on Lake Erie in the afternoon. He then presented Miss Jessie H. Brown, author of "Cleveland '94," and everyone sang the chorus of the song in a very happy manner.

Dr. Tyler then requested the audience to bow their heads in silent prayer for one minute, asking God's blessing upon our brothers and sisters in other lands.

Rev. Wayland Hoyt, D.D., of Minneapolis, was then introduced, and made an address on "Interdenominational Fellowship."

Interdenominational Fellowship.

Address of Rev. Wayland Hoyt, D.D.

Mr. President, Brothers and Sisters in Christian Endeavor, — Fidelity and Fellowship, fellowship because of fidelity. This, it seems to me, is the Christian Endeavor principle.

Do you know about Private William Scott? Private William Scott was a Vermont farm-boy. He enlisted. It was in the time of the war. There had been a long march all day. That night, all night, he had stood on picket guard. There had been a long march all the next day. That night a sick comrade was appointed on picket guard and he volunteered to take his place. He was not accustomed to be awake nights, and the fatigue overwhelmed him and he slept on picket guard. But it was at Chain Bridge, and the army was in a dangerous neighborhood and discipline must be preserved. He was apprehended, tried by court-martial, sentenced to be shot, and was awaiting the day before his execution in his tent. Meanwhile, the patient president, Abraham Lincoln, had heard about it; and, as private William Scott tells of it, he was surprised to see a great, tall man standing before him in his tent. "I knew him," William Scott said, "because of the medal of him that I wore. He was so kind. I never had talked with a great man before, but he was so kind he did not frighten me. He began to ask all about me, about the school I had gone to, about the farm, about my mother. I was very glad I had a picture of my mother in my blouse, and I drew it out and handed it to him; and he looked at it and said to me: 'You ought to be very thankful you have a

INTERIOR OF THE CONVENTION HALL, LOOKING TOWARD THE REAR.

mother, and you ought never to do anything which would bring the blush of shame to her cheek.' "

Says Private William Scott: "I did not understand why he should be talking to me so, when I knew I was to be shot to-morrow, and had made up my mind to ask him if he wouldn't just grant me the privilege of not being shot by the boys of my own regiment. I couldn't stand that. Just as I was going to ask him he stood up before me and said, ' William Scott, stand up;' and I stood up, and he put his hands on my shoulders and he said, 'William Scott, I have heard all about you. I don't believe you are a bad soldier; I believe you meant to do your very best. I am not going to have you shot. I am going to send you back to your ranks. But now, William Scott, who is going to pay my bill?'" And William Scott said: "Mr. Lincoln, I am very much obliged to you; I am taken all aback. I don't know but we can manage to pay you if it isn't more than $500 or $600. There is the mortgage on the farm, there is the bounty money in the bank, and I think the boys will chip in on pay-day and help me out." Said Lincoln: "William Scott, there is only one man who can pay my bill, and that man is William Scott. If from this time forward you are the soldier that you ought to be; if you are true to the old flag; and if at last I should be present when you died and you could say to me, 'Mr. Lincoln, I have kept this promise utterly, then, William Scott, you will have paid my bill.'" Thenceforward there never was such a soldier as William Scott. No man so obedient, no man so ready for difficult duty, no man so faithful. He refused promotion. There were the terrible battles of the Wilderness, and he performed deeds of valor. Officer after officer wounded to the death he carried to the rear, and forced himself again to the front. He was struck with a great shot and torn all to pieces, and they bore him back. The battle was done, and his comrades gathered round him; and William Scott said, "Boys, I think you can say to my mother I tried to do my duty. Boys, I fought my last battle; and, boys, if any of you should ever see Mr. Lincoln, won't you tell him that I was true to the promise I made in the tent, when he gave me the privilege of dying on the battle-field like a soldier, and not being shot to death like a dog. Won't you tell him I was true?" And he crossed his hands on his breast, and a bright smile overspread his face, and he said, "Good-by, boys," and it was all over. [*Applause.*]

Now, I am sure it is perfectly easy to see how this personal relation, established thus between William Scott and President Lincoln, marshaled and intensified every patriotic principle and impulse in him. I am perfectly sure you can plainly see how this personal relation, thus established between William Scott and President Lincoln, made his service of patriotism but the more anxiously painstaking, and the more accurately punctilious.

And now, this is precisely the way in which our Christianity acts, and this is the meaning of its at once exacting and yet joyful empire. Undermost, topmost, foremost, it is a personal relation.

What is your fundamental definition of Christianity? Devotion to a creed? No, not that primarily. Devotion to rights? Not that primarily. Devotion to a church? No, not that primarily. Devotion to the Bible? No, not even that primarily. What is your fundamental definition of Christianity? Devotion to the person. Personal loyalty to the personal Christ, that is Christianity. [*Applause.*] The Christ whom the Bible discloses; the Christ whom the church owns as its head; the Christ whom right symbolizes; the Christ who is the heart and center of its creed; him, our Lord Jesus Christ, who, when we were in darkness, came with the granitic certainties of his replies to our quivering and anxious question. Who, when not Socrates, nor Plato, nor Confucius, nor any one of the great teachers, was able to set before us the ideal and the exemplification of the perfect life, himself came to stand before us and to say, "I am the way and the truth and the life." Our Christ, who, when we were under the doom of sin, and manacled by its slavery, by his cross, and then by his death, and by his glorious resurrection and ascension, and by the giving of the Holy Ghost, made us free.

The fundamental Christian is the man who has personal loyalty to the personal Christ, and therefore adds to this Christ fidelity, fidelity about everything, and fidelity about church joining. This is the undermost principle of Christian Endeavor — fidelity to the local church and to the particular denomination to which you belong — because fidelity here means fidelity to him.

If any of you are one of these molluscous jelly fish — " It makes no difference to what church I belong " — be you sure you never got such a mushy notion as that from Christian Endeavor, never! [*Applause.*]

I once made, as his guest, a military march with Gen. Miles through a dangerous country; and I noticed that Gen. Miles was punctiliously anxious to obey the orders of his superior. And Christian Endeavor says: "The Bible is your order-book." Young man, young woman, intelligently, thoroughly, conscientiously, study that order-book, and join the church to which it seems to you that order-book points, in fidelity to Jesus Christ, and then conscientiously stand for your convictions. [*Applause.*] Christian Endeavor a poor and lazy way of unintelligent compromise and carelessness, sponging out denominational lines? Never! while denominational lines mean anything at all whatever. I dare affirm that Christian Endeavor, by its insistence on fidelity to the local church and to the particular denomination, has done more for an intelligent — not sectarianism, I like that distinction — for an intelligent denominationalism, than any movement under the stars, because it demands that you know the reason why you are what you are. If you don't know it, you are a poor specimen of a Christian Endeavorer, anyhow.

And now, interdenominational fellowship because of fidelity. For interdenominational fellowship is only faithful witnessing to a mighty fact. I say interdenominational fellowship; I do not say organic unity; I do not say a conglomerate hodge-podge of compromised convictions, but I do say spiritual interdenominational fellowship is only faithful witnessing to a mighty fact. "Ye are my witnesses," says our Lord, and it is our commanded duty to bear witness to a Christian fact; and that, outstanding, sublime, sun-enwreathed, is not that we have to become, but that we are one in Christ Jesus! [*Applause.*]

Thursday afternoon, in our Baptist denominational rally, Dr. Vedder, the editor of the *Baptist Examiner*, brought a message from the Moravian denominational rally, and he said that he was living in a town of Staten Island where there was no Baptist church; that he had therefore become a member of the Christian Endeavor society in the Moravian church in that town, and that they had sent him to bear this message to the Baptist rally: "We are brethren." And we, with one voice, sent back the message: "We are brethren." We are brethren in all deepest and truest senses. We are one in Christ Jesus, and interdenominational fellowship is the commanded witnessing to that mighty fact. Interdenominational fellowship because of fidelity; for interdenominational fellowship is girded and heartening for the conflict. We need to gird and hearten ourselves for the conflict, for the conflict is strong and even to be more terrible.

A young officer, after one of the great battles of the war, said that victory to him meant standing by his gun and keeping it fired at the enemy. And that was victory for him; but who shall say how much he was helped in that personal duty by hearing the boom of the companion guns standing with him along all that ridge and also firing? He was not alone; he was one of a mighty host, so he could be strong and true.

And one thing I get out of these Christian Endeavor conventions is a mighty hopefulness. I tell you this is Christ's world, and not the Devil's; this is a redeemed world, and this mighty host of Christian Endeavor means that this world which Christ has redeemed is to submit to him; and we get heart and hope from interdenominational fellowship.

Also, interdenominational fellowship because of fidelity; for we thus wipe off the reproach of Protestantism. Do you know, I think there is no more patriotic duty than the duty, when we come together in these vast assemblages, to declare our spiritual unity as against the slander, perpetual and persistent, of that hierarchy, not of freedom, but of absolutism, which takes its orders, not from America, but from the Tiber, and which means by various plotting to seize and destroy your public schools if possible, and so manage matters as that your institutions shall be adjusted to its demands. [*Applause.*] You may call me alarmist if you choose, but I tell you that is a cloud menacing the horizon. And there is nothing so certain to dispel it as our spiritual unity, expressed by this magnificent and mighty interdenominational fellowship; and we are serving our country when we do it.

And, last of all, interdenominational fellowship because of fidelity. For through interdenominational fellowship we are giving expression to the instinctive feeling of the regenerate and Christ-loving heart. It was something after this fashion: After the great battle of Pittsburg Landing, if I remember rightly, and a lot of wounded and dying men were turning imploring faces towards the cold stars; and one of them, a Christian, began feebly to sing, —

> "When I can read my title clear
> To mansions in the skies,
> I'll bid farewell to every fear,
> And wipe my weeping eyes."

He was an infantryman; and yonder there was a cavalryman, a Christian man, and he took up the song; and yonder there was an artilleryman, a Christian, and he took up the song; and yonder there was a poor fellow with the gray uniform, and yet a Christian, and he took up the song, and sang, —

> "When I can read my title clear,
> I'll bid farewell to every fear."

THE TENT.

The infantryman didn't have to put on the uniform of a cavalryman, the cavalryman to put on the uniform of the artilleryman, nor even the fellow yonder in the gray — he could keep his uniform; for great as was the chasm between him and the men against whom he fought, there was yet between him and them the deeper spiritual unity of oneness in Jesus Christ, and so he could sing, and all could sing, —

> "When I can read my title clear
> To mansions in the skies,
> I'll bid farewell to every fear,
> And wipe my weeping eyes."

You can't help it. We have got to love everybody who loves our Lord and Saviour Jesus Christ; and we can't help, and we won't help, saying that we love them all.

> "Like a mighty army moves the Church of God ;
> Brothers, we are treading where the saints have trod.
> We are not divided, all one body we ;
> One in faith and doctrine, one in charity.
> Onward, Christian soldiers, marching as to war,
> With the cross of Jesus going on before."

The conclusion of Dr. Hoyt's address was greeted with enthusiastic and prolonged applause, after which certain announcements were made, a hymn sung, and the session was adjourned.

SATURDAY AFTERNOON.

A large number of excursions both by land and water were arranged for the afternoon ; and the day being fair, all were well patronized. The only session of the convention was the Junior rally at Saengerfest Hall.

Junior Rally.

The morning session had hardly closed before the Juniors came trooping into the hall, anxious to secure good seats for the afternoon. Seats were reserved for them on the floor of the hall up toward the front, and by one o'clock they had filled all these seats and a good many more besides. The gallery and platform were also crowded with interested spectators. It was estimated that nearly five thousand people were turned away, unable to find even standing room in the hall. The song service naturally commenced early, and under Mr. Foster's lead the young folks had a great time. The two " Sunshine " songs were especially popular, and were sung enthusiastically.

Rev. James L. Hill, D.D., presided and conducted the opening exercises, which consisted of the repeating together of the Twenty-third Psalm, the singing of " America," and the reciting in concert of the Lord's Prayer. The well-known hymn, " At the Cross," was then sung, after which the audience listened to a temperance speech by a young boy in knickerbockers, Master Ernest Fisher of Washington, D.C.

Dr. Hill then gave the little folks a talk. He first asked the question how many of the children had ever seen a colt. Of course a good many hands were raised. Then he asked how many thought that colts were pretty. Again there was a generous response. Then he went on to tell them about his visit to a " colts' kindergarten." Said he : —

Train the Children.

Here they have their little trotting circuits, and here they are taught to develop whatever power they may possess. Little colts are trained to do something at a much earlier age than they used to be. So it is in the church. Boys can be trained best while they are little.

While I was in the West a man took the train with me. He had a bicycle with him, and was on the way to ride in a race. He said that a person could not become an expert rider who drank liquor. " Then you do not drink liquor? " — " No. I learned to resist when I was little." — " How was that? " — " Well, my mother had eight boys, and my father was a drunkard. My mother said, ' That is enough. I'll teach the little boys to say no.' So, just as soon as any of us began to learn to talk, mother would pick us up and stand us on the table and say, ' Now, what is mamma's boy going to say when anybody asks him to drink liquor? Say 'No.' Then the little fellow would say 'No.' Then she would say, 'Shout it louder,' and the boy would shout it louder. Then, as we grew older, when she would hear of the foolishness and cruelty and woe of a drunkard, she would tell us about it, and say, 'Now, get up on the table. What are you going to say when you are asked to drink liquor?' And the answer would come with vigor, 'No.' And it is so now. If a man asks me to drink liquor, or even talks about liquor, I find that my mouth begins to form at once to say no, and I begin to get myself together to say it louder." Oh, I believe in the work of the kindergarten. I knew of a boy who had the bad habit of saying, "I don't care." His mother would say to him kindly, " I fear my little boy will be late to school," and he would say, "I don't care." — "Why, look, my little boy has left his hat in the middle of the floor." — "I don't care." Finally she called him to her and said: "Mamma is grieved that her little son has this bad habit of saying 'I don't care,'" so she asked him to write out the words on a large piece of paper, "I don't care." Then she led him to an old well which had fallen into disuse. They wrapped a stone up in the paper; and the mother said, "Now let us drop 'I don't care' into this deep well, and then go away and leave it there forever." They did it. The boy dropped it. He never employed it again. That is the way for a boy to drop a sin. Drop it. Leave it. Forsake it. An old sailor said that he never knew a boy to get washed overboard at sea. A heavy man might; for a man weighs so much, that, if he catches hold of a rope, he cannot sustain his own weight as a boy can.

A boy is light and wiry and tenacious if he gets hold. Simply because he is a boy he can keep hold. He has less to sustain. So it is with the boy who by faith lays hold on Jesus. He has not the might of so many habits and thoughts to drag him down. This is the work we want to do among the Juniors. There is a redemptive work, but we emphasize to-day the preventive work. There is a work of reformation, but formation is better. We want every little Junior to some day thank God like David for what he has been kept from. The difficulty to-day in the Hawaiian Islands is this: Our missionaries converted a generation, but made no adequate provision for the generation which should next come upon the stage. One of the missionaries attending one of our conventions said that societies of Endeavor were the things needed in the Sandwich Islands. One of the choicest teachers in our Sunday-school came to me and said: "The boys in my class want to belong to something." If I were asked to compress the most significant thing I know about Junior societies into a word it would be this: Let the Juniors do the work in their own society. Do not lecture them. Let the organization be an autonomy. Let the chairmen read reports which their mothers can help them write. Let them feel a personal responsibility, like the little girl who came to the leader after the meeting and said, " Two girls got my chance, and I almost didn't say my verse." Cultivate such a spirit of *esprit de corps* that all will feel it a privilege to belong to it. The refrain which should spring spontaneously to the lips, beating in every heart, should be: " I'm glad I'm in this army." All the other departments of Christian Endeavor are marked by astounding growth and prosperity, but the Juniors have led all and surpassed everything. Like Henry Clay, I hear the sound of the coming millions. Notwithstanding the temptation, let us all be brief to-day. Two little girls in West Lynn were allowed to make a call on a friend the other afternoon, and stayed so long that their mother inquired the cause of the delay. The older one answered, "We didn't know how to leave off. How do people leave off when they call, mother?" It takes more vigor to stop an address than it does to begin it. Let us show that we have learned what the two little girls so much needed to learn — just how to leave off.

At the close of Dr. Hill's talk the Park sisters were introduced, and favored the audience with a beautiful cornet trio, winning round upon round of applause. Next came an address by Rev. Arthur W. Spooner of Camden, N.J., as follows: —

DELEGATES ARRIVING BY BOAT.

The Boy at the Throttle.

Address of Rev. A. W. Spooner.

Recalling my own boyhood, fast receding in the distance, but growing more and more sacred to memory as the years accumulate behind me, and remembering how my young life was influenced by the touch of hands long since stilled in death, and by messages of affectionate counsel which fell from lips now silent on earth, but vocal in heaven, I am profoundly impressed with the solemnity and grandeur of this occasion. Molten iron poured into the mold takes instantaneous and permanent shape; and just as surely will truths and impressions drop into the tender hearts and expanding minds of this vast army of boys and girls, whose power shall be felt far down into the years.

May God's richest blessing rest upon this great host of joyful, true-hearted, pure-hearted, brave-hearted Juniors!

I am to speak to you about "The Boy at the Throttle," and am confident that I shall have the attention of every boy in this vast audience; for where is the lad who does not admire the engineer, and wish that he could sit with hand on the throttle and control the snorting, puffing, mighty iron steed, as it speeds away over mountains and across prairies, leaping bridges and threading tunnels, wherever the shining track leads? I am also sure of the attention of the girls, because they are always interested in whatever concerns the boys, and are so polite that they would listen whether interested or not.

My subject seems to refer alone to the boys, as if they only were worth considering; but let me assure you that the girls are included in my thought and interest as of just as much importance as their brothers — stronger, perhaps, than they, but surely no smarter. What I say to the boys, I say also to the girls. Perhaps we can do no better than for all of us to think ourselves as boys — then the subject will be sure to fit. Hundreds of these bright-eyed girls have said again and again that they wished they were boys; so they will not object at all to trying to think they really are for just a few minutes.

My purpose in addressing you is not to make you laugh (although that is a good thing to do, and helps you to grow fat and beautiful), but rather with God's help to speak some earnest words which shall aid you, at least a little, in the development of a noble manhood and womanhood, and incite you to a heroic struggle for mastery.

God's plans for the human race are graded to an ascending scale.

Following the lead of his Spirit, the path scales the cliffs that pierce the clouds while it shines "brighter and brighter unto the perfect day." Not every man, and not every boy, seems willing to mount to these glory heights; but multitudes appear to prefer the down grade, with its misery depths and ever-blackening shadows. These are wandering stars, with no established orbit, whose only possible end is destruction.

This, however, is not what God desires for any soul. The boy who watches for heaven's finger-boards, and follows their directions, will find his whole nature vitalized with the ozone of the higher atmosphere, and his soul expanded with the ever-deepening joys of increasing and perpetual triumph. The times in which we live may properly be called the period of readjustment. Old creeds are being rigidly scrutinized, if not revised; social relations are being shifted, and in this general resetting of relations and readjustment of forces social and religious the boy has found his place. Can anything be plainer than that the true interpretation of the "handwriting on the wall" is this: "For the boys and the girls of the rising generation God has reserved tasks of transcendent importance."

Every generation is led up to some wide-open door of opportunity, by the same mighty though unseen hand that swings it back, and directed to some field of conquest where laurels await the victor's coming, as rich and fair as ever encircled a conqueror's brow. . At that open door, on the threshold of a new century just springing to birth, this generation is standing; and in the very van of the advancing host stand the boys and the girls, with sickle in one hand and sword in the other, ready to follow the great Captain either to yellow harvest fields of peace, or to the crimson plains of war.

One thing which the church of Christ is learning in these days of readjustment of forces, if not of creeds, is that for fighters in the army of the Lord, or for reapers in his harvest field, none can do better or more valiant service than the boys and girls. It

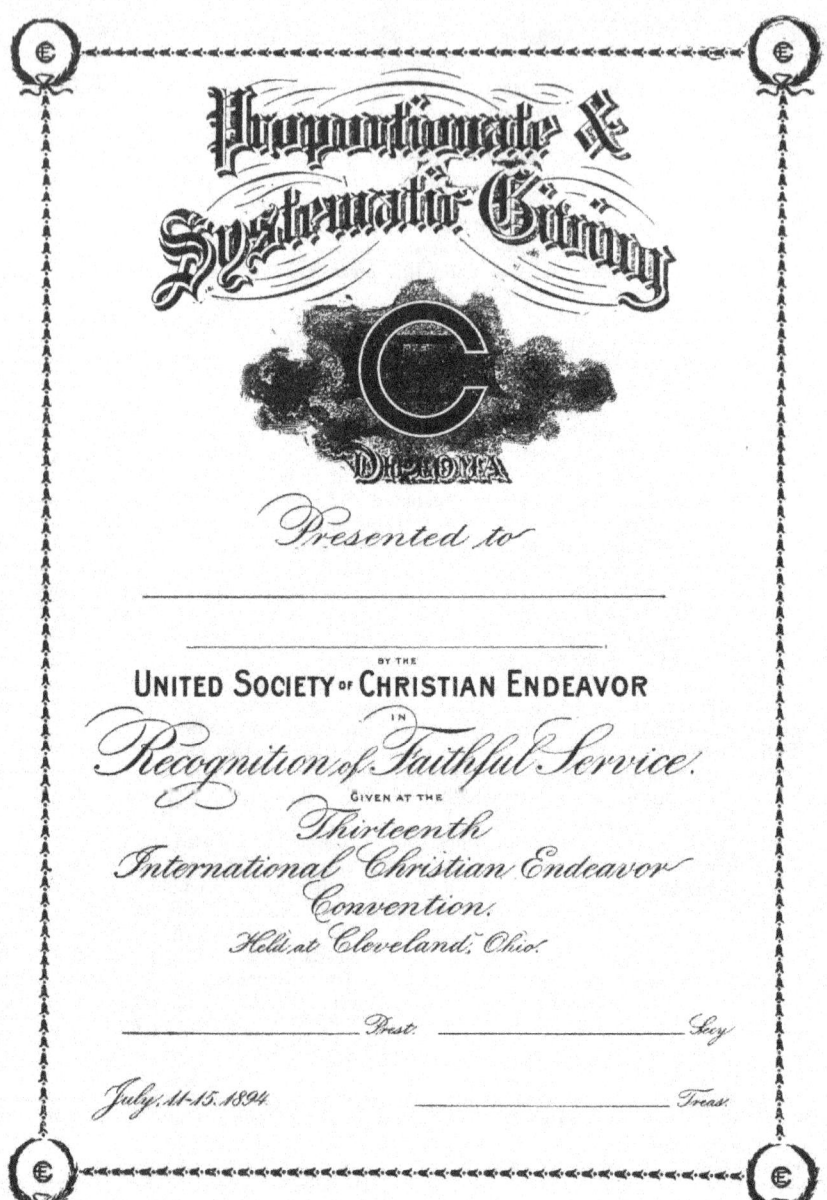

may not be possible to forecast in detail the future; but, as coming events do often "cast their shadows before them," so it seems easy to anticipate, in a degree at least, some of the approaching conflicts in which our sons, and our daughters too, will be called to engage.

May God prepare the boys and girls for victorious warfare! One of the grandest discoveries of this age of discoveries is the discovery of the boy.

The discovery of dynamics marks one of the chief material triumphs of this victorious century; and in the harnessing of these liberated giants of power to the wheels of commerce, and the looms and shafts and spindles of productive industry — transforming the lightnings of heaven into veritable "horses of fire," and chaining them to ponderous chariot wheels, turning tired beasts into the green meadows for long needed and richly earned rest. All this is wonderful, and pregnant with meaning, and freighted with promise to the race; but the discovery of the boy transcends it all. The world has always felt the foreign influence of this dynamic agency, but has signally failed to realize its potency, and almost to recognize it as a fact. The prophet foresaw the dawning of the age in whose outer circles we are living, and pointed out one of its distinguishing features when he exclaimed: "And a little child shall lead them."

The Bible recognizes distinctly the natural leadership of the children; and the Master himself holds them up high in his hands, and calls the attention of the world to them as models for all who would inherit the kingdom of God.

It is a sad thing to say, but true nevertheless, that the world at large, and Christians far too generally, have failed to recognize childhood as a productive period, a dynamic epoch in the history of the individual, and have regarded it rather as a necessary initial chapter to the book in which the record of maturer and more fruitful years should at length be written; not very interesting and not very important when considered by itself, and when the most that could be asked of a good boy was that he "keep off the grass," and be "seen and not heard." Oh, what a pity that child life, with its heaven-endowed principle of expansiveness, should be hampered and discouraged by such an unphilosophical and unchristian sentiment as this: "Children should be seen and not heard."

Say that of a manufacturer, and the wheels of his factory would stand still. Say that of the stone-cutter, and the marble or granite would never be shaped for the temple. Say that to the child, and insist upon applying the unwholesome principle, and you close up the avenues leading to intellect and soul, and, instead of training him to "mount up with wings as eagles," you compel him to crawl like a grub. Thank God the scales have been removed from the eyes of the church, and she has discovered to her great surprise that the boy is at the throttle.

There are two possible views to take of the boy as he stands at the throttle; i.e., we may consider him as related to himself, and as a factor in the mighty currents of intellectual and moral influence which are sweeping over the earth.

Standing at the throttle, the boy appears as the arbiter of his own future, giving it both shape and direction.

Looking at him in this light, he may be regarded not only as standing at the point of controlling leverage, with reference to his own character and career, but also as the throttle itself; or, still better, as a whole steam-engine, with fire-box, steam-chest, drive-wheels, bell, and whistle, all in splendid order, his whole nature expanding with suppressed power struggling to escape; or, better, waiting for some strategic point of application.

Just open the throttle, and see how the ponderous engine will leap to its task. Just give the boy a chance to apply his knowledge and power, and see how his whole nature will expand with the effort, and how nobly he will toil.

Possessed of a warm love for Christ, and an ambition to serve him, the boy will not be long in demonstrating that the assumption that he is good for little else than to worry the cat, tease his sister, and make a racket, is one of the most scandalous heresies of the nineteenth century.

Christian Endeavor has aroused the church to a realization of the fact that her mission is not done towards the children in her bosom when she has nursed them; but with the nursing she must couple training.

Towards the children within her pale the church must exercise the twofold function of nursing-mother and drilling-master. Instead of saying to the children, as in former years, "Run away, little children, until you are older and have more experience, then come to do a man's work in the vineyard," the language of the church is coming more and more to be this, "Come, little children, into the vineyard, and learn to do children's work now, so that when you become men and women you will be prepared to do heroic work for the Master."

Standing at the throttle, the boy occupies, with reference to his own future, and to the mighty movements of the age in which he lives, a position of great power and grave responsibility. His place in this world, and his position, either among the crowned or uncrowned hosts in the world to come, will be largely determined by the use made of the intellectual and moral lever which God has placed in his hand. The throttle is the point of control. By it the train is started and stopped. It possesses no power,

SCENE IN WADE PARK, ADELBERT COLLEGE IN THE DISTANCE.

produces none. All it is designed to do is to direct and control forces already developed.

How wicked would be the engineer who should open wide the throttle with a burning bridge in full sight, or an obstruction across the track calculated to hurl the train with its precious freightage of human lives hundreds of feet down the rocky abyss! What shall we say of the boy who opens the throttle of appetite and passion and greed, and focalizes all the powers of his nature in one dreadful race down the steep incline of depravity into the fires of remorse and despair, which never cease their burning? My boy, before you can make safe progress along any of the lines which stretch away into the distance you must learn to close the throttle.

It seems at first thought a strange act performed by the mother who one day set her little boy on the center of the table, and said to him, "Now, my son, say 'No!'" The little fellow obeyed, and then the mother said, "Say it again," and he said it again, and again, and again, and again, until he never forgot the hour or the lesson. The explanation given by the mother was that she wanted her boy to know how to say "No." He could easily say "Yes," but to say "No" at the right time would not be so easy. You boys are well aware that this mother was right. What she was trying to teach her boy was to apply the throttle. May God help you, my boys, to learn the same lesson! I have said that the boy standing at the throttle occupies a position of great power and grave responsibility. Let us think of this just a moment in conclusion. Now, my boys, in all seriousness, what are you going to be, and what are you going to do in this life? Tell me as you stand with your hand on the throttle of your destiny.

Don't tell me that it is too early in life to indulge in such serious meditations. I tell you that greatness begins in childhood if it begins at all, just as mighty rivers take their rise in tiny springs. It is stated that Lord Rosebery, the Prime Minister of England, was possessed of three ambitions early in life, and towards the objects of his desire he pressed his way till he won them all.

I knew a boy once, the son of a poor and obscure farmer, who, when a mere child, declared with an earnestness almost startling, that some day he would be rich. Now he is one of the rising merchants of a Western city, with a strong, healthy start towards the coveted goal of affluence.

As the roar of the ocean is thought to be reached from the polished surface of a shell, so the throbbings of coming manhood can be felt in the pulses of a boy. Two little boys were playing together one day, when one of them remarked with an air of incredulity, "Say, Ted, mother says there is 'lectricity in the old cat." — "Well," replied Ted, "so there is. Put your ear down to her and you'll hear the trolly." However true this may be as a scientific statement, of this I am sure, if you put your ear close to the heart of a boy of promise, you can detect the reverberations, faint, perhaps, but real, of hope and ambitions and purposes by which his life is soon to be controlled.

One word more to the boy at the throttle: Be steady, be true, be noble, and cherish none but holy ambitions. Close the throttle against all forms of vice and all shades of meanness. Let lying and profanity and vulgarity and intemperance and gambling be forever strangers to your lips, your hands, and your lives. It will be well for you to recall frequently the advice once given by Mr. Emerson to young men when he said, "If you see anything that you want in this world, pay the price for it and take it."

Never for one moment imagine that your future is to be a matter of chance, but remember that the strength of your character will measure the strength of your position in this world and in the next. Be sure, Juniors, that you are in the narrow path that leads to glory, then open your throttle and speed away.

After Mr. Spooner's address the Park Sisters played again, their selection this time being, "Nearer, my God, to Thee." Every one was greatly pleased with their rendering of the favorite hymn. Miss Pauline Root, M.D., of Madura, India, gave the next address as follows:—

Other Boys and Girls.

Address of Dr. Pauline Root.

As I have been thinking of this great gathering of boys and girls, I have seemed to see our friend Jesus standing here, gazing with tender love into your faces, and saying softly, "They have suffered the little children to come unto me. It is well — of such is the kingdom of heaven!" The kingdom of heaven, and you, the King's children! If you should see the dear Lord standing here, how eagerly you would listen to all his words; and each one of you would want to take his hand, and some of you would put your faces down upon the dear hands, and, with tears in your eyes and a big lump in the throat, you would tell him that you were sorry that you had not always done what he would have you do. You all know him so well that none of you would run away. You know his tender heart, and you would wait to be forgiven, and to be sent out again to show his love to those whom you meet day by day.

There is one thing very dear to Jesus' heart, and as he went away from earth he reminded his disciples or scholars that they were to carry on the work which he had begun; that they were to go into all the world, and tell everybody about God's gift to them; that they were to be kind and like Jesus, and that they were to heal the sick and teach the ignorant.

The world seems large to us; but as the teacher cares for her kindergarten, so to God the world is only a little school for which he can care easily. But for our sakes he gives us the great joy and privilege of helping. He says to you as you come to help, that some of the scholars have no money for clothes or books, and that many are hungry and have no shelter. He points out that some are sick and grievously tormented, that many are ignorant, and very many know nothing of a God of love. He says to you that you are happy and prosperous, and that you belong to a people moral and civilized, because his disciples long years ago lovingly obeyed his last command and visited the sick and the prisoners, clothed the naked, fed the hungry, and told all of God's love. He says to you, "You love me because I first loved you. Freely ye have received, freely give."

Whom are you to help? First, those at your doors, the boys and girls who are poor, the oppressed, the outcast, those sinned against, and those who sin. You cannot, perhaps, as children, visit them in foul, squalid tenements and in hospitals and in prisons; but you can remember them, love them, pray for them, and induce your older friends to work for them. Let your hearts go out, too, to the happy-go-lucky or discouraged colored children and their shiftless neighbors the poor "mountain whites" in the South, and to the bright Indian boys and girls, and the listless Mormons in the West. The Alaskans, too, should, because so near your home, appeal to you. The boys and girls have bodies that feel hunger and thirst and pain, and hearts that crave sympathy and love; and they are among the little ones of whom Christ says, "Inasmuch as ye did it to one of these least, ye did it unto me." In the islands of the seas thousands still do not know Jesus. Help to found schools, so that the boys and girls may start right. Your interest and help may strengthen the hands of the boys and girls who, in Christian Endeavor societies in such places as Micronesia and the Hawaiian Islands, are working as you work for Jesus. There comes before you that wonderfully beautiful and fascinating Japan, where wickedness and idolatry are so gilded that they seem less vile than in China and India, but where the people as truly need Christ.

Read Miss Bacon's book, read the quaint Japanese stories, read the missionary papers, and you will become wonderfully interested in Japan. You will love the dear Japanese babies as they ride on their nurses' backs, or as they toddle about in their long clothes. You will laugh and long to skip about on wooden shoes with the girls as they play at battledore and shuttlecock, and you will be delighted with glimpses into the festival of the dolls. The boys will long to join the men and boys as they fly wonderful kites; and they will want to know how the hidden reeds are placed which make such sweet music as the kite sails through the air. If you could go into a little boy's birthday party you would be instructed by one emblem, — a fish swimming against the current, by which sign the little boy is taught how to best overcome difficulties. You would doubtless be more gentle if you played with the young people, for their voices are more subdued; they rarely become excited or show anger, and they are scrupulously polite. If you are too young to see below the surface, Japan will seem most charming; but there is a defect at the core. Even in Japan it is not altogether easy for the young people to identify themselves with the Christian church. They are ridiculed and vexed, and yet they come out little heroes, loyal sons and daughters of the King.

The Christian Endeavorers of Japan have their home and foreign missionary gatherings and meetings for work, and to pray. In one missionary society I attended the graduating exercises of four boys who were about to pass from the Junior into the Senior society. There were speeches and music, and each boy read an original essay on a foreign country, after which he received a certificate or diploma from the society.

In China, where on one hand everything speaks of age and learning, and on the other where poverty, gross superstition, idolatry, and dirt are so prominent, very few know Jesus. What does he wish you to do for China? As school boys and girls, can you do more than to pray and give money? Yes; you can learn and know more about the people. They are worth studying. Read about the boys and girls — about those in the cities who have such odd notions as to the influence of wind and streams, of evil spirits, and of the spirits of the dead; about those curious houses in tiny boats, when the boats have eyes so that they can see to go, and the babies carry gourds on their backs so that they will float if they tumble overboard. You will see how the boys and girls make fire-crackers, and what they use them for. Read of the little girls and women with their tiny bound feet, of the slave girls, of the custom of casting dead babies into the streets or into baby towers, of the foundling hospital under the sign of a big red fish, where if a mother does not want to keep her baby she can put it in a little drawer and run away. In China you would be impressed with the steady devotion to study, and the ambition of every family to have at least one scholar; by the great examination halls, and the "halls of the classics," where tablets date back to Solomon's day. In the early morning one hears strange music, and sees overhead the pigeons in whose tails are fastened reeds which make music as they fly. During the day you might meet men carrying in their hands the cages of birds, to give their pets an airing. And at night, coming in from the country, you would have to make your little donkey gallop lest the sun should set before you are inside the city gates. It is in China that you would first learn to eat with chop-sticks, and where rare dishes of birds'-nest soups and sharks' fins might be given you. And it is in China that you might see the mourners' tears gathered in a basin. But I must not tell you all. You will see it more clearly if you read it for yourselves.

I would if I could tell you about Siam and Burmah, Persia and Koordistan, Arabia and Africa, Syria and Turkey. In all these countries there has been a time when women have been despised and untaught, and when men have sinned, and all have needed pardon, and many have craved sympathy and comfort. Christianity, with schools and hospitals, with preaching and societies of Christian Endeavor, has brought to a happy few a new brightness and joy.

As to Thibet and Mongolia, faithful have been the efforts to enter in the name of the Lord. In your day God will walk there also.

I have left to the last my own dear country, India. In all Eastern nations the dress of the wealthy people is usually rich and attractive, but the faces of the people do not always at first sight please us. In India we come upon many of our own type, — slender, graceful women, tall, handsome men. But here where the civilization is so ancient, caste reigns; the people are proud, and the women, often shut into close and unwholesome zenanas, lead lives that are often repressed and often sad. Infant marriages are still made, though husbands cannot claim their wives till they are twelve. But if a man dies before the young wife comes to his house, she is as truly a widow as if she had lived in his family for years. Little girl widows, not yet ten years old, have come to me as patients, — poor, sad-eyed little women, with shorn heads and somber garments. They have no joy to look forward to in life; and it hardly seems strange that some should try to escape the constant misery of being scorned and slighted, by throwing themselves into wells, by poison, or by eating pounded glass. One young widow was very happy, as she brought me a sealed brass jar containing water from the Ganges, telling me that so long as the water remained unevaporated before her god she would be free from sin.

When you are just entering the high school, my little women are caring for their poor houses, grinding and cooking rice or other grain, preparing the husband's food, but not eating with him, caring for their babies, rejoicing if they are the mothers of sons, condemned, despised, if only daughters come to them.

There is little of sanitary care even in the best of houses; and the huts of the low-caste people are in such filthy places, that when cholera or fever comes, they die by hundreds. The people have no other way to prevent the spreading of smallpox or cholera, except by offerings to their gods. As they die, their minds are so steeped in superstition, that they go away as they have lived, without hope and without God — in a country where gods are found and worshiped by the millions, but where women are considered too impure to hear the sacred books. In times of certain illnesses, the high-caste women are banished from the presence of those who are ceremonially clean. Often I have visited in Brahman families, where the young wife has had to suffer pain, thirst, hunger, fever, and maltreatment at the hands of the "barber woman," when life was passing away, and when no one dear to her has come to comfort her. It is not always so; but in very many cases no tender hand of love touches her head, no clasp of the hand is given, no words of comfort are offered, but near her the moans and death-wailing trouble the soul as it passes away. If she had heard of the love of God, she may, in her loneliness, turn to him, and as she passes into the shadow whisper, "I will fear no evil, for thou art with me." And many dear girls have gone joyfully, in perfect trust, because he has said, "Fear thou not, for I have redeemed thee; I have called thee by thy name, and thou art mine."

Boys and girls, you are looking forward eagerly to the time when you will be men and women, and leaders in the churches. You are going to live, many of you, to see mighty ingatherings in the mission fields. You will be loyal to your Christ. You may be called into the very work which we do now. How are you to be ready?

While you are in school, study and play. Cultivate your minds by good books, and by knowing the best people; your hearts by sympathy with God's poor; strengthen your bodies not by indulgence in "sweets," which by and by will bring a harvest of headaches, indigestion, and blue days, but by tennis and other outdoor games, by walks and climbing mountains or trees, by swimming, and by riding your horses or bicycles. Memorize portions of God's book and sacred hymns. By and by it will be less easy. Learn to sing, and play if you can on piano, organ, or violin. Then, in whatever way you enter into life's work with sound bodies, clear minds, God's word in your heart and his Spirit to guide you, you will be ready for honest service for your King.

You, the Junior Endeavorers of 1894, will many of you live to see marvelous things wrought in this world by our God.

Miss Root was followed by Rev. H. W. Pope of New Haven, Conn.

Show your Colors.

Address by Rev. H. W. Pope.

The influence of the national flag in a battle is said to be something marvelous. The sight of it fires the soldier with courage and enthusiasm. Its absence causes consternation and dismay. Hence the colors are never allowed to fall to the ground. If the color-bearer is shot down, another seizes the standard and bears it aloft. Lord Nelson, in a famous naval battle, nailed his colors to the masthead, so that he could not surrender if he would.

In the battle of life many a one falls because he cannot see the colors; because there is no one near to re-enforce his failing courage; no one whose clear, strong convictions make the truth seem truer, and right more righteous, and Jesus Christ more real.

Too many are living without convictions. They have opinions concerning moral questions, — good opinions too, — but they have no convictions. I mean by that, that they are not sufficiently interested in these causes to identify themselves with them, and, if need be, to suffer for them. Opinions can be entertained cheaply; but it costs something to hold convictions, because you are bound to defend and proclaim them. Mary Lyon had a conviction that women must be educated. That conviction cost her years of sacrifice, but it resulted in Mt. Holyoke College. Frances E. Willard, as a girl, had convictions on the subject of temperance. She thought strongly and felt deeply; and by her unremitting labors she has girdled the world with a circle of beacon lights, each of which blazes forth her own burning convictions.

Now, boys and girls, you are the natural color-bearers of society. Your home life has shielded you from many dangers to which your brothers and sisters are exposed. You have the Bible, which tells you how to live aright; and, above all, you have enlisted in the army of the Lord. Now show your colors. Stand up for the right every time. Do not allow a big boy to persecute a little one, nor a well-dressed girl to make fun of a poor one, without taking her part. Do not suffer any one to stone the birds, or abuse an animal, without at least a protest. They are God's birds, and no one has a right to kill them. Remember that Jesus has a place for you in his kingdom, and a work for you to do. He needs you in your school and on the playground, to show how brave and manly and true a Christian can be. He needs you in your home, to brighten it by a happy life, as he brightened his home when a boy. He does not expect you to be an old man before your time, but to be a Christian boy, with all a boy's love of fun and frolic. He expects you to run and romp and shout as loud as ever, but never to forget that you are a follower of Jesus Christ. Every Junior should have convictions on the subject of temperance. It is not enough for the girls to sing, "The lips that touch liquor shall never touch mine," but they should also put it in practice. Yea, they should even go farther, and say, "The lips that touch tobacco shall never touch mine; the lips that utter impure and profane words shall never touch mine; the hands that are soiled by bad habits shall never clasp mine; and the man who speaks slightingly of the Bible, or religion, or woman, shall never be mine." If you girls will show your colors in this way, the boys will find it easier to resist temptation.

Another cause which needs your championship is that of missions. A million a month are dying in China without a knowledge of Jesus Christ. Is it nothing to you, boys and girls, that you have the light of life while millions of your brothers and sisters are living and dying in darkness? Years ago a teacher in New York City was giving a lesson in geography. As she pointed out to her pupils the heathen and Christian lands, she spoke some very earnest words to them; and then and there a little girl eight years of age, named Eliza Agnew, resolved that if God opened the way she would be a missionary when she grew up, and go and tell the heathen about Jesus. She never forgot this resolve; and as soon as the way opened she went to Ceylon, where she remained forty-three years as the head of a girls' boarding-school. Over a thousand girls were taught by her, and more than 600 of them went out as Christians. All of you have opinions concerning the heathen; you have a great deal of pity for them; but little Eliza Agnew had convictions. She was willing to sacrifice for them. Are you willing to make sacrifices for them? and to what extent? I heard of a missionary meeting where a collection was taken. As the basket was passed to the little boy he said to the collector, "Put the basket lower, please." He did so, and the boy said, "Lower still." Once more it was lowered, and the little fellow said, "Put it on the floor." It was done; and the boy stepped into the basket, signifying that while the others gave gold and silver, he would give himself. God grant that many of you may follow his example!

Above all, little folks, have convictions concerning Jesus Christ. He is worthy of your love and loyalty. Never be ashamed of him or of his cause. The manliest thing a person can do is to stand up for Jesus. When President Garfield was a boy at Williams College he climbed Mount Greylock one day with a lot of his companions. Their plan was to spend the night on the mountain. Seated around the camp-fire they sang college songs and told stories all the evening. At length young Garfield took a Testament from his pocket and said, "Boys, it is my custom to read a chapter in the Bible and have prayer before going to bed. Shall we have it all together?" And they did. That is the kind of boy that you and I admire; one who serves the Lord and isn't afraid to say so. That is the kind of boys and girls I hope you all will be,— children who can say from the heart, —

> "I will go where you want me to go, Lord,
> Over mountain or valley or sea;
> I will say what you want me to say, Lord;
> I will be what you want me to be."

At the assault upon Fort Wagner in 1864, which was led by Col. Shaw of the Fifty-fourth Massachusetts Regiment, Color-Sergeant Kearney was the first one to mount the parapet. As he reached the summit of the fort he was terribly wounded by a shot which shattered his knee and thigh. As he fell he grasped the flag, and resting the staff against his body, and supporting himself by one foot and hand, kept the flag aloft until the assault was repulsed. Then he crawled off the field on one hand and foot, still holding the colors in the air. As he entered the field hospital where the wounded were being cared for they all cheered him. In response the brave fellow answered, "Boys, the old flag never touched the ground." That is the spirit of a true soldier, and that is the spirit which Jesus Christ expects in all his soldiers. Never let your colors trail in the dust. Have convictions and proclaim them.

Let your goodness be pronounced enough to interfere with other people's badness. There are 20,000,000 girls and boys in this country. What a power for good they would be, if all were outspoken defenders of truth and righteousness. Boys and girls, show your colors. Carry with you an atmosphere of purity and power which shall make it easy for others to do right in your presence.

> "Ye are called with a holy calling,
> The light of the world to be;
> To lift up the lamp of the gospel,
> That others the light may see."

Dr. Hill then introduced to the audience Mrs. I. M. Alden, known to all the world of young folks as "Pansy." Of course she received the heartiest kind of a welcome. She said : —

I am glad to be introduced to the Juniors. You may not think it, but I am a Junior myself. I have met with them every Sabbath morning during the winter, and every morning they were always there. I have had letters from Juniors in every State during the last winter, and not only that, but from every country in the world. So that I think that I may claim to be a Junior this afternoon. I attended a meeting here where they talked about what Juniors had done for other people, and I thought of a story which I heard since coming here of what one Junior has done. I will tell about it. I met a dear mother yesterday who said, "I want to know about the Mothers',Christian Endeavor meeting. I have not been interested in these things; I have not been in the meetings very much; but I have a little daughter, a little Junior, eight years old, and she is so faithful and conscientious about keeping her pledge and reading her Bible every day that she has set me to thinking. I want to keep track of the Juniors; I want to keep in sight of my little girl. Where is the Mothers' meeting." Juniors, go home and get the mothers all over the land to keep track of you. [*Applause.*]

Dr. Hill then introduced Miss Frances E. Willard, who was given a rousing Chautauqua salute. She simply said :—

All I have to say is, God bless you; thank you; good-by. [*Loud applause.*]

Miss Anna Gordon, Miss Willard's secretary, was also introduced and said : —

This is not a Methodist gathering, but I am going to say Amen to what Miss Willard has said. [*Laughter and applause.*]

One verse of "The Star Spangled Banner" was then sung, after which came a missionary exercise which interested the audience very much. It was entitled, "World-wide Juniors in Story and Song," and was prepared by Mrs. Alice M. Scudder of Jersey City, N.J., assisted by Miss Nellie Stockwell of Cleveland, Ohio. Mrs. Scudder was unable to be present, and her place was taken by Mrs. S. M. Perkins of Cleveland. Children dressed in the costumes of various nations were introduced, and took part in the exercise by brief remarks, reciting Scripture passages, and singing appropriate hymns. The exercise was as follows : —

World-wide Juniors in Story and Song.

By Mrs. Alice M. Scudder.

Leader. — We come to-day to celebrate our Third International Junior Rally, and to meet some representatives, both here and from abroad. As we look into the faces of these dear children, let us remember that in their lands child life is clouded by error and superstition, and to us is given the privilege of lifting them into a brighter and better life.

In several lands Junior Endeavor Societies have been formed; and as these are multiplied, we shall hope to see thousands of foreign children trained to work for Christ and the Church.

Our interest is always increased by acquaintance; so I wish to introduce to you a little Japanese friend, who will tell you about her life in Japan.

Japanese girl in costume. — Did any of you, when you were a baby, ever ride around on your mother's back while she guided the plow across the field, or stood ankle deep in a rice plantation? I know all about it, and it isn't a bit of fun to be tied in one place all day long. Still, it is nicer to be a Japanese than a Chinese girl; for our fathers think something of us, and we are not badly treated.

We have queer worship in Japan. I used to say my prayers to this tablet; but I don't now, for I know better. I used to think when I died I'd become a bug or an insect of some sort; but I know now that it is foolish to think so. Things are changing in Japan, and we are learning to love the dear Saviour. We have schools and a church; and ever since Dr. and Mrs. Clark were in Japan, we have a Junior Endeavor Society. Would you like to hear me say a Bible verse in Japanese? I will say, "God so loved the world, that he gave his only begotten Son, that whosoever believeth in him need not perish, but have everlasting life."

Leader. — Away over in the other hemisphere there is a benighted nation, that only the gospel of Jesus Christ can transform. Let us ask our little African boy if he would like to have a Junior Endeavor society in his land.

Africa (a colored boy). — I represent Africa, the dark continent; and if you should go among my people, you would find ways as dark as my skin. In Africa every man has several wives, and they buy them by paying so many cattle for them. My father had several wives besides my mother; and there is so much quarreling among them, that we were not a happy family.

You have no slaves now in America, but in Zulu-land slaves and men-stealers abound. I was stolen from my home when I was a very small boy; and they whipped and worked me until I was ready to die, so I just ran away.

A white man found me, and taught me all the good I know. I want to thank the good friends for sending such kind teachers to Africa. I intend to study and learn, so that I can go back and teach my people all I know about Christ and Christian ways. I want to have a Zulu Junior Endeavor society, and we want nice little Junior Endeavor pins. I like to sing this song, and it is my prayer.

Song, "Let my people go."

Leader. — A good many of the Juniors have seen Chinese boys; but not so many know how the Chinese girls look, so you will be glad to see our little friend in a Chinese girl's dress.

Chinese girl in costume. — I am a little Chinese girl, and I am glad I am alive; for sometimes they put the baby girls in a jar and throw them in the river to the god Amoy. I was almost dead when the missionary found me, and took me to his home, and cared for me. My two sisters still live; but they cannot play and run about as I can, for my mother began to bandage their feet, and they will have to wear a little shoe, such as I hold in my hand. Did you ever wear a tight shoe? Well, if you have, you will know how to pity the little Chinese girls. No one can tell what they suffer while their feet are bound. It is very cruel, and I want you to send missionaries to tell them of the wickedness of such foolishness, and we want to learn to be Christians; and if the Junior Endeavorers of America would save a little of their candy money, we could have plenty of religious teachers. Dear Juniors, won't you do this?

Leader. — I sometimes think that the country most to sadden our hearts is Turkey; and perhaps the Juniors will think so too, after hearing from our little Turkish friend.

Turkish child in costume. — Oh, dear! I'm nobody, and just because I'm a girl. My father loves none of his children but his boys; and I have heard that in America it is different, and that the little girls are loved even more than the boys. I hope I can stay in this country; for if I go back to Turkey I must soon be married to a man I never saw, and I must work for him like a slave. Then I must always have my face covered, no matter whether I am in the house cooking, or out in the hot sun. When my husband is present I must stand, and never open my lips until he bids me. I want to be loved, and I want nice books and playthings, and I want to go to school and church; and I want to live where they think woman and little girls are somebody, and where they promise us a heaven when we die. Please send more missionaries to teach the men and women of Turkey how to do right.

Leader. — Away off in mid-ocean lie groups of little islands, which I am glad to say are becoming Christianized, and we shall hear from a little maiden about Samoa.

Samoa child in costume. — I represent a little South Sea Island girl; and my home is at Samoa, in the Fiji Islands. I wish you could see our cocoanut and palm trees, and our queer little houses. Our people used to be very wicked, but there was a lovely ship called the Morning Star that brought missionaries and Bibles; and we learned that it was not right to worship gods of rain and lightnings and hurricanes, neither should we bow down to hideous images. So we learned about Jesus, and now we are very happy people. We are no longer cruel, but we try to keep peace with all; and we thank the dear children of America for sending the Morning Star to us, and we hope you will never forget to pray for the people of the South Sea Islands. I forgot to say that we wear Mother Hubbard dresses, and we like them; but in America you do not seem to care much for them.

Leader. — In India the people welcomed heartily the Christian Endeavor pledge, and already there are several Junior societies. Shall we hear from one who represents the children of that land?

India girl in costume. — I'm a little Hindu girl. Did you know that there were more than 80,000 people died last year in India from snake-bites. This is a cobra (holds up picture of snake); and the people where I came from think they are gods, and they won't have them killed. There are other queer things too. If the shadow of a poorer girl falls on me, I must go and wash many times. I'm a little Hindu widow, only ten years old; and, just think, I've been married. My mother-in-law was very cross, and beat me, and made me her slave. It is a terrible thing to be a widow in my country. Here in America everybody is kind to a widow, but way off in India everybody despises her. We have no dear Jesus to pray to: we pray to monkeys and cattle, and wicked gods that steal and lie. My people are very untruthful and say naughty words. I wish I had been born in a Christian land, so people would treat me kindly. I am happier since I have learned about Jesus.

Leader. — We saw a few moments ago a little Chinese girl; and now we shall hear from a Chinese boy, one who lives in America, one who often leads a very unhappy life because cruelly treated by the boys of our own land. Let us hear what he has to tell us.

Chinese boy in costume. — I am a Chinese boy, and I live here in America; and I want to say a good word to the Juniors of this land. You know how the children on the street plague us, and call us names, and chase us. Now, this is not right, for it makes us feel very badly. I know none of the Juniors do this, and I want to thank them for it; and I want to ask them to beg other boys and girls not to do so either.

We like our Sunday schools, and we intend to have Christian Endeavor societies. Please pray for us, and don't call out after us on the street, and pull our hair.

Leader. — The next young friend I shall *not have* to introduce, as you all know an Indian when you see her. She has great need of our love and prayers, for her people have been badly treated by white folks. Perhaps she will tell us what she thinks about it.

Indian girl in costume. — I am a little Indian, and I want to speak for my people. Lots of folks think Indians haven't any rights, but when you think about it you will remember this whole great land was once ours. When you have some spare time, my dear Juniors, I want you to sit down and write all the Indian names you can think of, and I want you to remember that Indians were once in every one of these places.

I know we were a warlike people; but if we had been treated kindly, we might have become Christians, for Jesus Christ came to bring peace. I wish you would think kindly of the Indians, for there are many good things about us. You never see my people except in wood near a cigar-store; but I am sure if you knew us better you would love us, and do more for us, and help us to have Junior Endeavor societies.

Leader. — There are a large number of children in our great cities that every Junior Endeavorer should love and pray for — I mean the dear little ones who live in wretched homes or are outcasts on the street. We shall listen to a song which will, I know, touch our hearts, and make us long to do more for the neglected little ones. (Song.)

Leader. — Let us show our love for all these unfortunates in some unselfish, practical way. Shall we see what the Juniors of Cleveland intend to do to show their sympathy for those who are less fortunate than ourselves? Shall we hear a piece called "Biddy Red Wing's Nest"?

A little girl came forward and recited as follows:

'Twas little Biddy Red Wing
 That wanted a new nest,
And while she was about it
 She meant to have the best.

So Sunday morning early,
 The church doors open wide,
Came pretty Biddy Red Wing,
 And put her head inside.

Straight up the aisle she tip-toed,
 And, far from noisy flocks,
She softly laid a nest-egg in
 The contribution-box.

At length the bells stopped ringing,
 The preacher rose to pray,
When up sprang Biddy Red Wing too,
 And cackled forth her lay.

'Cut-cut-cut-cut-cur-dah-cut!'
 Right out in meeting too,
Nor would her voice be silenced
 Till she had said it through.

She had done all a fowl could do,
 This noisy little hen,
To help the cause, and earned her right
 To tell it there and then.

And down the aisle and to the door
 She proudly cackled! while
A deacon passed the box around
 To cover up the smile.

And everybody something found,
 In pocket, purse, or vest,
To lay beside the nest-egg there
 In Biddy Red Wing's nest.

We have not Biddy Red Wing here,
 Her golden egg to lay;
And as she cannot be with us
 We'll do some other way.

We've brought to you this little nest
 To teach you all to give
To heathen children East and West
 So long as you may live.

We hope, like Biddy Red Wing's egg,
 That it will be a plea
To draw more money from you all
 To go across the sea.

If offering to-day you have,
 However great or small,
Just drop them in with Bible verse,
 As we your names shall call.

The exercise closed very prettily. The little girl holding "Biddy Red Wing's nest" stood at one side of the platform; and children, representing the various Junior societies of all the Cleveland churches, answered to the roll-call, and came forward, each one dropping a contribution into the nest, and then reciting a verse of Scripture. The offering amounted to $110 dollars, which was sent to the denominational Boards. Then all the children, home and foreign, standing on the platform, joined heartily in singing the hymn, "This is Our Endeavor."

After a few brief remarks by Dr. Hill, the parting hymn, "God be with You," was sung, and all joined in repeating the Mizpah Benediction.

SATURDAY EVENING.

No session of the Convention was held at the tent or the hall this evening. Instead, the customary State reunions were held at the various headquarters. These were exceedingly delightful, and the Cleveland hosts fairly outdid themselves in their endeavors to entertain the Convention delegates.

SUNDAY MORNING.

The early morning prayer-meetings were held for the last time, and were well attended in spite of the "dissipation" of the previous day. No session of the Convention was held; but at 10.30 the delegates attended the regular church services of the city, the custom being generally followed of the various State delegations attending the services of those churches where they were respectively entertained. The pulpits of the city were mostly occupied by pastors who were in attendance upon the convention.

Saengerfest Hall.

Nearly twelve thousand people were packed into Saengerfest Hall at the beginning of the praise service Sunday afternoon. It was an inspiring audience — and a perspiring one as well, for the heat was extreme. There was the usual enthusiasm, however, in the singing of hymns, although, it being the Sabbath Day, there was an absence of all demonstration. Mr. J. G. Warren led the praise service, which was varied by selections by the Christian Endeavor Male Quartet and the Park Sisters. Before the main programme began, President Dickinson was presented with a beautiful basket of flowers by Mr. Cheesman, representing the Cleveland Union. Mr. Dickinson accepted the gift with a few words expressing his gratitude and appreciation.

Dr. Smith Baker offered prayer, after which a hymn was sung under the direction of Mr. H. C. Lincoln. Rev. E. E. Baker of Dayton, Ohio, was then introduced as the first speaker. His address was as follows : —

Systematic and Proportionate Giving.

Address of Rev. E. E. Baker.

We are rapidly approaching the end of this great Convention. More marvelous than this series of meetings themselves is the greater and grander society that has made this Convention possible; and greater even than the society, circling the world as it does, is the Christ working in and through the society, whose we are and whom we serve. It is with a feeling of sadness that we come to these closing sessions; for we have drunk in of the inspiration from the very first meeting on Wednesday night, through the consecration services of the early mornings, and through all the various sessions of the day. I wonder whether we realize as we are here that we cannot return to our societies and our homes and our churches as we came; that we go back different persons, — different in soul, different in mind, different in ideas; that we have come here and received of God, and that we are under obligation, not only for that which we have received, but we are under obligation to return of that which we have received from him.

I heard a minister say a few months ago in a ministerial meeting that a convention like this was not profitable. He complained that there was not enough work done by the members of the convention. He said that all the members of that convention had to do was to sit and swallow and swallow. He had a pretty good idea of some delegates and some conventions.

The underlying principle of my subject to-day is that in proportion to our opportunity, in that same proportion is our responsibility; in proportion to our privileges, in that same proportion is the debt to give; in proportion as you and I receive here and elsewhere, we are bound in honor to give unto God and unto our fellow-men, and to those about us, that which we have received from him. It is peculiarly appropriate that the Christian Endeavor Society should take up this subject of systematic and proportionate giving; I say, peculiarly appropriate, because, first, of the origin of the Christian Endeavor Society. Dr. Clark himself said, in giving an account of the formation of that first society in Maine, that it was born in a church that was young and pliable and consecrated. The Williston church, in which the first society found being, had recently built a large and commodious house of worship, and had dedicated it to the honor of God free from debt; and the members of that church that welcomed the idea of Christian Endeavor had sacrificed for the Lord Jesus Christ by paying for that church as well as paying for the spread of the kingdom of God in the earth. It was in such giving and in such sacrificing that the first Christian Endeavor Society found warmth, encouragement, and growth. It is one of your advanced principles for the past year to have taught and to have studied and to have practiced the principles of systematic and proportionate giving. The secretary has already called attention to this magnificent roll of honor that is draped from the balcony. More than 5,000 societies are enrolled thereon, and the aggregate contributions of the 5,000 societies amount to more than $350,000. I say well done for the first year of systematic benevolence? I believe with the secretary, that if all the societies who had given had reported, there would be a grand aggregate of $500,000 on that roll of honor to-day. But that is nothing compared with what the church of Jesus Christ can do through consecrated manhood and womanhood. That is not anything compared with what the Society of Christian Endeavor can do with the possessions and earnings and the treasures of the members of this Christian Endeavor Society. The president in his annual report said that the earnings of the 2,000,000 members of this society last year were easily $150,000,000, and that if each one had given a tenth, the amount laid upon the altar for the propagation of God's word would have been $15,000,000; and I predict that the day will come, that the time is rapidly approaching, when Christian Endeavor everywhere will set apart unto God that which is his, and will give unto him that which he asked of the Jew to give in the years gone by.

I am pleased to find that there is an advance in the year that is to come. I am rejoiced to be informed that yesterday most important action was taken by the board of trustees, and that out there on the yacht, floating on the bosom of the lake, the missionary extension movement was indorsed and was encouraged, and was authorized for the future. Do you know what that means? That means the world for Christ. That means the whole round globe evangelized. That means every nation under heaven having heard of Jesus Christ, and having an opportunity to believe in him, and having the privilege of knowing him as we know him, rejoicing in him as we rejoice in him. That means in the year 1895, $1,000,000 for missions.

I wonder as I look into your faces to-day how many here have during the past year given one-tenth to the Lord. I was present in this great hall the other day when nearly every person in the hall stood up in token of their having taken the ironclad pledge; and I at that time wondered how many would stand up to-day, if I should ask you, in token of having set apart and having consecrated to God one-tenth of all you receive, of all that God has given you. I do not intend to put you to the test; I have not the right. I ask you to ask yourselves whether, as you sit here, it is not becoming to you to give attention to the claims of the church and the world and the missionary, and to the claims of those who are in darkness, and to the claims of God in the person of his Christ upon every one of us to give all that we can.

Why give unto God? I like the phrasing of this topic of mine. It is not proportionate and systematic giving unto the church; it is not proportionate and systematic giving to the Society of Christian Endeavor, nor to a system or to a board. It is giving to Almighty God, who has given us all that we have, and who has made us all we are. I wonder if you believe that all the giving of what you have, and the laying on the altar of what God has put into your possession, is accepted of God? I wonder whether you regard it as an act of worship? Sometimes we think our singing and our praying and our reading of Scripture and listening to the essay from the pulpit constitute all the worship we can render to God. We have made a great mistake when we have eliminated the taking up of the offering, and the giving it to him to be set apart and consecrated and used in his blessed service. I believe to give unto God is to worship him just as truly as praying unto him. I believe giving unto him is as acceptable in his sight as praying and honoring him, just as the word says, "Honor the Lord with thy substance;" and when we give willingly and cheerfully and lovingly we are honoring him indeed. I would that in our giving we might remember God as the beginning of it and as the center of it and as the consummation of it. I turn to God's Word, and find that he has a claim upon all possessions. He writes his name upon the heavens; they are his. He writes his name upon the earth; it is his. He writes his name upon all things on earth; they belong to him. He writes his name upon all possessions and property, and upon all means and upon all luxuries, and he says, "It is mine; I give it to thee for a little while; occupy till I come." And then in that great day of his coming, we are to give an account of those things we have, and we are to be rewarded according to our fidelity and our thankfulness with regard to that which he has given us. The teaching of God's word is that if we give to him of all that we have, that he is pleased, and he will accept it and bless the giver. Not only is this a part of worship and a part of God's claim, but it is Godlike. We have set before us the one great example of Jesus Christ. We know naught of God save as we know of him in his full revelation of Jesus Christ. We look about us in the world and see some evidence of his creative power; in the heavens we see other evidences of his creative power. But in Jesus Christ we behold the fullness of God; we behold in him the glory of the infinite, and the full expression of the love of God. That wonderful verse of the Scriptures explains it all (John iii.16), "God so loved the world that he gave" — there was no other way in which God could make known to us his love, except by giving, by sacrificing, by sending us the choicest treasure of his heart and of his heaven and of his eternity. When you and I, in our love for God and in our love for man, come to sacrifice and give, we are assuming likeness unto God, and becoming like unto Christ, and making ourselves agents of the Divine Spirit.

Some one has said that the watchwords of Christianity are watch and pray and fight and give. The lesson that Christ has taught to the world is the lesson of giving, and giving ourselves for him and for the world.

What proportion of giving is expected of us, as we lay our gifts upon his altar? I know that some of you have said it is not a tenth. You have said it in the stinginess of your heart. Some have said, "I will not give a tenth, even if you say God requires me to give it; it will cost me too much." I would say to you that I believe that the least a Christian man ought to give — the least a Christian man ought to give, is one-tenth of his income. [*Applause.*] I do not mean that that is all a man ought or can give; that that is all God will accept. I believe he will accept all we bring him, even though it be like the widow, all our living. I believe the man who comes into the presence of God empty handed goes away empty hearted. I believe the man who will take all that God gives, and give him nothing in return, is a poor kind of a Christian — if he is a Christian at all. You may say I have no authority or warrant for such a statement. Turn to the record for a little while. What do we find? In the beginning we find Abraham offering one-tenth unto Melchisedec, the priest of God, peculiarly and divinely appointed. Before the law we have Abraham giving a tenth, as if it were a divine instruction, to the head man of the race that he would accept a tenth, not in palliation nor appeasment, not in order that his wrath might be averted, but in acknowledgment of his goodness and love, and of his providence in bestowing that which he has bestowed upon us. I find after that the marvelous revelation where Jacob saw the ladder and the angels of God ascending and descending; and where he said, "This is Bethel, the place of God;" and when he got up from that place, he said, "Of all that the Lord shall give me, I will surely give unto him a tenth." Religion, revelation, beautiful visions, go hand in hand here with consecration of our substance and means. The law only emphasizes and reiterates that which had been previously practiced.

Some one said God has three reservations under a theoretic form of government: First, one-seventh part of our time; second, one-tenth part of our substance; third, communion daily with him in prayer. This has been beautifully expressed in the symbol of the holy place wherein we have the golden candlestick with its seven branches; consecrated time, where we have the plate of shew bread; consecrated substance, and the altar of incense; consecrated and unceasing prayer and praise to Almighty God.

But to come down to the Scriptures, what does Jesus Christ say about giving one-tenth? In the first place, I want to ask you a question. Do you think the New Testament dispensation requires less or more than the Old Testament dispensation? Do you think it requires less development on the part of a believer in Jesus Christ now than it did to belong to the Judaic Church? Do you think that you and I, because of Christ's cross, are exempt from consecrating all that we have and all we are to him? I think your answer has been that we are to give more; that we are to give all. The standard of entire devotement.

What would you think of a man who could be a member of the church for forty years and boast that it never cost him a cent? What do you think of a man who, when the offer is presented to him to help the propagation of the gospel and to extend the kingdom of Christ, buttons up his pocket-book from the outside for fear it might get out without his consent? What do you think when a man squirms and twists and makes faces because the cause of missions is presented to him? He has received all Christ can give, and gives nothing in return, that is, nothing that costs him anything, nothing but prayers and singing, and attendance on God's word. I believe Jesus Christ taught the entire consecration of body, mind and soul, and with the consecration of the three parts of a man's life are included his pocket-book, his bank-stock, his all that he has. Christ commended the gift of the widow, but without commending the Pharisees for having tithed mint, anise, and cummin. I believe that he has given us commendation of this method of regularly and systematically setting apart a portion of our income to the spread of the gospel. How much shall it be? I said a while ago a tenth. I do not mean to say that if you want to give a sixth you ought not; if you want to give an eighth you ought not; if you want to give a fifth you ought not. But if you want to give a third, you have the perfect right and also the great privilege of so doing. I do not mean to say that the method of giving that prevails in our churches and in our societies must give way to the method of setting apart some portion, however small or however large, for the salvation of men, and for the support of the church, and for the giving to charitable purposes. I want to say to you, that any man who has ever tried giving a tenth will not return to the old system for the world. I want to say to you if you step out upon the broad plank of God's promises, and trust him for temporal things as you trust him for spiritual things, you will come into a liberty that you never dreamed of. You will come into the broad light of his favor, such as you have never had before, and you will enter into the fullness of his blessings as you never have been blessed. I mean to declare to you that it pays in dollars and cents to give unto God a tenth of all you receive, of every dollar and every penny, of every wage, salary, and every present, and everything of value that comes into your life, laying aside on the first day of the week for the purpose of devoting to God and to his cause that which falls to you. I will give you an illustration of it. I know a man who has been regularly setting apart one eighth of all his business netted him after legitimate business expenses were taken out, not his living expenses, not his family luxuries, not his summer vacation money, not even his expenses to a Christian Endeavor convention. What he gave last year amounted to thousands of dollars. Now, notice, during these hard times, when the factories next to his were closed, when there was not a wheel turning, when there was not a man working for those other men, this man was running overtime and running all night, because he honored God and gave unto God. [*Applause.*]

I know a young man who went without his lunch in order that he might give more to a certain cause and interests that belonged to him, and I know that when the hour came when he needed all that money that he had given away, God put it right down there in his hand.

I can tell you of a man and his wife who last year had saved together money to go to the World's Fair, and just as they were about ready to go, a call came upon them to which they had to give all that money. You can imagine the situation; but they did not hesitate a minute about giving the money, and before the year was over God gave it back to the dollar.

I want to say to you from personal experience, if you trust God with money, he will not be in debt to you; he will pay it back. I want to say to you, if you are in debt, you may think you are not able to begin to lay aside a tenth, but begin to-day, take what you have and divide it into ten parts, and lay that one part over to God and never touch it, and he will pour out such blessings that you will not be able to contain them. I want to say that he has paid back to me every dollar I ever gave him and more. You trust God. Give to him that which he has given to you, systematically, regularly, conscientiously, and it will pay you in dollars. It is said that a hundred-fold is ten thousand per cent; and if you will only sow liberally, God, who keeps the books with greater accuracy than any man, will in that great day of judgment, if not here, give unto you a hundred-fold in proportion as you give to him.

And now I find my time is about up. I want to simply add one word, one earnest word of inspiration, and that is, having set apart money for God, give it conscientiously and faithfully and intelligently to him. You who thus give will have a joy, a pleasure, a happiness, a sense of performing God's will and God's purposes in this world, that will hasten the coming of Christ, the time when he shall be King of kings and Lord of lords.

MR. DICKINSON: Yesterday, on the blue waters of your beautiful Lake Erie, there was consumated a transaction, the influence of which will go around the world. The wheels of a dynamo were started yesterday that is destined to thrill the whole of this, our native land, and enlighten in due time the dark places of the earth. This is another of the surprises of this great convention. Some thirty missionary boards through their representatives struck hands with the Trustees of the United Society of Christian Endeavor, and pledged themselves to act together in this great missionary extension work which has already been alluded to. We are favored just now by having with us the treasurer of the Presbyterian Board of Foreign Missions, Mr. William Dulles, Jr., who will tell us about the transaction consummated yesterday.

MR. DULLES: Lake Erie is famous for battle. May we long remember it for something very different from battle, except it be the trumpet call to a continued battle on our part in the interest of truth. It was a glad and inspiring thing to find so many of the officers of missionary boards in union with the officers of your society; and we were so touched and thrilled by all this yesterday that one of your officers said, "Let us have prayer," and over Lake Erie there went up the voice of prayer to God for a blessing upon what had been done; and again another of your officers arose and said, "Let us repeat the Lord's Prayer, for it has in it 'Thy Kingdom come,'" and we joined our voices in that glad prayer. Missionary extension means that you combine and not scatter your efforts. Let all the Christian Endeavor societies in a neighborhood unite to arrange six public mass meetings about one month apart. Get all your pastors to preach about one or the other of the causes that will be presented. Our watchword for the year is $1,000,000 out of what God has given us for missions through our denominational boards. It will be for God, for Christ, and the Church. (For full outline of the Christian Endeavor missionary extension course, see Mr. Mershon's address.)

MR. DICKINSON: We have been talking about the duty that lies at our door. Now we will hear something about the other end of that duty. We want to hear what comes from proportionate, generous giving. We have with us two missionaries, Mr. and Mrs. Geo. H. Hubbard. They have been working in China since 1884.

Mr. and Mrs. Hubbard were given the Chautauqua salute as they stepped upon the platform. Mr. Hubbard read a cablegram from the United Society of Christian Endeavor of China, which held its first annual convention in Shanghai, June 23d to 25th. Mrs. Hubbard, dressed in the native Chinese costume, next gave a greeting from China, speaking in the native language, Mr. Hubbard interpreting.

A Greeting From China.

Address of Mrs. Geo. H. Hubbard.

Brothers, Sisters, and Friends of Christian Endeavor, — I bring you the greetings of the Foo Chow Christian Endeavor Society. All peace and all good to you. According to Chinese etiquette, a special salutation should be given to the host, so to you, Endeavorers of this fine city of Cleveland, all peace and every good. As I look about and see your preparations for our reception, my heart is filled with wonder. One thing in particular I notice, these two colors, the white and the yellow, not only in your great meeting place, but on your streets, in your shops, everywhere. What is the meaning of this? Let me give you my thought: white is the color of silver; yellow, of gold. Perhaps you would offer your silver and gold for Christ and the church. If this be true, praise be to God, and yourselves shall receive the greatest blessing.

It is now a little more than one year since my feet touched your shores. Of course, coming so far from the Golden Gate of the Orient across the great waters to the Golden Gate of the Occident, I underwent various trials and even fright, but all these are forgotten in that I now share with you in this day of Pentecost. During the first few days after my arrival I looked about to see what you have here like what we have in the Middle Kingdom. I find that you have the grass green and beautiful, also trees so great and tall with thick foliage affording grateful shade, and flowers so sweet and lovely. They seem to me like the smiling faces of friends; and the blue sky overhead, just like our sky in the far homeland, seemed to bring the two countries so much nearer. And in truth, by the way of heaven the two countries are as neighbors, and as neighbors ought to be mutually helpful. How helpful? One method is the Christian Endeavor society, which has already been established in China. Ours in Foo Chow, the first one, was begun in 1885. Many are the benefits that come from Christian Endeavor. One thing, it brings the young people of both countries nearer together, and makes them more like brothers and sisters in Christ Jesus. It is the Son of God who touches us. "Our Father," — my Father, your Father, — and so are we the children of God and joint heirs with Jesus Christ.

Another benefit is that it helps us to exercise ourselves with greater energy, that we may bring forth such fruits as these, — faith, love, joy, peace, long suffering, gentleness, goodness, meekness, and temperance. Of course, compared with your numbers, ours are very small, but growing. You remember Gideon's army was only three hundred men, but they were able to put to flight the hosts of Midian. Wasn't that an early society of Christian Endeavor? Let us, like Gideon's band, take the earth, and may the silver and golden rays of the Sun of righteousness shine forth into all the world, for the land of China as for all. God be with you till we meet again.

"All Hail the Power of Jesus' Name" was then sung.

MR. DICKINSON: We shall now have the pleasure of listening to one of the sons of the aborigines. We have with us Jonas Spotted Bear, a full-blooded Sioux Indian, in the uniform of the Santee Agency, who will now address us.

Christian Endeavor Among the Indians.

Address of Jonas Spotted Bear.

I am very glad to be present here before you, and for the opportunity to speak about my people. Many years ago the Indians were all wanderers. They did nothing but move from one place to another. Besides this, they hunted buffaloes and had wars. They did not know anything about civilization or the Word of God. They did not know there ever was such a God. Still, while these poor, helpless Indians were wandering around, they had some things to worship. They did not worship a true and living God, as they do now, but they worshiped things that they thought would help them. They worshiped the stones, the moon, the sun. These they worshiped like idols, just as the Egyptians did in olden times. They had no one to teach them and their children right, but they did the best they could; they taught their children themselves. They did not teach them to do what is right; but they taught them how to use bows and arrows, how to use the gun, and how to prepare themselves for war. But these are not the best things; the Indians did not know any better in those days.

My friends, I will say that there has been a very great change between the past and the present time; and all the old things that the Indians used to do are past and gone, and now they are getting full of a new life, and in this new life they are trying the best they know to help themselves and to help others. They are now becoming civilized. If you could have seen their children many years back, before you and I were born, if you could have seen the way they looked, and what they did, and contrast them with the children of to-day, you would hardly believe that some of them really are Indians. Now they have put off their blankets, pulled the feathers out of their hair, and dressed up like white people. Their children are not brought up as they used to be, but now they are brought up in a new way. Their children are sent to school to be trained in many ways. The boys are taught to be mechanics, farmers, teachers, and preachers. The girls are also trained in many ways. The students are interested in these things. They prepare themselves for the future, so that they can put themselves beside the white man. If you go out West you will see what they really mean, and what they want to be. You will see their homes and their farms. You will see they are not rough, long-haired Indians, with blankets over their heads and feathers in their hair, like they used to be, long before there were any whites in this country.

They are not only becoming civilized, but they are also becoming Christians. The Indians used to worship idols faithfully, but now they are trying to be honest and faithful in following Christ. It makes me happy to know that my people have learned to love their heavenly Father, and many of these heathen Indians love the Word of God. They read his words in the Bible; they realize the good that it has done for them; they see now how good it is to have such a friend, who is able to help and save them from their sins. They put their trust in God. They want their children to read, and to learn about him. There are many Christian young men and young women who are now workers for Christ among their own people. They are scattered all over in many different places, as far west as the Pacific.

The Christian Endeavor work is growing more and more earnest among my people. Thank God for the brave missionaries and for the faithful missionaries that he has given to my people, that they may learn the Word of God, and that they may believe that there is a true God.

We see now what an Indian is, and what he really means, and what he is trying to do. An Indian is a man with a soul; he is made in the image of God. But, in the first place, he was not trained like a white man. He was not born and brought up in a family where he could be trained and taught to read the Bible like the whites. So what the Indian wants is the Christian teacher. I am here as a representative; I am a full-blooded Sioux Indian; and, as a representative of my people, I ask you for Christian teachers and Christian patience, until we have learned the lessons that God would teach us.

I want your prayers for my people, that they may grow earnest and faithful in following God. [*Applause.*]

Mr. DICKINSON: Christian Endeavor has brought interdenominational fellowship without talking a great deal about it. While other people have been theorizing and arguing, we have been working. As a result, we are here in this hall to-day ten thousand strong, and we do not know from what denomination our neighbors next to us have come. We are all here as Christians; we are all here to emphasize the great truth that, while we are loyal to our individual denominations, we are tall enough to look over the fence and recognize our neighbor and fellow-Christian, and work with him as such.

We are now to have a practical illustration of this interdenominational fellowship. We have with us representatives of a large number of the denominational missionary boards, and five or six of them will address us during the next twenty-five minutes. Dr. McMillan of New York City, secretary of the Board of Home Missions of the Presbyterian Church of the United States of America, will be the first speaker.

Greetings from Representatives of Missionary Boards

DR. McMILLAN: *My Christian Friends,* — Into this great sea of humanity our various denominations pour tributary streams. I speak for one denomination, not because I am limited in my sympathies by the results of any denomination, for I do not think that a man whose piety is not active enough to jump over the denominational fence is strong enough to hold out all the way to the gates of heaven. I am willing to say their methods are as good as ours; but, since I am to speak for one of these denominations, I can only say that, in our sympathies, in our activities, and in our efforts, we are girdling the globe. Our foreign missionary board works in all the countries the church will give them means to work in. The home missionary board is working in all the States of our Union except four, and in all the Territories. We have in our church eight great boards, composing the eight principal lines of denominational benevolence. We are trying to do our part, shoulder to shoulder with our brethren, in regenerating our country, as the best and shortest way to the regeneration of the world. Our country stands here, all of our doors are front doors, and the world is pouring in here its worst and its best and brightest; and we are trying to receive it all into our great denominational life, and to mold it into our church life of sympathy and activity. We believe in Christian Endeavor most heartily, and we rejoice that you have come forward so grandly to our support. The Board of Home Missions received last year about $13,000, which was nearly double what you gave the year before; and when you catch the inspiration of that great missionary extension movement which was inaugurated yesterday, you will give twice as much.

REV. DR. J. G. FRASER of the Congregational Home Missionary Society: —

I am rather glad Dr. McMillan spoke first; for, practically, all I will have to do is to submit his address as the one I wanted to make. I am very glad to be here, especially because some years ago I stumbled upon a sort of earthly immortality by organizing the first Young People's Society of Christian Endeavor west of the Hudson River. A few years hence, when I get just a little older, I expect to be put under a glass case, and exhibited as "Fossil No. 1," in the cabinet of the Ohio Christian Endeavor Union; and people will say, "How astonishing that such a foolish looking man should have done so wise a thing as to introduce Christian Endeavor in Ohio!" As I go about the State of Ohio, I find everywhere the Christian Endeavor Society, and I find them always loyal to this great motto of theirs, "For Christ and the Church." Our home missionary societies are coming to recognize them as the best helpers we have in the work of evangelizing this land. I simply want to bring you the most cordial greeting on behalf of the Home Missionary Society of the Congregational Churches.

MISS M. V. WINGATE of Chicago, *Secretary of the Congregational Woman's Board:* Faith, hope, and love, but the greatest of these is love; not simply horizontal love that stretches out and touches all about us, but vertical love that goes down and down, clear through the earth to China, down to India, through to Japan and the Islands of the Sea. The greatest is love; "For God so loved the world that he gave his only begotten Son, that whosoever believeth on him might not perish but have everlasting life." "How shall they believe on him of whom they have not heard? and how shall they hear without a preacher? and how shall they preach except they be sent?" It is all made clear to us when Christ in his last command said, "Go ye into all the world and preach the gospel to every creature." Go ; yes, go in *person*, not alone by prayer and by gifts.

REV. W. E. C. WRIGHT, D.D., *of the American Missionary Association:* I look around on this vast assembly with something of the awe I felt when standing by Niagara, and in view especially of what was accomplished yesterday in conference with the missionary secretaries and the officers of the United Society. It is a spectacle not simply of Niagara as a thing of beauty to stir the emotions, but of Niagara with a part of its volume turned into channels of human industry to meet the wants of the human race. For the Christian Endeavor Societies, I believe, are to supply an enormous increase of motive power for the work of the church in evangelizing the world. We expect great help from the Christian Endeavor Societies of the Congregational Churches in the work which is committed to the American Missionary Association. By God's blessing upon this work we hope to make the Chinese population on our Pacific coast become a mighty force for evangelizing that great empire across the Pacific Ocean. We hope to make the Indian of the twentieth century a Christian Indian. We hope to fill the Southern mountains as full of intelligent religion and religious education in the very next generation as those mountains are certain to be then full of new industries and new towns. We hope to make the seven millions of our colored population no longer a problem in the nation's life, but a population that shall yield their due proportion of temperance reformers, of eloquent and trained Christian preachers, of artists, and faithful and useful citizens in all the walks of life, and yield also their due proportion of musicians that shall be an element of strength. For God's sake we hope to do these things in America; not for America's sake, but for the world's sake, and that they may all acknowledge Christ as the King of kings and Lord of lords.

The audience next sang, "Onward, Christian Soldiers!"

Rev. Dr. Berger announced that in the afternoon the hall and tent were filled, and that there were crowds upon the street who were unable to get into either place. Owing to this, two overflow meetings were arranged for the evening — one at Epworth Memorial, and the other at Woodland Avenue Presbyterian Church.

MR. BAER: At the request of the representatives of the press, I take pleasure in making an announcement. Before doing so I want to say this, and I think you will all agree with me, that the local papers of the city of Cleveland have done magnificent work in helping us to pass this Convention on to our friends at home. The representatives of the press, to the number of eighty, have united in a resolution of thanks to Mr. R. B. Hamilton and his associates of the Press Committee.

DR. DICKINSON: We will now listen to an address on the "Movement Among the Jews Towards Christ," by Rev. Herman Warszawiak of New York City.

Movement Among the Jews Towards Christ.

Address of Rev. Hermann Warszawiak,

Missionary to the Jews, in charge of the American Hebrew-Christian Mission, New York City.

Beloved Christian Friends, — I am to speak to you about the movement among the Jews towards Christ.

The church of our Lord Jesus has sadly neglected her duty with reference to the evangelization of Israel; nay, more, has even gone on to absolute prejudice against the Jewish people; and it is quite a common thing to hear the expression, "I take no stock whatever in the Jews." The history of this people in the past is evidence that they have greatly suffered at the hands of so-called Christians; and, instead of Christian kindness, violence, persecution, punishment, and even death, have been met with in almost every century, while to-day in some lands they are still oppressed and sorely tried because of their nationality and their faith.

Christian brothers and sisters, do you know that everything that is held dear and holy to the hearts of this great company, and of all Christendom as well, has been given to you through the Jewish people? The Bible, the church, the disciples of Jesus, the chosen apostle to the Gentiles, all came from among the Jews; nay, more than this, our precious Lord and Master himself was born of a Jewish virgin. In fact, whenever God wanted to send a message at large, he chose an Israelite as his messenger; and how wonderfully these men, like Isaiah, Jeremiah, David, Daniel, and others succeeded.

But look at the church to-day, with all her hundreds and thousands of faithful men and women who are trying to carry God's message to those who know it not; and, in spite of nearly nineteen centuries of ceaseless effort, she has sorrowfully to report more than half of the world still unevangelized. I think it would have been different had the Jews been the preachers instead! You cannot go out of the divine order, which says, "The gospel is the power of God unto salvation, to every one that believeth, *to the Jew first*, and also to the Greek;" and when you do so you will surely fail.

How badly off, in regard to the gospel, are the Jews all over our land! Take, for instance, this city of Cleveland. I am told there are about thirty thousand Jews in this city; and yet, if it had not been for one Jewish young man from our New York mission who had it put in his heart to come here a few months ago to testify of the Lord Jesus Christ to his brethren, no effort would have been made to reach them. All the two hundred thousand, or whatever the number of Christians there may be in Cleveland, cared nothing whatever about preaching the gospel to these their fellow-citizens. They surely would not have been so neglectful of any other nationality or people on the face of the earth.

And the saying is true, not only here, but in the towns and cities throughout the land. Indeed, there are many places in this country with thousands and tens of thousands of Jewish inhabitants, where the church has made not the least effort to bring these Israelites under the influence of the gospel. They seem to look upon the Jews as if they were a people who had long since been wiped from off the earth. In the city of New York where I am laboring, we have no less than a quarter of a million Jews, and only three or four converted Jewish brethren who are trying to make the gospel known unto them.

You say you have no interest in these cast-off people. Says Mr. Brown or Mr. Smith, "I take no interest in the Jews because they are such a money-making people." Well, I do not deny it. But is it wrong to make money? If it is, then many Christians are doing wrong; for most of those I know are just as anxious to make money as the Jew, only with this difference, that the Jew is usually more successful! But to make money is no sin; and I can tell you how the Jew is so successful in this respect. It is because when he makes $3,000 or $5,000 a year he does not spend $10,000, as so many Christians do, but he spends $500, and saves all the rest; and it is no wonder, therefore, that he prospers while others fail.

You have another prejudice against him. You say he sells too cheap. Well, this may be true; but when you say that he does it by swindling and stealing, I might as well speak out plainly and say that it is nothing but a lie. Were they dishonest, the police-forces and courts of this land are surely strong enough to put them where they ought to be; but visit the State prisons, and you will not find Jews there. True, you do not find many Christians there either; but those who are there are sure to be Gentiles, anyhow!

To tell you the truth, I think Christian people take no interest in the Jews simply because they are jealous of them. If this is not the reason, then I know not how to understand the Christian church, which tries to evangelize all classes, all people, and all nations, but keeps away from so noble a people, so able a people, so good a people, as is the Jewish nation. Why, you have never heard of a Jewish murderer, or a Jewish robber; neither have you ever met a Jewish drunkard on your streets, or seen a Jewish tramp or beggar at your doors. No, the Jewish people care for their own poor, and are not only philanthropic, but good-natured, always merciful and kind, and make first-class citizens wherever they are found.

Brethren, beloved, there is no society so able to help in the cause of Israel as you Christian Endeavorers. Why not invite the Jews to your regular meetings? They will certainly respond to your invitation, and listen attentively; and you will find in them, when you have won them, the best of qualities as soldiers in the great Endeavorer army.

Some say, however, that work among the Jews is not successful, and therefore it is no use to begin it. In answer to this I want to say that, having lived amongst the Jews all my life, and having preached to them the glorious gospel of Christ every day for the past five years, I find this work not only a success, but the most glorious, most hopeful, and most encouraging work of any with which I am acquainted. God never makes a mistake; and he has declared that "all Israel shall be saved;" and more than that, he said concerning them, "This people have I formed for myself; they shall show forth my glory." Oh, what a great future there is in store for this, God's chosen nation! — a future which is even now dawning upon them all over the world to-day.

You say it is useless to preach to the Jews? Why, only yesterday [Saturday] I went out to speak to some of the Jews in this city. I found sixty or seventy of them gathered in the Woman's Christian Temperance Union Hall, and, best as I knew how, I spoke to them of this glorious salvation in Christ; and not only did they most earnestly and attentively listen, but when I left the hall a number followed me out into the street, some crying, "Mister, Mister, can't you tell us something more about this Jesus?" One of them afterwards came to my room at the hotel, and spent two hours in conversation, asking all sorts of questions concerning Christ and his redemption.

You say that work among the Jews is not successful? Why, I am preaching every day to large multitudes of Jews in New York City; and I can truthfully report that for the past few years I have not preached once on a Sabbath Day, in the large De Witt Memorial Church, where our meetings are held, when even one single seat has been vacant. The Jews come in hundreds to the simplest preaching of the gospel of Christ, and frequently have been turned away for want of room to accommodate them. We have frequently had to put a sign upon the front door of our church which reads as follows: —

ALL SEATS TAKEN.
THE CHURCH IS FULL.
COME NEXT SATURDAY EARLIER.

And this is not a movement of a few weeks or even months, but has been going on steadily, without a break, for the past five years; and I can assure you that there are scores of Israelites, as the result, who have already given their hearts to the Lord Jesus Christ, and who have confessed him before men. Do you call this failure? and can you say such a work as this is not successful?

Then remember, too, that this movement is not alone in New York City, but we hear the same blessed news from almost all the principal Jewish Missions in the world. From Russia, Austria, Germany, Great Britain, as well as from many cities in the United States, come most encouraging reports of Jewish movement towards the Messiah and Saviour.

I beseech you, therefore, and I plead with you, beloved Endeavorers, in behalf of my brethren in the flesh, that you lend a helping hand to a work so near and dear to the heart of God, and of him who was himself, as to the flesh, a Son of David, Son of Abraham, an Israelite. Take these simple words into your hearts; and if my words fail to awaken your interest, I pray God that the Holy Spirit may arouse you, fellow Christians, to consider the claims of the Jews, who, though cast off now, are still beloved for the Father's sake, and are your brethren in the Lord Jesus Christ.

I am greatly thankful to the trustees of the United Society of Christian Endeavor for inviting me to present the cause of Israel before this great assembly of Endeavorers for Christ and the church. May God greatly use this opportunity for his own glory and for the blessing of his beloved people. Amen.

Mr. Warszawiak's speech was received with hearty applause. The audience then sang "I will sing the Wondrous Story."

MR. DICKINSON: America has not a few uncrowned queens, women of brilliant abilities, consecrated purpose, and tremendous energy, who, with unsceptered and as yet unballoted hand, are slowly but surely shaping the destiny of this great nation. We have with us one of these great reformers, a woman whose magnificent work in behalf of the cause of temperance has given her a world-wide reputation; and I take great pleasure in introducing to this Christian Endeavor audience Miss Frances E. Willard.

Miss Willard was greeted by the rising of the audience, and the Chautauqua salute. Her address was substantially the same as she had previously delivered at the tent. The services were closed with a prayer of thanksgiving by Dr. Beckley.

THE TENT.

As if realizing that this was "the last day, the great day of the feast," the delegates were on hand early, and an hour and a half before the beginning of the praise service a large audience was already gathered in the tent. The crowd kept increasing, until every particle of room in the vast enclosure was taken, and many were turned away. It was warm in the tent; on the platform it was inordinately hot; yet both speakers and auditors were very patient with the heat. Mr. Foster conducted the song service, and one after another various favorite hymns were sung with an enthusiasm which utterly disregarded the heat.

Treasurer Shaw called the meeting to order at 2.30 o'clock, and introduced, as the presiding officer, Rev. Thomas Marshall, D.D., of the Presbyterian Board of Missions. Dr. Marshall called on Bishop Fallows to conduct the devotional service. The One Hundredth Psalm was read together, one verse of "At the Cross" was sung, and Bishop Fallows offered a brief prayer.

DR. MARSHALL: I have great pleasure in introducing to you this afternoon Miss Frances E. Willard of Evanston, Ill., of world-wide temperance fame. [*Loud applause, and the Chautauqua salute.*]

Women and Temperance.

Address of Miss Frances E. Willard.

Beloved brothers and sisters of the great household of our common faith: —

> " In the cross of Christ I glory,
> Towering o'er the wrecks of time;
> All that's bright in woman's story
> Radiates from its form sublime."

Twenty years ago in November next, in this beautiful city of Cleveland, the women of the Gospel Temperance Crusade gathered to form the National Woman's Christian Temperance Union. For our sober second thought was organization, or systematic working according to a plan; and the very first debate we had, of very many that we have undergone during the time between that day and this, was whether the name "Christian" should be included in the name of the society. A few who were of the contrary part — as there are always some — said that "it would hurt our following." But the many said, "We are not here to seek a following; we are here to lift an ensign." The very first resolution adopted by that convention read as follows: "Resolved, that as our cause will be combated by mighty, determined, and relentless forces, we will, trusting in him who is the Prince of peace, meet argument with argument, misjudgment with patience, denunciation with kindness, and all our difficulties and dangers with prayer." It is in the name of faith and facts like these that I am glad to claim that our society is a sister beloved of the Christian Endeavor. Born of a Christian race, cradled in Christian homes, educated by the Christian pulpit, the women of the Crusade, and their successors of the white-ribbon movement, have evermore pointed man and woman, youth and maiden, boy and girl, to a wide-armed cross upon a lonely hillside, and have repeated with motherly tones those words of him who said, "And I, if I be lifted up from the earth, will draw all men unto me."

Now, beloved comrades, we live in an age when the Golden Rule and the precepts of our Master have begun to reach an equilibrium in the average mind. We live in an age when the Christianity of conduct is getting proclaimed as never before, when the heart of man has become so brotherly and friendly that he welcomes woman to his side in every avenue of life. There is no competition between men and women — or there ought not to be. Whoever speaks of competition has breathed out a curse upon the race; whoever speaks of co-operation has breathed out a blessing. If one eye should say to the other eye, "Let me do your seeing;" if one ear should say to the other ear, "You can just shut up shop, I will look after your hearing;" if one foot should say to the other foot, "I will outdo you in a walking-match," then might man say to woman, or woman to man, "We will see which one will get ahead." But God was before us in the matter; and in his blessed gospel — one of whose splendid object-lessons, one of whose brightest blossoming flowers, is this convention — he has taught us that "there is neither male nor female in Christ Jesus." The old English law said, "Husband and wife are one, and that one is the husband." The modern unwise agitator says, "Husband and wife are one, and that one is the wife." Christian Endeavor and the W. C. T. U. and the Church of Christ, whose children we are, says, "Husband and wife are one, and that one is — husband and wife." And this is said because "it is not good for man to be alone." Beloved friends, one of the mottoes of the society whose loving greetings I bring you to-day is, "Womanliness first; afterward what you will." I believe that is a motto born of the gospel. For I believe, although I do not know, that women will carry blessing and brightness everywhere they go, and that they will go everywhere. I believe the welcome of their presence and power will be the touchstone of the survival of the fittest in the age that is soon to dawn. I believe that the institution, the custom, the party, that cannot bear the clear daylight of a good woman's presence, deserves to die and will die.

Lady Henry Somerset, that great leader of women, that beautiful orator (who wanted to come here, as you were kind enough to ask her, and who will be here some day I hope), was looking into a liquor newspaper, because she is given to reading what they say in such papers, and she saw an open letter to herself, in which she was advised to remain within "the sphere of home," of which the letter proceeded to give her a diagram. Thinking of this kind advice, and idly turning over the pages of the paper, she next saw an advertisement which read as follows: "Wanted a barmaid. Must be good-looking, not over eighteen years of age. Photograph indispensable." Lady Henry now thought she understood how disinterested was the advice that had been given her, and was more than ever determined to go forth, with those women who with her have vowed by the help of Christ to make the world more homelike, hoping that some day she would be able to help the barmaids find homes of their own, far from the brutal haunts of the saloon. The hypocrisy of this newspaper is an illustration of the kind of opposition that is made to the active work of women in all those lines of reform that have centered around the cross. I once had occasion to present a petition to a Committee of the United States Senate, on behalf of the white-ribbon women, asking for the protection of the home, and that the safeguards of law be removed from the saloon. The attorney of the brewers' congress was there, and set forth his opposition after this manner: "Gentlemen, we brewers have vested interests you are bound to respect; and if you do not respect our vested interests, you will hear from us at the next election." While he was speaking, I thought about the "vested interests" I came to represent; I thought about the women whose names stand first on my calendar of saints; I thought about the mothers of the nation, who go down into the valley of unutterable pain and in the shadow of death, with the dew of eternity upon their foreheads, pass the sacred but terrible ordeal that gives to America her sons and daughters, and I said in my heart, "The vested interests of motherhood shall yet, in the estimation of Christian manhood throughout the republic, outrank the interest of the brewers' kegs and the distillers' vats."

It is for this reason that I wish to speak about women and temperance, though I confess it seems in this presence somewhat like carrying coals to Newcastle. You have taken a position on these subjects, and set a key-note that rings out true and clear; you have taken a position that might be illustrated by the story of the old lady in the schoolhouse, when the young people at singing-school were singing terribly out of tune. She, not listening any more than she could help, when the soprano soared through the roof, and the basso profundo plowed the gravel under the schoolhouse, set at work and got her fine old treble voice into order, pitched the key clear and sweet, while with her untrembling hand she beat the time of "How firm a foundation, ye saints of the Lord." Almost at once they had all fallen into line with her; they had caught the key, and they went on in happy harmony. In the tintinnabulation of the present time, there are sopranos who sing on a "high-license" scale; there are altos whose "regulations" are past finding out; there is a tenor that sings "tax," and a bass that basely declares for "nationalization;" but Old Lady Prohibition means to sing her tune right on in the same key, to walk by the same rule, to mind the same thing, and, bless your heart, all the rest will come into line and make a chorus of her solo one of these days! I do not know, but I believe that "the inviolate sea" shall yet salt down this continent to prohibition, and, by God's grace, I want to do the little that in one brief day's work one can do to help on that splendid consummation in the holy fight for a clear brain.

If ever an optimist lived, it was our Master, Christ. If ever an idealist drew breath, it was he who said, "Every plant that my heavenly Father hath not planted shall be rooted up." And it is to that marching song we must move forward. We must never know when we are defeated; we must never know when there are lions in the way; we must keep evermore our eyes fixed upon "the hills from whence cometh our help — Our help cometh from the Lord that made heaven and earth." Strike out into the forest of prejudice and blaze the trees, as your pioneers did in Ohio in the olden time. Slowly they march, they of the rank and file ; but they are following straight behind you. Do you not catch sometimes, away off there in the distance, the muffled music of their coming feet? It is the pioneer who fights out on the picket-line of duty. He is the soldier we must never recall. You number two millions; the white ribboners number but half a million. We have been working nearly twenty years; you only thirteen. But we have had to mold and work in the granite of character that was already formed; you work in the clay of the young character. You have the generous impulse of enthusiasm to carry you forward; and I thank God that in the world you have so many more than we, because yours being younger have so much longer to live than our motherly white ribboners, whose children many of you are.

So we will go side by side together, taking no half-way measures, not for moderation in drink, but for teetotalism; not for high license, but for prohibition; not for a double standard of personal purity, but for a white life for two. Because the drink-habit is enshrined in custom, we will strike out into society with our total abstinence pledge. Because the drink-habit is intrenched in the ignorance of the people, we will go with our scientific temperance text-books into the public school. Because it has defended itself behind towers and bastions of legislation, we will go with petitions to the legislature, municipal council, the State, the national Congress. Because it is in politics, we will follow it there; for we have declared that we will dissect out the alcohol nerve from the anatomy of the body politic, and where the scalpel takes us, there we will go. We have found that the nerve is neuralgic, and that the neuralgia is general ; and so we have had to go from head to foot in order to trace out its course. In the white-ribbon army we have seventy distinct lines of work, and one of our mottoes is the same that they had at the battle of the Boyne, "Wherever you see a head hit it," — that means that we have adopted the *Do Everything* Policy, since the curse is everywhere.

And so, brothers and sisters of the larger hope, I speak these earnest words because I believe that every brain is like an open furrow, and every word is like a seed dropped in. I speak to you because I know you are the burgomasters of the future, and I know that, when my voice fails and falters, you shall with clarion tongue take up the note and bear it onward to the larger multitude. I thank God for the opportunity of the hour. I thank him that we are nearer to the hour of victory "than when we first believed."

Good men say that municipal politics are in the most disgraceful condition, that home missionary work is greatly needed, and we all believe it. Men say they cannot put down the saloon, the gambling-house, and the haunt of infamy; yet all the time they have at their command, as I believe, the forces that would help them to do just these things.

"'Oh, ship ahoy,' rang out the cry ;
'Oh, give us water ere we die.'

> A voice came o'er the waves afar,
> '*Just drop your bucket where you are.*'
> Then they dipped, and drank their fill
> Of water fresh from mead and rill;
> And then they knew they sailed upon
> The broad bosom of the Amazon."

My brothers, you have got the votes you need. Dip them out of the home-life of the nation. Call the home-guards to the front. Let Barak once more go forth side by side with Deborah. I speak these words on Sunday because they are, as I believe, words that could never have been spoken except for Christ and his gospel. Lucy Stone spoke words like these in a little schoolhouse in the State of Maine, one Saturday night long years ago. On Sunday morning, to refresh her spirit, she went to church, and the minister took for his text, "And this Jezebel has come among us." Let the fact that you listen to me kindly show what a distance we have marched since the days of that brave and royal heart.

General Phil Sheridan, in the great crisis of one of his battles, saw that the enemy wavered; he saw that his hour had come; and in his dashing fashion he cried out, "Let everything go in, — artillery, engineers, bands of music, cavalry, infantry, everybody." Your Christian Endeavor sends out the same cry. I thank God that you send it. Flying cavalry of youth go in; let the artillery of argument go in; let the women and children go in; let the sweet singers go in; and out from the climax of the battle, by Christ's dear grace, shall come a disrupted liquor traffic, a protected home, and a redeemed republic, where Christ shall rule in custom and in law.

Again and again thunders of applause greeted the telling points made by the speaker.

One verse of "Onward, Christian Soldiers," was then heartily sung, after which Dr. Marshall introduced Rev. Gilbert Reid, for ten years a missionary of the Presbyterian Board in China. Mr. Reid came forward dressed in his Chinese robes, with queue and wooden shoes, and spoke as follows : —

A Greeting from China.

Address of Rev. Gilbert Reid.

I give the salutation of China to the young people of this great American continent. Extremes meet. An anxious, rushing, worrying, nervously prostrated American becoming a dignified, august, long-robed, long-lived Chinaman — this by the principle of adaption is the greeting which Christian America gives to the empire of China.

China and the United States — the one an ancient nation long before Rome ruled in Gaul or Britain, and the other a young republic of a little over one hundred years; the one intensely conservative and proudly exclusive, and the other rich, enlightened, progressive, liberty-loving; the one tolerant towards all religions — Confucianism, Taoism, Judaism, Buddhism, Mohammedanism, Nestorianism, Romanism, and all the sects of Protestantism, and the other known as Christian; the one looking to the past and living in the past, and ignoring the possibilities and demands of the future, and the other living in the future and forgetting too much her own glorious past — these are the two nations facing each other to-day, and greeting each other across the blue waves of the Pacific, and demanding the clearest, broadest diplomacy, the truest, bravest convictions, and the calm of a conscience which will be true to itself and yet fair to others.

During my stay in the United States I have noticed that many of our people don't like the Chinese quite as well as they like the Japanese; they don't like the Oriental quite as well as the Occidental; they don't like the English quite as well as the Americans; they don't like other people quite as well as they like themselves.

A certain statement used to read, "Every man for himself and God for us all;" but a negro quoted it this way, "Every man for himself and God for himself." True Christianity, however, means self-preservation by devotion to others and obedience to God, "Trusting in the Lord Jesus Christ for strength."

What, now, is the real greeting which China gives to America in return for the greeting which America gives to China? Let us consider the facts just as they are, whatever the robes we wear or the country where we may dwell.

Think first of all of a matter of history. The United States has certain laws on her statute-books excluding from further entrance to our gates all who are called Chinese laborers, and compelling all those who now live in America to register, to be photographed and identified, on pain of deportation. Now, in the same spirit of magnanimity and unparalleled fairness, a treaty is negotiated between the governments of the two countries, whereby the Chinese government can make similar laws and negotiations against American workingmen, skilled or unskilled, who may desire to cross the Pacific and gain a livelihood in China, while as for the rest of Americans in China, merchants or missionaries, a complete register must be furnished the Chinese emperor every year, as to who we are, what we are doing, and where we dwell. To the exclusiveness of the Chinese are now added the exclusion laws of the United States.

Every nation being an independent sovereignty has the right to make her own laws, and establish the character of her own citizenship. For the sake of self-preservation as a nation, laws of limitation and restriction are indispensable; but when those laws are based, not on questions of character and merit, but on nationality and race, they cease to show forth that courtesy, that comity, and that fairness which are the essence of true international relationship. Three things, as it seems to me, need to be kept in mind in the solution of the difficult and serious problem of immigration, whether it be European or Asiatic or African: First, more rigid regulations concerning the time and mode of naturalization; second, the extension of this limited favor equally to all, not only to the white man, but to the black man, and not only to the black man, but also to the red man, born on our own soil, and to the Mongolian from across the Pacific; and third, rigid laws of exclusion, both on the side of the Atlantic and the Pacific, to all aliens who intend to remain aliens, and have no real capacity to become true, loyal, peace-loving American citizens. This is good citizenship; and as good citizenship is bound up in good Christianity, every social and political problem needs to be studied and handled by the ministry and the laity; so those wider social and political problems which relate to the peace of nations and the enlightenment of the race, are inseparably connected with the great missionary undertaking and the universal kingdom of our Lord.

And what, now, is the real greeting which China gives to the Christian missionary? Is the religion of our Saviour either needed or wanted by the four hundred millions of Chinese? Is there any chance of success? Just as cheering as the promises of God, no more and no less, is the outcome of missions in China. Any man who is a pessimist, and any minister who has blue Mondays, is not needed to preach the gospel in China.

But be it remembered, though the work is radiant with hope, it is beset with difficulty; and any one who has not the grace of grit, the power to hold on, whose enthusiasm is merely that weak, namby-pamby, wishy-washy, limp, sentimental conglomeration of gush and bosh, can never stand China, or work in China.

The Chinese have no liking for the foreigner, any more than the average American has for the Chinaman. This dislike, nourished by suspicion and superstitious fear, by slanderous rumors and villainous lies, expands again and again into intense hostility, until it stirs up the howling mob to tear down the foreigner's house, to plunder the foreigner's goods, and, as only a year ago, in the case of the two Swedish missionaries in the very center of the empire, to cruelly butcher their lives, and then leave their bodies for four days on the main street of the city under the hot July sun. So far as protection in China from the interference of foreign powers is concerned, the foreigner's life is less safe and his name is less honored to-day than it was twenty years ago. As good citizenship in America needs to be molded by Christianity, so does good citizenship abroad; every kind of social problem is legitimately a part of Christian missions.

When, in the apostolic church, the message went over from Europe to the Apostle Paul: "Come over into Macedonia and help us," it did not mean that the Macedonians themselves were asking for the gospel or would receive the messenger, but that God, who dwelt in them and sought their good, gave the call and the opportunity. The call was not a human call, but a divine one; and the opportunity was not human, but providential. Always and everywhere the call of duty is best obeyed when it is the call of God, like the negro slave, who, in the dream of something divine, cried out: —

> "Man wills us slaves;
> God wills us free;
> I will as God wills,
> God's will be done."

In all the history of China, God's hand is plainly seen beckoning every true soul to deeds of charity and righteousness, of peace and good-will. When we consider a nation coming down from the earliest history, a vast population, holding its own in the face of rivalry of great governments, and to-day, with all the impetuous trend and non-resistance of its character, still maintaining its independent sovereignty, surely God has a meaning for the existence and perpetuity of this race, and somewhere in his scheme of universal redemption is found the salvation of this ancient people. As Christ became incarnate "in the fullness of time," so to-day seems to be the time when Christ shall become incarnate among the people of China. First of all, then, the providential call of China is in the race itself.

2. China is providentially prepared in her religious teachings. No religion outside of Christianity presents such high morality as Confucianism. No people given to idolatry worship beings so pure, so elevating, so reasonable as the Chinese. Not a single idol is the representation of vice or impurity. Thus reaching forth in the search for truth and peace, for God and heaven, Christianity, when rightly presented, in all the tenderness of its life, the satisfactoriness and breadth of its teaching, and the divine uplift of its inherent power, will in due time be gladly accepted and as faithfully proclaimed. Christianity was meant for man, as man was meant for God.

3. China is providentially prepared in the social make-up of the country. There are over 1,800 cities, and every one is a center of influence such as few cities in this country can be. The capital of every province is emphatically the center of that province in official life and political influence, in education and in commerce. Likewise all the smaller sections of the country have cities to which to go and around which to gather. By placing the light of our religion in one of those cities, it does more than shine within those walls which surround that city, it radiates in every direction through the country around. Christian influence is thus facilitated and magnified by the very social constitution of the people.

4. China is likewise providentially prepared by the political make-up of the people. Certain men stand out as leaders, while others content themselves with being the followers. Socialism is only a minor key to be struck in the body politic. As provincial capitals are the places of central influence, so the officials of the government located at the capitals are the persons of central influence. Every little community has one person or a few, to whom all the rest look for advice and for guidance. Surely the conversion of such men to Christianity is in harmony with the providential arrangement.

5. China is providentially prepared in her educational ambitions. For some time, even in the early days when our ancestors were roaming around in the woods of Britain, China has had her schools and her literary examinations. Books are always revered by her people, even by the illiterate. The printed characters of her Confucian classics are never to be soiled or trampled upon. Education is the door to influence. Within the last few years Western science, through the edict of the emperor, has been incorporated in her examinations, and it remains to be seen whether skeptics or agnostics from our Western land shall be quicker than Christians to enter the open door.

6. China is providentially prepared in the Christian constituency already secured. Fifty thousand Protestant communicants and 150,000 Protestant adherents; these form the nucleus for the future. At the same slow rate we have been going the last forty years in China, you will find at the end of the next forty years 40,000,000 Protestant communicants and 100,000,000 Protestant adherents. Our schools are established, hospitals are built, books are prepared, the Bible is distributed, churches are formed. The forces are gathered, the strategic points are seized, now for the final conflict.

We need your pledge, the whole church needs it, not only because it describes in clearest language in the first sentence the essence of Christianity, but because it makes every member a conscientious participant in church activity. We need your service of consecration, so that souls beset with trial, opposition, and persecution may again and again renew their allegiance to the Great Head of the church, the Friend of humanity. We need your interdenominational fellowship, so that heathenism may not laugh to scorn our divisions and our rivalries. We need denominational loyalty, though not to any large degree, until such time as by the leadership of God's Spirit we may present the one church of Christ in China. Missions need Christian Endeavor, and Christian Endeavor needs missions.

In the outlook that lies before us in the solemn, dim vista of coming years, difficulties colossal and defiant may surround our path, and he who tries it will best understand them; but with the spirit of patience, kindness, and hope; with the principles of adaptation, conciliation, and love; wearied never by the waiting, nor baffled by calumnies, misunderstanding, annoyances, and persecution; magnifying the truth, and imbued again and again with the spirit; cheering each other, and dwelling together in the bonds of peace, we may rest assured that God himself, in his own time, will, with his hand of supreme benediction, own the work which seeks to heed his commands; and when his truth and grace have been proclaimed and made known, then Christianity, young still as the morning, and full of an undying energy, will conquer and reign with the grip and scope of a divine power, until from land to land and sea to sea we shall hear the sound of the music of the Lord's triumph.

The next speaker was Mr. S. L. Mershon of Chicago, through whose efforts the missionary extension plan has been so prominently emphasized. He was welcomed most cordially, and his address aroused very great interest.

The Christian Endeavor Missionary Extension Course.

Address of Mr. S. L. Mershon.

Christian Endeavor was born of an evangelistic revival and a mission band. If there is, therefore, anything in heredity, an evangelistic movement along missionary lines is the logical development in Christian Endeavor.

Do you pray every day, "Thy kingdom come"? Do you read the Bible every day, "Go ye into all the world and preach the gospel to every creature"? Do you, in your consecration meetings, say, "Here am I, Lord, send me"? Then the missionary extension must be the result. The past has charged the Endeavor life-blood with it. We breathe it in the very atmosphere of the present; while the future, with its eternity, beckons us on to it.

So long as missionary effort shall be the theme of the gospel, missionary extension will be the genius of Christian Endeavor. When a sinner comes to salvation, his overwhelming desire is to tell his associates that he has found the Lord. When a great organization becomes filled with the Spirit of God, the impulse for the universal proclamation of the gospel possesses it.

In addition to these all-powerful, inherent factors in our organization, we have:—

1. The crying need of the Christian church for a missionary evangelistic crusade.
2. The crying need of the unreached masses in the world for missionary effort.

The apathy of the church imperatively demands a missionary evangelistic movement.

A startling statement (an awful statement) is made in that recent "Epistle to the Churches" sent out by a committee of twenty of the denominational boards of foreign missions. Listen to what they say is the cause of the limited progress of Christianity in heathen lands. "If the truth be told, one obstacle now outweighs all others; it is found not in outside oppositions, but in the worldliness and apathy of the church herself. If she were to rise up to the full measure of her power, all the opposing forces of earth and hell could not resist her triumphant march."

The crying need of the church for a missionary evangelistic movement is shown—

1. In the lack of consecrated wealth in proportion to the church's resources.

A Methodist authority states that in the Methodist Church one million of its members give nothing to missions; while the enormous amount of wealth unappropriated to God, piling up in the coffers of the Presbyterians, makes my soul cry out as a Presbyterian.

If such is the condition in these two mighty denominations, what must we say of others who average below them in gifts of men and money?

These facts should scourge the consciences of the children of God, and should awaken us to some new form of missionary evangelistic effort.

The crying need of the church for a missionary evangelistic movement is shown —

2. In the lack of missionary volunteers in proportion to the world's needs.

Our normal schools are graduating swarms of Christian teachers scrambling for places in our overcrowded lists of applicants for positions as teachers in our public schools.

Our colleges and seminaries are graduating men into God's ministry with a pastor to every 200 souls in our thickly populated rural districts, while city slums, frontiers, and foreign lands teem with appalling seas of Christless souls, passing to Christless graves into a Christless eternity.

Medical colleges are granting diplomas to armies of Christian medical students, sending them into a profession already suffering in this country from congestion of brains, while the despairing cry of physical and spiritual agony goes up unceasingly from the great ocean of life in heathen lands. Relief can only come from those who for Christ's sake are willing to deny themselves, and follow in the footsteps of the greatest medical missionary of all the ages.

The crying need of the church for a missionary evangelistic movement is shown —

3. In the lack of missionary information in an otherwise intelligent church.

Here we strike the very key to the situation. Lack of missionary information in both pulpit and pew is a condition to which the missionary extension idea responds with an adequate answer.

We must have wider information as a basis for missionary giving, missionary going, and missionary praying. He who gives without knowledge is a spendthrift. He who goes on an errand without knowing why he is going is a fool, while he who prays for a cause about which he is willfully ignorant is a hypocrite. It is bad principle as well as bad practice for a man to give without knowledge. We believe that God Almighty has no use for an unconsecrated dollar, and willful ignorance is no basis for consecration.

It is a pertinent question, Why this amazing ignorance of missions in the Christian church? The solution must be found somewhere in the answers to three questions.

1. Is the pulpit dead?
2. Is the message dead?
3. Is the conscience of the church dead?

In other words, is it the fault of the pulpit or the pew — or both? Has the pulpit lost its power to educate along missionary lines? Is it possible that 12,000 Methodist pastors are preaching missions, and one million Methodist laymen are not contributing one cent for that cause? Can it be that 6,000 Presbyterian pastors are preaching the great commission, while the unused wealth of that church is piling up mountain high? Well may we ask a similar question of the other denominations.

It will be an awful time when the pastors who don't preach the last command shall march to the judgment seat with the millions of their denominations who don't give, and shall stand face to face with the heathen of their generation who have never heard of the Christ.

O Sinai, with thine awfulness! O death, with all thy possible sea of sorrows! O bleeding heart of Christ, with all thy lost power to save, what will it all mean? It seems to me that heaven, earth, and hell will recoil from the tableau ere it burst into a scene the like of which no mind can picture or tongue speak.

We met a pastor lately whose glibness on the subject of a late heresy trial was simply marvelous, yet who went down to a Waterloo when called to face five questions on China, where his Lord is in desperate conflict for the winning of one-third of the population of the world to a Christ crucified, and where his own denominational board is now facing the awful question of recalling missionaries because the denomination that pastor represents does not do its duty in sustaining its board of missions. Does that pastor's mouth and heart need opening? or do his people need to have their hearts and consciences opened, or both? That pastor's biography might help us to an explanation of this vexed question. His early professor in church history lectured long and deep on the apostasy of the early church, and forgot the apostasy of the modern church from the doctrine of our Lord regarding the world's evangelization. He graduated from a college and seminary from which the student volunteer movement had been exiled by a faculty who have their faces to the sunset; and he accepted a call to that large church, where a former doctor of divinity had left him a spiritual casket in the form of a church with a taste for literary essay Sabbath morning, with a text for a pretext, a sacred concert Sunday evening, and a very exclusive social function at their midweek gathering.

This missionary evangelistic movement, called missionary extension, proposes to stencil on the hearts and consciences of such a church God's notice of foreclosure. "His blood will I require at thy hand."

Those faithful, godly pastors, who, at the head of their self-denying churches, are now raising the men and money for the missionary cause, have a right to demand a movement to aid them in stirring other churches to help hasten the coming of the final day of Christ's triumph.

The denominational boards of missions need missionary extension.

On one side of them we have hundreds of millions of starving, perishing souls; on the other side a church capable of supplying the bread of life.

The church has appointed certain of its leaders, called secretaries, to stand in this breach and distribute the supply of food. Day and night the ceaseless cry of dying multitudes crowds their ears and tears their hearts; but the church is slow in passing up the supplies. What is to be done? Lethargy on one side means death, — awful death on the other side. In this crisis hour missionary extension has been sent, born of God, endowed with a courage from on high. It makes its cry to the armies of Endeavor and to all lovers of Christ's kingdom to fall into line for the final rally of the century. Let the pastors preach and the young people work, while a procession of missionary evangelists moves from city to city.

The debts of our missionary boards illustrate their terrible needs. God bless these debts! It means that hundreds of thousands of immortal souls heard the gospel last year because our secretaries had too much heart to snatch away the bread of life when the church did not put dollars enough into their treasuries. God doubly bless every secretary and committee who voted in the face of an empty treasury! Send on the gospel; we will not flinch.

Endeavorers, every one of you, will you stand by those men of God as they have stood by the cross of Christ, and pay those debts, thereby saving our boards from retreat? Look at the way your pastor is becoming gray over the care of a single church. What must be the weight on the hearts of those secretaries, some carrying a heathen world, while others carry the unreached millions of our own beloved lands.

In order to lay this responsibility where it really belongs, our overworked secretaries and physically worn-out missionaries, home for a much needed rest, have heretofore gone to a limited number of our churches with a cry for help; but look how they have gone, either —

1. By invitation from these particular churches, or —
2. By their own invitation to these particular churches.

When pastors invite missionary speakers to come, it usually indicates a church already interested in missions. When the representatives of our board solicit the privilege of speaking on missions in a certain pulpit, it indicates a church already contributing largely to the missionary cause. Churches not interested seldom send invitations; while our secretaries, like good fishermen, cast their hooks where, on previous occasions, they have found good fishing. This leads to certain pastors being driven almost distracted by applications from missionary speakers, while others are utterly neglected. With the great pressure on our boards to keep up the supply of funds, do you wonder that before starting out to speak our secretaries may look over the Conference association, or General Assembly minutes, for the churches that have given liberally in the past to the missionary cause, and then make a "bee-line" for those pulpits? They naturally want to use their time for the greatest financial results. In this way the churches that have not done their share are overlooked, and no material gain is made. The problem before the boards and churches is: How can the boards reach the churches not interested, while not losing their hold on those already secured, and without investing their revenue in cost of missionary education? The answer that will solve this problem will double the financial returns to our boards, and lift the whole church to a higher plane of missionary life. The missionary extension course will do it if enthusiastically adopted and re-enforced by our boards with the added co-operation of the pastors. The missionary churches in a community constrain the non-missionary churches to unite with them in the extension course.

Thank God, we have the confidence of our boards! Thank God, we have the help of the pastors! Thank God, the heart of the Endeavorer is loyal to both! Then, tie the knot, and tie it quick.

The boards have still another way of reaching the churches; and that is by a direct appeal to the pastors and church officials in their ecclesiastical assemblies, such as in conferences, synods, and presbyterial gatherings. The secretaries go a long distance to impress upon the pastors and elders and stewards in those gatherings the appalling need of the world. This appeal must come in with all the other topics crowding these august assemblies (unless crowded out by that scheme of the devil, a heresy trial).

Missionary extension does not propose to preach at church officials, but before them. On every circuit our speakers come in contact with more pastors, elders, and stewards than can be reached in the average presbyterial, synodical, or conference meeting. This is repeated six times in succession during the extension course of addresses.

These church officials, in place of being theorized to on the importance of preaching along these lines, have an object lesson before them. They see the people of their own parishes, and the members of their own communities at large, swarming and crowding into the largest auditoriums, while speaker after speaker holds these vast audiences spellbound by the hour on the very topics which some of them have refused to present to their own people, or have presented half-heartedly. One such missionary extension circuit enthusiastically held in a single district is worth a dozen addresses in a synodical gathering, is it not, especially where it creates a popular demand in the communities that compels consideration for this, the greatest work in the world?

We urge another argument as to why our denominational boards need this missionary movement.

A good child refrains from criticizing its mother, but a child's right to ask questions is universally recognized. Therefore, Christian Endeavor, with all its denominational loyalty, may well ask why it is that the churches of one of our most powerful denominations devote over two-thirds of their contributions to undenominational objects, while its great missionary boards are carrying appalling debts.

Other denominations are equally indictable.

We have already too many irresponsible strangers wandering about with plaintive missionary appeals, draining the resources of our Christian churches for alleged missionary work that certainly exists in the imagination, probably exists on paper, possibly exists in the ambition, but more likely exists in the pocket, of the advocates. An ocean of consecrated money goes in this way every year to man's cupidity, instead of to God's glory, because it is not sent through the regular channels of the church.

Missionary extension will help to calk up this leak by furnishing missionary advocates in the interest of our denominational boards of missions.

The boards need this movement to co-operate with these young people along these lines of denominational loyalty, and to guide many of our older people back to these lines of thought and action. The already aroused and rapidly increasing demand for missionary information in our mighty armies of young people will create a supply of missionary advocates from some source. Will it be through an organization loyal to the boards, controlled by the boards, and working for the boards, or by independent organization? This is a momentous question.

Student life needs the missionary extension course.

The missionary extension movement is sweeping into our colleges, universities, and seminaries, but always in aid of, and in no way hurtful to, that wonderful organization, the student volunteer movement.

In nearly every educational center will be found a powerful Christian Endeavor Union, while in all of the best educational institutions will be found, or should be found, active Endeavorers. Christian Endeavor has no use for a college campus fence between that institution and the church of Jesus Christ. The highest educational institution in the world is God's church. Christian Endeavor believes that when a Christian student enters college he is not absolved from his vow to the church to which he belongs and the denomination he represents.

Every Christian student, be he in preparatory school, college, or seminary, owes his allegiance to the church of his denomination. The college chapel is a poor substitute for a fully equipped church of Jesus Christ in a college town. The missionary extension course presumes that the Christian student is a part of the Christian church, and in entering a college community we seek the co-operation of all the students as well as the town people.

The tendency of student life in our higher educational institutions is isolation from church life, neglect of the social prayer-meetings, and non-attendance upon the Sunday School.

The missionary institute believes most heartily in the broad catholicity and interdenominational instruction of the student volunteer movement, but believes that in addition to the same, the students should be brought by our distinctively denominational missionary movement into active work in our churches, for their denominational boards, and into the blazing firelight of the local missionary life of the church. Their local church has the right to claim their allegiance, needs their help, while they need the influence of the practical religious life of the church. It can be readily seen that these two movements are complements of each other in every respect, and the most vigorous activity on the part of either will prove helpful to the other.

The world needs missionary extension. O Endeavorers! two million strong hearts beating with the Christ love, listen, listen, "Feed my sheep, feed my lambs." Mount up to the altitude of your Master's prayer, "I pray not for these alone."

The plan of the missionary extension course is very simple.

The Christian Endeavor Missionary Institute agrees to send upon application six speakers to present the great problems of missions, city, home, and foreign. It will send them without compensation, on three conditions:—

1. That all the pastors will preach missionary sermons in harmony with the course.

2. That the Endeavor Societies will pay the traveling expenses of the speakers, and a slight assessment for cost of correspondence. Both these amounts are always very small, as we arrange circuits of cities; and as speakers travel on ministerial rates, which means reduced fares, the proportion of extra costs amounts to but a few cents, a total never in excess of full railroad-fare and entertainment. This is divided between all societies on each circuit.

3. That the speakers shall be given grand mass-meetings, well advertised; and, while under the auspices of the local Endeavor Societies, they shall be understood as popular mass-meetings for everybody. Co-operation is invited from every organization that loves the extension of Christ's kingdom among men. These mass-meetings are generally arranged to be held about a month apart.

Missionary extension is sound along the line of economics.

The Endeavor Societies pay the traveling expenses of the speakers, thus saving our boards of missions a heavy item in a year's work.

A careful scrutiny of missionary itineraries will disclose a few facts helpful here. It is found that by a very large majority missionaries speak to women's meetings in afternoon gatherings, where, on the average, less than thirty women assemble, and those only who are regular members of a missionary society. Generally the boards pay the traveling expenses, and the collection averages less than five cents for each one present. It is stated on good official authority that one board's traveling expense account is over three times the receipts from the meetings visited. That policy would be most happily vindicated if different people assembled each time, and were open to conversion, so that a growing organization of missionary workers resulted; but the evidence is against it.

Missionary extension is sound along the lines of conservation of force. Each board of missions desires (some denominations have five or six boards) to be represented by a special address to each church during the year. It has been heretofore impossible, in the larger denominations, to accomplish this in one-half the churches. Let it be remembered now that each board in each denomination has its own speakers to speak on its own work.

Now, imagine a town of five churches, representing five denominations each, with their five boards of missions. It will take twenty-five speakers to present the different phases of missionary work in that community. Most of the meetings will be held in the afternoon; and while no sign "For ladies only" is displayed, the effect is the same, and an average attendance of thirty women is a liberal estimate for the usual afternoon meeting.

Missionary extension enters that town with its course of addresses. It will take but six of those twenty-five speakers, and they will be well advertised. It will pack a large auditorium six nights with the best brain, thought, and energy of the religious, social, professional, and commercial circles in that town, which, of course, includes those noble lady missionary workers accustomed to meet in the afternoon.

Notice, now, very carefully, what more it will do. It will enlist five pastors into preaching a course of six missionary sermons, a gain of thirty missionary sermons there. It will take the nineteen speakers already saved from the old-style method, and carry the missionary extension course into three other cities of the same size, and secure from the pastors of those three towns six missionary sermons, each making a net gain of ninety missionary sermons in the other towns.

This gives us a total gain of one hundred and forty-four missionary sermons and addresses delivered before packed houses, with all traveling expenses paid by the Endeavorers in place of by the boards, and one speaker left over. This simply is a result of Endeavor methods in missionary effort. Is this not conservation of force, in addition to economy? and does this not answer to the needs of the church?

We invite the financiers of our missionary boards to do some calculating on this proposition, and we ask them to figure out the additional value to the cause of the solid columns so generously given in reports of these meetings by the press in the various cities.

We might remark that experience has proved that college presidents, prominent pastors, and other platform talent of exceptional ability, have generously rallied in enthusiastic support of this movement; so that the charge that the pulpit, the bar, the counting-house, and bank will not respond to the missionary needs is set at rest by the representatives of all these spheres of activity furnishing eloquent advocates in the interest of our denominational boards of missions on the missionary extension platform.

We ask what will be the atmosphere in the churches with all those proverbial ministerial barrels loaded with missionary sermons? Will we not have in a few years in the ministry an army of missionary advocates armed as it were to the very teeth, ready to step in and take their places on the missionary extension platform to which they are already volunteering in large numbers?

Missionary extension meets the requirements for co-operation between the great denominational missionary organizations.

The secretaries of the great denominational boards have the power of absolute control over the missionary extension course. Missionary extension is, therefore, the servant of the denominational boards.

Now, a step farther. To be strictly up to the times, every Christian Endeavor Union should have a superintendent of missions. These superintendents become the representatives of the missionary extension movement in the respective States. The various denominational women's boards of missions have a State missionary secretary, and young people's missionary secretary residing in each State. These representatives of the denominational boards furnish a State committee of advisers for our missionary extension State representative, just as our honored and beloved missionary board secretaries furnish the counsel for the work of missionary extension at headquarters. No new machinery, and no new line of work are created.

It is, therefore, an interdenominationa movement, under the control of the denominational boards of missions. As a State movement, it is under the supervision of the State representatives of the denominational boards of missions. It is strictly interdenominational, but never undenominational. Every dollar that it raises goes to the denominational boards, without any mixing of funds. Every volunteer that it enlists, it points to the denominational boards. It is "in the church, of the church, and for the church."

The bell has struck a crisis hour for missions in Christian Endeavor, and Christian Endeavor has struck the bell that tolls a crisis hour in missions.

After Mr. Mershon concluded his address, the appropriate hymn "Bringing in the Sheaves" was sung. Mr. Shaw then made the following statement : —

MR. SHAW: It is not necessary for me to enlarge on the work of this great Christian Endeavor Missionary Extension Course that has been laid before you this afternoon. As Dr. Clark has said, this "son of thunder" has kindled fires all through Illinois, Iowa, Wisconsin, Tennessee, New York, and many other States; but what we want is not blazing patches of missionary enthusiasm, but a whole nation ablaze with missionary fire and power. [*Applause.*] The trustees of the United Society of Christian Endeavor have most heartily and unanimously indorsed the Christian Endeavor Missionary Extension Course. [*Applause.*] We have pledged to this course our utmost support, and we shall call upon all our unions and societies to co-operate in every possible way. This course will spread throughout this land and throughout the world, I believe. Perhaps that is enough for me to say in regard to the missionary extension course. It has our full, hearty, and unqualified approval, co-operation, and support. Now, one thing more. Where is the money to come from to send these scores and scores of young people who are volunteering for missionary work to their respective fields? Christian Endeavor did nobly last year. Five thousand five hundred societies reported that they had contributed over $135,000 to their denominational boards. I don't know how much the other societies have given; but this year we set for our standard one million dollars [*applause*] from Christian Endeavorers to the denominational boards of missions. [*Applause.*] I want to emphasize this fact, that the money is to be given directly to the denominational boards. It seems to me that the time has come for us to put our money into the channels that we have organized. I should judge, from reports that have come to me, that there are enough natives of one country across the sea who are seeking an education with a view to return as missionaries to give that country a missionary for every hundred people. We want to stop this. Unless a man has the indorsement of our denominational boards I do not believe that he has any right to be turned loose among our young people. [*Applause.*] One million dollars for missions: is that too much? [*Cries of No, no!*] Why, my brothers and sisters, it only means one cent a week from the members of our Christian Endeavor Societies. The smallest coin that we know anything about in this country, given by every member per week for one year, would mean a million dollars. Shame on us when we spend more money for chewing-gum than we give for missions! [*Loud applause.*] God help us to realize the mighty import of this movement; and to be willing that if we cannot go we will send. And we will send not our copper, but we will remember that the Lord God Almighty said that the silver and the gold are his, and he didn't say a word about the copper. [*Laughter and applause.*] One million dollars for missions! Let this be our watchword. Let us give until our hearts are where they ought to be in the cause of missions, and until God can look down upon us and say, "Ye have done well; ye have brought in all the tithes into the storehouse, and now the windows of heaven shall be opened," and a blessing such as our churches have never known will be poured out upon us. Oh, that we may have hearts to receive it, that we may be able to rejoice in the blessing of God! [*Applause.*]

DR. MARSHALL: Let us bring these grand remarks to a climax. All who will say, "By God's grace we will try and do it," please stand on your feet. (*The entire audience rose.*) God bless you! Do not forget it to-night at the consecration meeting. And now we are anxious that you should know something of the character of those boards that have received of your support. We shall now introduce to you some of the representatives of those boards who are here in this great Convention. Half of them are to speak at the Saengerfest Hall; we have the other half here on the platform. First, I introduce to you Rev. A. N. Hitchcock, D.D., representing the American Board.

Greetings from Representatives of Missionary Boards.

DR. HITCHCOCK: Some one being asked what those strange letters, "A.B.C.F.M.," stood for, said that it must be, "Any Body Can Feed Me." I suppose the allusion was to the fact that by original constitution and historic example the American Board, being the oldest and first distinctively foreign society in this country, it had to receive its food from any source that saw fit to yield it, and so American Christians generally, of all denominations, were at first its regular contributors. A farmer living in the suburbs of Chicago, driving into the city, so I have been told, was asked by his wife who saw those letters upon a large placard what those letters stood for; and the farmer replied, "I don't know what they stand for, unless it is because they can't sit down." Ever since the American Board was organized, in 1810, it has found it impossible, in the face of such startling facts as have been brought to our thought to-day, to sit down. [*Applause.*] And so, in bringing to you to-day the greetings of this first foreign missionary society of America, I bring you the greetings of a society that has been at work from the first year of its organization. I bring you greetings from twenty large missions, extending from Japan to the far South Sea Islands; from more than 40,000 living Christians in our churches; from more than 50,000 pagan children and youth in our schools; from more than 2,600 native workers, who are not only converts, but propagandists like yourselves; from more than 125,000 adherents of our churches. [*Applause.*]

DR. MARSHALL: When Judson lay seventy months in prison in Burmah, he woke up the Baptist Church in America. I introduce to you a Joan of Arc in the field, Miss Ella McLaurin, who represents the Baptist Missionary Union at their request as one of their secretaries. [*Applause.*]

MISS MCLAURIN: The American Baptist Missionary Union, from a small beginning in 1814, has gradually developed, until to-day her missionaries have scaled the almost inaccessible fastnesses of paganism, and are holding up the banner of our King in twenty great nations. We have 2,158 native preachers, who are carrying the gospel to the regions beyond; 1,200 schools, with 25,000 heathen boys and girls preparing for future work, besides our theological seminaries. We have a great Sunday-school society, with 90,996 students in our Bible schools. This year we are confronted by a crisis; but in the name of our God there is no reason for discouragement. We are confronted, as we believe, by a crisis of unutterable moment. Every door is thrown open wide for approach. Every heathen country in which we are laboring is calling for men and women to come and tell them of this Jesus doctrine. In the name of our Master seventy-four of our number have knocked at the door of our Board this year; and trusting in our Lord Jesus Christ we mean to send them forth, believing that the Christian Endeavor Societies will rally to their support. [*Applause.*]

DR. MARSHALL: What shall we say of the followers of John and Charles Wesley? Rev. Dr. Leonard, who was to speak to you, sits beside the dying bed of his brother. Also Dr. Merriman of the Reformed Church in America has been providentially called away. I introduce to you Rev. John Prugh, D.D., who will speak for the foreign mission board of the Reformed Church in the United States.

MR. PRUGH: I represent a denomination largely composed of German people and German descendants. It is well known that the Germans do not move hastily, but they are a people of warm hearts and deep sympathies. [*Applause.*] "Sir Oliver," said prim George Fox to the Protector, "if thee and I came to know each other we would love each other;" and as the Reformed people are coming to know the Christian Endeavor society and what it is, they are loving it strongly. Last Monday at Tiffin, Ohio, the board of commissioners of foreign missions of our church said, "In spite of the hard times we dare not retrench; we must extend our work," and two more missionaries were elected, one of whom, an Ohio boy, is to be supported by the societies of Christian Endeavor in our church. [*Applause.*] Everywhere the conviction is deepening that the Christian Endeavor society has been called into being of God for missions; and, Mr. Chairman, in this magnificent programme as outlined by Mr. Mershon, and in the great progressive movement inaugurated yesterday on board of that now famous little steam yacht, you will find the people of the Reformed Church standing shoulder to shoulder with you in hearty co-operation. [*Applause.*]

DR. MARSHALL: In this grand campaign for Christ we have representing the Christian foreign missionary society, Rev. B. B. Tyler, D.D., of New York.

DR. TYLER: The Disciples of Christ as a separate people originated in a profound desire to unite God's children for aggressive evangelistic work. The prayer of our Saviour in the 17th chapter of John, "That they all may be one, as thou, Father, art in me and I in thee, that they may be one in us, that the world may believe that thou hast sent me," was the inspiration of this movement. The General Christian Missionary Convention for home and foreign work was organized in 1849. By and by it gave up work in the foreign field, and the Foreign Christian Missionary Society was organized in 1875. The Christian Woman's Board of Missions for home and foreign work was organized in 1874. The Foreign Christian Missionary Society supports now in the foreign field 125 missionaries. This year, notwithstanding the stress of the times, the number of churches contributing to our treasury is 25 per cent larger than ever before. [*Applause.*] Our Christian Woman's Board of Missions has raised and expended more than $400,000, and they have not heard of the hard times. [*Applause.*]

Dr. MARSHALL: The missionary board of the Reformed Episcopal Church will be represented by Bishop Fallows of Chicago.

BISHOP FALLOWS: The Reformed Episcopal Church, as you know, is perhaps the youngest of the churches. It was born when the Evangelical Alliance met some years ago in Chicago — born out of a passionate desire of evangelical Episcopalians to come into closest spiritual contact for the Master's service with all who love our Lord and Saviour Jesus Christ in sincerity. [*Applause.*] Its board of foreign missions, I may say as its representative, most heartily and unequivocally joins with the boards of these great denominations of Christendom in this new movement, this Christan Endeavor missionary extension movement. God bless it! Christ will go with it. [*Applause.*]

DR. MARSHALL: We shall next listen to the treasurer of the Board of Foreign Missions of the Presbyterian Church of the United States, Mr. William Dulles, Jr.

MR. DULLES: I gladly bring you greetings from our board — grateful greetings, earnest greetings, hopeful greetings. You already are doing noble work for us and with us, and I thank you in the name of the Master. In the support of individual missionaries, 725 societies are already grouped, so that there are 29 representatives on foreign fields in our board work representing you and receiving the gifts that you send. The thirtieth group has been begun, and I trust that out of this new suggestion will come many more of these groups. Others of you are giving. New York State leads with 169 societies contributing, giving last year $2,387. In all, last year your societies gave, as far as we can trace the gifts, and we can do it quite accurately, $29,000. [*Applause.*] Let it be multiplied many times. I will tell you again, as you have already been told, there will never come to your societies, never come to your hearts, or to the hearts of any of God's people, the rich, full blessing, until you have reached out to the farthest places, and carried the gospel over land and sea to those in darkness and gross ignorance. May we indeed remember it to-night when in consecration we bow, that we may feel that whatever we are doing we must do with our might, and do always for the glory of our Master. So may we lift up this banner, Christian Endeavorers the world over, Christian people the world over, that this world may be won to our Master, and that the glory of his great kingdom may come in our hearts and in the hearts of those known, unseen, unheard millions, unheard by us, but whose voices even at this moment rise up in appeal to the Master, and through that Master their appeal comes here to you. [*Applause.*]

DR. MARSHALL: The followers of William Penn will be represented by Rev. M. M. Binford.

MR. BINFORD: The Friends' Church in the United States have their various missionary boards, subdivided somewhat after the order of the States. While we may thus lose in concentration, we certainly gain something in the diffusiveness of our system. Our Christian Endeavorers are closely allied with the various missionary boards throughout all our church. The total amounts given for the past year do not seem very large, and yet we are climbing up rapidly toward the one dollar per member for our Endeavorers. [*Applause.*]

This closed the missionary greetings, so far as the tent was concerned. Mr. Shaw then made a number of announcements, included in which was the following:—

MR. SHAW: How many people do you think have come to Cleveland in spite of the strike? There have been registered — those who have actually signed their names — from outside of Cleveland, 18,790. [*Applause.*] In this city of Cleveland, of Christian Endeavorers and their friends, 21,210 have taken the trouble to register their names in order to get admission to these meetings — a grand total of 40,000. If there had been more badges to give out, more would have been glad to register in order to secure admission. [*Loud applause.*]

DR. MARSHALL: We have kept the good wine until now. I introduce to you one who will speak on the inspiring and strategic elements of modern missions, Rev. N. D. Hillis, D.D., of Evanston, Ill. [*Applause.*]

The Strategic Element in Missions.

Address of Rev. N. D. Hillis, D.D.

Last week, when one of the officers of this nation looked down upon a whole body of soldiers confronting a mob of men, he remarked that one Bible and one missionary were sufficient to accomplish more than a hundred bayonets with a hundred soldiers back of them. The other day one of the great leaders of English thought said that modern missions are the Gulf Stream of modern history. One of our great writers has recently spoken of this movement, foreign missionary extension in connection with the societies of Christian Endeavor, as the epoch-making movement of this generation. It was in connection with the word that I am to use this afternoon — strategic, and the strategic element in particular — that the words to which I wish to call your attention were first spoken: "In the fullness of time God sent forth his Son." Now, the fullness of time is the ripeness of time; it is the strategic, the epoch-making time. For the farmer there is an epoch-making time when soil and sun and rain and seed unite in growth in April or May. When once that strategic moment is gone, the farmer finds it gone forever. There is an opportune moment for the man who works as a molder. The iron is cold, and then a little time after it is cold again; but midway between there is an opportune moment when the iron will take its particular set. There is an opportune moment in connection with the sickness of a child or a friend, when the fever passes away, and when the medicine will have its effect. There was an opportune moment in the history of the world, when the old nations were weary, when the Roman language had turned the world into one great whispering gallery, when Roman soldiers were in every city, and Roman judges were in every community — then, in the ripeness of time, "God sent forth his Son."

We are to study for a little while the ripeness of this time, when suddenly God hath brought the world to a great epoch-making moment in connection with foreign missions. First of all, note how God hath broken down all the barriers between the nations. A little while ago every gate was shut, every harbor was locked, the walls were round about the cities; and now, suddenly, all the walls have fallen and every gate is open. Japan used to hate us so that at one time she said, through the lips of her emperor, that if any foreign missionary ventured to set foot on her soil, — yea, if God Almighty ventured to come within the confines of that island, — he would do so at the cost of his head. When the first representative of the English government landed in China, he was compelled to stay in the cellar of a great mercantile warehouse, and there he studied the language for seven years. He tells us how, upon the first morning that he ventured out upon the streets, he saw the wheelbarrows of the scavengers coming out of the alleys laden with little naked female babies, with a cord tied around their necks — strangled to death during the night. If you had gone to certain other nations, like Corea, or the dark continent of Africa, you would have found everywhere trouble, danger, obstacles, enemies, disease, destruction, and death. Now, suddenly, God hath thrown down every barrier; there is a highway into every city; and God hath given us the hearts of the foreign peoples. This represents the first element in the great strategic moment of opportunity for the Christian church in connection with foreign missions.

In the second place, note how, as if to guide that first element, God hath developed the instruments that enable us to enter in. There are no more foreign nations; the great countries are brought near to us. The triple expansion steam-engine brings Liverpool to our doors. Think of telegraphy, enabling one of these treasurers to send the money raised this afternoon, and before to-morrow morning pay it over the counter of some bank in India or in the very heart of Asia! We speak of steam-engines becoming missionaries. Men worship idols; but when you have a steam-engine going through the country, people can no longer worship a little idol of stone or wood. If a man is going to worship any kind of a god, he will worship one that breathes out smoke and flames. So the steam-engine and the telegraph have broken down caste, and are working powerfully in connection with the evangelization of the world. Then there are these wonderful instruments such as the printing-press. How marvelously they are helping! I saw a press the other day that printed 40,000 copies of the Christian Scriptures in a working-day of eight hours, — all done by one man. Consider how the languages have all been changed as barriers to work. There is no language more difficult to learn than the Chinese. You speak of our language as having twenty-six letters, and as difficult of acquisition for some children ; but the Chinese language has two hundred and forty-eight characters, and one of them is made with fifty different strokes of the pen. Now we have four hundred languages and dialects reduced to order, and all manner of books translated and printed in them, — not simply the Bible, but poems, the best works of fiction, of history, of law, and of literature. All this is preaching the gospel to the people in connection with these missions. Not simply are the barriers down, but the great tools are invented and the instruments given into our hands that enable us to carry the gospel to these peoples.

In the third place, note how wonderfully God hath wrought upon the hearts of the young men to enter into the work in connection with this great movement. We have had indirect reference to the student volunteer movement — how many there are of these young men! They do not represent anything except the best brawn, the best brain, and the best culture of our Christian colleges. You ask sometimes who they are. If you should inquire into the foreign missionary movement in Great Britain, you would find there a man who carried off all the honors at Oxford in Semitic languages, who married the daughter of the wealthiest commoner in the House of Parliament, and they two went as foreign missionaries into Arabia, and there laid down their lives after four and a half years of work. If you should go to the center of England you would find there wealthy young men in this movement able to take half a million dollars with them into the interior of China and spend it there for Jesus Christ. Coming to this country, you will find, as Dr. McCosh and President Patton have said, that the best orators, the best classical students, and the most finely cultured students that have gone forth from Princeton University, have given themselves to this movement. They recognize this magnificent opportunity, the crying out of the nations for the gospel, the sudden invention of the instruments that enable us to enter in, and the call of God to them.

In the fourth place, note how suddenly God hath raised up in every one of these peoples one epoch-making brain that capitalizes all that is divinest and best in connection with each one of these nations. Carlyle has said that God always condenses an abstract principle into some one human brain, and lifts it up and flames it forth into all society, so that one man stands for liberty, another for self-sacrifice; one woman stands for temperance, another for Christian Endeavor, another for patriotism, and so on. We learn best by example. Art pupils look at art masters. The young children of generals feed upon the glorious qualities of their parents. We learn, best of all, by looking up to Jesus Christ. God in his providence condensed before Burmah the example of Judson. The magnificent principles for which he stood flamed out all over Burmah. He was at one time sitting at table, and a man slipped in and knocked him senseless. For months he was chained in a mere outhouse. He was placed in a little wooden jail one hundred and twenty feet long, with a roof only twelve feet high, where fourscore other men were confined as prisoners, without ventilation, without any sewerage, in the midst of unspeakable filth, with a lion chained just outside. After three months, when the lion died, his wife obtained permission for him to be locked up in that lion's den. When at last he passed away he had lifted before that people everything that was noble and divine and Christlike. He incarnated Christianity; he translated it, and sent it out to the people. Dr. Duff did the same for India; Africanus for the south of Africa; Dr. John Paton for the people of the New Hebrides; Morrison for China; another is doing it for Corea, and another for Japan. Again and again these men and women have lifted up Christianity, and made it attractive and beautiful and supernal. They have translated Jesus Christ into practical life, and given the people the advantage of their example. That very fact, that Christianity has been condensed at length into one splendid flaming example in every nation, means a great strategic moment for the church.

And, last of all, notice how God, having opened the doors, and laid a pathway into every city, and made the peoples heart-hungry for the gospel, with a great line of contrast between their religions and their social and political condition and ours, and having given to us the instruments by which we can enter in, and having lifted up for us these great examples of splendid Christian manhood, and having laid it upon the minds and hearts of so many young students to enter this work, hath finally given us the money—

money poured into the coffers of the American people. Did you ever stop to think how much this people is worth? Just seven billions of dollars! The steam-engine alone multiplies the power of the men of this country over twelve hundred times. One working-man, with the help of steam, is able to do the work of twelve hundred men. Every working-man in this country has on an average sixty steel slaves working for him, — spinning for him, printing for him, weaving for him, running for him. Suppose we stop and consider how much is our wealth compared with the wealth of foreign peoples. This single nation has money equal to all the wealth of Norway and Sweden and Germany and Russia and Holland and Belgium and Switzerland and Italy and Portugal and Spain and all of North Africa. All this money has been given unto us in lands, in vineyards, in orchards, in splendid husbandry, in magnificent prairies, in great forests. Given into our hands for what? Why, for such a time as this, that, in connection with these splendid forces, we might move out into the world and capture the world for Jesus Christ. And what is the duty of the hour? To meet these strategical elements by giving ourselves first and our money afterwards, that we may immediately match the opportunity by our obedience and our fidelity in entering thereinto.

Now, there are very many of us who, as young men and women, are planning to go into certain lines of work, — some of us as lawyers, but there is a lawyer for every two hundred men in this country; some of us as doctors, and yet I saw the other night two hundred young doctors graduate in the single city of Chicago, and the general health of the community still survived the shock. Now, young men and women about to choose your profession, what shall you do? Go where your brain power will go the farthest. Will you put it in wood? No, put it in iron if you can. Will you put it in butter? No, put it into steel. Will you put it in ice? The heat will melt it. Put it into that which is hard and permanent. The permanency of the material is the measure of the value of your work. Will you put, then, your brain power, your genius, your knowledge, into things that rot, into iron that rusts, into steel that corrodes, into brick buildings that storms bring down and fire destroys? Put it into manhood, into reason, into imagination, into conscience, into faith and aspiration. Put it into the divine elements that make for the future.

When I heard that there are 350,000 people abroad for every Christian man and woman, and that out West there is one preacher to every seven hundred people, I felt like a man out in a great vineyard where all the grapes are plucked within half a mile, and where everybody is running around for a stray grape or a little chance cluster, while half a mile outside the circuit there are great vines laden to the ground with splendid clusters. We are staying at home and picking around the edge, calling it a special providence of God if he converts one or two souls in five or six weeks' time, when on every side there are to be found hundreds of thousands abroad. Too many preachers are like the physician who mixes up tonics for people who are already stuffed. Our churches cannot eat any more gospel bread until they have lost a little of their fat by exercise. The people's garments are saturated with the water of life, and you cannot saturate them any more until they have wrung out some of the water by hard work. That is the trouble in this country. We are doing too little for the amount we are receiving.

And here comes the epoch-making moment for young men and women in connection with their choice or a profession or occupation. Take these people in India, for example. If you feel skeptical about their intellectual caliber, open some of the books representing the work of foreign missionaries among them. Any man who is a lawyer and has studied law-works knows that there is one book that he must always read side by side with Blackstone. It is the work known as "Ancient Law and Early Institutions," by Sir Henry Maine. It consists of lectures delivered by the professor of law in the missionary university at Calcutta that was founded a little more than sixty years ago. This indicates the quality of brain they have. This shows the largeness of the work for the college educator, for the journalist, for the writer, for the splendid brain among the rank and file of life. There never was a diviner opportunity than this, when the doors are opened, and the instruments invented, and the peoples hungry, and the money given, and 4,000 young men and women in the volunteer movement ready to go. It is God's epoch-making hour; it is the ripeness of time. God sent his Son, and ordered all the world to make a forward movement; he has sent another ripe time, an epoch-making age, when now at length the battle of Gog and Magog is on, and upon our fidelity and consecration and gifts and prayers shall depend the issue of this splendid opportunity.

May God write the principles upon our hearts, teach us obedience to what we know to be right, open our pocket-books, consecrate our children, consecrate ourselves, and teach us all that the great strategic moment of advance for foreign missions has come, when we are to take the world with a noble Christian civilization, and enthrone Jesus Christ in the home, in the street, in the market, in the forum, in all the cities and villages of God's round world that has been redeemed by Jesus Christ, until at length he that was lifted up on the cross shall put his arms around the world and lift it up to his Father, redeemed by his blood into the likeness of himself.

After Dr. Hillis's inspiring address, which was frequently applauded, the audience sang the missionary hymn, "Speed Away." At Dr. Marshall's request all then resumed their seats, while he offered a brief prayer and pronounced the benediction.

SUNDAY EVENING.

The last session of the great Convention, the consecration service, always attracts the largest audience of the week. Many of the delegates, in anticipation of this fact, did not return home at the close of the afternoon service, but remained either at the hall or the tent until the hour for evening service. So many were there of these prudent ones, that a good-sized song service was in progress at the hall as early as 5.30 o'clock. Soon after the crowd began to rapidly increase; and it was not long before both auditoriums were completely filled, and late comers had to be referred to the overflow meetings which were held at the Epworth Memorial and Woodland Avenue Churches.

Saengerfest Hall.

Half an hour before the time of service Mr. Foster appeared on the platform and gave direction to the singing impulses of the congregation, which had hitherto been entirely spontaneous. "Jesus, Lover of my Soul," "Jesus, Saviour, pilot me," "Scatter the Sunshine," and other favorite hymns were sung. A very beautiful effect was produced by singing the hymn, "Bringing in the Sheaves," in sections, one part of the audience singing one line of the refrain, another, another, and so on, the whole congregation joining in on the closing line. The chorus was then repeated softly, with marvelous impressiveness. After this Mr. Foster thought the audience would enjoy a few moments of rest, but the delegates were irrepressible. Some one started the hymn, "Beautiful Zion," and immediately all joined in and sang as if they hadn't sung for a week. Opportunity was given, however, for the Cleveland Male Quartette to render a selection, "This is the Gold Seed-time," which was highly appreciated. Mr. Foster reminded the audience of the invariable rule not to indulge in applause on the evening of the consecration service, but to confine all demonstrations of approval to the waving of handkerchiefs. This was at once accepted by the delegates. "At the Cross" was then sung superbly, and again Mr. Foster waited. The audience had no use for "Quaker pauses," however, but started "O Saviour, hide Me," and sang it through splendidly. President Dickinson concluded not to wait any longer for the schedule time to arrive, but called upon Bishop Fallows to conduct the devotional exercises. The One Hundredth Psalm was read responsively, and Bishop Fallows led in prayer.

The committee on resolutions next reported through Rev. W. H. McMillan, D.D. The resolutions, which were unanimously adopted, were as follows : —

"*Resolved*, That the thanks of this Convention are hereby given to the Cleveland Committee of 1894, to the pastors and churches, to the city officials, and all others who have aided in making these exceptionally complete arrangements for the comfort and success of the Convention.

"*Resolved*, That the thanks of the Convention are also given to the public press for the full and acurate reports they have published of our proceedings, and especially for their earnest editorial indorsements of the purposes and work of the society.

"*Resolved*, That it was with especial satisfaction that we received our welcome to Ohio from the lips of her Christian Governor, who, being himself a faithful servant of the Lord, was able to express a sincere and ardent interest with us in all that is done for Christ and the Church.

"*Resolved*, That we recognize the sale and use of intoxicants as the greatest evil of the times, and the chief enemy of the physical, moral, and spiritual well-being of man; and we hold ourselves pledged, as Christian Endeavorers, to seek the utter overthrow of this evil, at all times, in every lawful way.

"*Resolved*, That we reaffirm our solemn purpose to remember the Sabbath Day to keep it holy; that we regard its right observance as essential to the civil and religious interests of man; and that we resist, to the utmost of our powers, the mighty efforts now being made by the enemies of God to desecrate and utterly secularize the Lord's Day.

"*Resolved*, That we accept as timely and important the suggestions contained in our president's annual address, concerning special lines of Christian Endeavor effort during the coming year, and it will be our purpose to carry them out in our work.

"*Resolved*, That we note with special pleasure the presence of so many representatives of our denominational missionary boards, and rejoice in the rising tide of missionary enthusiasm. We heartily indorse the plan of the Christian Endeavor Missionary Extension Course, and pledge our hearty co-operation in carrying it to success.

"*Resolved*, That we extend to our beloved President and leader our tenderest sympathies in his present affliction, and assure him that our prayers shall continually be offered that his life may be spared and his health restored, that he may be long continued in the place of special usefulness to which the providence of God has called him.

"*Resolved*, That gratefully recognizing the providential rise, development, and possibilities of the Endeavor for Christian citizenship, we commend to all our societies the appointment of a committee to secure the arousement, instruction, and co-operation of their members, churches, and fellow-citizens in the effort to secure civic righteousness, industrial peace, and the social unification of their respective communities, and that their work in behalf of Christian citizenship may be so done as to be an incentive to and expression of that power with God which alone can give us power with men, and is to be secured only through united prayer and personal consecration.

"*Resolved*, That in the face of present distrust and recent breach of human relationships, we reaffirm our faith in the future, our confidence in the law-abiding and liberty-loving spirit of the people, our unshaken trust in the Christian solution of present problems, and our abiding hope for the coming of the kingdom of God on earth.

"*Resolved*, That we reassert Christ to be the center of social unity; his righteousness to be the only basis of industrial peace; his cross of self-giving in service to be the only means of social solution; his church to be his mediator for the reconciliation of men; and his spirit in human hearts to be the only power adequate to maintain or establish the brotherhood of man in the coming readjustment of human relations.

"*Resolved*, That we will seek and will respond to opportunity to co-operate with all individual and organized efforts to promote civic righteousness, industrial peace, and social development.

"*Resolved*, That we recognize a popular educational propaganda in Christian social economics to be one of the most pressing needs of the hour. We therefore recommend to the editor of *The Golden Rule* the publication of monthly studies in Christian citizenship, supplemented by lesson leaves, which shall be adapted to Christian Endeavor Societies in training their members for social service and in spreading the principles of Christian citizenship among the people."

Two verses of the hymn "Blessed Assurance" were then sung, after which President Dickinson introduced, as the preacher of the sermon, President B. P. Raymond, D.D., LL.D., of Wesleyan University, Middletown, Conn. As President Raymond came forward, he was greeted by a hearty salute from the Connecticut delegates. He spoke as follows: —

Sermon by Pres. B. F. Raymond, D.D., LL.D.

TEXT : "To every man his work." (Mark xiii. 34.)

This text needs to be read three times, and peculiarly emphasized each time. First of all, "To every man *work*." That is nature's law. Every atom in this universe of ours is wonderfully active. Again, we may read it and say, "To *every* man work." No one may be excused. It would be a misfortune to any man if society were to excuse him. It would be worse than a calamity for any man to excuse himself, for that means a process of decay and death at the very summit of his being. Or we may read it, and that is really the climax of the text, "To every man *his* work." In the emphasis upon that word "his" the individuality of the worker is emphasized.

I propose to speak this evening on the culture of the spiritual unit in this conquering host. There are two sides to this theme. One is the external side of our work. But you have been hearing about that in every gathering since you arrived here. Your work along the lines of Christian citizenship, in the way of reform, and in every other way, has been set forth, and it will be hardly necessary for me to emphasize that side of your work. I do not know whether I shall reach it at all or not. But I am not going to lose my opportunity on this occasion to say a word about the culture of the individual, for the great army is made up of individual men and women. And, by the way, the text ought not to read, "To every *man* his work;" for if you will look into the original itself, or into the revised version, you will find that it says, "To every *one* his work;" for the Scriptures recognize the fact that woman has something to do in this world of ours.

The individual is in peril in this age in which we live. He is in peril in the vast lines of industry and manufacturing interests. In the olden time, before the division of labor, a man did a great many things, and gained an outlook on life in many directions; but when the making of a pin is divided up into a dozen different parts, and each man does one insignificant, infinitesimal part, week in and week out, and year in and year out, there is peril to that man's spiritual life.

There is peril in the crowd in which we live. When the fist of calamity smites one of our little group of half a dozen, we feel that we, too, are attacked; but when the brazen fist of calamity comes down upon some individual man or woman in the crowd yonder in the great city, who thinks of it, or of its significance, beyond the passing instant when it may be read in the daily news? And how easy it is for us to lose our sense of individuality and responsibility when we get into a crowd! We measure the unit of force, in this age of ours, by horse-power. I read the other day, in the newspaper, that 18,000,000 cubic feet of water, falling 300 feet over Niagara Falls, generates 10,000,000 horse-power. We estimate the power of things by the amount of horse-power to which they are equivalent. But we must not forget that there are some things in this world of ours which can neither be weighed on hay-scales nor measured by horse-power. The Lord Jesus Christ chose not horse-power, but man-power. The man or the woman who incarnates something of the divine life and love of our Saviour is the unit for work in his kingdom.

Now, I have great respect for Niagara Falls; but I stand here to-night for the individual man, — the man who can turn this Niagara flood into power to run the machinery of the noisy industries of Buffalo, or transform it into motor power for transportation purposes in Syracuse. The man who can transmute Niagara's cold flood into the furnace, heated seven times hotter for the smelter's purpose, or can temper our luxuriant palaces against the cold north-west blast of the winter time, the man who by pressing a button can change this dark flood into rivers of electric light to illuminate the dark streets traversed by our law-makers in Albany, is the real force. I have great respect for great Niagara; but I take off my hat to the man who commands, and Niagara listens, hesitates, and obeys.

The Lord Jesus Christ made no mistake when he chose for his unit of power the man and the woman.

I wish, then, as I try to emphasize this thought this evening, that this mighty army of Endeavorers whom you represent might take into consideration the subject of their own personal culture and growth; for the work that the army does depends upon the culture and elevation of the men and women who make it up. Given an army of slaves or mercenary soldiers, such as Xerxes drove at the end of the lash across the Hellespont, and they amount to very little; but given a body of men and women with trained intellects, pure hearts, a righteous purpose, and a consecrated will, and the army we already have is "remnant" enough to carry Isaiah's hope to the uttermost parts of this world.

We have peculiar advantages for Christian culture, and the unfoldment of our personal life. The Lord Jesus Christ seemed peculiarly anxious to show himself in every aspect of his character to his disciples. He did not make very much of a success in gathering multitudes about him. He had no such army of followers, when he left this world, as that which is gathered here this evening. But, as some one has said, he spent much time with twelve men; and I would like to go farther and say that he spent much time with three men — an inner circle to whom he communicated his truth and sought to show every aspect of his character. If you look through the history of the church you will find the old Greek church fathers trying to get some conception of him from a philosophic point of view, and they formulated a mighty creed; much work was done by them that will never need to be done again, though not of great value to most of us. The early fathers in the Roman church took up the same subject, and they sought to formulate the thought of the Christ and the character of the Christ in the old Latin terminology. They carried Christ into the forum; and the result is that we have a lot of legal terms running down through the centuries that do not begin to tell us of the significance of the atonement, and of the meaning of the nature and of the character of the Lord Jesus Christ. It is sometimes the case that a theology gets itself incarnated or incarcerated in a word, and that word perpetuates some false view of the truth through long centuries. Then the Scholastics came on a few centuries later, and they thought they could shut it all up in a syllogism; but you cannot hide life in a syllogism. We have peculiar advantages in our age for coming to a true understanding of the Lord Jesus Christ; and while I believe in mathematics, and wish every Endeavorer could have a thorough collegiate course in mathematics, in science, and in the classics, for the results that would come to them, still I am well aware of the fact that the culture which you need for your work is that culture which comes from contact with and knowledge of the Lord Jesus Christ. Our advantage is, that we are coming to look at the Christ through the historical sweep of his work, not through the terminology of the old Greek philosophy, not through the terminology of the Roman lawyer, or through the syllogism of the Scholastic.

Now let me turn for a few minutes to that thought — the sweep of Christ's work. Paul the apostle tells us that all things revolve around the Christ. Go to his Epistle to the Galatians, and you find him assuring you that everything moves forward toward the fullness of the time when Christ should come. Go to the Epistle to the Ephesians, and you find him pointing to the time when all is to be summed up in him, and he is to be Head over all. Go to the Epistle to the Philippians, and you find that every knee is to bow, and every tongue is to confess him. Go to the Epistle to the Colossians, and you find that in that epistle Paul relates the whole cosmos to the Christ. Go to the Epistle to the Romans, and there you find that the whole creation goes groaning and travailing on, reaching out after the coming of the Son of man. And Paul's thought is formulated really by his experience, and by his training in the Old Testament Scriptures.

Go back to the very earliest chapters in the Book of Genesis, and you read there that mysterious passage about the seed of the woman that shall bruise the serpent's head. We speak of that as a kind of first gospel. I suppose, as you have read it, you have said to yourself, "I see nothing in that that looks like the gospel of the Lord Jesus Christ." We sing, —

"See, from his head, his hands, his feet,
Sorrow and love flow mingled down,"

and we put this old mysterious promise and that hymn alongside of each other, and we say that they do not look at all alike, they have no relation to each other; but that is a superficial judgment. You may go out into the forest and pick up an acorn; and as you look at it you may say to yourself, "I see nothing in this that looks like an oak." You may put it under the microscope, and there is no root or trunk or branch or twig or leaf to be found there; and you may say, "I do not believe that it has anything to do with the oak." But put it under the conditions that nature has provided for it, and ere long you find it manifesting itself; and after a few years there it stands before you on the hillside, and you know that that acorn had to do with that oak. Or go to the mountain side, and take the eagle's egg and study it. You may put it under a microscope, the most powerful instrument that was ever made or ever will be made, and there is no eagle there. You may say, "I do not believe that this egg has anything to do with the eagle." But provide the conditions which nature has provided for it, and ere long you find the parts, as the scientist says, beginning to specialize themselves; and in a few weeks you have your eagle floating above his native crag, and you know that that egg had to do with that eagle.

Precisely so the word of God is a growth, an unfoldment of a series of germs; and if you follow along to study its unfoldment you find ere long God calling an old man to come out from his native land and go to a land of which he knows little or nothing; and as the night draws on and he bows down to worship, the Almighty says to him, "In thy seed shall all the families of the earth be blessed." That, I think, is one of the most remarkable communications that is made in the whole Word of God. That, my friends, will stand against all higher and all lower criticism. When you pass back along the line which the old prophets have made for us until you reach the ninth or tenth century before Christ, far above the whole level of criticism, you find them looking back into that dark past and laboring at the problem which was developed in the covenant made between Abraham and Jehovah; they carried forward the unfoldment of that problem toward the Christ. But look at the particulars a little. The Almighty did not leave the promise there. In a little while Abraham became discouraged. He did not see how this promise was to be realized, and God said to him, "Go out and count the stars of the night." Again he became discouraged; and the Lord said to him, "Go out and count the sand by the seashore; so shall thy seed be." In the course of a few years that old promise, either implicitly or explicitly, is given to Abraham and his descendants some twelve or fifteen times. It looks to me like the mother heart of the Almighty coming down to this man and this family, determined somehow to sing this old song of hope into the heart and life of Abraham, that it might become the song of hope for all the world.

And we strike three distinct lines of development. The one may be called the prophetic line, the line of the teacher — for the prophet was a great teacher. Moses said that the Lord God would send them a prophet like unto himself, and that prophet they would hear. Now, it is not altogether clear whether an individual prophet is referred to, or whether a line of prophets is intended. The context looks as though a line of prophets was intended. In any case, the line of prophets came to them, and proved to be inspired men. They knew the will of God, and they continued to communicate and teach that will to the people. But the night passed by amid many vicissitudes, and at length we rise to the height which Isaiah has reached, and from his point of view the future is clear; there is no difficulty in understanding who that great prophet is who is to come at last, and be the teacher of all the nations of the earth.

But the people desired a king, — this gives us another distinct line of development, — and the prophetic mind begins to brood over that idea of a king; and as the successive kings come and go they are looking out to discover if they are the ones who are to realize the promise of the King to rule Israel and bless the world. The years pass by, and you do not know always exactly where you are in the Old Testament history; but when you have risen to the time of David and his Psalms, and to the time of Isaiah and his songs, and look out from that period into the future, there is no difficulty in determining who it is that is to fulfill that expectation concerning the Messiah who is to rule over all the nations of the earth. No other man rises in all history that dares for a moment to assume that he is the fulfillment of these expectations of the old prophets.

Just one more illustration of the line of thought running through the Old Testament Scriptures. You do not read very much in the Book of Leviticus, do you? You think it a very dry book; and to some extent it may be. And yet you know that deep down under the sands of the desert are sometimes found the sweetest springs of water. So in this old Book of Leviticus, there is a line of revealed truth that moves toward the future. Take those sacrifices that relate to sin. Take the scapegoat as an illustration. One of the things that the people needed to know above all others was that sin could be forgiven. That is a difficult truth for us to receive; it was far more difficult for them. They selected a scapegoat; and a man chosen for that purpose confessed the sins of the people over the head of that goat, which was then sent away into an unknown land, as though it could bear their sins away, never to return. That was the supreme truth which that people needed to know if they were to be the bearers of revelation to men; and to put that truth in that way shows the profoundest knowledge of the true method of teaching; for we are just coming to the method that underlies all the ritual and ceremony of the Book of Leviticus. Let me illustrate. In the early history of our country it is said that one of the Indian chiefs made up his mind to declare war upon the settlers; and he took a rattlesnake's skin and filled it with arrows, and brought it into the settlement. It was not necessary for him to go through any very long explanation as to the significance of that dramatic act. The settlers took the rattlesnake's skin, and filled it with powder and ball and returned it. Do you think they needed to explain the meaning of that act? Or take another illustration. It is said that old Commodore Esek Hopkins, in the early history of our nation, before the Stars and Stripes had been settled upon, constructed a flag and floated it above his vessel. In the center was a pine-tree; underneath was a coiled rattlesnake, with head erect and tongue extended, and underneath the rattlesnake were the words, "Don't tread on me." Do you think that it was necessary to send a diplomat to England to explain the meaning of that flag? Now, this way of putting truth before the eyes of men was the method which God adopted with these old Israelites to teach them the doctrine of the forgiveness of sin, and to anticipate, in this vague way, as they were able to receive it, the Coming One, who should atone for the sins of the world. But however obscure may have been the meaning of those old ceremonials to the Jewish mind, as you move forward under the tuition of the prophets, you come at last to the sublime passage in the fifty-third chapter of Isaiah. In that revelation he grasps the whole content of revelation by the root, and out from that chapter immediately arises the song of victory. Israel is called upon to sing, to spread abroad and possess the nations.

I say, then, that, as we look along these several lines of development, from that germ in Genesis, along the lines of prophecy, of the history of the kings, and of the sacrificial system, we see the whole movement steadily reaching on toward the hour of the Christ. Standing now, with these thoughts before our mind, by the side of that chapter in Genesis, I think we ought to have no difficulty in singing,

"See, from his head, his hands, his feet,
Sorrow and love flow mingled down;"

for God has given to us in the Book of Revelation some eighteen centuries of historic illustration of the mighty forces that move forward toward that sublime culmination.

And now, my friends, I want to point you to another illustration in secular history. Starting in at the time of the Christ, when the old Roman civilization was going to pieces, it seems to me to be of marvelous significance that just then and there the Christ stood up with his disciples to organize the new and the coming civilization; for so he did. But the dark ages came again, and it seems as though the truth could not live. The fires of persecution are kindled against the representatives of the faith. Huss of Bohemia, and Savonarola of Florence, are burned.

But the truth was saved by a body of young men trained in the schools of that time. They were taught to think. The schools were organized for the purpose of proving that the dogmas of the papish church were rational. They did not succeed, but they taught men to think. Emerson has said, "Beware how you let loose a thinker into this world." As the result of their thinking, the whole atmosphere of that age was surcharged with Protestant thought. Sometimes, when an iceberg comes floating down toward the deep sea, it seems so solidly anchored in the deeper currents that nothing can disturb it; but as it goes on its journey southward the warm waves wrap themselves around it, and little by little the center of gravity is changed, and suddenly over it goes. The warm waves of Protestant thought are thus changing the center of gravity in the dominant church of the fifteenth century in Germany; and if you could have looked up through those years you might have seen a mount, and on that mount a man, standing with the Word of God in his hand and holding it aloft. That man is Martin Luther, and that book is the Bible: the inspiration of the new civilizations went out from that center, passed on to England, and Christ came to the front again, in new power for the conquest of the world. To master these achievements of Christianity, to get the sweep of the prophet's thought, and see the dominance he has in the progress of the great civilizations, is to attain a culture which will secure us against all the currents of superficial criticism. We shall be made strong in him and for him.

It is supposed that this world of ours is somehow very strangely hostile to the supernatural. Suppose we had an eminent geologist here this evening, and suppose we could induce him to go back over the history of the past, and teach us all he knew about geology in five minutes. He takes his geological hammer along, and he goes down through the various strata of rock, until he comes to the oldest, and says, "These are called the azoic rocks." Why are they called azoic rocks? "Because there is no life here; that is what the word means." He passes on a little, and comes to the lowest form of life, and then on to another period, and he says, "This is called the Devonian Age, or the age of fishes." What are we to think of that age? "Why, we find it just a little developed beyond the earlier life, a little more complex, interacting with its environment at more points." Then he carries us on to the Carboniferous Age, when the great coal strata were laid in; then on to the Reptilian Age, with life a little more highly developed and organized; and then on to the age of mammals and of man. Now, if any scientist wishes to shut himself up to the narrow line which he is cultivating, of course he will find it hostile to the gospel of the Lord Jesus Christ; but we never see anything truly when we isolate it. To isolate any Scripture text is to misinterpret it. To isolate any view of the universe is to misinterpret it. We exist in relations; the whole universe is made up of relations. If we view this process of development as it is represented in relationships, then it has quite another lesson. The geologist may say to us that it is five hundred thousand years from this azoic period up to man. If he so say, it seems to me to be only an argument five hundred thousand years long, every link of which reaches on toward the Christ. If he choose to call it five millions or five hundred millions of years, I am unable to see that it makes a bit of difference. The argument is only so much the longer; and every one of these wonderful creatures that goes stalking over the rocks of the old Devonian and Reptilian periods seems to me to stand upon its tiptoes and say to its successors, "Stand upon my shoulders, and behold the Lamb of God that taketh away the sin of the world," because the march is steadily through all these long æons of time, from the azoic period up to man, and from man up to the divine man, Jesus Christ.

Now, these phases of thought touch many of the popular objections of our time, and some of the more serious objections. I commend to you the study of the subject of human history in its relation to the Christ for the personal culture of your intellect, and your faith in him. It is the first business of every Christian to grow. We must cultivate our affections. The Scriptures teach us that we are to set our affections on things above. God has set forth his love and his character in such a way in the Christ as to draw out our affections toward him. Just as the æsthetic nature responds to the beautiful in nature, and needs only to be directed toward it, so the higher affections are called out by fixing them on the Christ. He is set before us for the very purpose of calling out our love for God. Look to him for the culture of the affections as well as of the intellect.

The will is to be trained by obedience to the law which Christ expressed, when he taught his disciples that he came not to be ministered unto, but to minister. The central law of life is Christian service. The gospel is thus related to the whole man, intellect, affection, and will. Our first work is to make the most of these powers for Christ.

I turn aside now to say one word with reference to our external work. You are organized for Christian work. What is the meaning of the individual unit in the organization?

God waits for men and organizations. The Almighty waits for fitting conditions in which he is to do his work. Did not the Lord Jesus Christ teach us that there were places in which he could do no mighty work because of their unbelief? Turn back to the Old Testament Scriptures and you will find that it took about twenty-five hundred years to make the first book of the Bible, a book that you can read through in an hour or two. There was not enough of revelation given in those twenty-five hundred years to make a book that would last you two hours. But then the Lord God brought his people into the promised land, and organized them, and then the prophets began to appear.

The communications are now no longer sporadic. The message that came from the Almighty to the prophet went out through the scribes and the priests to every synagogue in every little village throughout the length and breadth of the land; and from that synagogue the religious significance of that communication was communicated to all the people in the community. Not only so, but the teaching of the prophet went to the judge who sat at the gate to adjust relationships between man and his fellow-man; and the teaching of the prophet became the precedent in his code for the administration of justice among the people; and we are just getting around to this idea, that God's law and the gospel somehow must come into Christian citizenship. From the great religious festivals the people went back to every corner of the land; and in every drop of their blood beat a new enthusiasm for the realization of the hope that had come to their father Abraham. We ought to bear with us just such an enthusiasm from this religious festival.

As the result of the organization of Israel into a national life, within the next few hundred years we get a book that the ages have been reading for nineteen centuries, and it has not been read through yet; and when all of the infidelity of the world shall have been buried forever, when the pagan monuments and the heathenisms of the Oriental world shall have been long forgotten, this old book will be the study of Christian men and women, and still will live on to inspire the faith of the ages that are to come.

God waits for organizations. Would it be too much to say that the Almighty waited for this organization? I think not. I think the history of the past will justify me in saying that there is an aspect of truth in the thought that God waited for you. For was he not in at the birth of this organization? I look at these organizations not simply as representing the Endeavorers to-night; I look at them, rather, as epoch-making, as a worldwide movement in their significance; I look at them as the quickened heart-beat of the young Anglo-Saxon blood of this Western world. Did you ever marshal this army, and study its significance? Go back just fifty years, and take the Young Men's Christian Association, and see that splendid organization as it has gone out into the world to tackle the forlorn hopes in our great cities. Or take the rise of the Chautauqua movement, which is another means of training the young people for the work of Christ. Or take the organizations in the other churches, such as the Epworth League, and we may add the Sunday-school; for it is on the same line, and deals with the same class of people. Did you ever think of this army, millions strong, marshaled for a common cause? How shall we explain it? Shall we explain it by saying that Dr. Clark brought together a few of his young people to pray and to talk about Christian work? Why, you might as well seek to explain the origin of the Reformation by saying that Martin Luther had a little quarrel with the Pope, and the Reformation followed! What about the tidal wave of Protestantism that rolled its resistless current over that whole continent, — over France and Italy and Bohemia and Germany and the Dutch Republic and the Netherlands, and then crossed the channel and invaded England, and unlocked her rusty cathedral doors, and made its way up into the glens and lochs and mountain fastnesses of old Scotland? Is that to be explained by saying that Martin Luther had a little quarrel with the Pope? Oh, my brethren, we must learn that God is in this world of ours! We are just getting back to the old philosophy of the prophets. If I were to name four of the most eminent philosophers of the past fifty years, and to ask them what is their theory of the relation of God to this world, they would all stand up and say, "In him we live and move and have our being; he upholdeth all things by the word of his power." God is in this world of ours, and in these movements of our time. You might as well attempt to explain the birth of our republic by saying that the people of Boston emptied a cargo of tea into

Boston Harbor. Does that explain the birth of our republic? No, no. Our very soil was fecund with forces that wrought, Titan-like, to lift this young republic to the level of a national life, and invisible hands reached down from on high to pull us out of our tutelage and make us a nation. Nothing but the most abject cowardice on the part of the men of that time could have saved us from being a nation. No; God is in this world of ours, and is carrying forward its history in national life, and in ecclesiastical life as well.

So I say, these organizations, this splendid army before us to-night, which represents millions of other young people, are a part of God's plan; and in these organizations these individual units are to find opportunity to make the most of themselves; for only as we put ourselves into relation with the forces about us can we make much of our work. A man standing alone on the Western prairie cannot accomplish much; but just as God has filled this world with coal and oil and electricity, and has made it possible for man to connect himself with all these agencies, and so make himself mighty, so he has surrounded us in these organizations with a spiritual environment, and we jostle on every hand against spiritual forces that are mightier far than the forces which Elisha saw. They come to us to create high ideals as to the meaning of our life. They come to us to awaken courage and give us strength for work. They touch us to kindle enthusiasm for the cause. The common blood of Christian life circulates in all of our veins, and with it all we are related to the Lord Jesus Christ as the center and source of our power. God has called these organizations into being for the culture of the spiritual unit, and also for the purpose of making that unit effective in the Christian work of the world.

And as these organizations have meaning for the individual, so they have meaning for the world. This is my closing thought. The world was waiting for these organizations. The church was not doing its work on this question of Christian citizenship, in the lines of reform, quite as it ought to have done, and God has called you to take up that work. And the missionary spirit which has taken possession of you points to the conditions which are already being provided for you in the foreign land. The millions of China and India stand waiting for you; and I think that if by some magic process we could get telephonic communication with the whole heart of heathenism, its heart-beat would say, "Show us the Father; bring to us the Christ: we are waiting for this gospel that saves."

I congratulate you on the history of the past; if you are loyal to yourselves and your own spiritual development, you will be loyal to the work which Christ gives you to do in the world. Growth and work forever go together. May the blessing of God be upon you and make you in the years to come a thousand-fold more mighty than you have ever been in the past!

The delegates expressed their appreciation of President Raymond's sermon by a generous Chautauqua salute. The Cleveland Male Quartette then sang a selection, "One Sweetly Solemn Thought," after which the audience rose and joined in singing, "Jesus, Saviour, Pilot Me."

Rev. J. T. Beckley, D.D., then presented a resolution with reference to the absence of Dr. Clark, which he had been authorized by the trustees to draw up.

Dr. Beckley: Fellow Endeavorers, God has given us a great and blessed Convention. How wonderfully his hand has guided us and guarded us in all these gatherings, so that no harm has come to us! The absence of our leader has been a great disappointment to us. It is said that every institution is but the lengthened shadow of a man; and I have felt that Christian Endeavor in its beautiful spirit embodied the spirit of our leader, for it seems to me that God has seldom given to any man a finer, sweeter, stronger soul than he has given to Dr. Clark. And now it seems eminently fitting that in the closing moments of this Convention we should hold him in special memory. So I ask you to pass this resolution: —

"*Resolved*, That we send to our President the expression of our deep and abiding love, assuring him how keenly we have missed his presence, which has always been one of the benedictions of these great conventions; and how sincerely we pray and fervently hope that he may be speedily restored to the most vigorous health. Thankful to the heavenly Father that he has used him to inspire one of the mightiest movements of modern Christendom, we invoke upon him utmost blessings."

The resolution was adopted by a rising vote, accompanied by the enthusiastic waving of handkerchiefs. Prayer was then offered by Prof. Howe of Louisville, Ky.

DR. BECKLEY: I want to say this word further, that, in the absence of one leader, God has raised up another, a man of like spirit. We know how devotedly he has watched over this Convention, how admirably he has presided and how his own spirit has pervaded it. Now I feel that, as we close this Convention, we will all want to say to Mr. Dickinson, "We thank you;" and so, every Endeavorer who wants to say that, please wave his handkerchief.

The whole audience responded with a most vigorous salute. Mr. Foster then sang a solo, at the request of the choir, entitled "In the Secret of his Presence." He was given a cordial greeting.

Consecration Service.

MR. DICKINSON: We have now come to the superlative moments of this great Convention; we have come to the summit of our mount of privilege; and if we be filled tonight with the spirit of these meetings, I am quite sure that we shall see the transfigured Christ, and that we shall go away from this beautiful city with transfigured lives. "Out of the abundance of the heart the mouth speaketh." I have three things in my own heart to-night which I must speak out, and very briefly. First, I have felt inexpressibly sad and lonely through all this Convention because of the absence of one who has been present during the whole series of these great meetings excepting this last one. My eyes were filled with tears to-night while Dr. Beckley was speaking to you, and it seems fitting that I should say to you that my sorrow is a personal one. For more than twenty-five years I have known and loved Francis E. Clark ; for more than twenty-five years we have been bosom companions; and during all these years, while I have known him and loved him, I have ever found him true and loyal, sincere and faithful, brave and determined. He is a grand man, and God has sent him to fill a great place in this last half of this nineteenth century. I have been sad because he is lonely in his own home on the Atlantic coast, sending telegrams and letters to us, expressing his deep interest in this great Convention, and telling us how all day he is praying for all of these Endeavorers. I have here his consecration message to the more than 40,000 people who are gathered in Cleveland to-day in the name of Christian Endeavor, his consecration message especially to you who are here to-night in this hall. Dr. Clark says:—

"While you have been learning many lessons of hope and cheer, I have been trying to learn my lesson from the providence which keeps me away from the one place where I most long to be,— a lesson of patience and willingness to bear as well as to do God's will. I trust I have learned it. May this consecration meeting which closes the Convention be the crown of all the glorious meetings that have gone before, and during its progress may you every one see Jesus and commune with him. My message is from Colossians ii. 5 and 6: 'For though I be absent in the flesh, yet I am with you in the spirit, joying and beholding your order and the steadfastness of your faith in Christ. As ye have therefore received Christ Jesus the Lord, so walk ye in him.'

"With sincere affection,

"FRANCIS E. CLARK."

I remember so well the first Convention of Christian Endeavor. It was held in the Williston church, in Portland; and I remember how Dr. Clark stood up before that little body, numbering hardly one hundred and fifty, expressing his thanksgiving to God for the work that had been done in that church during the year, and personally reconsecrating himself to Jesus Christ, never even dreaming of any such convention as this, never even dreaming that Christian Endeavor in a little while would be larger than the State of Maine, ay, larger than New England and the United States. This Convention he was especially anticipating, and I know that our hearts go out with that resolution to him; and the supreme wish of every one here to-night is that he may speeedily recover.

With this feeling of sorrow there is also a feeling of thanksgiving in my heart to-night. I thank you every one for the co-operation and the forbearance which I have received at your hands during the sessions of this Convention. My heart goes out in gratitude to the Committee of '94, to Dr. Tyler, Mr. Cheesman, Mr. Darsie, and all of the efficient members of that committee, who have done so much to make it a pleasant thing for us to be here in Cleveland. My heart goes out in gratitude to this chorus, and the members of the orchestra, who have done so much to add to the interest of these great meetings; to all of these ushers, who have helped so efficiently in controlling these great congregations and in adding to their convenience and comfort; to these members of the press, who have been unsparing in their efforts to publish in full all of the details of this Convention, giving us better reports than we have ever had before; and to the hospitable people of Cleveland, for their open doors and their open hearts. But more than all this, my dear friends, my heart, and I know your hearts with mine, goes out in thanksgiving to Almighty God, that, in spite of all the disappointments which we anticipated, in spite of all the hindrances which we apprehended, some of which we have experienced, many of which we have not experienced, — in spite of all our fears, he has made this Convention one of the grandest conventions of the whole series. Without doubt this has been in many respects without its equal in this series.

And one other thought before I leave the meeting with you. It is a sincere desire, born of this meeting, that I may make a new consecration of myself to Almighty God, a new and larger consecration of what I am and have to him. I have been thinking very much of the great truth that the miracle of Immanuel which we hear about in the first part of the Gospels is still going on here among us to-night. It is a continuous miracle. It began when Christ came into the flesh, when he, the divine Son of God, became incarnate. It entered its second stage on the Day of Pentecost, when God took possession of human hearts and made his dwelling there, and it has been going on ever since whenever a heart has been open to receive him. Immanuel God with us. This is the great truth, it seems to me, of the Gospels, the truth around which all other truths swing. "Ye are the temple of God." And this is what Paul meant when he said, "For me to live is Christ;" "Christ in you the hope of glory," and to his Corinthian church you remember he said, "Ye are the body of the Lord Jesus Christ." Christ working in and through us; let this be the key-note of our thought and of our prayer to-night, that we may live Christ as we go out from this Convention, that we may take the magnificent thoughts of the sermon to-night into our lives, and make them part and parcel of our very souls and of our characters; that we may go out to work for Christ wherever he may call us.

And now it is simply impossible for us all to speak out of the abundance of our hearts to-night. I know there are thousands who would like to stand up and give testimony for Christ, and who would like to say what this Convention has been to them; but of course, there being so many, we are obliged to make some arrangement by which a large number may express themselves representatively. So the congregation has been divided into States and Provinces, and I am going to ask the various States to take part in this meeting as the roll is called.

At Mr. Dickinson's request, a number of sentence prayers were offered by ministers on the platform, after which the roll of States was called, the various State delegations rising in a body, and responding with a verse of Scripture or a hymn.

ALABAMA: "Bear ye one another's burdens, and so fulfill the law of Christ."

ALASKA: "Born in heathenism, yet saved by Christ, Alaskan Christians send greetings and good wishes to this Convention, which has now come to a close. A good work has begun in our country, and by the help of the Almighty we will keep it going. Come over and help us. 'Whither thou goest I will go; thy people shall be my people, and thy God my God.'"

ARKANSAS: "Behold, how good and how pleasant it is for brethren to dwell together in unity."

CALIFORNIA: "We are but a band of feeble folk, yet we have made our home in the Rock; and although the American Railway Union would not permit California to come in force to the Convention, we hope and believe that, in spite of the General Managers' Union, the Convention will come to San Francisco next year. We hardly feel competent to speak for the State, inasmuch as we represent only one-twentieth of those who proposed to come; but speaking in the spirit of the State convention held but a little while ago at Riverside, I can voice the consecrated spirit of California, perhaps, in two ways. First, deepened earnestness to make the life of each Endeavorer to be the utterance, not of self, but of Jesus Christ. 'I am crucified with Christ, nevertheless, I live, and yet not I, but Christ liveth in me.' Second, the passing through enthusiasm into practical energy. 'I must work the works of him that sent me while it is day.' And over all the sunshine of our blessed State." Delegates singing. "There is sunshine in my soul to-day."

COLORADO: "We shall return and try to lift ever higher and higher that emblem which nature has so beautifully placed on the side of one of our famous mountains, the Mountain of the Holy Cross."

CONNECTICUT: "'This one thing I do,'" etc.

DELAWARE: Hymn, "Though your sins be as scarlet."

DISTRICT OF COLUMBIA: "Come with us and we will do thee good." Hymn, "Our fathers' God, to thee."

FLORIDA: "He that dwelleth in the secret place of the Most High shall abide under the shadow of the Almighty."

GEORGIA: Scripture verse.

IDAHO: "Idaho did not come to the Convention in force, but she expects to return in power."

ILLINOIS: State song, "Glory, hallelujah, for Christ we'll win the world," accompanied with the waving of flags, and responded to by the whole audience.

INDIANA: Hymn, "More Love to Thee." Dr. Darby of Indiana led in prayer.

IOWA: "We believe in the truth of Christ Jesus, and it is making us free."

KANSAS: Song, "We can hear the Saviour calling."

KENTUCKY: "Kentucky is making progress. Those who came through the perils of the railroad will return to stand more thoroughly for Christian Endeavor than ever. Our motto is, 'Kentucky for Christ and the Church.'"

LOUISIANA: "We claim Louisiana for Christ. 'I will say to the north, Give up; and to the south, Keep not back,'" etc.

MAINE: "Behold, how good and how pleasant it is for brethren to dwell together in unity."

MARYLAND: One verse, "Send Showers of Blessing." "All things work together for good to them that love God."

MASSACHUSETTS: A delegate: "The Massachusetts delegates last year pledged themselves to do all in their power to each bring at least one soul to the Lord Jesus Christ during the year. They propose to double their efforts this year; and, with the help of God, each will try to bring at least two souls to the knowledge of Christ. We have faith to believe that at the next convention we can report success in our efforts." (Delegates joining.) "I can do all things through Christ which strengtheneth me." One verse, "Bringing in the Sheaves."

MICHIGAN: "I can do all things," etc. State song, "We are the Michigan Army of Christian Endeavor," to the tune, "What a Wonderful Saviour."

MINNESOTA: "I know whom I have believed, and am persuaded," etc. Hymn, "Gathered with the Saints in Glory."

MISSOURI: Pledge repeated. State song, "Keep the Flag Flying."

MISSISSIPPI: "Let the words of my mouth," etc. Ps. xix. 14.

MONTANA: "As the mountains are round about Jerusalem, so the snow-capped mountains of Montana surround many earnest Christian Endeavorers, who are working that that magnificent State, with her veins of silver and gold, shall be given to Christ and his Church."

NEBRASKA: "Create in me a clean heart, O God, and renew a right spirit within me." Hymn, "Dear Jesus, I long to be perfectly whole."

NEW HAMPSHIRE: Hymn, "I consecrate my life to thee."
NEW JERSEY: Each delegate with Bible uplifted. "Thy Word have I hid in my heart, that I might not sin against thee."
NEW MEXICO: "The voice of one crying in the wilderness, Prepare ye the way of the Lord." Hymn, "Hold the Fort."
NEW YORK: "Ask what ye will, and it shall be done unto you." Two verses of State song.
THE CHOIR: Hymn, "Consecrate me now to thy service, Lord."
NORTH CAROLINA: "The land whither we go to possess, it is a land of hills and valleys. By God's grace we will win North Carolina for Christ."
NORTH DAKOTA: "There is no State in the Union where hearts beat more warmly for the Christian Endeavor work and movement than in North Dakota. I am glad to say we are growing in North Dakota, and the work is progressing rapidly. 'Pray ye for the peace of Jerusalem; they shall prosper that love thee.'"
OHIO: "Let your light so shine before men." State song.
OKLAHOMA: "Though the fig tree shall not blossom, neither shall fruit be in the vines; the labor of the olive shall fail, and the fields shall yield no meat; the flock shall be cut off from the fold, and there shall be no herd in the stalls; yet will I rejoice in the Lord, I will joy in the God of my salvation."
OREGON: "Oregon will greet you with two thousand delegates at San Francisco. I hope to carry the enthusiasm of this Convention over these plains and mountains, and down into our fertile valleys. Our motto is, 'Our city for Christ, our county for Christ, our State for Christ.' We can do all things through Christ which strengtheneth us."
PENNSYLVANIA: "Pennsylvania for Christ." Declaration of principles. One verse of "All hail the power of Jesus' name," waving the State flags in closing.
RHODE ISLAND: "Remember now thy Creator in the days of thy youth."
SOUTH DAKOTA: "We are looking upward and trusting. Our motto is, 'Our State for Christ.' We hope to carry back the enthusiasm of this Convention to our cowboys, our miners, and our farmers."
SOUTH CAROLINA: "Behold, God is my salvation. I will trust, and not be afraid."
TENNESSEE: "Tennessee for missionary extension and good citizenship." State song, "Where he leads us we will follow."
TEXAS: "If God be for us, who can be against us." State song to the tune, "Blessed Assurance."

"This is our burden, this is our plea;
Texas for Christ our motto shall be;
Praying and working only to see
Texas to Christ in love bow the knee."

UTAH: Song, "Bringing in the Sheaves."
VERMONT: "I am not ashamed of the gospel of Christ," etc. Hymn, "What a Friend we have in Jesus."
VIRGINIA: "Lord, I am thine, entirely thine." "The Old Dominion for Christ."
WASHINGTON: "Five thousand Endeavorers in the State of Washington send their greetings to this Convention. They ask that on your journey to San Francisco, one year from this time, you will go by way of our State, and leave us a double portion of your spirit, so that we can say with the Psalmist, 'Bless the Lord, O my soul, and all that is within me, bless his holy name.'"
WEST VIRGINIA: "Let the words of my mouth," etc. Hymn, "My Faith looks up to Thee."
WISCONSIN: "What shall we render unto the Lord for all his benefits?" etc. Hymn, "But Drops of Grief can ne'er repay."
CHINA: "'Behold, these shall come from far: and lo, these from the north and from the west; and these from the land of Sinim.' Christian Endeavor has increased in China this year until we now have a national Christian Endeavor Society meeting in Shanghai. We have no doubt but that China shall be won for Christ and the church."
FLOATING SOCIETIES: Hymn, "Jesus, Lover of My Soul."
CANADA: *A delegate,* — "The Christian Endeavorers of Canada wish to thank the Christian Endeavorers of the United States for the great hospitality shown to us since we came among you. Already our hearts are annexed in the great Christian Endeavor movement." (*All the delegates.*) Hymn, "Just as I am."

Greetings were received from : —

ADELAIDE, South Australia.
WELLINGTON and AUCKLAND, New Zealand.
BRISBANE, QUEENSLAND, Australia.
CONGO FREE STATE, West Africa.
OSAKA, Japan.
BATH, England.

REV. N. BOYNTON, LONDON, England.
SANTIAGO, CHILE, South America.
MADAGASCAR.
MONROVIA, LIBERIA, Africa.
PARIS, France.
JERUSALEM.

Mr. Foster then started the hymn, "Blest be the Tie that binds," and the whole audience rose and sang the hymn amid the waving of flags and handkerchiefs. The scene was a very beautiful and impressive one.

MR. DICKINSON: I remember very well standing on the platform of the great Exposition Building in St. Louis beside Dr. Hoyt, after we had listened to Mr. Mills's sermon and to the testimonies of consecration, and he remarked to me, "This sight moves me to a passion of tears." After the benediction was pronounced, away over in one corner some one started the beautiful hymn, "Alas, and did My Saviour bleed." I remember how that song, started by a single voice, began to roll over the congregation in a mighty tidal wave of harmony, until it seemed fairly to dash up on the platform where we stood. Down through the aisles, out into the corridors, out into the dark streets of St. Louis, the thousands of Christian Endeavorers went singing, "At the Cross." I never shall forget the impression it made upon me. Let that be the song of your hearts and of your lives, "At the Cross." Stay at the cross and work, impelled by that mighty power, during all of these coming months. "To every man his work," says Dr. Raymond. How many are there here to-night who feel that a part of their individual work during these coming twelve months will be to try to bring at least one soul to Jesus Christ? How many are ready to raise their hands as a solemn pledge that, God helping them, they will try to win one soul to Christ? [*Hands were raised all over the audience with hardly an exception.*] This means that if this purpose of yours is carried out thousands of souls will be saved; for the Lord God will help you carry it out.

Now let us all bow for just a moment in silent prayer, and I will ask Dr. Hoyt to lead us in a closing prayer, after which I declare this Thirteenth Convention of the Society of Christian Endeavor adjourned *sine die*.

After a moment of silent prayer, Dr. Hoyt led in prayer, closing with the benediction. The audience then rose and joined in singing the parting hymn, "God be with You till We meet Again." Then all repeated the Mizpah Benediction, and the Convention was adjourned. But again some one started the hymn, "At the Cross," as the delegates turned to leave their seats, and again the hall was filled with the melody of the beautiful song while the audience dispersed. It was carried out into the night; and as the long line of street-cars carried away their crowds of delegates, the echoes of this hymn were heard.

THE TENT.

SUNDAY NIGHT.

The crowd on Sunday night began to gather early, the different delegations singing different hymns as they came in, all apparently anxious to get the most out of the last and best session of the Convention. Finally the choir drowned their voices with "Never say Good-by."

Secretary John Willis Baer presided over this meeting; and Rev. M. L. Berger, pastor of the Park Congregational Church, opened the meeting with prayer.

MR. BAER: I have pleasure in introducing the Rev. A. J. F. Behrends, D.D., pastor of the Central Congregational Church, Brooklyn, N.Y., who will preach the sermon.

Sermon by Rev. A J. F. Behrends, D.D.

I ask your attention to-night for a little while to certain thoughts suggested by the Scripture that you will find recorded in the Gospel according to Luke, in the ninth chapter, at the thirty-third verse. It is part of the description of our Lord's transfiguration before the three disciples, Peter, James, and John; and the words are these: "It came to pass, as they departed from him, Peter said unto Jesus, Master, it is good for us to be here: and let us make three tabernacles; one for thee, and one for Moses, and one for Elias: not knowing what he said."

It is very easy to criticise Peter; but I think if you or I had been there, we should have felt just as Peter did. It had been a long and a wearisome day. The journey up the mountain-side had been hard, as all mountain climbing is. I have no doubt that they greatly enjoyed the rest and the quiet of the summit of that hill; and, when the glorious vision appeared, it seemed to Peter that it was infinitely better to tabernacle upon the mountain with nothing but the open sky for his roof, if only the Master and Moses and Elias could bear them fellowship, than it would have been to go back into the valley and to live there in the palaces of the kings. But it was not so to be; for at the very moment when Peter made his suggestion, there at the foot of the mountain was an agonized father, who had brought his lunatic child to the disciples that Jesus had left behind, and he was waiting with anxious heart for the return of the Master, in order that his boy might be restored to physical soundness and mental sanity. Jesus felt — and this is what I want you to remember if you remember nothing else — that the place where he was needed was the place where he ought to be. It was a hard climb, I have said, up that mountain slope; but it was a harder thing to go down into the valley where sin and suffering were, where misery and wretchedness pained the eye and burdened the heart. And Peter, toward the close of his life, learned the lesson of the Master, and was content to be where he was needed, though the vision of that mountain glory and the memory of it were an inspiration to him all the rest of his life.

Now, my dear friends, for the last few days you have been having your transfiguration experiences; you have come up here to this mount of privilege from all parts of this great land; the atmosphere of heaven is the air that you have breathed; you have tented under God's blue sky upon this mountain-top of opportunity; and to-morrow morning will begin — I will not say the long and wearisome journey, but the rapid journey, downhill into the valley where the common experiences of life and the drudgery of every-day service will be crowding themselves once more upon your minds and upon your hearts. Perhaps some of you are saying to-night, "Let us build here our tabernacles; though it be a tent, it is better for us to live here than to go back into the places whence we came." But no, my brethren, no, my friends; the places where we are needed are the places where we ought to make haste to go. This mortal life of ours, with its few and fast-fleeting years, was not intended to be for you and for me a haven of rest, but an opportunity for service. By and by the coronation shall come, by and by the silver trumpets shall ring out their coronation hallelujahs, by and by we shall wave our palms and shout our victories; but to-day, and every day until life closes for each one of us, is meant for earnest, enthusiastic, aggressive, and unceasing action. The great world needs us; and we should go down from our mount of privilege like this, carrying with us something of the enthusiasm of the hour, the better to be furnished for the work to which life summons us.

Now, there are these contrasts and contradictions in our life, in every human life, — the mountain with its peace, with its ethereal atmosphere, with its restfulness, and the valley with its weariness and want. You and I are called upon to make our choice. What shall be our choice? If we choose both valley and mountain, if we are unwilling to part with either, then the question comes, How shall we hold them in just relation to each other? There are four ways open to us.

In the first place, you may make up your mind that you will not have anything to do with the mountain anyhow, that it is all a useless task to ascend to the summit, that you will be content to make your home in the valley, — in other words, to live in the world and live for the world, and to live for the world only and all the time. Or you may choose to make the mountain summit your home; that is to say, to give your time and attention and energy to what we call the salvation of the soul, to make your religion first and second and last and uppermost, and to be utterly indifferent to the things that are going on in this busy, workaday world. Or you may say, "I will have two residences; I will have one in the valley, and another on the mountain summit," just as some people flit from the city to the country, and never are at rest anywhere. Or you may say, "I will carry the glory of the mountain into the deepest and darkest shades of the valley, and I will make it my business, so far as God gives me opportunity and it lieth in me, to transfigure this earth into a heaven." What shall it be?

Surrender to the world and indifference to the world are the extremes; and of these extremes the first is the easier, apparently the more natural — to be indifferent to eternity, or to heavenly things, or to the demands of God in his service, to let all thought and energy be wrapped up in the things that perish with the using. I say this is the most natural thing to do, the easiest thing to do; the most natural, because it requires the least degree of resistance.

Yet, when I say that, I check myself and I say no; it is the most unnatural thing in all the world that a man can do, to live only in and for the life that now is, because that will be most sure to starve and shrivel all that is best and noblest in him. The men and women that live only for what they can get in this world, for the riches that they can amass, for the pleasures that they can enjoy, for the popular applause they can win, are the men and women toward whom my heart goes out in infinite pity. They know not what they are doing, the tremendous sacrifices that they are making for the flitting joys that last only for a moment. I recall the conclusion of an Old Testament writer, who, personifying himself as a great king in Israel, tells us that he marched over all the pathways of pleasure, and through all the avenues of popular applause, and again and again as the conclusion of his experience, he wrote this epitaph, "Vanity of vanities, all is vanity." I have known a good many men and women, who, having come to threescore years and ten, immersed, saturated, in the joys that mortal life can give, have said at last, "It does not pay." It never has paid.

After all, the soul that you are is infinitely nobler and greater than the whole world in which that soul finds its temporary abode, and where it receives its temporary discipline and schooling. And this is the kingdom that you and I are to subdue, a greater task than that to which ever Cæsar or Napoleon or Alexander set his hand. This is the globe whose contents you are to master, whose mines you are to search for wealth, whose seas you are to explore for pearls, whose vast acres you are to cultivate, until they become radiant in divine fruitfulness and beauty. The longer I live, the more settled is this my conviction, that every man makes his own hell, and every man makes his own heaven; and not all the forces in heaven and in hell combined can damn him if his own heart within him speaks the absolving and the saving word. Yes, I tell you it is true that the whole race of man is incompetent either to crown you or to discrown you. Every one of us must weave his own crown, or we shall never have a crown. The sweetest words that can breathe their celestial music into your hearts are not the words that other people speak into your ears, or the words that other people speak of you to others, but the words that your own soul speaks to itself, the words that in the silence of secret prayer God whispers to your waiting ears when he says, "Well done, good and faithful servant, enter thou into the joy of thy Lord."

I say, then, that the man is foolish who says, "I will live only in the valley, I will have nothing to do with the mountain summit; let other people climb the mountains if they want to, I don't want to." You are surrendering your royalty, all that is best and noblest in the life with which God has gifted you.

"Well," I can hear somebody else say, "for myself, then, I will have nothing to do with the valley; I will make my home upon the mountain summit; I will have nothing to do with the world: I will be indifferent to it; I will treat it as the enemy of my soul's salvation." My friends, that is not a new suggestion; it is a philosophy almost as old as the history of the human race. The history of the Orient is packed with the attempts of men to secure sanctity of life by the destruction and the defacement of the body, and even into our Western religions this idea has crept, that we must go to fasting, and to watchings, and to flagellations, in order that the body itself may be reduced to slavery, so that it shall not resist the higher instincts of the soul. And what is the history of that theory of religion? It does not need a very large amount of knowledge of history to answer the question. It has filled the earth with monasteries and convents and religious retreats. What has been the result? Your ascetic in every case has become a glutton and wine-bibber. Your mystic, whatever his reveries of divine contemplation, has at last become guilty of the grossest acts of sensualism. The body that he tried to enslave has mastered him, and has brutalized his soul. No, you cannot starve the body into subjection, you cannot fill the veins and arteries with healthy blood if you refuse to breathe the pure air of heaven. I say to you, young men, drink and eat, and sleep on a comfortable bed, the most comfortable you can get; and, if you do that, you will be able to keep the body under a great deal more easily than if you attempt to ignore the laws that God's own hand has written on nerve fiber, and on muscle and artery and vein, and upon every organ of your physical organism.

It is an utterly impossible thing for a man to refuse to have anything to do with the world. Why? Why has this attempt of religion that has regarded the world as an enemy always failed? The answer is a very simple one. Because every man of us carries the world with him wherever he goes, in these hands and feet, in this head and heart, in this body of ours, which some men in the name of religion have undertaken to defile, and to treat with contempt; and that body goes with you wherever you go, into your seclusions. You may bar and bolt the doors where you pray, but the body will be a hanger-on, from which you cannot be delivered; and so it is with what we call the world. The domestic ties, the social relations, the industrial occupations, the political institutions of life, are not things concerning which any one of us can say, "I will be indifferent to them;" for we ourselves are the outgrowth and the product of them. They are there in spite of us; and they shape our lives, whether we will or no. You may say, "Well, I am not going to work any more; I am going to give all my time to praying." Suppose everybody should do that! We would soon starve, should we not? so that there would not be anybody left to pray. So the simple fact is, if you want to pray, you will have to work too; and if you do not work, somebody else has to work, in order to make it possible for you to pray. You may say, "I do not care what becomes of society; let anarchy run riot; let the red flag wave; let the law be trampled under foot; I am going into my spiritual retreat; I am going to live on the mountain summit; I care nothing for the valley." Yes, but somebody else will have to take care of the valley, or you will not have any mountain-top on which to live. There must be men to build the churches; and, to have them, there must be men that follow the plow, and keep the factories busy, and that are intent, day after day, for six days in the week, upon their secular toil. You may say, "I will live in the valley, and I do not care anything for the mountain-top." But it is impossible for any man to say, "I will live only on the mountain-top, and have nothing to do with the valley." You can have a valley without mountains, but you cannot have mountains without valleys. When the valley recedes, the mountain goes with it; and your religion collapses the instant you secure universal indifference to the prosaic things that concern this earthly life.

Well, what shall we do, then, to be true to ourselves? It is plain that we must treat the world as it deserves to be treated, and we must not be indifferent to the higher spiritual welfare of our souls. What shall we do? Well, we can have two homes, one in the valley and the other on the mountain-top; and every once in a while we can put on our pilgrim suits, and say, "I guess it is about time for me to leave the valley and spend two or three days on the summit of the mountain."

There are not a few people that divide their lives in that way, by artificial lines; so many hours, so many days, so many weeks, perhaps, to be spent in things that concern their religious welfare, and all the rest of the time they are utterly forgetful of God and their religious obligations. But a life like that is a broken life. You may say, "I will pray every morning, I will keep the Sabbath conscientiously, I will enter with all possible zeal into the annual revivals of religion; when the days are short, and when business is dull, then I will begin to think of God, and get myself a little better prepared for death, and for what comes after death." That sort of thing is a great deal better than indifference. I believe in revivals of religion; but I tell you my heart is always pained when I think that men think of God and turn their attention to their spiritual welfare only when business is bad, and when the days are short. I am firm in this conviction, that revivals as we now know them, a series of occasional emotional outbreaks, mark a transitional period in the history of the church of Jesus Christ. We are going to outgrow them one of these days. Then it shall be just as natural for a man to be religious as it is for him to eat and drink; then the confession of Jesus Christ will be just as natural a thing for a man to make as for any of you to confess, and to be proud of the fact, that you are a citizen of the American republic. We shall come to that conception of religious duty one of these days, and then our revivals will be steady and continuous.

Now, I believe in regularity in religious habits, just as I believe in regularity in everything else. No business man can succeed if he is irregular in his business habits. No man that counts religion to be of any worth can make his religion a thing effective for himself, or effective for others, unless he puts the principle of regularity into his religious life. But set times for prayer, the religious and conscientious observance of the Sabbath Day, keeping it holy — these religious habits must grow out of a continuous life that never has either ebb or flow, but which is as steady as the pulses of my wrist and the beating of my heart, or else this will come to pass: by and by the man will get tired of putting on his pilgrim garments to make another ascent of the mountain, and he will say, "Well, it does not pay; I will stay in the valley." We must find some other way of bringing the mountain and the valley together, something different from the relationship of occasional contact. What is it?

I can put it into a single word. Suppose we try this plan and method. Let us carry the glory of the mountain into the darkness and dreariness of the valley; let us do all that we do, eating and drinking and toiling, to the glory of God; let us enter into the wide sweep of that magnificent vision that Peter had on the housetop, when the sheet from heaven was let down with all manner of four-footed and creeping creatures in it. When God said to him, "Arise and eat," Peter said, "Lord, nothing unclean has ever entered into my mouth;" and the voice from heaven came, "What God hath cleansed, call not thou unclean." I tell you, friends, there is nothing mean in this world, there is nothing unclean in any of its relationships, there is nothing degrading in any of its tasks, however humble they may be. Every one of them, through the fiery and devoted energy of a sublime consecration, may be touched and be made to glow with the radiance of heaven itself. Bring the glory of the mountain down into the valley.

I have said you cannot get rid of your body; you are in it, and will have to stay in it until you die and get the body of the resurrection glory. What then? I will keep this body pure, so help me, God; I will make this body the instrument of a pure heart and of a cleansed spirit, so that it shall render service unto Him that made it and intrusted it to me. You are in the world, and you cannot get out of it. What then? Why, make the world an instrument of righteousness wherever it is possible for you to do it.

You know that the landscape gardener converts the primeval forest into a lovely park, with vast stretches of lawn and shady retreats. He does not begin his work by leveling all the eminences and by filling up all the valleys. No, no; he says, "Let the configuration that nature has given to these broad acres remain; I will make my paths wind in and out and over that chasm; I will throw a bridge over that trickling stream; I will preserve all; yes, the freaks of nature I will use for artistic effect." Cataracts and waterfalls and caves and rocks and cliffs — all these he uses deftly in order to enhance the beauty of his art. He might say, "Nature has done everything wrong, is working against me;" but no, he says, "These are features that I can work into a more comprehensive and varied plan, so as to give a larger beauty to the works of my hands." My dear young friends, there is nothing in human life that is not divine, that cannot be made to glow with divine beauty; nay, it is divine in its essential constitution; it is divine if men only will not mutilate it. It is because we make such bad work that we turn the forests of God into deserts, instead of converting them into celestial parks, the Edens that by and by shall blossom into the Paradise regained.

Some of you I presume, many of you probably, have followed the flight of the seagulls in the wake of a great ocean steamer; and you have noticed that they never fly in a straight line; they make long, circling sweeps, and their broad pinions are almost motionless, simply swaying hither and thither, and compelling the force of gravity, that would draw them down into the sea, to do their work for them, sending them on their path. They might say, "This force of gravity is my enemy, and pulls me downward;" but no, the instinct of the sea-gull teaches him better. Without that force of gravity which would pull him down into the sea as into a premature grave, there would actually be no leverage for the use of his muscular energy. Thus, I say to you, the things that seem to be against you, under God are the things that are for you. It is your business as a rational being, it is your business as a son or daughter of God, to make these environments and these tremendous energies that seem to be dragging you downward, momentous ard mighty for giving you added zeal, added enterprise, and increased success.

So I say, let us make this choice. "Our conversation is in heaven," said one of the apostles. That word "conversation" ought to have been translated, and is translated in the Revised Version, "citizenship." "Our citizenship is in heaven." Remember that. But while your citizenship is in heaven, your residence and your work are on the earth. Remember that too. Remember that the mountain and the valley are very close together. It does not take a day to go from one to the other. The natural and the supernatural do not merely impinge; they are concentric circles or spheres. The earthly and the heavenly are always close together; the one overlaps, pervades, and permeates the other; and the earthly ought always to have its root in the heavenly so that the energy of the heavenly impulse in your soul ought to be the directing and the glorifying force by which you take hold of and transfigure all that is terrestrial. Where does your religion call you? To the drudgery of your every-day work, whether it be in the kitchen, or in the schoolroom, or in the counting-room, or in the councils of empire, — I care not where it is, wherever God in his providence has put you to do your work as a man among men, as a woman among women, there, however lowly the lot, however humble the task, there is the place to exhibit your divine courage and patience and faith and zeal and hope. Oh, what a world this will be when the glory of the mountain is carried into every valley of the death shade, until every burden becomes a crown, and every sorrow is changed into a flashing jewel, and every grave becomes the monument of a divine and imperishable victory! God grant that it may be so with every one of us!

The resolutions were then read by Rev. Rufus W. Miller of Hummelstown, Pa., and adopted by a rising vote. Next came a cornet trio, by the Park Sisters, with piano accompaniment, rendering "Nearer, my God, to Thee," in a very beautiful and touching manner.

Consecration Service.

SECY. BAER: With hearts full of gratitude to God for so many mercies and blessings, all crowded into four or five days, it will be a difficult thing for you and me to return proper thanks, or to express from our hearts all that we feel in these closing moments of this great Convention. Praise God for the committee and its consecrated work. Praise God for the citizens of Cleveland, well known through all the world for their homes and their home comforts, and they have freely shared them with us during these passing days. Praise God for the great numbers that have come to this wonderful gathering, the largest that has ever been held in the series of great conventions, and this in spite of the fact that the country was disturbed in many ways. Praise God for all the teachings that have been given to us by the earnest and eloquent speakers from these platforms. Praise God for their having stirred our hearts to a deeper appreciation of the fellowship of meetings like this. Praise God for the thought that we have had that you and I can be helpful in winning the boys and girls for the Lord Jesus Christ, and that our Junior army, marching along in large numbers, can be strengthened and increased by our loyal service. Praise him again for all the good thoughts that have come to us along the line of missions. As the fields have been emphasized over and over again, may we go to our homes and our societies, and not only pray for missionaries in the field, but that some of us may be among the recruits that shall go; and more than that, that every one of us shall have a certain part in helping our missionary boards to raise money, so that next year our missionary money will be not less than one million dollars. Praise God for all the incentives along the line of good citizenship. You and I will go now to the primaries of our parties better instructed how to vote.

I would ask you, as I ask myself, again to stand in the presence of my Maker, and to be true and honest, or not to say one word.

There is one to-day by the seashore in New England who has missed this Convention, and you have missed him more; and it is pleasant for me to read a greeting from Dr. Clark, which came yesterday, and he asked that it might be read to you in the closing consecration service. Every one of us looks to him, not only as a leader, divinely led of him who is leading us all, but as one who is a deep, earnest, personal friend. And so I will ask you to bow your heads in silent prayer. May there be ten thousand prayers to God at this moment, that he will speedily restore to strength our beloved leader, Dr. Clark.

The audience bowed in silent prayer, after which a greeting from Dr. Clark was read by Secretary Baer.

MR. BAER: Let us all reach out as we never have before, ever looking to our divine Leader, and work and pray, that ours may be a more evangelistic movement than it ever has been before. May the coming year bring hundreds of thousands into the churches of our land.

The roll-call of the States came next. Each delegation arose as its name was called, and repeated words of consecration or sang a hymn. The delegations having been divided, the responses were similar to those given in the hall.

Overflow Meetings.

The Epworth Memorial M. E. Church was crowded to its utmost capacity with an audience which failed to find room in either of the main places of meeting. Many, too, were turned away from this church, and the Woodland Avenue Presbyterian Church was opened for a second overflow meeting. Both meetings were deeply interesting. Dr. B. B. Tyler of New York preached at the Epworth Memorial Church, and the consecration meeting which followed included a great number of personal testimonies. The meeting at the Woodland Avenue Church was entirely in the hands of the young people, and was carried on in characteristic Christian Endeavor fashion. Brief addresses were made by Mr. John Buchan and Mr. John Sencebaugh, members of the church, and all who attended the meeting enjoyed it greatly. Special services were also held in many of the Cleveland churches, presided over by members of the Board of Trustees of the United Society, or by visiting pastors; they were all largely attended.

WHAT THEY SAY.

The Greatest of All.

THE convention was an entire and most happy surprise from beginning to end. It was held under unprecedented difficulties. There was the great disappointment and loss caused by the absence of the president and founder of Christian Endeavor. There were the great strikes, that detained thousands of delegates and many speakers. Yet, in spite of these hindrances, the convention was in many important respects the greatest in Christian Endeavor history. Its numbers were unsurpassed. Its enthusiasm was never equaled. Never was a Christian Endeavor convention so thoroughly satisfactory. From no previous convention have the attendants gone away so well pleased and so greatly blessed. That Christian Endeavor could hold such a convention, under such circumstances, is the clearest possible proof that the movement is founded on a rock, and rapidly lifting gigantic walls toward heaven. The news from Cleveland, as the press and the returned delegates carry it throughout the world, will fire Christian Endeavor hearts everywhere with fresh ardor. And surely this news will operate as an incentive to wider and deeper endeavor, during the coming months, throughout the entire Christian Endeavor world. Christ's followers will treat every success merely as the vantage ground from which to conquer more success, every advance merely as the argument for further advance. So let our song arise: "More work for Christ! Better work for the church! Forward march, Endeavorers, into a glad, strong, faithful new year of Christian Endeavor!" — *The Golden Rule.*

We Forge Ahead.

THE Christian Endeavorers got to Cleveland, just the same, in immense numbers. A little thing like a railroad strike doesn't discourage a Christian Endeavorer from going ahead and accomplishing his purpose. This characteristic accounts in a large measure for the magnificent success of this organization. — *The Boston Herald.*

The Convention and the Strike.

IT may seem like a "far cry" from Chicago to Cleveland, from the great strike which so signally failed in the closing hours of last week to the great Y. P. S. C. E. Convention, which in the last half of last week achieved such a magnificent, stupendous, and auspicious success. But the two events are not wholly devoid of relation one to the other; for it is certain that if the objects that are aimed at by the latest and greatest of significant religious movements were to be speedily accomplished, there would soon be an end of man's inhumanity to man, of envy, malice, greed, lawlessness, of the bitter brood of passions from which spring, on the one side and on the other, such scenes as those at which mankind stood aghast when the Chicago mobs were doing their evil work. — *The Boston Advertiser.*

A World Influence.

FEW conventions of Christian workers call forth greater interest than this one. Not only is it important as being composed of the young men and women of the churches, but on account of the high character of the work which the organization represents. The young people's societies are, indeed, to some, not free from objection because of the novelty of the movement, and because of a feeling that they are governed within themselves, and not entirely amenable to the control of the sessions, yet these very objectors have nothing but good wishes for the members, and if their approval be qualified, the qualification itself springs from kindness. And, moreover, we are getting more and more accustomed to the innovation; and it is safe to say that the better the work of the societies is known in its wider scope, as a world influence, the more apparent becomes the great good accomplished. — *The Presbyterian Review.*

A Vast and Vital Power.

A VAST number of Christian people have come to look upon these annual conventions of the Christian Endeavor Society as one of the most important, if not *the* most important and interesting religious gathering of the year. These meetings bring together the youth of the churches, the flower of the army of Christ. They represent the most hopeful, most enthusiastic, and the most aggressive elements of the evangelical denominations. They stand for unity, for work, and for advancement along all lines of Christian activity.

While the conventions have no legislative powers and no authority of any kind over the churches represented, their resolutions and expressed desires carry great weight and have an important influence with the Christian community. The Endeavor movement is a vast and vital power on the side of all that is best, truest, and purest in Christianity, and it cannot grow too large or stay in the world too long. — *The Christian Work.*

Marching Orders from on High.

No convention ever met under more adverse conditions and forbidding circumstances than this convention of Christian Endeavorers. The whole system of traffic and travel was practically paralyzed, and notwithstanding the fact that the frenzied agents of this outrage upon the country stepped aside with bowed heads before the advance of this splendid army, in unconscious acknowledgment of the supremacy of the Christian principles which they were violating, it seemed almost impossible that this vast multitude of young Christian soldiers could reach their destination at the appointed time. But difficulties and dangers melted away at their approach, and their very presence seemed to have the effect of "oil cast upon troubled waters." As with Israel of old, the waters withdrew at their coming, and "they passed over dry-shod." It seemed that their gathering, at this opportune moment, was by the appointment of Providence, and that their marching orders were directly and literally "from on high." — *The New York Mail and Express.*

For Missions.

IT is interesting to record that at one of the conferences on missions over one hundred young men and young women pledged themselves to go out as missionaries to the foreign field. Equally pleasing as an incident of the gathering is the fact that on Saturday morning the trustees of the United Society held a meeting on board of a yacht belonging to Mr. White, of Cleveland, who took the trustees and the representatives of the mission boards of the several denominations assembled at the convention for a twenty-mile sail. During the trip plans for a united aggressive movement in missions were discussed. It is expected that the outcome of this conference will be initiative of a great and important series of operations against the forces of evil the world over. — *The New York Observer.*

A Remarkable Gathering.

Our Forest City has just been the scene of one of the most remarkable gatherings of human beings in modern times. It was not a political convention, drawn together by the desire for the spoils of office. It was not a mediæval crusade, bent on a futile and purely sentimental mission, to rescue an empty tomb from vandal hands. It was not a martial host called to battle with shot and shell. It was the International Convention of the Societies of Christian Endeavor, the representatives of over two million young people who, in the last thirteen years, have been organized for Christian work in this one organization. — *The Evangelical Messenger.*

A Megatherium.

Big? The word is feeble. It is immense, stupendous; it is the megatherium of conventions. The most that is possible is to give a few impressions of such things as one man can see or hear; for such a convention is like a great battle,— no one man sees it all, or can tell its whole story. — *The Examiner.*

Even the Beer=Garden.

The Committee of '94 receive words of praise on every hand for the admirable manner in which the arrangements for this convention have been managed. The city is gay with white and yellow, the colors of the Cleveland Union; they are seen everywhere, from the large convention halls and churches to the express-cart and the movable peanut-stand. We even noticed a beer-garden theater decorated with Christian Endeavor banners, and the colors that stand for courage and purity; but this is only carrying out the Christian Endeavor spirit, which has the courage to enter even such places as these, and purify them in the name of "Christ and the Church."— *The Interior.*

The Attraction.

The multitudes were drawn to the city by the lake through their personal attachment to Christ and his church. There were no honors to be distributed, no position or material gains to be acquired. Love to a single person, the matchless Christ, was the impelling influence. — *The Lutheran World.*

The Singing.

Singing, cyclones, avalanches, landslides of singing. Singing on the train en route, on the street-cars in Cleveland, in the hotels, in the halls, everywhere there were Endeavorers, and such songs! Multiply a good solo by 12,000, and add the inspiration and enthusiasm of the occasion, and you may form some idea of what the singing was. — *The Cumberland Presbyterian.*

More About the Singing.

We cannot close without speaking of the singing. The choruses at the Tent and Saengerfest Hall consist of one thousand voices each, and all the people sing. Waves of melody burst forth on either hand. One part of the vast audience, then another, takes up the song, and song and response swell back and forth, and it is grand beyond description. — *The Christian Advocate.*

What, Indeed?

IN view of all these hindrances the remark was made over and over, "If *this* is a Christian Endeavor Convention under unfavorable circumstances, what would it have been without these obstacles?" — *The Christian Standard.*

An Offset.

SURELY this is a remarkable showing, and a wonderful testimony to God's blessing upon this world-wide movement. An army of more than two millions. More than six hundred thousand converts in the thirteen years. Over against anarchy, bitterness, and all pessimism we put this great fact. An Englishman sitting by me when Governor McKinley was received, and when his patriotic utterances were applauded to the echo, remarked in surprise, "I had no idea there was so intense a patriotism in this country. Yes, in what the Christian Endeavor army represents lies the hope of the republic." — *The Standard.*

A New Project.

THE Young People's Society of Christian Endeavor has undertaken another great project, which is nothing less than an attempt to enlist all the members of that organization with the leading denominational mission boards in a wide-reaching and thorough campaign to arouse the missionary spirit among all Christians. — *The Presbyterian Banner.*

Missions and Good Citizenship.

"A MILLION dollars a year for missions!" That is not a bad, or an inapt, or an untimely watchword to let go ringing down the lines of the nearly two million members connected with the International Christian Endeavor federation. Nor does it seem to us to be at all an impracticable one. This "missionary extension" movement is a very reasonable one, and will readily commend itself to all. Meanwhile it is to be hoped the "civil education" movement, which was begun in some places during the past year, will be generally taken up and pressed until the municipal corruption and misrule shall be no longer possible in face of the new citizenship and the more conscientious patriotism. — *The Advance.*

Loyalty and Fellowship.

THE chief feature of the Christian Endeavor movement is that it requires and promotes loyalty to Christ and to the churches respectively to which its members belong, without fostering the narrow sect spirit which is averse to fellowship and co-operation with other Christians. Thus the social power of Christianity is organized and quickened into activity to promote faith, piety, and all manner of good works. For generations the social elements of the churches lay dormant for lack of cultivation, and the Christian world was waiting for this Endeavor movement to awaken them into life and activity. This is the work which it has done, and it is marvelous in our eyes. — *The Lutheran Observer.*

Never Before.

IT is doubtless the fact that never before in the history of the world have such immense audiences assembled beneath one roof for a distinctively religious purpose, while the enthusiasm awakened by these conventions is something wholly unique in modern religious life. — *The Kingdom.*

Faces Illumined.

WE believe that the Christian Endeavor convention at Cleveland was the grandest expression of the church, pure and simple, that earth or heaven has ever seen among men. That sea of faces was illumined by fires of the Holy Ghost. — *The Herald of Gospel Liberty.*

A Significant Incident.

AN incident occurred in Saengerfest Hall, at the Christian Endeavor convention in Cleveland, on Thursday forenoon of last week, that aroused much interest. In a lull in the exercises there was a call for State songs. The delegates from one of the States had sung their State song, and there was a call for Maryland. A large colored man, pastor of a colored church in Baltimore, with a voice like a trumpet, stepped forward and began to sing the song composed by Paul M. Strayer, entitled "Baltimore, '96," it being an invitation to hold the Convention of '96 in the Monumental City. Something occurred to interrupt him for a moment or two, when Rev. F. C. Klein, a Marylander, but at present pastor of Trinity Church in Allegheny, stepped to the side of the colored songster, and joined in with him to complete the song. The idea of a colored man and a white man standing side by side, representing the old slave State of Maryland, was too much for the audience, and they burst out at every pause in the song with tumultuous applause. It was an incident that represented the leveling and the harmonizing spirit of Christian Endeavor. — *The Methodist Recorder.*

No Need to Explain.

No one asks at Cleveland as two years ago at New York, "What is Christian Endeavor?" Everybody in Cleveland knows what it is and heartily welcomes it. A marked development is manifest since that meeting. No longer does it need to explain its ideas or apologize for its existence. It has become a constituent and necessary part of the churches in all denominations. It is now telling what it has done and planning greater work. It is aggressive. The young people have a place and a work in and for the church. — *The Evangelist.*

A Christian Endeavor Missionary.

MR. S. S. SNYDER, who spoke at our Reformed Church rally on "Christian Endeavor and Missions," by a providential coincidence was in a position to be introduced as our Christian Endeavor missionary elect, the board having chosen him for that post on the previous day. — *The Christian World.*

For Discouraged Elijahs.

THE great meeting at Cleveland, which has been held this last week, also suggests that the Christian forces of American life are much greater than we are wont to suppose. This Young People's movement has done much to propagate the Christian impulse among young people. It has brought many within the circle of church life and work; but it has done a larger service in giving common expression to the Christian fidelity of multitudes of young men and women. They would have been Christians without it, but they would not have known each other, and they would not have had the inspiring consciousness that comes from the knowledge that there is a vast community of Christian conviction and service. — *The Watchman.*

For Presbyterians.

THE favor with which Endeavor principles are received by Presbyterians was indicated by a vote taken at the denominational rally presided over by Rev. R. V. Hunter. A resolution indorsing the movement was adopted by a unanimous vote of Presbyterian ministers, North, South, and of Canada. The movement is found now in not less than thirty denominations. It has made itself felt in all our church life, and now, by means of the good-citizenship committee, proposes to make itself felt in philanthropic and municipal and State and national affairs. Let us devoutly thank God for this work, and pray for his gracious guidance of it in all the future. — *The Herald and Presbyter*.

Hosts, Children, and Gush.

AN unkind critic said, some time ago, that the three main elements in a Christian Endeavor convention were hosts, children, and gush. That critic was a little right and much wrong. The little that was correct in the criticism was favorable to the friends of Endeavor. They do mass the multitudes as no others do. No other organization of a religious kind on earth can bring together men and women as can Christian Endeavor. No organization of any other kind, labor, political, scientific, in Europe, Asia, Africa, or America, can present the testimony of enthusiasm and increasing interest, year after year, like this one composed of the friends of Jesus. The "children" part of the criticism displays ignorance and misstatement, as well as unkindness. The hoary heads are seen, day by day, in these audiences by the hundreds. Christian Endeavor, under God, is manned by men and women, plus the young. The scientists of the day, the wise men of the times, the leaders of thought, the ornaments of the pulpit, the picked ones from the universities, the strong from the seminaries, the choice of the generation, are present, and enjoy and help on the conventions and the work they tell of, and advance. And as for "gush," if it is to be found anywhere, the most unlikely place to look for it under the sun is at this convention. True, one hears the hyper-ornate in language and the extra-analogical in presentation now and then. But from an extended experience in conferences and conventions of religious and secular kinds in this and in European lands, the testimony is soberly given that in an annual Christian Endeavor convention there is less of the unsubstantial than in any gathering of modern times that is numbered by the thousands. Take these Canadians who come down from the Dominion, these representatives who come up from the South, and these delegates who represent the districts lying between, and you have "the pick" of the century. The leaders of genuine reform are here; the conservators of the best that now is are of the number; the churches' best workers are represented in convention; and here are they of whom the present workers, to whom the world owes a great debt, can say sincerely, "The generation that is coming is better than ours that is passing away, because the God of the generations has bestowed newly and largely through this blessed agency of Christian Endeavor." — *The Outlook*.

Impressive, Inspiring, Uplifting.

THUS closed one of the most impressive, inspiring, and uplifting conventions ever held in this or any other land. It was remarkable for many reasons, — for its members coming and going like a mighty army with none but peaceful ensigns; for its enthusiasm, which was deep and promises to be permanent; for the profound undertone of reverence and piety that characterized all the sessions, even amid storms of applause;

for its *personnel*, many of the most gifted and celebrated men and women having part in the programme; for the splendid talents, before either obscured or undeveloped, that were brought to the fore; for the noble exhibition of powers of the highest character devoted humbly and utterly to the service of Christ. — *The Lutheran Evangelist.*

Defeat for Skeptics.

THE Christian Endeavor Convention at Cleveland has been a grand religious ovation. In attendance, eloquent addresses, and earnest enthusiasm it was a wonderful gathering. In spite of skepticism and rationalism, so long as the young people of the Protestant churches manifest such enthusiastic interest in Christian work and Bible study, no anti-Christian opposition can prevail against the army of the living God. — *The Christian Guardian.*

A Cheering Sign.

CHRISTIAN ENDEAVOR keeps on its prosperous course, always increasing in volume and power. It maintains the simple standard with which it began, of loyalty to Jesus Christ and activity in his service. It has avoided denominational conflicts, and has steadily promoted the strength of local churches. The enthusiasm of its members is unbounded. Even the great railroad strike could not block their way, and the annual meeting at Cleveland was in every respect a success. The addresses, prayer-meetings, and plans for the work of the coming year, were evidently pervaded by the Holy Spirit, and their impulse will be felt for good throughout the whole country. There is not in the whole world a more cheering sign of the coming of the kingdom of our Lord Jesus Christ than the Christian Endeavor Society. — *The Congregationalist.*

It Pays the Local Churches.

BUT can the local church and preacher afford such an expenditure of energy? When we learn what the Cleveland churches have lost, we will answer that unequivocally. Our first judgment is that a church that will devote itself to carrying out such a work will earn a standing in its community that it would hardly hope to win in any other way. The churches in Cleveland that have lost by this convention have not been those that have made the most of it. That we will vouch for. — *Christian Standard.*

Debs or no Debs.

"WARS and rumors of wars" had no power to turn back the Endeavor hosts from the rallying-point of their annual pilgrimage. "Cleveland, '94," had been the cry way back in the New York convention; and now that the time had come, to Cleveland the Endeavorers were going, "strike or no strike, Debs or no Debs." And "The Forest City" was ready for the incoming hosts. Arrayed "like a bride adorned for her husband," with the Cleveland Christian Endeavor colors fluttering from the housetops, streaming from the balconies and verandas, flying even from the trolley-wires and poles, a bewildering and beautiful commingling of red and white and blue and gold, bathed in sunshine and sparkling with electric lights, the fair city welcomed her guests with a cordiality and perfection of preparation that has never been surpassed in any of the wonderful series of Endeavor conventions. Truly may Cleveland's guests look back upon the week spent in the enjoyment of her superabundant hospitality, and, with the memory of St. Louis and Minneapolis, of New York and Montreal, still fresh, say to Cleveland, "Many daughters have done virtuously, but thou excellest them all." — *The Christian Intelligencer.*

On Earth as in Heaven.

THROUGH all this church love and loyalty ran strong and clear throughout the convention a rapidly rising stream of interdenominational fellowship, which enabled each delegate to honor every other delegate's supreme devotion to his own church, and, at the same time, compelled each delegate to recognize that every other delegate was worthy of affectionate sympathy and respect in his labor for the cause of our one Lord. It was akin to the interdenominational fellowship which will make heaven the happy home alike of Presbyterians and Baptists, of Methodists and Congregationalists, and of all the other slightly differing creeds in Christendom. Not less of denominational spirit, but less of sectarian bitterness, is the tendency of Endeavor, and one of the results of this convention. — *The Cumberland Presbyterian.*

Unity in Diversity.

IN addressing the convention on "Interdenominational Fellowship," the Rev. P. R. Danley took very strong ground for unity in diversity and for co-operation in place of competition. No one has more effectively set forth the evils of division which weaken the working force and moral influence of Protestant Christianity. "That the world may know that thou hast sent me," states the most weighty argument for a united church. The Christian Endeavor Society has, by the acceptance of such a platform, and by its increasing efforts to promote unity of feeling, done much to prepare the ground for the "United Church." — *The Churchman.*

No Bosses.

THERE were no dry readers of manuscript, no dreary sermonizers — no perfunctory performer can hold a Christian Endeavor audience. Some of the speakers were slow, but, in the main, few mistakes are made in selecting speakers. The flighty speculator, the ecclesiastical politician, the religious boss, gets no place. Busy schemers, one-sided schismatics, cranks, and hobby-riders, who seek to pull wires and get indorsement in church courts, are repudiated at a Christian Endeavor Convention. Indeed, I hope Christian Endeavor will strike a death-blow to bossism in our churches. There's no place given to ecclesiastical "buncombe," and no notice taken of defunct dignitaries and pietistic fossils, except to label them and lay them "on the shelf," as specimens of museum curiosity. — *The United Presbyterian.*

Get the Best Returns.

THE Christian Endeavor movement is gaining ground. Presbyterians are a large and important factor in it. Their influence will prove helpful. Pastors and elders must keep pace with it, and wisely and lovingly control it in the individual church. Give it a God-speed, and utilize it to the highest spiritual and practical results. Let the church get the best possible returns out of it. — *The Presbyterian.*

Always Memorable.

THE Cleveland convention will always be memorable because of the action of the trustees, whereby the entire society will be enlisted in missionary extension, similar to the plan of the well-known university extension movement. The aim is to arouse, through the great missionary boards, in a wide-reaching and thorough campaign, the missionary spirit among all Christians. — *The Christian Inquirer.*

Permanent.

ONLY thirteen years of history has the Society behind it, but never has movement grown so rapidly. Better still, it has the elements of permanency, first, because it is Christian, and second, because it is not an independent organization, but a mode of the life and work of the church of Christ, which "ever shall remain." — *The Presbyterian Record.*

Phenomenal.

IN point of attendance, the convention is an unmistakable evidence of the growth and mighty power of the Christian Endeavor army in the world. This organization has had a phenomenal growth, and its power and usefulness as a Christian agency for good have been alike phenomenal. — *The Religious Telescope.*

Couldn't fry It Out.

A reporter said: "The sun could not fry out the least bit of enthusiasm with which the Endeavorers are continually running over. They might be packed into cars like Holland herrings in a keg, jabbed in the ribs with umbrellas, and their favorite corns trampled all over, but nothing dampens their ardor." — *The Christian World.*

Their Reward.

THE reception of Cleveland was royal. It can never be forgotten. But the city will feel the spiritual impetus for years to come. They will find that it is more blessed to give than to receive, for they thus received something far richer than any mere financial or toilsome outlay could purchase. — *The Mid-Continent.*

Reform and Fellowship.

WHEN forty thousand young people, representing two millions of their fellows, come together into one place and cheer themselves hoarse over the most radical reform utterances of John G. Woolley and Frances E. Willard, look out. Something is bound to happen. But when it is remembered that these millions of young people are the Sabbath-school teachers and religious leaders of the coming generation, we are ready to shout Hallelujah! Thank God, that in this time of anarchy and saloon rule and political corruption, he is raising up a host to stand for righteousness.

There is another thing this movement means which is not less desirable. It means the vital, spiritual union of evangelical Christendom. It is to be regretted that it has been deemed wise on the part of some of the denominations to attempt to alienate their young people from this distinct movement. Christian Endeavor is the most practical answer to our Lord's dying petition, that his people might all be one, that the world has witnessed since the time of the apostles. We should not lay a straw in the way of this glorious fellowship. This is one of the divinest things about this great movement. It is well enough for each denomination to have its own rallies, and take advantage of the youthful enthusiasm awakening at great conventions to forward its own legitimate work. But there is a force springing from this blessed fellowship which nothing else can supply, and it ought not to be tampered with or weakened. — *The Christian Statesman.*

Now, to do It!

IT is wonderful to think that just when the church attendance had so fallen off as to cause serious apprehension in the minds of good people, and just when the prayer-meeting had become perfunctory almost beyond the point of endurance, a movement should have come to the rescue whose characteristic feature was the emphasis it placed on *doing the will of God.* An old lady of our acquaintance went down the aisle of her home church at the close of a great sermon by her pastor, murmuring to herself, " It has all been said; it has all been said, — *now it has got to be done.*" This may be called a rough rendering of the Christian Endeavor motto. The purpose of these young people is to work out their own salvation, " while God worketh in them to will and to do of his good pleasure." — *The Union Signal.*

The Convention a Tremendous Success.

THE great success of the Christian Endeavor Convention was assured in advance; but the immense proportions of the gathering in this city of the hosts which have made it their rallying-point was not to be understood until the tremendous meetings which marked the formal opening of the work to be done here by the representatives of a most wonderful organization.

When the great tent and the big Saengerfest Hall were filled to the doors yesterday morning, and the churches in the vicinity were found too small for the overflow meetings, the true size and impressiveness of the convention became apparent. Now the whole city understands the tremendous size and power for good of the organization which is able, in hard times and in the face of a strike which would have destroyed many conventions, to bring together a host of enthusiastic and zealous young men and women, the like of which was never seen before. The demonstration of the vitality and vastness of the forces enlisted on the side of religion and morals was calculated to move the most thoughtless and awe the most hostile.

We congratulate the Christian Endeavorers, from the leaders to the latest recruits of their magnificent army, on the unbounded success of the convention of 1894. May they remember their visit to Cleveland with such pride and satisfaction as the people of this city feel as they contemplate the greatest gathering of any kind which has ever been seen in this part of the world at a meeting of any organization whatsoever. — *The Cleveland Leader.*

Farewell.

THE convention has been the greatest in the history of the Christian Endeavor. It has been the greatest in enthusiasm and the greatest in results. There is a great deal lies back of those commonplace words. There is very much more than any words can express. The Christian Endeavor is made up of workers, organized to work; and they do work with an earnestness and a force seldom seen before in this shadowland of sin.

The result is not to be seen by the eye, but felt in the heart. It is an awakening, a reviving of spirit, a clearer conceiving of purpose, a strengthening of resolve, and an improving of methods. Every State in the Union, every church represented, and, it may be added, all members of those churches, will reap their share of the benefits.

One of the results particularly demands special comment. The closer alliance with the mission societies of the several churches which was resolved upon must give a fresh stimulus to all Protestant missionary work.

It is earnestly hoped that every one of these delegates has derived pleasure and profit from his visit to Cleveland outside of that supplied them by the convention. Cleveland has done her best to entertain them hospitably. Certainly the people of the city have been pleased with them, have rejoiced in their presence, and now bid them farewell with the greatest of good-will, and wish their glorious cause Godspeed. — *The Cleveland Plain-Dealer.*

OFFICERS

OF THE

United Society of Christian Endeavor.

OFFICE:
646 Washington Street, Boston, Mass., U.S.A.

President.
Rev. FRANCIS E. CLARK, D.D., Boston, Mass.

General Secretary.
Mr. JOHN WILLIS BAER, Boston, Mass.

Treasurer.
Mr. WILLIAM SHAW, Boston, Mass.

Trustees.

Rev. C. A. Dickinson.
Rev. R. W. Brokaw.
Rev. N. Boynton.
Rev. J. F. Cowan.
Rev. John H. Barrows, D.D.
Rev. E. R. Dille, D.D.
Rev. Teunis S. Hamlin, D.D.
Rev. P. S. Henson, D.D.
Rev. J. T. Beckley, D.D.
Bishop Samuel Fallows, D.D.
Prof. J. L. Howe.
Rev. W. W. Andrews.
Rev. J. Z. Tyler.
Rev. Canon J. B. Richardson.
Rev. J. M. Lowden.

Rev. James L. Hill, D.D.
Rev. H. B. Grose.
Mr. W. H. Pennell.
Mr. W. J. Van Patten.
Rev. Wayland Hoyt, D.D.
Hon. John Wanamaker.
Rev. William Patterson.
Rev. H. C. Farrar, D.D.
Rev. W. H. McMillan, D.D.
Rev. W. J. Darby.
Rev. M. Rhodes, D.D.
Rev. Gilby C. Kelly, D.D.
Pres. Wm. R. Harper, Ph.D.
Rev. D. J. Burrell, D.D.
Rev. Rufus W. Miller.

Rev. M. M. Binford.

Auditor.
Mr. F. H. KIDDER, Boston, Mass.

COMMITTEE OF ARRANGEMENTS.

Rev. J. Z. TYLER, Chairman.
Miss MIRIAM C. SMITH, Secretary.
Mr. A. E. ROBLEE, Finance and Treasurer.
Mr. J. E. CHEESMAN, Hall.
Mr. N. E. HILLS, Entertainment.
Mr. F. MELVILLE LEWIS, Printing.
Rev. S. L. DARSIE, Music.
Mr. R. B. HAMILTON, Press.
Mr. A. W. NEALE, Reception.
Mr. J. V. HITCHCOCK, Auditing.
Rev. R. A. GEORGE, *Ex-officio.*

SCRIBE.

REV. H. W. GLEASON, Minneapolis.

MUSICAL DIRECTORS.

MR. P. S. FOSTER, Washington, D.C.
MR. H. C. LINCOLN, Philadelphia, Pa.
MR. J. G. WARREN, Cleveland, O.

CORNETISTS.

THE PARK SISTERS, New York City.

STATISTICS.

JULY 1, 1894.

THE following is the official enrollment of Christian Endeavor Societies *to date* (July 1, 1894). If your State, Territory, or Province ought to be credited with more societies, it is no fault of mine. The societies have not enrolled, and, consequently, have not been counted. I know that there are many hundreds of societies in existence, particularly Junior societies, that have never enrolled. Enroll, *enroll*, and be counted. The list is as follows: —

UNITED STATES.

	Young People's.	Junior.	Total.
Alabama	94	17	111
Alaska Territory	2		2
Arizona Territory	12		12
Arkansas	103	23	126
California	632	320	952
Colorado	194	75	269
Connecticut	530	144	674
Delaware	56	16	72
District of Columbia	75	30	105
Florida	124	14	138
Georgia	128	13	141
Idaho	28	11	39
Iowa	1,062	296	1,358
Indiana	1,217	317	1,534
Illinois	1,571	678	2,249
Indian Territory	27	1	28
Kansas	839	254	1,093
Kentucky	239	37	276
Louisiana	43	9	52
Maine	483	116	599
Massachusetts	918	311	1,229
Mississippi	25	3	28
Maryland	279	72	351
Montana	41	19	60
Missouri	720	236	956
Minnesota	568	257	825
Michigan	734	184	918
Nebraska	460	159	619
New Hampshire	267	49	316
Nevada	3	1	4
New York	2,646	673	3,319
New Jersey	682	253	935
New Mexico	24	4	28
North Carolina	106	15	121
North Dakota	89	14	103
Ohio	1,852	415	2,267
Oklahoma Territory	83	15	98
Oregon	226	85	311
Carried forward,	17,182	5,136	22,318

	Young People's.	Junior.	Total.
Brought forward,	17,182	5,136	22,318
Pennsylvania	2,738	717	3,455
Rhode Island	135	49	184
South Carolina	35	11	46
South Dakota	175	43	218
Tennessee	248	100	348
Texas	239	36	275
Utah	43	25	68
Vermont	304	87	391
Virginia	118	12	130
Washington	185	55	240
West Virginia	229	36	265
Wisconsin	542	159	701
Wyoming	13	5	18
Floating Societies	50	1	51
Mothers' Societies	9		9
Intermediate Societies	30		30
	22,275	6,472	28,747

DOMINION OF CANADA.

	Young People's.	Junior.	Total.
Alberta	8	5	13
Assiniboia	16	1	17
British Columbia	29	2	31
Manitoba	111	15	126
New Brunswick	107	8	115
Nova Scotia	364	27	391
Ontario	1,131	150	1,281
Province of Quebec	178	37	215
Prince Edward Island	44	2	46
Saskatchewan	2		2
Newfoundland	5		5
	1,995	247	2,242

FOREIGN AND MISSIONARY LANDS.

	Young People's.	Junior.	Total.
Africa	23	2	25
Australia	795	39	834
Bermuda	2		2
Brazil	1	1	2
Columbia	1		1
Chile	3		3
China	21	2	23
England	1,430	23	1,453
France	9		9
India	67	5	72
Ireland	28	4	32
Japan	56	3	59
Madagascar	30		30
Mexico	22		22
Norway	1		1
Persia	3		3
Samoan Islands	9		9
Carried forward,	2,501	79	2,580

	Young People's.	Junior.	Total.
Brought forward,	2,501	79	2,580
Sandwich Islands	6		6
Scotland	55	3	58
Spain	1		1
Syria	3		3
Turkey	32	6	38
West Indies	41	3	44
Burmah	9		9
Siam	1		1
	2,649	91	2,740

RECAPITULATION.

	Young People's.	Junior.	Total.
United States	22,275	6,472	28,747
Dominion of Canada	1,995	247	2,242
Foreign and Missionary Lands	2,649	91	2,740
WORLD-WIDE TOTAL	26,919	6,810	33,729

JOHN WILLIS BAER,
General Secretary.

INDEX.

	PAGE
Address of Welcome. Rev. J. Z. Tyler	65–67
Address of Welcome. Gov. William McKinley	67, 68
Alden, Mrs. I. M. (Pansy): Remarks	182
Annual Address of President Francis E. Clark	78–81
Annual Report of General Secretary John Willis Baer	70–76
Announcement of Conventions, '95, '96; by Rev. James L. Hill	81–83
Babcock, Rev. Maltbie D.: "Glorifying God"	86–89
Baer, General Secretary John Willis: Annual Report	70–76
Baker, Rev. E. E.: "Systematic and Proportionate Giving"	187–190
Baker, Rev. Smith: "Christian Citizenship"	105–109
Barnes, Mrs. Frances J.: "Joel's Prophecy"	44–46
Bear, Jonas Spotted: "Christian Endeavor among the Indians"	192
Beckley, Rev. J. T.: Remarks	223, 224
Behrends, Rev. A. J. F.: Sermon	229–233
Binford, Rev. M. M.: "Spiritual Life of Endeavorers"	38–41
Boardman, Rev. George Dana: "St. Paul's Endeavor"	27–33
Boy at the Throttle, The. By Rev. A. W. Spooner	173–177
Brett, Rev. Cornelius: Open Parliament — "The Junior Society"	143–146
Brokaw, Rev. R. W.: "Christian Endeavor for the Times"	48, 49
Chappell, Rev. E. B.: "Christian Citizenship"	112–117
Christian Citizenship. By Rev. E. B. Chappell	112–117
Christian Endeavor and Christian Citizenship. By Rev. H. B. Grose	18–22
Christian Citizenship. By Rev. Smith Baker	105–109
Christian Endeavor Among the Germans. By Rev. Theo. F. John	160–163
Christian Endeavor Among the Indians. By Jonas Spotted Bear	192
Christian Endeavor Among the Life Savers. By Rev. J. Lester Wells	9–12
Christian Endeavor as a Training School. By Rev. Teunis S. Hamlin	22–27
Christian Endeavor Missionary Extension Course. By S. L. Mershon	203–208
Christian Endeavor vs. the Saloon. By John G. Woolley	98–103
Christian Endeavor for the Times. By Rev. R. W. Brokaw	48, 49
Christians in the Twentieth Century. By Rev. W. H. McMillan	57–61
Christ, the Worker: A Model for All Endeavorers. By Rev. John Potts, D.D.	128–133
Claims of an Educated Life, The. By Pres. William J. Tucker	124–128
Clark, President Francis E.: Annual Address	78–81
Clark, President Francis E.: Letter to Convention	64
Committee of Arrangements	246
Committee Conferences	119–122
Comstock, Anthony: "Environment of Our Youth"	12–18

	PAGE
Cowan, Rev. J. F.: "Principles, Enthusiasm, Methods"	50–53
Common-Sense in Church Life and Work. By Rev. Jos. K. Dixon	136–142
Consecration Service — Hall	224–228
Consecration Service — Tent	233, 234
Danley, Rev. P. R.: "Interdenominational Fellowship"	151–155
Deepest Thing in Christian Endeavor, The. By Rev. Gilby C. Kelly	41–43
Denominational Rallies	146–149; 158–160
Dixon, Rev. A. C.: "Heroes of Faith"	91–95
Dixon, Rev. Jos. K.: "Common-Sense in Church Life and Work"	136–142
Dulles, William Jr.: Remarks	190
Environment of Our Youth, The. By Anthony Comstock	12–18
Farrar, Rev. H. C.: "Grit and Grace"	35–37
Floating Societies of Christian Endeavor. By Miss Antoinette P. Jones	46–48
Glorifying God. By Rev. Maltbie D. Babcock	86–89
Golden Opportunities for Christian Endeavor. By Mrs. Ellen J. Phinney	33–35
Good Citizenship. Open Parliament	110–112
Greeting from China. By Mrs. Geo. H. Hubbard	191
Greeting from China. By Rev. Gilbert Reid	200–203
Greetings from Representatives of Missionary Boards	193, 194; 209–211
Grit and Grace. By Rev. H. C. Farrar	35–37
Grose, Rev. H. B.: "Christian Endeavor and Christian Citizenship"	18–22
Hamlin, Rev. Teunis S.: "Christian Endeavor as a Training School"	22–27
Heroes of Faith. By Rev. A. C. Dixon	91–95
Hill, Rev. J. L.: Announcement of Conventions '95, '96	81–83
Hill, Rev. J. L.: "Train the Children"	170, 171
Hillis, Rev. N. D.: "Strategic Element in Missions"	212–215
Howe, Prof. J. Lewis: Open Parliament — "Benefits of Interdenominational Fellowship"	156, 157
Hoyt, Rev. Wayland: "Interdenominational Fellowship"	165–170
Hubbard, Mrs. Geo. H.: Greeting from China	191
Hunter, Rev. R. V.: Open Parliament — "The Pledge"	96–98
Interdenominational Fellowship. By Rev. P. R. Danley	151–155
Interdenominational Fellowship. By Rev. Wayland Hoyt	165–170
Interdenominational Fellowship. Open Parliament	156, 157
Introduction	5–7
Joel's Prophecy. By Mrs. Frances J. Barnes	44–46
John, Rev. Theo. F.: "Christian Endeavor Work Among the Germans"	160–163
Johnson, Rev. W. D.: "The Negro and the Endeavorer"	134, 135
Jones, Miss Antoinette P.: "Floating Societies of Christian Endeavor"	46–48
Junior Rally	170
Junior Society. Open Parliament	143–146
Kelly, Rev. Gilby C.: "Deepest Thing in Christian Endeavor"	41–43
McKinley, Gov. William: Address of Welcome	67, 68
McMillan, Rev. W. H.: "Christians in the Twentieth Century"	57–61
Mershon, S. L.: "Christian Endeavor Missionary Extension Course"	203–208
Movement Among the Jews Toward Christ. By Rev. Herman Warszawiak	194–196
Negro and the Endeavorer. By Rev. W. D. Johnson	134, 135
Officers and Trustees of the United Society of Christian Endeavor	245

Index.   253

	PAGE
Open Parliament — "Benefits of Interdenominational Fellowship." Conducted by Professor J. Lewis Howe	156, 157
Open Parliament — "Good Citizenship." Conducted by Edwin D. Wheelock,	110–112
Open Parliament — "The Junior Society." Conducted by Rev. Cornelius Brett	143–146
Open Parliament — "The Pledge." Conducted by Rev. R. V. Hunter	96–98
Other Boys and Girls. By Dr. Pauline Root	177–180
Overflow Meetings	234
Patterson, Rev. William: Response to Addresses of Welcome	68–70
Phinney, Mrs. Ellen J.: "Golden Opportunities for Christian Endeavor"	33–35
Pledge — Open Parliament	96–98
Pope, Rev. H. W.: "Show your Colors"	180, 181
Potts, Rev. John: "Christ, the Worker: a Model for all Endeavorers"	128–133
Presentation of Banners	84–86; 103, 104; 163–165
Presentation of Diplomas	117, 118; 149–151
Principles, Enthusiasm, Methods. By Rev. J. F. Cowan	50–53
Raymond, Pres. B. P.: Sermon	217–223
Reid, Rev. Gilbert: Greeting from China	200–203
Resolutions	216, 217
Response to Addresses of Welcome. Rev. William Patterson	68–70
Rhodes, Rev. M. M.: "Sources of Power"	54–56
Root, Dr. Pauline: "Other Boys and Girls"	177–180
Sermon. By Rev. A. J. F. Behrends	229–233
Sermon. By President B. P. Raymond	217–223
Scudder, Mrs. Alice M.: "World-wide Juniors in Story and Song"	182–185
Shaw, William: Remarks	208, 209
Show Your Colors. By Rev. H. W. Pope	180, 181
Smith, Rev. C. F.: Remarks	135
Sources of Power. By Rev. M. Rhodes	54–56
Spiritual Life of Endeavorers, The. By Rev. M. M. Binford	38–41
Spooner, Rev. A. W.: "Boy at the Throttle"	173–177
St. Paul's Endeavor. By Rev. George Dana Boardman	27–33
Statistics	247–249
Stitt, Rev. R. Haywood: Remarks	158
Strategic Element in Missions. By Rev. N. D. Hillis	212–215
Systematic and Proportionate Giving. By Rev. E. E. Baker	187–190
Train the Children. By Rev. J. L. Hill	170, 171
Trustees' Meeting	8, 9
Tucker, Pres. W. J.: "Claims of an Educated Life"	124–128
Tyler, Rev. J. Z.: Address of Welcome	65–67
Warszawiak, Rev. Herman: "Movement of the Jews toward Christ"	194–196
Wells, Rev. J. Lester: "Christian Endeavor among the Life-Savers"	9–12
What They Say	235–245
Wheelock, Edwin D.: Open Parliament on Good Citizenship	110–112
Willard, Frances E.: "Women and Temperance"	197–200
Women and Temperance. By Frances E. Willard	197–200
Woolley, John G.: "Christian Endeavor vs. the Saloon"	98–103
World-wide Juniors in Story and Song. By Mrs. Alice M. Scudder	182–185

ILLUSTRATIONS —

	PAGE
Committee of '94	65
Convention Hall (Exterior)	162
Convention Hall (Interior) looking toward platform	164
Convention Hall (Interior) looking toward the rear	166
Delegates Arriving by Boat	172
Diploma	174
Officers and Trustees	FRONTISPIECE
Scene in Wade Park	176
Tent	116

JUST OUT
Our New Hymn=Book
Christian Endeavor Hymns

... By Ira D. Sankey ...

The new book was introduced to the public at the Cleveland Convention, and scored an immediate success. It promises to be the most popular hymn-book ever issued. Those who have examined advance copies are enthusiastic in their praise. It is substantially and attractively bound, and contains 223 hymns and 208 pages.

   The **Topical Index** with which the book is supplied will be a great convenience.

PRICES.

Sample copy, postpaid.. $.35.
In quantities, by express, at purchaser's expense.................. .30.

Cash with order, or sent C. O. D.

DON'T PURCHASE UNTIL YOU HAVE EXAMINED THIS BOOK.

Publishing Department, United Society of Christian Endeavor,
646 Washington St., Boston. ✕ 155 La Salle St., Chicago.

www.ingramcontent.com/pod-product-compliance
Lightning Source LLC
Chambersburg PA
CBHW022355040426
42450CB00005B/189